ANALYSIS
OF
GROUPS

Contributions to Theory,
Research, and Practice

Graham S. Gibbard

John J. Hartman

Richard D. Mann

Editors

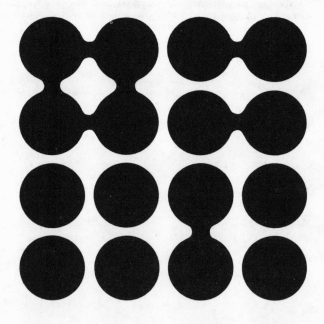

ANALYSIS

OF

GROUPS

Jossey-Bass Publishers
San Francisco   •   London   •   1986

ANALYSIS OF GROUPS
Contributions to Theory, Research, and Practice
Graham S. Gibbard, John J. Hartman, and Richard D. Mann, Editors

JACKET DESIGN BY WILLI BAUM

FIRST EDITION
First printing: January 1974
Second printing: September 1976
Third printing: November 1978
Fourth printing: December 1981
Fifth printing: February 1986

Code 7345

The Jossey-Bass
Behavioral Science Series

Preface

A*nalysis of Groups* reflects a collaboration between the three of us which began thirteen years ago. We constitute a small work group studying other small groups, and over the years we have supported, enlightened, and criticized one another. This collaboration has in fact been one of the many professional and personal experiences which have extended our understanding of what occurs when individuals attempt to pool their efforts to work in a group. One of the central themes of this book is that such collaborative efforts are difficult, but that they are possible and that they can offer the individual opportunities to learn, to work, and to enjoy his work which are not available to the individual working in isolation.

Our involvement in this book grew out of a shared concern with contemporary theory, research, and practice in experiential groups. We were impressed both with how much was happening in the field and with how little was understood about it. The recent blossoming of curiosity and experimentation in experiential groups is matched only by a widespread uncertainty about the nature, purpose, and effects of such group experience. A sampling of some of the recurrent questions about these groups is sufficient to demonstrate the point: What is a therapy group? A T-group? What typically occurs in these kinds of groups? What are the essential

similarities and differences between them? Do all emotionally involving small groups develop in much the same way? What is the
best way to conceptualize and study the role of the individual group
member? What is the most effective stance for the group leader to
assume?

At the same time, one often encounters an implicit (and not
so infrequently an explicit) opposition to the analytic appraisal of
small-group participation. This opposition includes a failure to
endorse or support thoughtful, systematic investigation of small-group
phenomena. Even more importantly, there has been an unfortunate
tendency for different traditions or schools of thought in small-
group work to establish relatively self-contained conceptual systems
and literatures, without much effort at cross-fertilization.

Analysis of Groups is offered as a corrective for some of these
obstacles to comparative group studies and as a spur to the development of a more inclusive theoretical view of experiential groups. We
do not aim to cover all this territory, but rather to focus in some
depth on the theoretical and empirical work that seems to us crucial
to the development of more inclusive theory and more fruitful research.

This book is intended primarily for professionals and students, for the classroom teacher, the group therapist, the organizational consultant, and other members or leaders of small groups
and larger social systems, who are interested in sophisticated,
methodologically varied approaches to group psychology. It offers
sections on the observation of groups, on group process and development, on the relationship between the individual and the group, on
the function of collective fantasy and myth in group formation, and,
finally, on authority and leadership.

Although we are listed as editors in alphabetical order, we
settled on a division of labor in which Gibbard assumed primary
responsibility for Parts Three and Five and Hartman for Parts One,
Two, and Four; Mann contributed to the formulation and development of each of the five sections.

While we have in other publications expressed our debt to
teachers, fellow researchers, and various others who have encouraged
and influenced our attempts to understand groups, the publishing of
this book prompts us to identify a handful of men who have had a

profound impact on our work. The writing of W. R. Bion has informed our thinking about groups for many years. Because his work is so wide-ranging we could not find any single, short contribution that would encompass enough of his point of view to justify including it in this collection. Similarly, the depth and scope of Philip E. Slater's substantive contributions to group psychology cannot be captured in a brief article or excerpt. Since we are all products of an undergraduate education in the Department of Social Relations at Harvard, our debt to Gordon Allport, Henry A. Murray, and Robert F. Bales takes precedence over all others. Allport's devotion to the idiographic patterning of human personality and the autonomy of the ego and Murray's respect for and understanding of fantasy and the unconscious aspects of behavior have contributed immeasurably to our efforts to understand the idiosyncratic styles of individuals and the evolution of collective fantasy in small groups. Finally, it should be clear that for the field of small groups in general and for us in particular the work of Robert F. Bales has for more than twenty years provided a model of scholarship and conceptual innovation.

Earl Baughman, Grant Dahlstrom, Laurence Hemmendinger, Martin Lakin, and Jacob Levine offered support and advice at critical points in the evolution of the book. We extend our thanks to Linda Shepard, Cheryl Keemer, and Carol Nardini for typing the final version of the manuscript. Our thanks go also to Albert J. Silverman, Chairman of the Department of Psychiatry at the University of Michigan, for helping to defray the expense of manuscript preparation.

We would like to dedicate this book to our most significant small groups—our families—for teaching us the most basic things, for good and for ill, about the vicissitudes of group living.

New Haven, Connecticut GRAHAM S. GIBBARD
Ann Arbor, Michigan JOHN J. HARTMAN
September 1973 RICHARD D. MANN

Introduction

*I*t is important to place the present collection of studies in the context of contemporary work in small groups, so that the reader will understand what we hope to accomplish.

Kurt W. Back (1973) has written an insightful analysis of the encounter group movement. He describes the movement as a reflection of certain rituals and myths, and in this sense as an essentially millenarian movement aimed at creating utopian relations between individuals. Unlike other millenarian movements, all of the utopian action in a small experiential group is compressed into a brief period of time. Thus, the encounter group experience provides a microcosmic societal experience which substitutes for macrocosmic social change. Back also notes the anti-intellectual, antiscientific, antirational, and anticognitive aspects of such groups, their leaders, and proponents.

As Back observes, the spirit of the encounter group movement is a reaction against the equation of knowledge with work in the "hard" natural sciences. The polar opposite of the encounter spirit *is* the experimental social psychological one, which is in fact inclined to equate knowledge with experimental, hypothesis-testing, laboratory-based research. This approach to small-group research—with its reliance on statistical data, laboratory manipulation of "variables," and social psychological "laws"—has maintained only a tenuous relationship to the experiences of real people in real groups. Such research has tended to be sterile, dry, and of little direct value to those professionals who deal with groups on an everyday basis. We are in great sympathy with those who would humanize research and broaden the definition of scientific knowledge to include approaches other than those based on narrow conceptions of scientific method. We are in complete agreement with those who would have research be relevant and useful to professionals and students, and with others who want to know more about how groups function and how individuals function in groups. We would not, however, exclude research and cognitive understanding from our more humanistic and holistic approach. Our fundamental methodological commitment is to the naturalistic observation of groups in a variety of settings. We believe that subjectivity and clinical inference are essential to the process of observation, particularly when the phenomena under study are influenced by unconscious feelings and fantasies. But we are also convinced that the intuitive, imaginative, and often speculative thinking of the clinician is compatible with serious and systematic intellectual work.

In addition to an overreaction to scientific approaches to group research, resulting in an anticognitive stance, there has been a persistent tendency toward ethnocentrism in the group field as a whole. Even in the more traditional areas of group work, distinct schools—with their own language systems and ways of conceptualizing group phenomena—have developed. There have been few attempts to integrate these schools or to offer comparative analyses.

It is our intention to bring together a series of articles representing a midpoint in the continuum of small-group work, a position which is neither anti-intellectual nor tied to a particular millenarian or utopian vision of the world.

Our overall intent is to present theory and research grounded in a psychodynamic view of personality while at the same time offering contributions from distinctly different traditions. For that reason this collection includes articles by psychoanalysts, group therapists, teachers in self-analytic college classrooms, and sociological researchers. What all of these contributors have in common is a belief that valuable and exciting small group research is possible without narrowing the focus of study to a micrometer of statistics and without rejecting a cognitive approach in favor of largely emotional experiences. To our mind, the encounter movement has too often been caught up in its own enthusiasm and has quite wrongly lost faith in intellectual attempts to understand group experience.

Because much of the encounter group movement reflects a disenchantment with psychoanalysis and a psychodynamic view of man, we believe it is important to state our commitment to a psychodynamic psychology of individual and group behavior. This adherence to a point of view which is rapidly losing favor in the face of newer approaches to therapy, training, and encounter is worth some mention here. Our endorsement of psychodynamic psychology is one aspect of an effort to bring the irrational, the illogical, the exclusively emotional under rational understanding and control. This entails a respect for and a nurturing of intellectuality, of study, of scholarship, and of research broadly defined. For us, the experience is not the method. Another factor in our lack of defection to the utopianism of the new movement is our allegiance to *work,* in Mann's sense of the term (Mann and associates, 1967, 1970), rather than to *fun,* as Strupp (1972) and Back (1973) have characterized a core value of the encounter group movement.

Our intention is, then, to juxtapose and facilitate a comparative study of theory and research from three distinctive traditions in small-group practice and research: the group psychotherapy, the sensitivity training, and the self-analytic classroom traditions. In so doing, we hope to move closer to an understanding of several facets of group life which have a significance that extends far beyond any single setting or type of group. We have selected sixteen articles. Several selections are established "classics"; several have been published only recently; still others are pieces of current work which have not been previously published. The list of contributors attests to a diversity of backgrounds, training, and professional responsibilities: recent Ph.D.s, a college president, psychoanalysts, sociologists. Three contributors are from England, one from Canada, and one from Australia. With this diversity, and with the diversity in the field as a whole, we found it necessary to provide more than cursory introductions to each section. The introductions are offered not as thorough reviews but as selective and critical overviews which aim to identify the central issues exemplified by the work chosen for particular parts of the book. We hope to provide a foundation for the integrative and comparative efforts we believe necessary, but by no means do we deprive the reader of the opportunity to do his share of the work.

The book is structured in the following way: Part One deals with different strategies of observation of small groups and with several methods of data analysis. Most students of small groups have tended to adopt either a *quantitative* approach, reflecting ties with traditional empirical research in the social sciences, or a *naturalistic-clinical* stance, reflecting a commitment to participant observation and a more holistic frame of reference. There are gains and losses inherent in either strategy. We shall provide the reader with a discussion of the methodological issues involved, paradigms of the quantitative and the clinical strategies, and a balanced appraisal of some recent efforts to integrate naturalistic and quantitative strategies.

Part Two focuses on group development and social change. Small-group researchers and participant-observers of psychotherapy and training groups have devoted considerable attention to the "phases" or "stages" in the development of small social systems. To this end many different kinds of groups have been studied. One perennial goal of such research has been the articulation of principles of group development which can be applied to the phenomena of small social systems and much larger social groups. One chronic difficulty in the study of developmental shifts in small groups is the lack of agreement about what might, or should, change over time, for example, patterns of overt behavior, tacit norms and attitudes, affective structures. A second, related problem has to do with the assessment of developmental shifts, particularly when significant changes are not easily tied to identifiable milestones or are not prominently reflected in the manifest content of group interaction. Finally, there are important distinctions between general and specific conceptualizations of group development. The more abstract and generalized developmental schemes tend to become disconnected from what is observable in a particular group setting. Alternatively, a more detailed analysis of the development of a particular group or type of group may confound significant developmental trends with setting-specific situational influences. This section of the book provides an overview of research in this area and a sampling of developmental studies.

Part Three deals with the interaction between individual dynamics and group process and structure. Small-group researchers have long sought to identify and explain the distinctive individual roles which develop in most small groups. One of the most intriguing characteristics of relatively unstructured groups is the evolution of a constellation of informal roles which serve important social and psychological functions for the group. Three central goals of work in this area are (1) the identification and analysis of the "casts of characters" which evolve in specific types of groups; (2) the formulation of more general conceptualizations of interpersonal style and role differentiation; and (3) the specification of the relationship between role differentiation and the phases or stages of group development. This section of readings includes contributions addressed to all three issues and also offers articles in which the study of the relationship between interpersonal style and social structure is a major focus.

Part Four deals with a relatively neglected issue in small-group research, that of the role of shared fantasy and myth in group development. This section deals with the collective fusions of individual fantasies, which constitute the basis for the growth and maintenance of collective projective systems. Some of the correspondences between large and small social systems are striking and permit a variety of comparisons. At the same time, the systematic study of collective fantasy is really only beginning, and there is as yet no coherent theory of collective fantasy and its evolution in social systems. Our aim here is to present several clinical and naturalistic studies of collective fantasy, to make some effort to distinguish between significant consistencies across groups and the eccentricities of particular groups, and to point the way toward a more systematic view of collective fantasy. We hope also to sensitize the reader to the subtle manifestations of shared fantasy in all social systems and to clarify both the organizing and system-maintaining functions and the disruptive effects of fantasies in small groups.

Part Five, the concluding section, deals with the all-important topic of authority and leadership. Our concern in this section is more pragmatic but no less complex than that of the preceding set of readings. Here we look closely at the position of the formal group leader (therapist, trainer, or teacher) and—more generally—at the formulation and implementation of goals and tasks in small experiential groups. Each of the three major traditions has a good deal to say in this regard, though the delineation of clear boundaries between various styles of group work continues to be exceedingly problematic. The articles chosen include, first, some impressive efforts to articulate personal and professional aims, the inherent difficulties facing any group leader, and the styles of leadership which work best for particular leaders; and second, research on what actually occurs as group leaders attempt to implement the goals which they have endorsed.

Contents

Preface   ix

Introduction   xiii

Contributors   xxi

ONE: STRATEGIES OF OBSERVATION AND ANALYSIS   1

1. The Identity of the Group Researcher
   Richard D. Mann   13

2. Observation
   Theodore M. Mills   42

3. Methodological Issues in the Assessment
     of Total-Group Phenomena in Group Therapy
     Dorothy Stock, Morton A. Lieberman   57

4. Some Problems Regarding Exemplification
   Philip E. Slater   75

TWO: GROUP PROCESS AND DEVELOPMENT   83

5. Therapy Groups and Training Groups:
   Similarities and Differences
   Seymour R. Kaplan   94

6. A Theory of Group Development
   Warren G. Bennis, Herbert A. Shepard   127

7. Anxiety, Boundary Evolution, and Social Change
   John J. Hartman, Graham S. Gibbard   154

THREE: THE INDIVIDUAL AND THE GROUP   177

8. Interracial Dynamics in Self-Analytic Groups
   Sara K. Winter   197

9. An Investigation of Group Reaction
   to Central Figures
   John W. Ringwald   220

10. Individuation, Fusion, and Role Specialization
    Graham S. Gibbard   247

FOUR: SHARED FANTASY AND MYTH   267

11. Social Systems as a Defense Against
    Persecutory and Depressive Anxiety
    Elliot Jaques   277

12. Phases, Roles, and Myths in Self-Analytic Groups
    Dexter C. Dunphy   300

13. A Note on Fantasy Themes
    in the Evolution Group Culture
    John J. Hartman, Graham S. Gibbard   315

FIVE: THE DYNAMICS OF LEADERSHIP   337

14. Leadership: The Individual and the Group
       Pierre M. Turquet   349

15. Strategy, Position, and Power
       Dorothy Stock Whitaker, Morton A. Lieberman   372

16. The T-Group Trainer: A Study of Conflict
       in the Exercise of Authority
       Rory O'Day   387

    Bibliography   411

    Indexes   429

Contributors

WARREN G. BENNIS *has been professor of organizational and management psychology at MIT and vice-president, State University of New York at Buffalo; he is now president, University of Cincinnati.*

DEXTER C. DUNPHY *is professor of business administration and head, Department of Behavioral Science, University of New South Wales, Australia.*

GRAHAM S. GIBBARD *is clinical and research psychologist, Mental Hygiene Clinic, West Haven Veterans Administration Hospital, and professor of psychology, Department of Psychiatry, Yale University.*

JOHN J. HARTMAN *is professor of psychology and coordinator of group and family psychotherapy, Department of Psychiatry, University of Michigan.*

ELLIOT JAQUES *is a practicing psychoanalyst and group consultant and director, Institute of Organization and Social Studies, Brunel University, England.*

SEYMOUR R. KAPLAN *is professor of psychiatry, Albert Einstein College of Medicine, Yeshiva University, and also heads the division of Community and Administrative Psychiatry, Montefiore Medical Center.*

MORTON A. LIEBERMAN *is professor of psychology, Department of Psychiatry and Committee on Human Development, University of Chicago.*

RICHARD D. MANN *is professor of psychology, University of Michigan.*

THEODORE M. MILLS *is professor of sociology, State University of New York at Buffalo.*

RORY O'DAY *is professor, Department of Human Relations, University of Waterloo, Canada.*

JOHN W. RINGWALD *is professor of psychology, Departments of Psychiatry and Psychology, Yale University, and is on the staff of the Connecticut Mental Health Center.*

HERBERT A. SHEPARD *teaches at several colleges and is a consultant to industrial, governmental, educational, and health institutions.*

PHILIP E. SLATER *has taught sociology at Harvard and Brandeis; he has left academia and established, with Maurice Schwartz, a training and consulting group named Green House, in Cambridge, Massachusetts.*

PIERRE M. TURQUET *is chairman, Adult Department, Tavistock Clinic, and consultant, Centre for Applied Social Research, Tavistock Institute of Human Relations.*

DOROTHY STOCK WHITAKER *is professor of social work, Department of Social Administration and Social Work, University of York, England.*

SARA K. WINTER *is professor, Department of Psychology, Wesleyan University.*

ANALYSIS
OF
GROUPS

*Contributions to Theory,
Research, and Practice*

PART ONE

STRATEGIES OF OBSERVATION AND ANALYSIS

The group researcher—be he therapist, educator, consultant, or student—often finds himself at a loss when he attempts to make sense of the events in the groups with which he deals daily. Professionals and students alike are confronted with a variety of methodologies and observational techniques which offer some guidance. Unfortunately, all of these techniques and methodologies have shortcomings, and in the end each of us must choose to follow one path rather than another. What are some of the factors that influence such a decision?

It has occurred to us on several occasions that the problems encountered by the researcher trying to understand the flow of events in groups are analogous to those of the historian trying to understand history. Small-group research has concerned itself with two major issues: (1) developmental changes in group process and structure; (2) the role of individual "leaders" or "role specialists" in dictating the direction of social change. The former reminds one of all-encompassing politico-economic theories of historical causation, and the latter of the "great-man" theory of history.

In the Second Epilogue to *War and Peace*, Leo Tolstoy attempts to deal explicitly with the problems of historical causation.

1

He expresses cynicism about the possibility that the life history of humanity or of a single nation can ever be described in a comprehensible way. He argues that causation in history rests on so many variable factors that we can never know what causes historical change. A reconstructive view of history, a systematic synthesis of historical facts, is impossible because human beings can neither perceive all the facts nor synthesize them into a coherent explanation. Consequently, Tolstoy disparages the attempts of theorists like Compte and Marx to formulate a science of historical laws. He believes that the facts of history are atomistic; they rest on the actions of a great many individuals and nonhuman forces. In *War and Peace,* Napoleon, the great man of history who feels that he alone can change it, is defeated by the Russian people and the ubiquitous Russian winter.

In a brilliant analysis of Tolstoy, Isaiah Berlin (1957) delineates two types of thinkers: those who aspire to a unifying view, those who know "one big thing," and those who know a great many little things but have no unifying world view. The former he calls *hedgehogs*; the latter, *foxes.* Berlin's thesis is that Tolstoy was in actuality a fox but wanted very much to be a hedgehog. It is this conflict that lies at the heart of Tolstoy's ambiguous philosophy of history. Despite his cynical assaults upon those who wished to synthesize the particles of history into an atomic theory, Tolstoy yearned for such lawful historical formulations. His language at the end of the Second Epilogue is replete with scientific analogies. He wished to explain all phenomena in terms of first causes and expressed a faith in the rationalistic approach of natural science. Berlin summarizes Tolstoy's view in this way: "Our ignorance of how things happen is not due to some inherent inaccessibility of the first causes, only to their multiplicity, the smallness of the ultimate units, and our inability to see and hear and remember and record and coordinate enough of the available material" (Berlin, 1957, p. 50).

Tolstoy's view of history has relevance for contemporary social science in general and the question of methodology in small-group research in particular. Methodological strategies in small-group research can be described as "clinical" or "statistical" (Meehl, 1954). Critics of the clinical approach regard it as intuitive, subjective, artistic, and unscientific. Those committed to a clinical approach argue that most quantitative efforts obscure the richness, variety, subtlety, and complexity of human behavior. For purposes of distinction here, the clinical approach may be termed that of the hedgehog. The clinician is most likely to have or to seek a more unifying view of things and to employ a method which is more global and impressionistic. The statistical approach can be regarded, then, as that of the fox. The statistician collects systematically a great many data that do not necessarily come together into a unified scheme. There is a third group of researchers who have tried to combine the two approaches—either as a compromise or as a hybrid incorporating the strengths of each into a more powerful methodology. For purposes of clarity (if not elegance) we might term these workers hedgefoxes.

There is a risk in drawing these distinctions too sharply. For one thing, pure types do not exist in reality. Most group researchers employing statistical methods have as their goal the discovery of general laws of group behavior. Likewise, the clinician, despite his endorsement of a unifying theoretical stance, most often approaches a group session with an open mind, letting the data accumulate to confirm or deny hypotheses. In writing about group events, even the most clinical marshal evidence and order data in a systematic although not necessarily quantitative way. There is a further risk that these distinctions can portray more polarization than exists and thereby create unnecessary controversy. However, these distinctions are useful enough, we believe, to justify such a risk. The field of small-group research actually highlights the statistical-clinical problem. Studies can be arrayed along this continuum fairly easily. Some approaches are rich in clinical, anecdotal observations and theoretical formulations. Others emphasize a methodology resting on complicated act-by-act scoring and ingenious quantitative analysis of data.

THE FOXES

The methods of the fox are best exemplified by the work of R. F. Bales (1950a) in his development of an act-by-act scoring system for group interaction, interaction process analysis. Working primarily in the sociological tradition, Bales categorized verbal interaction on various dimensions with a high degree of reliability. His coding system can be used to score many kinds of verbal interaction in diverse groups. Laboratory, therapy, classroom, and other types of groups have been studied by means of this method. The categories by which the observations are coded call for relatively objective criteria, achieve good reliability, and are easily quantifiable. This system has yielded remarkable generalizations about group development, role differentiation, and individual differences in a variety of settings. (For a detailed discussion of this scoring system see Chapter 2 of this volume.)

Others have continued in this tradition by developing scoring systems with different emphases. Mills (1964) utilized his sign process analysis to study the development of self-analytic classroom groups. Mann and his associates (1966, 1967, 1970) developed first a member-leader and then a member-member scoring system to assess the feelings of members in various classroom groups. These approaches all serve to reduce group events to their component parts, which can be coded and then treated statistically. These scoring systems reflect the conviction that if one can record enough of the atomistic events in groups well enough and can manipulate the resulting data ingeniously enough, the laws or patterns of group life will emerge statistically.

Numerous other schemes have been devised for coding interaction in groups, as Weick's (1968) review of the literature shows. Bales and Mills are the most exemplary for our purposes here and perhaps the most influential in our own thinking. Several other methodological approaches deserve mention here, however. Leary (1957) postulated two orthogonal bipolar dimensions: the dominance-submission and the love-hate dimension. Efforts have been made to extend this scheme into a scoring system for groups, but the overall results are not encouraging. Schutz (1958) used an observer rating form and observation system based on the needs for inclusion, control, and affection. Thelen (1954) developed a scoring system for group interaction based on Bion's theory of group basic-assumption activity. All these studies have in common the attempt to code verbal interaction systematically, according to a scheme derived from theoretical assumptions about interpersonal behavior, in

order to identify more nearly universal dimensions of social interaction.

Others of an essentially foxy disposition have eschewed the
direct scoring of verbal interaction and have concentrated instead
on postmeeting variables. This technique has the advantage of
sampling activity of all of the members, not simply the verbally
active ones. Wechsler and Reisel (1959) and Stock and Thelen
(1958) employed such postmeeting ratings. Dunphy (1964, 1966,
1968) utilized the postmeeting write-ups of the week's events in two
self-analytic groups in his extensive study of group development and
role differentiation. He utilized a computer-based content-analysis
system, The General Inquirer, for his data. (For details see Chapter
12 of this volume.) Content analysis allows for the breakdown of
verbal behavior into smaller units and is especially well suited for
statistical treatment. It has the disadvantage of failing to take into
account the context and connotation of the content being coded.

THE HEDGEHOGS

Those who aspire to a larger, more unifying view of groups
may not take explicit or systematic intervening steps in arriving at
their conclusions about groups. They employ less obviously "scientific" methods in arriving at their conclusions. Bion (1959), Bennis
and Shepard (1956), and Slater (1966) best exemplify this approach. Bion's theories, for example, derive from his therapeutic
experiences with groups and his theoretical training as a Kleinian
analyst. His unifying view is that group process is a function of
defense against psychotic anxiety and that the group-as-a-whole is
unconsciously perceived as the mother's body. He further notes that
the group is capable of certain "basic-assumption" activities—
fight/flight, dependency, and pairing—that interfere with constructive work. Others have attempted to test out these ideas in more
systematic and quantitative fashion (Stock and Thelen, 1958). But
Bion's theory was not originally derived by quantitative means but
rather from more intuitive and theoretical processes.

Bennis and Shepard likewise employed a more global, impressionistic—clinical—approach in arriving at their observations
about group development. (Their paper appears as Chapter 6 of

this volume.) Theirs is a comprehensive theory which involves the group-as-a-whole, subgroups, individuals, and "barometric events." They contend that group development proceeds in two areas of "internal uncertainty": dependence, which involves authority relations, and interdependence, which involves personal relations. (These are essentially the power and love dimensions noted by Leary.) Despite the systematic nature of this theory, the methods by which it was derived are global rather than atomistic and impressionistic rather than statistical.

Slater (1966) utilized a more systematic way of recording his observations of self-analytic groups. He kept postmeeting logs in which he recorded his observations, impressions, and theories. His unit of analysis was the session as a whole. Out of these impressions and ruminations he elaborated a complicated yet elegant theory of group development which touches importantly on issues of personality formation, cognitive development, and religious evolution. It is truly the work of a hedgehog, because many disparate phenomena in his groups and far beyond are integrated in an overarching conceptual framework. His unifying idea is that group development is a function of group and individual boundary establishment and maintenance. There is a desire for boundary establishment in groups, yet a contrary wish/fear involving the loss of individuality by fusion with the group-as-a-whole. Slater translates Bion's nondevelopmental scheme into a developmental model and integrates Piaget's stages of cognitive development and Neumann's stages of religious development with his own group-development theory.

The focus of the hedgehog is thus more global, more impressionistic, and ultimately more subjective and idiographic than that of the fox. Much of the group therapy literature that is case-study oriented fits this description. Most psychoanalytic work, except that which is subjected to experimental study, also falls into this category. The issues with which the hedgehog is ultimately concerned are difficult to operationalize and quantify for statistical treatment. When unconscious processes are a main focus, as they tend to be in these kinds of studies, quantification issues become even more acute. How can it be demonstrated that such processes exist? How are they to be measured? Or should they be? It is around these kinds of questions that the battle is joined. The statistically minded call out for quantifiable verification of these global processes, theoretical structures, and unconscious mechanisms. The clinicians, hard-pressed to do so, argue for the essential value and integrity of their approach without such constricting measurement.

THE HEDGEFOXES

This ungainly term is used to denote those who have sought to combine the methods of the fox and the hedgehog into a single approach, to integrate the clinical with the statistical. This is where such delineation becomes particularly risky, since pure types simply do not exist. Bales (1970) in his recent work has combined his interaction process analysis approach with more in-depth studies of individuals via a factor-analytic method. Through a complex factor analysis of a multitude of data, he has arrived at a notion of a three-dimensional interpersonal space: status and power, likeability, and task commitment. He has included in this work a method to quantify fantasy activity in groups as well. Bales in many respects epitomizes the Tolstoyan dilemma and has perhaps progressed further than anyone else in trying to resolve it. Bales' work reflects the hope that laws of group behavior will emerge from the analysis of larger and larger amounts of small samples of data. Out of this ability to observe, code, and analyze these atomistic behaviors will come the unifying view of the hedgehog. His latest work comes closest to this ideal.

Dunphy, too, utilized a system of content analysis which broke the verbal reports of group members into categories of words. By using factor analysis to reconstruct these data, Dunphy was able to develop an intriguing theory about the role of individual specialists and the development of group mythology in social change. This work, too, reflects the desire for a formulation in which role differentiation, fantasy activity, and group development fall in one more inclusive framework.

Mills (1964) also used his scoring system as a stepping stone to a more global theory of the development of a working group. His methodology was by no means an end in itself. For our purposes here it is important to note that these studies in their *methodology* did not combine clinical and statistical approaches. They utilized a statistical method to achieve a hedgehog's goal—that of achieving a more unifying theory of interpersonal and group behavior.

It is clear that one method which has facilitated the construction of more unifying views from atomistic data is factor analysis. Carson (1969) has written a thoughtful review of efforts to reduce the vast domain of interpersonal behavior to a few universal factors. Gibbard and Hartman have recently (1973a)` commented on the success of this strategy for small-group research. We have argued that one shortcoming of attempts to classify universal factors in interpersonal life is that they proceed at a relatively high level of abstraction. In addition, interpersonal behavior varies so much across situations that, rather than reflecting universal dimensions, a factor analysis may reflect the uniqueness of the setting from which the behavior was sampled. Thus, the dimensions which emerge from one study or series of studies may have considerable validity as abstract conceptualizations but offer little help in pinpointing the central issues or the most salient categories of behavior in a different setting. After all, what comes out of a factor analysis depends on what system of categorization of behavior was utilized initially. Scoring systems relevant to one type of situation may not be appropriate for another. An investigator may, legitimately, set himself the primary task of understanding one type of setting—say, a patient-staff meeting—and for this task a general system of classification may be largely irrelevant. Alternatively, it may well be that strategies designed for specific interpersonal settings *will* lead to clarifications, refinements, or revisions of the more general conceptualizations.

So, although factor analysis seems to promise the possibility of combining the methods of the fox with the goals of the hedgehog, such an integration is not easily achieved—it is still dependent on the nature of the variables used and the method of recording such variables.

Two further sets of studies deserve mention here because they are distinguished by efforts to utilize quantitative techniques to code behavior such as feelings, unconscious processes, defenses, and group climate. The coding process thus begins to have much in common with clinical inference. One has to make "subjective" judgments and inferences about what is going on between two people or in the group-as-a-whole.

The first of these efforts is the work of Dorothy Stock Whitaker in her collaboration through the years with H. Thelen and M. Lieberman (Stock and Thelen, 1958; Stock and Lieberman, 1962; Whitaker and Lieberman, 1964). One study was an attempt to operationalize and concretize Bion's highly impressionistic concepts about group life—work versus the basic-assumption activities of fight/flight, dependency, and pairing. This study was in the spirit of those many attempts to subject psychoanalytic concepts to more rigorous tests of validity. The scoring system used in this study was geared specifically to those behaviors which are of interest to the clinician. The researchers, however, attempted to record these behaviors for quantitative evaluation. A paper with Lieberman (Chapter 3) explores methodology involved in assessing the kinds of global clinical inferences necessary in the conduct of "group process" group therapy. How can one concretize group "climate" or a group "focal conflict"? Whitaker and Lieberman explore a rationale for doing just that.

The other studies that deserve mention here are those of Mann and his coworkers (Mann, 1966, 1967; Mann and others, 1970; Gibbard and Hartman, 1973a,b,c). These studies employed an act-by-act scoring system in the tradition of Bales, but this system was based on "clinical" variables reflecting the observation and interpretation of group members' *feelings* toward the leader. This system was later modified to include member-member feelings as well. The system has been applied to self-analytic and traditional classroom groups and, in an exploratory fashion, to therapy groups. Much of the scoring involves inferences about the symbolic meaning of discussions of concerns external to the group, discussions which are seen as disguised statements about or messages to the leader or members. The categories include four kinds of hostility (moving against, disagreeing, withdrawing, and guilt-inducing), four kinds of affection (moving toward, identifying, agreeing, and reparation), three kinds of power relations (submission, equality, dominance) and "ego states" (expressing and denying anxiety, depression, and guilt). In addition, four thematic categories (nurturance, control, sexuality, and competence) are scored.

This scoring system, based primarily on psychodynamic theories, has as its focus feelings, impulses, moods, and attitudes. Scoring becomes more akin to recording the flow of clinical inferences than to quantifying content in a more "objective" fashion. The aim of these studies was to show that variables useful to the clinician could be systematically observed and scored with reasonable reliability. Not everyone, however, can score using this system; it is not like counting words. One has to be trained to listen with the "third ear" to make these kinds of inferences. But despite the subtlety and complexity of this system trained scorers have achieved adequate levels of reliability.

Factor analysis was then employed in the various studies to reduce the category and thematic variables to a more manageable number. The factor analysis was then used to generate factor scores on those interactions that best exemplified the factors. By going back to the tape recordings of the actual interactions, we used a more global and clinical approach to make sense of the factors. That is, the studies did not stop with the factor analysis; they began there. The factor analysis allowed us to look more systematically at the rich and complex human interactions, to order our understanding of the vast array of data. Listening to the tapes allowed us to animate and enliven the numbers, which we had almost come to believe *were* the interactions.

In this way the studies were attempts to combine and interweave the clinical and statistical approaches to small-group research. After over ten years of work with this methodology, we can say with some detachment that the Tolstoyan ideal remains. Trying to combine systematic observation and quantitative analysis with variables familiar to the clinician is a worthy goal that has yielded worthwhile results. At times, though, it seemed as if the work had too many numbers for the working clinician and yet was too impressionistic and subjective for some experimental social psychologists.

Which of these broad approaches to small-group methodology is best? Which should a researcher use? The ultimate answer to these questions lies in the needs, values, and particular questions of the individual researcher. We have simply stated the alternatives. In addition, in this section we present papers representative of different positions in the hope that the reader will decide for himself which approach suits his particular situation.

Mann begins with an openly personal statement about the place of research in his own identity, ultimate values, professional commitment to groups, and social concerns. He feels that research should be responsive primarily to personal, professional, and social needs rather than to a more abstract and dispassionate notion of what constitutes science. The latter he regards as narrowing and constricting for students, professionals, and researchers. Mann's previous work has reflected a desire to integrate the clinical and statistical, the scientific and the artistic. This present paper is to some extent a move away from that position. The paper seems to be written with the same general goal in mind—to be a hedgefox—but in a spirit less bound to the assumptions and values of science. It is an attempt not to solve the clinical-statistical dilemma but to transcend it.

Mills's paper, in contrast, represents the measured voice of the fox, outlining the procedures of a science and describing those techniques which have been the basis of most group research. He presents a useful summary of Bales' technique of act-by-act scoring and outlines Dunphy's method of content analysis as well. Mills' paper articulates a rationale for objectivity, systematization, and quantification—in contrast to Mann's support of the artistic and subjective.

Stock and Lieberman, in the third selection, offer a thoughtful approach to the issue of concretizing variables such as "group focal conflict" or other hazy clinical concepts. They attempt to deal with issues of reliability and validity in clinical observation and interpretation. How does the researcher know that what he says he has observed—a group focal conflict, say—really exists? Can he achieve reliability for these kinds of observations, or do the inferences come out of a textbook or even out of his own neurosis? Questions such as this are posed by skeptical experimentalists and patients alike. They constitute the core issues for all enterprises which involve variables that must be inferred from direct observation and are the questions most relevant to all research based on psychoanalytic theory. Stock and Lieberman accept the traditional scientific criteria for systematic recording of observation, for reliability, and for attention to issues of validity. They outline a procedure which, while accepting these criteria, allows for a flexibility and a breadth compatible with the concerns of the clinician. The spirit of the paper is on the whole conciliatory to the scientific approach but is firm in its commitment to investigating and utilizing concepts of a highly impressionistic sort. It is therefore a hedgehog's approach but with an appreciation of the values and goals of the fox. It is akin to the earlier work of Mann, which sought to reach a viable compromise between scientific criteria and clinical concepts and concerns. It represents a middle ground between the positions of Mann and Mills as articulated in their papers in this section.

Slater's paper concludes the section with a description of the merits of naturalistic observation as opposed to experimentation, of hypothesis developing versus hypothesis testing. This short paper was selected as the methodological statement of an arch-hedgehog. Without quantification or the strictures of hypothesis testing, Slater has presented a group theory which seeks to integrate cognitive development, religious evolution, and group development. His is a unifying view of seemingly disparate phenomena, and in this paper he articulates and defends the methodology which brought about such an integration.

The Identity of
the Group Researcher

RICHARD D. MANN

*I*t may be time to rescue group re-
search from the hands of the scientists. It may be time to create a
new vision of what it means to try to undersand things that really
matter, things in which you are involved but which continue to
baffle or upset you. When one considers how many people are deeply
involved in group events whose meaning they can scarcely comprehend, and then considers how few of these people do research to
enlighten themselves and others, it begins to seem likely that the
problem lies not with the people in groups but with the definition
and conduct of research.

Just the other day a graduate student who called on another
matter announced toward the end of the conversation, "I think I'm
going to drop out of the university this year. I can't find any research to do that doesn't seem either silly or sterile." We do not need
to know which part of human reality most engaged this student to
share her exhaustion with the struggle to bring together her own

13

sharpest insights and concerns on the one hand and the professional literature, the sanctioned methods, and the scientific frame of mind on the other.

When a first or second grader in a traditional classroom finally shouts out his pained awareness that it really isn't any fun in school anymore, the teacher says, "Oh, Johnny, you know we have fun-time for the first half-hour before we get down to the regular work, and there's a long recess on Tuesdays and Fridays." When a graduate student finally blurts out his pained awareness that what he most wants to do is utterly deprived of legitimacy, the instructor of the methods course says, "Oh, but you know how much we value exploratory, clinical, impressionistic studies as a first step before the really solid research gets under way." And so all of us learn, all our lives, that what we call our work is trivial in their eyes, that it is nowhere near as serious and valid as what they do, and try so hard to make us do. The very things we most want to do become, in their eyes and gradually in our own as well, some kind of vague, sloppy self-indulgence which they hope we will transcend as quickly as possible.

It may be time to say that all that pressure to shape up is unhelpful and misguided. It derives from the wrong assumptions about who we researchers are, what we need in order to grow and to understand, and where we should be heading. It is not the voice of surgency and creativity. It is the voice of a bureaucratized and deadened spirit, which has somehow adorned itself with the trappings of science.

Research activity need not define for the person doing it an identity or an ideal which resembles the all too clearly drawn image of the researcher as scientist. That constraining and alienating definition of who we are can and should be replaced by a definition that validates our reality as seekers who embrace their not-knowing, as fellow participants in life, as facilitators of the growth of certain real persons, as partisans in a vital social movement, as friends, and as persons capable of relating to the world in many complex ways all at once. There is absolutely no need for people to approach the world of research only through the portal of science. It is time to illuminate the other portals and to demonstrate their accessibility before even more people come to the wrong gate and turn away, unwilling to pay such a heavy (and unnecessary) price for acquiring the techniques and even the pleasures of the researcher-scientist.

It is possible to turn away from the identity of the researcher-scientist without discarding everything that the scientific tradition has created. If some of us researchers choose to end our poignant struggle to achieve respectability in the eyes of those whose operating values are so alienating, we need not leave behind the various skills and equipment we have already mastered. For myself at least, the great challenge lies in assembling a new and more liberating identity as researcher, keeping what is useful from my training and discarding only what now seems mistaken and narrow about the world of science. I am fully aware that I am under no obligation to change my self-description. I recall the academic ceremonies in which it is claimed that, despite our occasional differences, we are really all one big happy family. Science has room for all, we are told. But when the ceremony is over, many return to the workaday world still maintaining that some styles of research are more scientific than others and therefore more faithful to the great family mission. And others return from the family banquet unreassured, just as blocked from doing what they are impelled to do, and just as unable to feel good about their work as ever before.

I have no proposal for a new family name. I know only that I will no longer cringe at being called unscientific. I will no longer hide my subjectivity in order to pass by the guardian at the portal of science. I am, quite simply, a person who spends much of his professional life in groups. Some we call self-analytic groups; others are political. Even in my family, with my friends, or when serving on faculty committees it sometimes seems crystal clear that this is the slice of reality I want to know more about. What is going on in these groups? How did we get here? What can I do to get this group moving? Have others come this way before? Do their footprints give any clue as to how to get out of this thicket? Am I growing into a more generally useful person in groups? Do I deserve my paycheck or my reputation? At their core these and the hundreds of other questions I ask myself about groups are not a scientist's questions. They bear some resemblance to the concerns of a scientist, perhaps, but I must redefine who I am when I ask these questions. Who am I—who are we—when we work within and try to learn from groups?

The core of the identity which I am trying to clarify is this: I am a person who is driven to enlarge my own sense of the meaningfulness around and within me. Some of my greatest pleasures are utterly personal, and they derive from the sudden realization that the person over there has a reality separate from his effect on me. Suddenly my sense of the continuity and integrity of separate people, each acting in deeply expressive and purposive ways, overwhelms me. Where before there had been only my irritation, my impatient or scornful assumption that I knew who they were and what they were about, now there is an awed realization of the dignity of individuals and their developing relationships. The lights go on. The fog lifts. People come into focus. And that apparently endless struggle to locate oneself in a world of meaning, a world of real people, has, at least for the moment, yielded some measure of success.

It seems to me that any effort to understand why I and some others do research must start at precisely this point—the struggle to live in a world of meaning. That dual sense of exhilaration and occasional relief, of vigilance and of calm, is the root experience for the kind of research I want to do.

Can we begin, then, to explore this struggle and to understand how our work as researchers derives in part from these root experiences? I can still recall with chilling vividness the first group I ever "ran," a Soc Rel 120 group at Harvard in the fall of 1960.[1] I knew that my role as instructor meant I was supposed to "intervene" from time to time. But I sat there in paralyzed confusion for days as the group got under way. "My God," I thought, "I'm just not going to be able to do this thing. I don't have one single coherent thought in my head, except this one." Certainly one reason we do research is to reduce the terror of those inevitable moments when we simply do not grasp the meaning of what is going on around us.

If research is ever to assist us in our search for the coherence of what is happening in groups, we will need to be very clear about

[1] For a description of the self-analytic groups alluded to here, see Bales (1970), Mann (1967)), Mills (1964), or Slater (1966).

what constitutes an appropriate methodology for this search. Several examples come to mind: Henry Murray working alone for hours over a TAT protocol he has just gathered; Phil Slater closeting himself with his private log of what just occurred in the group session the hour before; a group watching a video replay of a particularly intense interaction. The two great enemies of successful research at this level are the universal inclination to resist awareness of how meaningful things are and the inability of people, even with the best of intentions, to keep up with the flow and complexity of human behavior. What a long list could be assembled of the reasons why we choose to dismiss much of what we observe as meaningless, trivial—not worth further inquiry. We are quickly overwhelmed, and the terror we have learned to master since childhood creeps back into our consciousness. The terror stems from the sense of falling further and further behind, of understanding no more than a tiny fraction of what is being said and intended. Some people go blank; some turn to their inner fantasies and become increasingly self-absorbed; and others construct elaborate filters which allow only certain issues or meanings to seem important. But the sense of missing things that I would rather understand is what impels me to turn to the stylized but wonderfully helpful world of research.

Research can slow things down. Projective techniques, tape recordings, and interview notes provide us with something we can go over slowly, at a rate which matches our feeble powers to process the meaningfulness of people's expressive activity. We can go over and over the same material. If we are lucky and have at least some talent for this kind of work, the chaos turns to scattered islands of comprehension. The redundancy of life becomes more apparent.

I never learned more about what goes on in groups than during the time spent creating and analyzing a verbatim transcript of one self-analytic group. The act-by-act scoring methodology my colleagues and I have used for the past ten years is our way of searching for meaning.[2] I know that I need to be able to go over the material many times. I know that I need to force myself to ask about every utterance: "What does that mean? What is the person saying and feeling?" I have learned that I can sense the complex meaning

---

[2] For a detailed description of this scoring system see Mann (1967, 1970) and Gibbard and Hartman (1973a).

in what people say if I can take seriously a notion developed by Freud in his interpretation of dream material—the notion that many feelings gain expression only after considerable symbolization and disguise.

The question becomes: Why is this person saying this thing at this moment in this context? I need time to answer this question, and scoring takes a long time indeed. Just as Murray would work to unscramble the complex identifications and projections which connect the person with his TAT protocol, we work to uncover at least some of the symbolic equations between the speaker, the others in the group, and the speaker's references to apparently external events. When a person suddenly launches an attack on the psychiatrist who tried to prevent Hemingway's suicide, it may be our task as researchers to see whether any part of the meaningfulness of his remarks can be traced to his feelings about himself or the group leader or a male rival or anyone else.

Back in the days when I thought that the highest calling of the researcher was to follow the path of science, I felt it necessary to justify my research in ways that scientists find acceptable: I was constructing exhaustive, universally applicable categories; I was adding to the data base of the field, and so on and so forth. Those weren't awful goals, and I still have them somewhere in my hierarchy of wishes, but they were quite minor goals. My research was, and still is, one part of my deepest needs to understand particular people in particular groups.

It was not enough, for me at least, simply to slow down the action with my tape recorder and verbatim transcript. That was just the first step. I found that three things happened when I went over a transcript: (1) I could sense at least some of the meanings and symbolic interactions far better than during the group session (and this was enormously exciting and rewarding). (2) My capacity to retain what I had uncovered was pretty feeble. I could recall that I had had a lot of interesting thoughts but either I was doomed to forget most of them or I would have to create a document five times the size of the transcript, and then what would I do with that? (3) Even more disconcerting was my growing awareness that the great excitement of each successive day's absorption with the material was

thematically discontinuous with the great insights of the next day.
I found myself to be terribly distractible, pulled one day into an
exploration of one aspect of the meaning of it all, and then pulled
the next day into an equally engrossing but quite different aspect.
And even beyond my concern for the comparability of data so dear
to the scientist's heart, I was concerned that each day's adventure
with the data reflected my own shifting mood, my own love of
novelty, or even my unwillingness to explore some issues beyond a
certain point.

I was in the market for a research technique which could
reassure me that I would not have to repeat my analyses under all
possible variations of my own inner moods and preoccupations.
But what were my questions? What did I really want to know?

It all seems very clear to me now, in retrospect. I was a
novice, running my first few groups. I knew that things of great
meaning to me were going on, and I wanted to be able to have a
clearer sense of their basic form. I wanted to know what those
people in the group felt about me. Did they feel some kind of
hostility? Is that what they were saying, even if not in so many
words? Were they defending me, pulling away, flirting, identifying,
or what? And then an entirely different set of questions: What
was their relationship to me as an authority in this group, as the
instructor, the group leader? And finally, how were they feeling
about themselves? Were they expressing fear, self-reproach, a degree
of self-satisfaction; or were they working hard to conceal and
master their own mistrust, guilt, or depression? These were my
questions in 1961. Plus one other: How was I indicating my awareness of what they were feeling? What was the content of the mirror
I held to the group, and was I telling them it was all right to feel
such things or not?

Later, others came along with other questions. Others began
to record what the leader was feeling toward the group and what
the various group members were feeling toward each other. I
never doubted the importance of these questions; they just were
not my primary concerns. It got a little tiresome having people
suggest to me that I was unaware that the group contained more
than member-leader relations. But my research was a reflection of

what was on my mind and what I felt I needed to understand better than I could merely by being in the group and listening. No apologies needed.

What I learned at that time about the search for meaning now forms an integral part of my feeling for all research. Research is, or can be, merely a somewhat stylized representation of the great insight that I (the researcher) am not the center of the universe, that the meaningfulness of what others say and do stems from their own integral centrality. In new or confusing encounters with others, however, I seem always to begin with an egocentric view. For example, if someone is trying to relate to some aspect of me which I am blind to, I tend to dismiss his intended meaning and to substitute my own. If he is working on something quite apart from me, I tend to come up with quite inaccurate estimates of what is going on. The magnitude of my misperceptions is often quite astounding. But the truly astounding thing is the difference it makes to grasp one truth of interpersonal life: that each person is spinning on his own gyroscope, his own meaning system. One is more able to comprehend the meaningfulness of a person's actions if one traces them back to that person's needs, values, experiences, and symbols and if one takes account of how that person perceives the context of his actions.

I recall a residents' seminar at which the presenting resident made brilliant conjectures about the probable meaning of one central symptom; the analyst leading the discussion responded to these conjectures by remarking, "Well, those were *your* associations to the symptom in question; what were the patient's associations?" Those long silences in the analytic hour sometimes reflect a remarkable research methodology in action: When you don't understand yet, listen some more—listen to the patient before leaping in with your own meanings, however brilliant or fascinating they may seem at the time. The idea that it is the other person whose elaborations will clarify the meaning of his own thoughts and actions is one which is very hard to translate into formal research methodology. In other words, the requisite skills of a researcher come to include patience, respect for the integrity and expressive capacities of others, and above all a willingness to value the capacities of others to generate and to comprehend their own meaning. Perhaps one reason why people turn away from naturalistic research is that the researcher's stance of attentive passivity is somehow less comfortable than the active, meaning-imposing stance of the experimenter or the survey researcher with his interview schedule all worked out. However that may be, all I am asserting here is that the identity of the researcher can (but need not) include a deep commitment to an interpersonal world in which the separateness and the self-generated meaningfulness of each person is affirmed.

In some ways, then, the researcher recapitulates that painful developmental crisis which Melanie Klein (1957) sees as starting in the earliest months of life. The emergence of the infant from a totally undifferentiated, egocentric world into a world containing others is accompanied by the first horrible hypothesis of interpersonal life: the distinct possibility that the other has meaning as one's mortal enemy. The best sense we can make of the world at times is that someone out there is enraged at our tenuous hold on life and seeks only to deny or destroy us. The paranoid position, as Klein calls it, is horrible enough; but this construction of reality is soon joined by a second hypothesis, which is tantalizing in its capacity to make sense out of life's bewildering complexity. If the first locates evil in the other, the witch-monster of our deepest fears, the second locates the evil and the malevolence in ourselves and suggests that we are the greedy, inevitably hurtful monster of our deepest depressions. As the infant moves into the interpersonal world, it does so via these awful possibilities; and clearly our adult lives are never free of the reverberations and the newly created variants of these twin horrors: fear of the motives of others and fear of our own motives in dealing with others.

Research is obviously not the only way to soften the impact of the fears we bring to interpersonal life. Research is but one of the ways we manage to take another and a longer look at reality. The phantoms with which I populate my interpersonal world, the portents of danger which I think I see behind this remark or that silence, are as vulnerable to the light of scrutiny as the ominous shadow cast by the lamp in my darkened and frightening nursery. It was Freud who illuminated the mistrustful world of the Victorian doctor. The poor doctor had it all figured out—his hysterical patients were faking and carrying on in order to gain his sympathy and heaven knows what other compromise with his professional identity. Parents thought their children's terror of horses was just some fanciful effort to provoke them to the point of utter frustration and rage. But Freud's research offered to his patients and their relatives, and to himself as well, a reassuring sense of the meaningfulness of each symptom. It turned out that his patients' strange behavior made sense if only one could understand their inner worlds. Suddenly the advances of the seductive patient were more than a devious effort to destroy the reputation of a too-trusting doctor. The parents of Hans turned out to have much more than a bad or silly boy. What Freud did, and what any researcher can do, is to offer the world, including himself, a way to break the hold of various unhelpful hypotheses.

It seems clear to me that groups are a simply marvelous place for paranoid and depressive hypotheses to develop. There is so much evidence to confirm one's fears that the leader is deliberately trying to frustrate or harm the group. The leader, too, has his worst fears confirmed. Everyone in a group seems so capable of saying precisely the wrong thing, the thing that unaccountably wounds or alienates people.

I do research because the hypotheses which otherwise lodge in my brain after days of intense group participation are not only troublesome but wrong. They are hopelessly oversimplified constructions of reality which I cannot dislodge because I cannot untangle the current reality from the residue of all my previous relationships. To be liberating and conducive to sustained work, the commonly accepted definition of a researcher's identity must make room for the intensely private activities of a person struggling with his own past. Research which is widely sharable may be so because our pasts are sometimes congruent, but this sharing of insight is not the only goal.

My colleagues and I do research on groups partly because we find that what happens in groups offers us a chance to unravel the intertwined realities of our present and our past. I know all too well how open I am to this confusion of realities, but somehow I am challenged by the prospect of risking this confusion. Research is but an adjunct of a full life in which my commitment is to the people in the groups, not to the archives of a professional literature. I have found that research has more than repaid the effort involved, simply because it permits me to sort out some of the unique variations on life found in any new situation. In general, after an intense period of research, people seem deeper, less malevolent, more sensible, more courageous, less silly, better set in the context of their own history, more creative, and much more attractive. Perhaps if I had found otherwise, I would not have found research so useful to my professional and personal life. But that is how it has worked out, and that accounts in part for why it now seems so important to rescue research from those who would find such a result irrelevant or even disqualifying.

So far, I have made it sound as though research is useful either when I am completely confused or when I need some help dispelling some of my worst fears and misperceptions about group life. And if my sense of myself as a scientist is strained by even these definitions of research, it is nearly shattered by one further realization: that although we often know too little, there are times when we know too much. We know so much, we are so flooded with meaning, that we are overwhelmed. Research is, or can be, a somewhat stylized version of our commitment to ride the whirlwind, to let the meanings in, and to risk feeling terribly crazy. For meanings that are too discordant, too challenging to what we think we know, set in motion that process of mind we learn to call madness. When all the usual ways of making life seem trivial and incomprehensible break down, we are often left at the mercy of a veritable overload of meaning. At that moment the world of the scientist's null hypothesis looks like heaven itself. But often the scientist's pretense of knowing nothing seems a clever but not very helpful way of stalling, a deliberate effort to turn away from the truth. It is quite an accomplishment that scientists have managed to convince themselves (and a few others) that the state of knowledge is still nearly zero. But at what a cost this grand intellectual structure is erected. The price science would seem to exact is that we agree not to see the worlds of meaning which are dancing before our very eyes.

The question is: Is there some third way to relate to the meaning before us, some way which leaves us neither overwhelmed nor barren? Is there some way to grow in our capacity to take in the import of others' (and our own) sometimes alien-seeming meanings?

What the researcher must do, it seems to me, and what the

scientist is seldom trained to do, is to develop the capacity for metaphor, symbolization, playfulness, and all the familiar human skills that make one more capable of tolerating meaning. What the journal editor or the research-methods teacher censures as imprecise and poetic is what the human mind often produces when it is confronted with a new and stressful awareness. We learn to toy with scary things. We learn to say what is known, but in a disguised and tentative way.

When Skinner put the lid on the box, the better to block his view of the rat's delicate, exploratory behavior, he offered one path: the path of reducing the meaningfulness one apprehends to practically the vanishing point. The better to determine the lawfulness of behavior, he contends. But this model for how to proceed is of no use to a person in a group. Even the researcher pulled away from the group, left with a mere tape recording, had better not yearn for Skinner's closed box. What then?

Suddenly all the structures for putting human inquiry into separate boxes, all the ways to divide social science from the humanities, all the ways to split off scholarly work from the creative arts seem like a colossal hoax. To do research without allowing oneself a full identity—one that includes modes of thought commonly ascribed to poets, scientists, rationalists, and crazy people—is to meet the stress of meaningfulness with unnecessary handicaps. Research can be mighty heady stuff. If a linguist and a therapist can become so enmeshed in the meaningfulness of five minutes of an initial interview that it takes a whole book to explore the phonetic protocol, it is no surprise to find that research on groups leads straight to the precipice (see Pittenger, Hockett, and Danehy, 1960).

Some days we scorers (meaning Maxine Bernstein, Graham Gibbard, John Hartman, and I) would open up vistas of what lay behind the manifest content of the group transactions, vistas which seemed about to engulf us. Would we ever get out alive? If you once listen to what people really mean, and experience the pain, the unexpected coherence, and even the beauty of what someone is feeling and doing, will you ever extricate yourself? The threat when scoring is not one single danger, but certainly part of what one fears is self-loss. First one loses one's own bearings. The sense a person had seemed to be making when viewed from one external perspective fades away and is replaced by how it all looks from the inside out. Stressful as this may be, it is manageable in part by experiencing oneself as a partisan of the other. But the tape rolls on, and a far greater stress awaits you. This one person you feel so identified with is engaged in a struggle or an encounter with a second person. If one abandons both one's own prior perspective and the perspective of the first person, if one moves to see the world from within and on behalf of the second person, the danger is not only self-loss; the danger is fragmentation.

There is nothing unique about this sequence. It is one of the special tortures of interpersonal life, of what Bion (1962) calls the three-body problem. Shifting perspectives, each creating unique and divergent realities, are the stuff of group life from the family onward. And who says a person is capable of generating only one coherent meaning system? The more deeply one probes, the more a "person" resembles a whole panel of sometimes convergent and sometimes warring subsystems of meaning and pressure. One mother can generate such divergent messages—one message, for instance, telling the child to drop dead; another telling him never to mention the first message to anyone, including the mother herself—that the child simply collapses into illness. Two parents, or two or more group members, pressing in on a person can create an endlessly complex swirl of meaning. To enter this maelstrom, either as a participant or as an observer-researcher, is to risk a great deal. What is a person to do? When we are in groups or even when we contrive via research to get some distance from the scene, we must find a creative solution to the stresses of understanding so much.

The conduct and the fruits of research reflect one of our greatest assets: our appreciation of form. We can bind in our frenzy with one or another use of form. Whether we use haiku or iambic pentameter, we can transform our self-consciousness into that of the passive servant of pure form. The words appear to be pulled from us; nature appears to speak through us. We become more the servant of the lord of creation and less the vulnerable Icarus. We know, but our knowing is not a blasphemy. We disguise the source of our knowing by grasping for the form of tarot cards, sun signs, and sometimes even the form of scientific research.

We tend to reject expressive behavior that is not bound by

some sense of form; we call such behavior "word salad" and dismiss it as too subjective. And partly to avoid this chilling reception, partly to hide even from ourselves our power to grasp the truth, we develop an appreciation of form. The familiar rhythms and rhymes of the hymns we sing reassure us. We borrow a prayer from here, a psalm from there. And when all is going well, we manage to say what is really on our mind with little fear that someone will turn on us and ask, "What did you just say? What do you mean by that? Who are you?" The form of science is equally reassuring to some. The journal article is as stylized as the mass or the limerick, the fugue or the sonata. Good form is appreciated. Generous references to the currently popular concepts and methods permit the speaker to speak and the listener to hear. But forms die. Rituals drift away from the original, creative compromise between form and content. New meanings explode the old vessels.

There is no point in blaming science as such. It still serves many people very well. And those of us who rankle at its glorification of the invisible observer and who feel the dead weight of theory and method too acutely can simply move on. Besides, at one time its form matched quite nicely my timidity and my unwillingness to own my awareness.

A category system, an act-by-act methodology, and the presentation of results in a manner suitable for framing are forms. They solve one set of problems and they create another. We are from earliest infancy caught between our needs to figure out the regularities of life and our need to appreciate and be part of the particular, the immediate. The search for order and lawfulness is a matter of desperate priority. What leads to what? When is the stove hot? Can I get the Red Sox to rally in the ninth if I watch the picture through the dining room mirror while standing on one foot?

A category system is a compromise, obviously. Its promise is comparability across events, the better to foster recognition of patterns, the better to discover the orderliness, if any exists, of what leads to what.

The redundancy of my perceptions and concerns was my guide. I seemed to ask somewhat the same questions and to probe for somewhat the same hidden meanings over and over again. And after ten years of familiarity with the form of Freed Bales's observational research (see Bales, 1950a), it is not too surprising that my own grasping for form followed this path. The content of the categories was my own expressive task. I was no longer interested in how each act served or thwarted the small group in reaching its adaptive and integrative tasks. Rather, my preoccupation had shifted to the feelings experienced and somehow expressed by individual group members. The redundancy of my many efforts to grasp this set of meanings was one source of the categories; my absorption with the theories which seemed to have the most power and depth was the other. Klein (1948, 1957, 1963), Bion (1959), Bennis and Shepard (1956), and Bibring (1953) were part of the great compromise. However much they might have lost in developing their ideas, they had still retained, it seemed to me, a level of awareness and a capacity to grasp meaning which made their concepts useful to my own search for meaning and order. One category, guilt-inducing, landed in the final system simply because of my acute awareness of how exquisite a form of hostility this could be in the hands of my stepfather. My life had sensitized me to this, and so naturally it seemed to belong in the catalog of expressive acts. I mention this partly to emphasize my disagreement with those like Daniel Katz (1971), who are critical of group research because we do not settle on one or two category systems for a couple of decades. The identity of the researcher, if not that of the scientist, should not be hemmed in by such counsel from afar. If the progress of science is slowed by researchers' need to shape their observation system to their particular setting and to their particular concern, so be it.

The scientist and the artist, to name but two possible reference persons, give us quite different answers to the question: What should I work on? For example, the scientist is quick to caution us against exploring paths that meander through our personal fears and passions, whereas the artist urges us to risk this engagement, to avoid wasting time with the flatly obvious, and to be concerned only to stop short of formlessness. Overinvolvement becomes less the issue than uninvolvement, which is one danger, and madness, which is the other.

Every researcher must somehow juggle these cautionary messages and find some personal range of functioning that feels comfortable to him. What shall we do about the issue of love and hate in interpersonal life? Many researchers design recording devices so narrow in their band-width that it is as if there were no such thing as hostility, and barely any affection. Their accounts of group dynamics make one wonder whether only a few bizarre folks see so much destruction, so much courting, and so much anxiety and depression around these very issues. The portraits painted by many researcher-scientists seem lifeless, the inner worlds of the subjects studied so pathetically responsive to the stimuli presented via the carefully prepared tape recording. Are these subjects, as they present them to us, people whom they care about?

Research can be a stylized version of the diffusely erotic, constructive, and life-affirming process that we call love. It can be many other things too, but why pretend that it is *only* other things? In Bales's writing (1970), there is deep esteem for the group member who can help the group along, for the person who can bind in his egoism and join with others in making the larger collectivity a success. If in Bales's account the more rebellious, hostile people are treated somewhat unsympthetically, so be it. We need only look at Slater's (1966) work to see a quite different set of preoccupations: the operative metaphor is not Bales' "initially leaderless group" but the primal family or the despot at court. Slater's sympathies are ferociously antisycophant. Narcissism is not just wickedly anti-system. The autonomous male rebel, Joseph's big bad brother, and especially the women who lead the group away from enthraldom and toward autonomy are portrayed with affection and respect. In our own earlier work (Mann, 1967), by far the greatest sympathy and fascination went to the hero. The hero's explosive mixture of rebellion and depression, identification and autonomy, pulled from me as a researcher, as it had as a group leader, a strong need to paint the sympathetic portrait that I felt should be put before the world. Research can be done because of, and often in behalf of, the very people we have felt most drawn to and have engaged most deeply. Research is one way to rework a relationship so intense that one does not grasp more than the tiniest part of what has happened. The process of research can cool things off, but it can clarify them as well. Why shouldn't we wish to preserve and understand more fully the most meaningful aspects of group life?

As one's distance from the group increases, the hold of one's partisan identifications seems to lessen. In my own experience, although many of my final portraits were superficial and even mocking, my range of sympathy and respect as a researcher was far greater than when I was in the group. And in each subsequent group, I became less and less inclined to settle for shallow, unsympathetic constructions of people. What kind of research is it that enables one to feel drawn toward a larger number of human beings than before? What kind of research makes one want to show others a new way to look at this or that person—a way that transcends the most obvious first assessments of a person's meaning and his own private struggle? Whatever its label, it is a kind of research which does not define as illegitimate that general human pursuit whose motive power is love. Rather than research that just incidentally belittles and dehumanizes its subjects, why not expand the volume of research that draws upon one's own unique pool of understanding and affection?

If one part of my identity as a researcher defines as important the development of affection and/or an empathic understanding of others, it is all the more important to be clear how complex is the path to that goal. The great enemy of sympathy is not anger or lack of sympathy; it is superficiality, a preoccupation with a person's behavior and a reluctance to look behind the externals to the inner meanings and intentions. So, to permit myself as a researcher to carry on my normal strivings for deep, affectional relationships with others I must avoid freezing myself into a stance where I must think sympathetic thoughts all the time. I am not particularly proud that many people irritate me or leave me cold; but to suppress or ignore these feelings would not do much good. If such pretending were effective, the world would be a mighty loving place. There is no short cut to the erratic course one follows before one strikes the spark of sympathy and thereby reorders and replaces one's previously held images of another person. It is the path of engagement, and its main characteristic is that the other person comes to matter. One comes to hold any image—the ugly and the idealized alike—with some tentativeness. It is the other's reality that comes to matter, not just one's own need to feel that this other person has been nicely figured out. But what a long, difficult path it is. How begrudgingly we abandon our first inclinations to accept or reject others on our own terms, to see others mainly as different approximations to our own ideals or to our best or worst selves.

Not only is it difficult to share control over the meaning and direction of relationships; it is difficult to hold on to whatever gains are made in this direction. I suspect that one feature of group research which makes any published report of group research as repulsive as it is appealing is that the report is both an affirmation and a betrayal of human relationships. The reader, in identifying with the people in the groups under study, experiences the promise and the disappointment of one person's efforts to understand another human being. Students in later groups read the accounts of prior groups, and they can barely tolerate what they learn about the inner workings of the group leader's mind. Slater captures only part of the meaning of the experimenter myth when he points to the need of group members to locate purpose and control in the person of the leader. As his and other writings on group process show, the members of a group are correct that the leader's goals are "acquisitive and inquisitive." The members of the group are expressing a reasonable fear, the fear that the leader only seems personally engaged, whereas in reality he is gathering material for a new book. The experimenter only seems solicitous and attentive; perhaps behind that façade he is scornful or bored; perhaps he is using people.

An incident drawn from my own experience is relevant here: I knew that I was supposed to take my pay voucher and leave after participating in Bales' three-man problem-solving group. That was in 1951, and I was just starting my sophomore year in college. I stood there, outside the observer's room. Chris Heinicke had already ducked back inside the curtains and closed the door, taking our postmeeting reaction questionnaires with him. I just stood there. I wanted to talk to somebody about all this. Could one really study why some people are liked and some rejected? How had the other two subjects rated me? These were two of the things on my mind. And could I get in on this study? I don't think I misjudged the look of panic and confusion on the faces of the observers when they finally emerged, thinking the coast was clear. The voyeurs were confronted by the object of their observations. We all transcended the starkness of that moment, and I did get in on the study, thanks to Freed's great kindness. But the residual memory of that encounter haunts me whenever a person brings my book to class and it is clear that I too am caught in the act. What does it mean to study another person? How does it feel to walk through the wax museum of dead groups on the way to today's session?

One important reaction to being studied is to feel belittled and objectified to the point of lifelessness. It is evident that we human beings are prone to yield to others the power to define and evaluate the meaning of our own existence. We may later become embarrassed or enraged; we may reclaim for our own that power to define and evaluate. But before we do, we may yield to others in the interest of opening ourselves up to truths about ourselves which we hope will assist our personal development. When we discover, or think we have discovered, a fundamentally cold, exploitative observer behind the mask of concern, our chilled horror at what we have done is matched only by our rage.

The form of scientific method is certainly not the only form that leads to this ugly scene. People exploit each other all the time, and only *seem* to care. But since one may be dealing in group research with many of the forms of scientific productivity, one had better recognize just how alienating all those numbers can be. Many people cannot manage all the ten-dollar words, fancy graphs, and categories without feeling that chilled apprehension which warns them to get away fast.

It is only reasonable to expect research to share with all developing relationships a certain fumbling awkwardness. "Where 'ya from? What are you majoring in?" asks one undergraduate, as the other cringes at the thought of being known forever in only these superficial ways. But the knowledge of others does not always stay at that level. How might research be defined if we are to get beyond the superficial, mechanical approach to knowing? One good clue is found in the work of Searles (1965), Freud (1905, 1909a, 1909b, 1911, 1918), and Winnicott (1958), and a second in the work of Hinton (1970), Fanon (1963), and Gitlin and Hollander (1970). The first clue comes from the world of the clinician/researcher, the second from the world of researchers who are working to understand, join with, and serve a whole community that they did not know very well at first. We are able to see in Searles' narrative the interconnections between trying to understand a person, coming to respect that person's struggle to survive and grow, and trying to find an effective mode of relating to that struggle. The clinician/ researchers listed all make it clear that they are capable of being awed by their patients. They are capable of losing the trail and going off on useless tangents. They learn from remaining in contact with the other. And they confess freely that much difficult introspection was necessary before they could accept whatever truths they finally came to. These characteristics of the clinician/researcher are also apparent in William Hinton, when as a young UNRRA representative he found himself at work within the new Chinese revolutionary society. They are apparent in Fanon's dramatic transformation as a young psychiatrist in pre- and post-revolutionary Algeria. And Todd Gitlin and Nanci Hollander, strangers and organizers in Uptown Chicago, leave the same impression. Commitment to being an effective person in the continuing presence of others and their struggle explodes the confining self-definition of the observer/scientist.

Where can we find these qualities of commitment and deepening relationship in the world of group research? I would look first to the work of W. R. Bion (1959). The struggle which he describes (and which he is involved in) is not exactly the struggle for sanity and self-control described by the clinicians, or the struggle for survival or the revolutionary remaking of society described by Hinton, Fanon, and others. It is the struggle of a group to work— that is, in Bion's special use of the word *work,* a process of seeking to embrace the particular reality of all the group members; a process of seeking to create a social order that will be democratic, rational, and yet deeply expressive of human needs and emotions. Slater's (1966) writings cast this struggle in somewhat different terms, as do Mills's (1964), Bales's (1970), and our own earlier publications (Mann, 1967, 1970), but I do see a common theme and commitment throughout.

The issue is one of values. Bion's values are right out in the open. Work is a precious, if fragile, accomplishment. Slater calls one final chapter "The New Order"; and he makes it clear that, although he is no utopian dreaming of permanent perfection, he is attached to the unstable process which increases the "equality, fraternity, and autonomy" of the group members. Mills, too, talks of the evolution of the group's capacity to work, to achieve intimacy, to alter the authority relationship, and to create something worthy of an enduring commitment.

The injunction of the scientific tradition to remain value-free has two serious effects on the vitality of research on groups. The first, and less serious, effect is that the reader is left to guess where we stand and whether we even know that we stand anywhere at all. The more serious effect is that, since we cannot reveal our hopes for the group, we also cannot reveal our disappointments. We tend not to reveal in public the many ways that we prevented the group from reaching shared goals. And we withhold from view the content of our self-criticism and our awareness that our unique personal failings were part of the inevitable failures of the group to achieve or sustain its (and our) valued goals. Compared with the frank openness of Searles and other clinicians, or compared with the complexity of Hinton's self-criticism, our work is strikingly empty of the very material that other mortals need if they are to learn how to be effective group leaders. The group leader is a unique, and very limited, participant; and we who then become researchers as an adjunct to our work as group leaders might do well to be more open about our values and our unique limitations, as well as our unique contributions to our groups.

What keeps us from being more frank and revealing about our own participation in the groups we describe? The tradition of social science seems to me to express both our timidity and our immodesty at the same time. On the one hand, we hide behind our research methodology: But what can we put in the place of the infamous "passive voice" of the research report? I for one recoil from those narratives in the group literature which seem overly boastful or propagandistic. But grandiosity can be expressed in many forms. One can turn away from the presentations of flawless infallibility offered by Schutz (1967), John Mann (1970), and others in the encounter group literature, only to be confronted by the immodesty of the scientific tradition. If I write as though my groups were all groups, as though I had discovered a piece of universal truth, then I am tempted to conceal the uniqueness of the group's leader, members, setting, contract, and the like. The journals do contain, in very small print, a description of these particulars, but the discussion

section usually soars above these nasty details and makes pronounce-
ments about the functional relationships of the variables and concepts
which interest the author. Somehow our attachment to the form and
the covert grandiosity of science needs to be loosened.

One crucial aspect of the researcher's identity comes into
focus at the moment when the researcher tries to communicate the
results of the investigation. Who is his audience? Is it a national
network of fellow scientists interested in the same problem? Or is it
only the patient, client, or group with whom a continuing relationship goes on? The latter sort of research report, when delivered
orally, is usually called an interpretation or an intervention. Somewhere between these two communications lies the more usual and the
more stressful situation of the group leader whose reference group
includes both fellow researchers and the members of each particular
group. To experience one's several audiences as placing incompatible
demands on one's expressive activity is to drift toward that form of
academic catatonia we know as the writing block. Or else we
oscillate between periods of addressing our groups and addressing
our scientific colleagues and judges via books and articles.

Anyone who deviates from the official code is prone to think
that he or she is utterly alone. That's one reason why there's so much
furtiveness, dissembling, and self-doubt abroad in the world, even in
the world of the researcher. If the official code sanctions the search
for regularities which are generalizable across a range of comparable
conditions, one feels deviant if in fact he thinks it quite sufficient to
understand one particular person or one particular group. Despite
the frequent failures of the researcher/scientists even to replicate
each other's key findings, the official code is that we must press on
to discover the general laws which have thus far eluded one of the
most massive search parties in human history. The fact that the trail
periodically runs cold and the pack dashes off in some new and
wonderfully promising direction is not supposed to cast any doubt
on the merit of the search.

But what if I am not alone in my doubt that I can adopt the
official code and still remain true to my other audiences (audiences
other than fellow scientists; audiences such as a patient, client,
or group) and to my real reasons for doing research? I do not read
Slater or Searles or Hinton in order to discover universal truths. No

group in which I serve as the leader/instructor has ever been or, I suspect, ever will be very much like Slater's groups. But from his research reports I learn how it goes for him. My vicarious experience of his groups changes my sense of what is possible. It enlarges my sense of the meaningful, and it sharpens my perceptions when I return to my own groups. And it is helpful to use his experience and perceptions when somewhat similar things happen. I cannot honestly say that I make systematic use of his or anyone else's observations. The particular people in front of me in the particular group are much better at shaping my perceptions than someone else's research report. But there are times when my own perceptions and insights crystallize around an incident or a concept which I know derives from someone else's work. The observations of my colleagues in a staff meeting, or in print, enlarge for me the possibilities of metaphor.

If we could break the hold of the scientific model, we could learn to say to our groups, "This, as best I can comprehend it, was (or is) our actuality," and at the same time we can say to our colleagues, "This is another variation on what is possible." The research report which claims to be no more than a glimpse of the possible adds to the pool of meaningful apprehensions of the world; any reader can use such a report as the basis of understanding his own particular reality.

If we adopt this modest view of our research reports, we are not limited to "descriptive" or concrete statements about our particular groups. Consider Ted Mills's marvelous portrait of a classroom group's final moments: "Yearning for a benediction from some source, the group dies" (Mills, 1964, p. 79). Do all groups yearn for a benediction? No, certainly not. Some groups generate a perfectly satisfactory benediction and yearn, if they yearn at all, for other things before they die. Other groups know that they have failed; for them a benediction would be an intolerable lie. What is Mills saying then? He's saying, in the cryptic and poetic way we all use when we have hold of a particular truth: Groups die, yearning for a benediction (*or else they don't*). Or they don't? That's right, they might. It's *possible*. It's enough to say what's possible. While the corps of scientific proof-seekers might descend on Mills's statement, absorbed with their task of seeing if all groups do this or, if not, then under what conditions, we who read and connect with Mills's elegant observation can add what he says to the pool of meaning from which metaphors are drawn.

The scientists' search for universal laws, derived as it is from the ancient preoccupation with *essence,* is but one of the noble efforts of people cast adrift in a very confusing and exciting world. It is not necessarily a deadening search or even a fruitless search, as the exploration of the "physical universe" has shown. But for me the scientific model is not the best way to resolve what once seemed incompatible demands derived from my connectedness to particular groups and my connectedness to my colleagues in the field. Rather, I would now choose to have my research and my research reports serve my continuing relationship to the groups I work in; if these reports enlarge or alter my colleagues' sense of what *can* happen in groups, then I would feel I had joined them in our mutual and growing appreciation of the possible. We do learn from each other's experiences. But when we do, we do so only rarely in the way that a scientist learns from the results of a colleague's experiments. More often we learn as we might from a good novelist or a friend whose construction of reality we find useful. Their ideas seem less like an addition to our knowledge than like the pellet which crystalizes the super-saturated solution of our previously unarticulated perceptions. We knew it before, usually. Our indebtedness to our colleagues is that they contribute to the relief of conscious recognition. At the very least, their work stirs in us a sense of familiarity when we are confronted by similar events.

It would be possible to overdo the extent of our attachment to the particular group. We arrive alone and we leave alone, even if we have created indelible mental traces of people and events. It is not surprising, then, that one of the things we do with our experience, and one of the reasons we return for more, has to do with that elusive network of fellow human beings called a social movement. Any definition of the identity of the group researcher which leaves out the researcher's connection to one or more of the social movements of the day would be unnecessarily constricting.

One factor that has deterred peasants from rising up against their oppressive landlord is the set of fantasies of what would happen if they tried. And one factor that pinned the leftist youth of

China in the cities was their fantasy of what indifference or resentment awaited them if they ever went to the aid of the peasant. William Hinton's (1966) research in Long Bow, however, reveals that the peasants can win, although the battle in this instance was prolonged and took many unexpected forms, and that young city folks can be useful to villagers. In short, revolution is not easy, but neither is it impossible. As a result of such research, certain defeatist fantasies lose their hold over our vision of what mankind can accomplish.

What are the defeatist fantasies to which group research has been addressed? As I read Slater, Bion, Mills, Schutz, Stock, Benne, and Bennis, and as I mull over the work that my colleagues and I have been doing, it is clear to me that we are addressing some or all of the following widely shared conclusions about group life: Groups are impossible; they never work out. Groups are always oppressive, and there are always scapegoats, cliques, victims, and bullies. The thoughts that are not normally shared in groups are best left unshared, because the only choice is between rigid control and the anarchic, destructive orgy of lust and sadism that is just around the corner. Leaders have a special stake in keeping the lid on, because the people under them would take advantage of any sign of weakness. Either the leader is on top or the whole thing flips around; the members are on top, and then, sure enough, someone will rise up and recreate the whole structure all over again. Cooperation is possible only when people create and maintain formal roles, contracts, and sanctions because mutual respect and genuine concern for others are endlessly elusive goals. Unexpected eruptions of anger or sensuality leave behind a legacy of mistrust, and the task of any group is to prevent any but the most pallid verbal allusions to the possibility of strong feelings. And, finally, since failure and impasse are the natural states toward which all groups gravitate, the most a group can do is to find some condition or person who will end up being blamed for it all.

Anyone who would dare contend with these defeatist fantasies had better be prepared to find that he himself has succumbed to them at times. They fit some of the data some of the time. But the energy of any social movement derives in part from a collective realization that they are unnecessary. The proselytizing and perse-

verance so characteristic of a surgent movement are bound up with
the discovery that one or more defeatist fantasies have been reduced
to a mere possibility. They have lost their certainty.

Everyone knew that you could entertain all kinds of weird
ideas about your body, but they were equally sure that no one in the
world would ever want to hear about them, and, besides, those kind
of ideas, if indulged, just make you crazy. So when Bill Schutz came
out with *Joy* (1967), it was for some people at least a direct confrontation with their certainty of what would happen during a
"guided daydream" which explored their own bodies. *Joy* was a
very important book for them. Some people, myself included, felt
the challenge of this statement of the possible but were still unwilling
to abandon their previous position. Something in me, which I incorrectly labeled "the scientist," demanded to be shown all the
negative evidence, all the disasters which I was sure were being
suppressed. It's like asking Fidel Castro to tell us all the gory details
about the disastrous attack on the Moncada barracks, the better to
protect our own already formed fantasies of what happens when you
buck authority.

If we can look beyond the impact of graduate training, and
our compliance with that training, we can focus on the driving force
of one social movement, the experience of the group members and
the professionals/researchers who have joined together to create a
new group. The ways in which a developing group can disconfirm
everyone's worst fears are endless. The moments when one sits back
in awe of the creativity of a group as it roars past one flimsy road-
block after another are unforgettable. And there are times when it
all seems like an incredible ballet. The cycles of tension and resolution create an intense, aesthetic experience and one learns again how
interpersonal life has its own natural sense of form and grace. What
would be more comprehensible than that the researcher would develop a commitment to what he or she has seen and would emerge
from the particular experience eager to use that experience to forge
a verbal tradition which affirms the validity of what has proven to
be possible?

What, then, is good research? How many different answers
to that question will we tolerate? Given their purposes, some scientists
do good research. But there are other purposes, other identities; and

the question for me becomes "How can I use my research to serve my purposes and express my identity?" If this is my goal, I would be no better served by rejecting science than by following only that one path. There is a point of articulation between my continuing role as a professional, my training as a social scientist, my need to experience and express the aesthetic intensity of interpersonal life, and my commitment to the implications of all this for how the world must change. The point of articulation seems to be that many purposes are served by observation.

The professional who works in groups and the scientist who studies them have overlapping interests in observing what happens. It may be that the professional will include more self-observation or that he will have to wonder about the usefulness and timing of the observation when used as an intervention in the ongoing life of the group. The scientist may prefer observations which seem conducive to his wish to generalize and make abstract models with predictive power. But there is overlap at times.

The professional and the artist have other purposes in common. They must capture without killing. Their observations must serve their reality but not at the expense of losing the paradox or the instability of any interim report. The apparent accuracy of the captured truth is meant to be an illusion. It is meant to give way to the complexity which can and should burst its contours.

And the professional shares with the organizer and the brave cadre a vision of what can be done. Their observations tend to keep alive the honor roll of past victories, or else they tend to focus upon the strengths, the outrages, and the urgency which they think will lead on to action or change.

But in none of these cases need we assume that success is sought through untruth. To be sure, partial, limited truth is all that any can claim. The professional, the scientist, the artist, and the organizer each limit their observations and embrace only part of what they find. To each words like discipline and competence have quite different meanings. But to each there are such things as good research and useful observations.

Although we are obviously free to change it at will, we are capable of sensing an emergent priority to our various identities and purposes. I will move with the scientist as far as we can go together.

We can develop techniques for observing groups. We can perform intricate statistical analyses which reveal how things go together or change. We can share the excitement of confirming or extending the previously known body of theory and observation. But our paths will diverge when our common efforts obscure my vision of the next group more than they sharpen it. We will have to go our separate ways when my perceptions drift into areas not yet included in our common agenda. The highest priority for me is that my research become a useful extension of the time spent in groups functioning as a professional or an educator.

The built-in tension between the professional and the scientist will not disappear overnight, and we need to know the probable limits of our collaboration. I can, as a scientist, build or borrow categories which transfer usefully to my work as a professional, but the built-in tension is revealed when the group members find me more absorbed with using my precious pigeonholes than with seeing them as unique individuals. Sometimes their resentment at being categorized causes me to back off; sometimes it doesn't. How and with whose help I can assemble the most useful set of conceptual tools for use in groups is still a mystery to me.

Even more problematic is the array of correlations and time trends which I find in the research literature. For a while it seemed clear that, at least in the groups I studied, the most rebellious males were not only hostile; they were depressed and struggling to work out a stable form of identification with authority. Now I keep turning over in my mind an essay called "Where Have All the Heroes Gone?" Have I changed so much as a leader? How has the women's movement changed the meanings and options available in a college group? Are we a branch of contemporary history?

The professional may have quite a different feeling than the scientist about both the need to be original and the need to have one's findings hold up over time. The professional and the organizer can remain absorbed with the same issues and the same obstacles to change, as long as they present themselves, without fear of the journal editor's pithy note: "It's been done." The need felt by the scientist/researchers to stake out new territories which will differentiate them from all others leads too often to an absorption with minor technical variations. And if at the same time there is a need to have the statements endure, to hold up under different conditions and occasions, the result may be a literature particularly unsuited to the professional. The conclusion I draw from a dozen years of working in groups is that very few generalizations endure and the ones which are most clearly original endure least of all. It isn't long before each new group has disconfirmed most predictions or created such a unique set of symbols and preoccupations as to make most of the going hypotheses untestable within this new context.

The need for a new definition of research is bound up with the need for a new literature. The beginnings of this literature are already apparent in journals which permit professionals to exchange their observations. Even doctoral dissertations are less bound in than before by the criteria of excellence appropriate to the identity of the scientist or the scholar. The complex and never constant identity of the group researcher will take as many different forms as we are different people, and that fact makes me wonder how we can get in touch with each other and exchange our answers to the questions: Who are we when we do research? Where are we headed?

2

Observation

Theodore M. Mills

*F*or the essentials in building a science, the eminent physiologist L. J. Henderson (1953) suggested three ingredients: first, intimate contact and a habitual, intuitive familiarity with the phenomena; second, means for systematically collecting and ordering data; and, third, an effective way of thinking about the phenomena. The relevance of his proposal for widely separated fields is apparent when, for example, we compare the astronomer and the sociologist of groups.

In the first place, through search, scanning, and repeated observation, the astronomer soon acquires a "feel" for the heavens, and a cognitive map of its particulars: objects, dimensions, relations, movements, and so on. Although at any one time he may not be able to reproduce all of its particulars, his map is of enormous service in locating where he is, in allowing him to concentrate in a selected area without losing touch with other areas, and, of course, in helping him to sense immediately any new and strange object. A comparable "feel" and "map" is acquired by the sociolo-

From Theodore M. Mills, *The Sociology of Small Groups,* © 1967, pp. 25–35. Reprinted by permission of the author and Prentice-Hall, Inc., Englewood Cliffs, New Jersey.

gist through direct and repeated contact with groups, through observation of a wide variety of groups, and through active participation in them. In time, and as figure and ground separate, he becomes sensitive to what is and is not happening in a group, to what the group is forgetting or avoiding, to shifts in rules, to changes in direction, and to conflicts before they become otherwise apparent.

Second, both astronomer and sociologist make systematic observations. While the astronomer takes readings on mass, density, rotation, speed, and direction of movement, the sociologist observes and records indicators of what group members do, say, feel, and think. Both use such readings as workable facts.

Third, both attempt to construct conceptions of their phenomena—abstract, simplified models, or theories, which account for, or help to explain, a proportion of the facts. The heliocentric theory of the solar system is an example for astronomy; the boundary-maintaining system tending toward a state of equilibrium is one from sociology.

In short, although astronomy and sociology are clearly different in subject matter, refinement of techniques, and theoretical sophistication, they are comparable in the types of procedures by which they make science out of their respective inquiries. Both require intuitive familiarity with the phenomena, systematic data, and an effective way of thinking about the phenomena.

Notwithstanding these similarities, however, an important procedural difference remains. Since sociology is man studying man, it is highly reflexive. As a human being, the sociologist cannot exclude himself from his inquiry, nor can he practically exclude how the men he studies influence him, nor how his study of man affects man. He can, of course, but to do so is, as Cooley (1926) suggested, to discard one of his strongest assets—namely, his affinity with his object of study, his capacity to empathize with him, his opportunity to talk with and to learn from him. Because of this affinity and because of the reflexivity of sociology, we are obliged to add to Henderson's list a fourth ingredient: a collaborative exchange between the investigator and the investigated. As we know, even the most rudimentary description of a group requires a reciprocal relation between sociologist and group; the sociologist must contact the group and the group must open at least part of itself to the investigator. Beyond that, the growth of the field requires a skillfully devised social relationship wherein groups permit the investigator to become not only familiar but increasingly familiar with their operations, where systematic data may be collected not only on obvious and public matters but over an increasingly wide and deep range of phenomena, and where the ideas in the minds both of group members and sociologist about how groups operate may be exchanged, applied, tested, and reformulated. . . .

THE OBSERVER AND THE GROUP

Many scientists, as we know, use special instruments (the microscope and the telescope are common examples) to bring their phenomena closer to them. As the worlds these instruments open became familiar, the scientist senses additional realms, and often devises new instruments (such as the electron microscope and the radio telescope, to maintain the example) to reach these new realms. In such instances, technology and the investigator work together both to increase the intimacy of contact and to extend the realm of phenomena with which the investigator may familiarize himself.

Much the same may be said for the social scientist, whose concern with groups causes him to find ways to be brought into ever closer and broader contact with group processes. But the technology through which this is accomplished is of a special kind. Because group processes occur within and among persons, and because both persons and groups surround themselves with boundaries which regulate access to these processes, the barriers separating groups and their investigators are more social, emotional, attitudinal, and cultural than they are physical. Consequently, the barriers must be transcended by social, psychological, and cultural means. The special technology (and the first technical procedure) of the investigator of groups is to devise that quality of social relation between himself and groups which allows him to come into sustained and intimate contact with the group.

Since effective construction of such a relation depends upon a comprehension of the boundary that separates the group from him, and more generally upon an understanding of the dynamics between insiders and outsiders, and since comprehension of these dynamics comes best through actual contact with groups, let us imagine an apprentice beginning his career as a sociologist, and trace the highlights of his experience in confronting groups.

THE DYNAMICS OF FAMILIARITY

The apprentice's training program may take him to any of a number of different settings: the wardroom of a ship, a nursery school, a group therapy session, a training seminar for senior military personnel, a family conference in the living room.[1] Wherever, one of his first discoveries is that he is in direct and immediate contact with unique, concrete, unrehearsed, and largely unpredictable human processes. Events are disorderly, and often incoherent, appearing to him in raw form, unfiltered by anyone else's interpretation of their meaning. Although he may be confused by lack of order and pattern, he can sense the possibility for independent observation and analysis. His first discovery, then, is the opportunity to become intuitively familiar with the phenomena—Henderson's first requirement.

Soon, contrary to the expectations of the popular belief, the apprentice is surprised by the extent to which people under observation reveal themselves. He finds that they are not always on guard, and as a consequence inadvertently becomes privy to information that, in certain circumstances, could seriously affect their lives. A military officer's castigation of his commander could ruin his own career; a corporation executive's offhand admission of illegal tax procedures could lead to his imprisonment; wives' intimate talk in group therapy could estrange their husbands; a young psychiatrist's ineptness in a training group could destroy his patients' faith in him. And in the laboratory, even the most attractive young lady, preening before a mirror, could mar her reputation as well as the image of her beauty by carelessly or absentmindedly probing deeply into her nose with her little finger. The apprentice learns that, to be sure, some guards are up, but many others are down.

This experience of discovering the unexpected, the apprentice

[1] On the observer's relation to groups in the field see Whyte (1951b) and Rosenfeld (1958).

finds, affects his personal composure. When he sees more than he expects to, and more than members intend to reveal, and when there are no limits on what he should see or on what he should do with what he sees, he feels uneasy and embarrassed, as though he were stepping out of bounds—as if he were some sort of transgressor. (Such doubts about the right to observe were reflected in the dream of one observer following his first day with a therapy group: dressed in a doctor's white coat, he was in a courtroom being tried as a Peeping Tom before a greatly oversized microphone, which as the dream progressed seemed to him in his state of confusion to represent the judge.) Seeing too much violates childhood taboos and associates oneself with the spy, the snooper, or the voyeur—or with lonely persons who are neither entirely inside or outside. And not only the right to observe but one's motivation in observing comes into doubt. One could even come to see himself as a pervert or a blackmailer and become further upset by the jokes about observation laboratories and about those who work in them—jokes that play on the voyeuristic potentials. Anxiety over precisely this matter causes some apprentices to leave the role of observer altogether. Others, of course, overcome such occupational hazards and become perceptive observers of human processes.

Apprentice sociologists who stay discover that group members attribute to them superhuman powers. In their imagination, the observer misses no signals and forgets nothing. He is an all-seeing, all-knowing judge, and frequently is thought to be in collusion with the authority figure in the group, and aligned with those who have jurisdiction over the group. Members often warn their fellows against the power of the observer, as in the following quotation of a military officer, in which the ostensible reference to someone at a distant base turns out to be a comment on the observer who is present in the room: "The important thing to remember here is that Sherril is just a spy, no more. He can't do anything—can't produce anything solid. He's just going around getting the dope and sending it over his hot line up above. Everybody should realize that he can make or break anybody on the base. A snooper like that can tear an organization apart." Is not this officer's concern generally shared by those being observed? (What is being done with the information about me? Can it be used against me? How safe are we? Who has the observer under control? Until we know, we either close ranks against him or fall apart.)

One interpretation of these disturbances is that observation confuses traditional notions about boundaries. Whereas the observer's sitting on the side and being excluded from group activity affirms the existence of a boundary, his access to inside information denies the boundary. Although he is an outsider, he wants inside information and wants it without becoming an insider. And, while privy to the group, he remains outside its jurisdiction. In all these ways, and more, his presence implies a privileged position, with the right to take away information without giving anything in return, and to be above the group while it is "subject" to him.

It is a curious fact that groups both define the observer as being above them, and feel he takes something away from them. The mechanism is somewhat as follows: if *he* is the observer, then we need not make observations of our own; if he is a superior observer, then we'd *better not* make our observations; if he is the judge—a superior judge—then we'd better not make our own decisions. They more or less delegate to the outsider their own responsibilities, perhaps in the hope that he will oblige by performing them —for to observe, judge, and predict what happens is indeed a difficult task. When, however (in keeping within the limits of propriety recognized by the well-trained observer), he does not accept these responsibilities, they not only resent him but in the meantime have allowed their own capabilities to atrophy. They have become more watchful but less observant, more critical but less evaluative, more controlled but less committed. They often attribute their loss of these powers to the presence of the outside observer. The maneuver is defensive, for there is no technical reason why group and observer cannot make independent observations, judgments, and decisions.

The apprentice next discovers that the group wants to observe *him*—a discovery sometimes made when it is least expected. For instance, on one occasion, a training group in a laboratory stopped abruptly and announced that it would go no further until the several observers were brought out from behind the mirrors, identified, and "given the opportunity" of explaining their *real* purposes in being there. This was a first step in "getting to really know the observers." Group members want to contact the observer

—to have him respond and reveal himself—partly, of course, to correct their vague and oversized image of him, and partly to find out about themselves and to detect the standards he uses in judging them, but also, we suggest, to bring him into the group and under its jurisdiction.

Should it surprise us that in the meantime the observer discovers within himself a desire to join the group? Increasingly he wants to express his feelings toward members—his warmth toward some, his coolness toward others, his admiration for some, his distaste for others. Increasingly he empathizes with the leader, wanting to prompt him or advise him or discuss with him the philosophy of leadership. Increasingly his emotional state follows the emotional swings of the group. In the extreme he may identify with the group to the extent that he comes under all the influences it is under—as, for example, in taking the same experimental drugs the group is taking.

Our purpose in relating and discussing these things is to suggest that the presence of the observer contradicts the traditional notion of the boundary separating insider from outsider: the observer, to repeat, is an outsider wanting inside information without becoming an insider. The group can solidify its boundary and seal itself off against him, or the boundary may be dissolved bilaterally, to be re-formed to include him within its jurisdiction and thus to make him a member of the group. Note, however, that in either case science loses, for in both instances the apprentice vacates the role of independent scientific observer.

This all suggests that the balance of forces tends to move the investigator out of his role of scientist. His technical problem is to counteract these forces. His solution, in general terms, is to help reconstitute the group boundaries so that they may be both maintained and transcended: *maintained* through mutual respect for the legitimate and distinct purposes, first of group development, and second of scientific observation; and *transcended* through mutual appreciation of the essential kinship between the observer and the observed arising from their affinity as members of the human community. *How* this is to be accomplished will vary from one circumstance to another, but note that a solution is *critically important* to the sociology of groups. On the one hand, if the boundaries are not transcended, the group will repel the investigator, and if they are not maintained, it will incorporate him; on the other hand, if they are both transcended and maintained, then entré into one area of inquiry tends to a greater chance of further entré.[2]

THE SYSTEMATIC COLLECTION OF DATA

For the apprentice who emerges from the phase of open, un-structured observation into a new phase where he formulates ideas about how groups tend to operate, and seeks evidence against which to check these ideas, the second procedure is to devise methods for taking disciplined readings on what occurs.[3] Methods of measurement and techniques for collecting data—if they are to be of more than transitory interest—derive from a conception of which facets of group phenomena are relevant and important both to the immediate group and to the general universe of groups. Few methods exemplify the connection between a conception of groups and a method for gathering empirical readings better than Bales' (1950a) *interaction process analysis,* one of the more cleanly devised, and certainly one of the most widely used, techniques for categorizing overt behavior in groups.[4]

Interaction Process Analysis

Each overt act that occurs in a group is classified in one of the twelve categories shown in Table 1. The boiling-down of all possible ways of interpreting group events into this set is a product of a highly ordered conception of group processes; some main features are paraphrased as follows:

1. The small, face-to-face group is one instance of a more

[2] The issues in becoming an observer of small groups are paralleled in the general sociologist's relation to societies. They are discussed in the latter context by Edward Shils (1961).

[3] For an early review of observation schemes see Roger W. Heyns and Ronald Lippitt (1954), and for a review of more recent techniques see Weick (1968).

[4] For examples of the application of Bales' method see Talland (1955), Psathas (1960a), and Lennard and Bernstein (1960).

general type of system (the social system) which includes organizations, communities, societies, and nations. As such, the small group possesses many features comparable to features found in social systems, such as an organization of activities, differential contact among members, division of labor, norms and means of social control, power structure, subgroups, ideology, ceremonies, and patterned means for coping with both internal and external problems.

2. The origin of these features and their dynamic relation may be studied relatively simply in the small group, not only because groups are relatively easy to observe but because the structural features (such as a division of labor or a given power structure) are solutions to issues arising out of a specific context of interaction. Through detailed study of the interaction process one is able to identify such issues, to specify the group's response to them, and consequently to account for the structural features of the system. The more detailed the analysis of process, the clearer it becomes that the structural features and interaction process are simply two aspects of the same phenomenon.

3. A wide range of interpersonal encounters can usefully be conceived as problem solving. When people meet, there are differences to be ironed out and decisions to be made—whether the occasion is an argument among roommates, a family at dinner, a community meeting, a university seminar, a board of directors' meeting, or a council of war.

4. If a group is to solve its problems and arrive at its decisions, certain basic functions must be performed at a minimum level of proficiency: (a) *communication*: through exchange of information, members must arrive at a common definition of the situation they confront; (b) *evaluation*: through exchange of ideas and opinions, they must arrive at a more or less shared attitude toward the situation; and (c) *control*: in the face of competing alternatives, they must choose and decide upon a single course of action.

5. Meanwhile, freedom to work on the problem depends on certain interpersonal processes: there must be a periodic feedback from members, indicating whether movement of the group in a particular direction is acceptable or unacceptable; the tension level within and between members must not get too high; and the group must be held together.

Table 1. BALES' SET OF OBSERVATION CATEGORIES[a]

Socio-emotional area:

Positive reactions	1. Shows solidarity; raises other's status; gives help and reward
	2. Shows tension release; jokes, laughs, and shows satisfaction
	3. Agrees, showing passive acceptance; understands, concurs, and complies

Task area:

Attempted answers	4. Gives suggestion and direction, implying autonomy for others
	5. Gives opinion, evaluation, and analysis; expresses feelings and wishes
	6. Gives orientation and information; repeats, clarifies, and confirms

Task area:

a   b   c   d   e   f

Questions	7. Asks for orientation, information, repetition, and confirmation
	8. Asks for opinion, evaluation, analysis, and expression of feeling
	9. Asks for suggestion, direction, and possible ways of action

Socio-emotional area:

Negative reactions	10. Disagrees, showing passive rejection and formality; withholds help
	11. Shows tension and asks for help; withdraws out of field
	12. Shows antagonism, deflating other's status and defending or asserting self

Legend:

a. Problems of orientation   d. Problems of decision
b. Problems of evaluation   e. Problems of tension management
c. Problems of control   f. Problems of integration

[a] From Bales (1950b).

6. Finally, Bales suggests that the instrumental functions in 4 above, and the socio-emotional functions in 5 above, are dynamically related: attempts to solve the task tend to break up the group, thereby necessitating reintegrative activity; and attempts to pull the group together tend to weaken task efficiency, thereby requiring renewed emphasis upon the task.

With these six points in mind, a review of the twelve categories shows that Bales' method employs the fewest possible categories in order to collect data relevant to the concept. Acts primarily relevant to the problem of communication are classified in either category 6 or 7; those relevant to evaluation, either category 5 or 8; those relevant to control, or decision, in either category 4 or 9. Reactions to these instrumental attempts which facilitate forward movement are classified in the "green-light" set (category 3 when an agreement to a statement, category 2 when a sign of tension reduction, and category 1 when a manifestation of interpersonal or group solidarity). Reactions which impede forward movement or which indicate resistance to that movement are classified in the "red-light" set (category 10 if a disagreement to a statement, category 11 if a sign of increased tension, and category 12 if a manifestation of hostility toward a person or the group as a whole).

The scoring procedure is simple: the observer (1) gives each group member an arbitrary number; (2) screens each act or gesture to determine which of the functions it is most directly relevant to; (3) records the act by placing it in the appropriate category, indicating both the number of the person initiating it and the number of the person to whom it is directed; and (4) continues this procedure as acts occur, keeping scores in an order corresponding to their occurrence (and often using as an aid a machine with a moving tape).

With training and considerable practice, and after having scored process in a given set of groups, the apprentice may arrange his data in order to answer the following types of questions:

1. Does interaction follow an ordered sequence—for example, from the beginning to the end of a meeting? Bales and Strodtbeck suggest a general, and ideal, sequence wherein instrumental

emphasis shifts first from problems of communication to problems of evaluation, and finally to problems of control (Bales and Strodtbeck, 1951).

2. Is there a dynamic relation, or covariation, between task activity and socio-emotional activity? Again Bales and Strodtbeck suggest that as the group moves through problems of communication, evaluation, and control, "red-light" activity will increase, and that after the point of decision and as a manifestation of consolidation, "green-light" categories will increase (Bales and Strodtbeck, 1951).

3. Is there a pattern in the distribution of interpersonal interaction? Is the communication network structured? Bales and associates have collected evidence suggesting a tendency for each actor to distribute his action among others according to their output, resulting in a network wherein the relative frequency of acts between any two parties can be estimated by their total output relative to other members (Bales, Strodtbeck, Mills, and Roseborough, 1951).

4. How do members divide among themselves the performance of the various behavioral functions represented by the categories? Slater and Bales find a tendency, under certain conditions, for one active member to push toward solving the problem while the other active member attempts to hold the group together—a division of functions corresponding to the major distinctions among the categories and, accordingly, to the basic functional problems outlined in Bales' original formulation (Bales and Slater, 1955).

5. Conceiving of the interaction process as a more or less ordered system changing through time, what variables affect the characteristics of this system? Here the apprentice may be led in any one of a number of directions. For example, consider the effect that the following factors would have: the kind of problem the group is working on; the personalities of the members, taken individually and as a configuration; the size of the group; sex, age, and social class of members; age of the group; relation of the group to other groups, and its relation to the observer. One could extend the list, but the question remains essentially the same—namely: If we view the overt interpersonal behavioral process as the result of the convergence of a number of forces at a particular time and place, what

factors affect those forces which, in turn, alter in a determinate way the interaction process?

OTHER DIMENSIONS OF GROUP PROCESS

The value of Bales' method to the apprentice goes beyond the data produced. First, it sharpens his eye and disciplines him to attend to each event that occurs. Though he may score only one aspect of each act, he leaves out no acts. Second, the method introduces a conception of the ongoing interaction system, the problem-solving aspect of which is clearly formulated and rationally connected to the scoring operation. The good scorer employs this conception and, as he improves his scoring, tends to refine his own conception of the system. With the conception of the system on one hand and the appearance of an event on the other, the scoring operation is, in the end, a judgment about what each event does to the system. In making such judgments the apprentice tends to become more keenly aware of the intricate patterns and ordered sequences that characterize interaction. Like the student of music who learns an orchestral score, he begins to comprehend the design underlying its interaction: the sensing of a "score" by the apprentice tends to open to him a new world of interpersonal process. Third, Bales' method does not try to capture the richness of all these processes. From the full score, as it were, it abstracts one line: it selects the problem-solving relevance of activity, leaving other dimensions, or other lines in the score, to other methods. The value to the apprentice is that what is picked up and what is not picked up is clearly and unambiguously formulated. Consequently, Bales' method throws into sharp relief the untouched dimensions which require special methods of their own. Some of these follow: (1) the substantive *content* of statements: the ideas that are conveyed; (2) the intent of the actor: the aim, purpose, or motivation behind actions; (3) feelings experienced by others, as well as the actor, while someone is acting; (4) thoughts in the minds of members stimulated or evoked by the action, such as: Is what is going on good or bad, appropriate or inappropriate, effective or ineffective, desirable or undesirable?

Sociologists interested in "what is said"—interested in classifying the types of ideas, in tracing their order of appearance, in registering their acceptance, rejection, or modification, and in following their accumulation as part of group culture—such sociologists require a separate scheme especially designed to abstract the *content* line of the "score." One example of such a method is Mills' (1964) sign process analysis; another is The General Inquirer, which uses language translation techniques to select and to simplify the content, and the modern computer to speed up categorization, storing, ordering, and retrieval (Stone, Dunphy, Smith, and Ogilvie, 1966). When an investigator combines data from one of these methods with data from interaction process analysis, he has information on both "what is said" (inputs to group culture) and on the action's effect upon the problem-solving system. Therefore, he may explore in the small group an aspect of one of the classical issues of sociology; namely, the dynamic relation between culture and social structure. For example, does change in a person's expressed ideas affect his position in the group? Does a shift on the part of the group as a whole from one type of thought to another affect the distribution of interaction? Are there structures of interaction that restrict the realm of expressible thought? Are there others that expand the realm? Investigation of this type of issue is a second step in the dynamic analysis of group process. There are additional ones.

Beneath the overt act lie covert feelings, and behind the explicit statement are unexpressed thoughts. Beyond this, the overt act and the explicit statement evoke in other members feelings and thoughts, a large proportion of which are not clearly manifest—at least not to the ear and to the eye we are accustomed to use in observing groups. This means that much of the iceberg of group process is below the surface: feelings of pleasure or displeasure; wishes to affirm or to disaffirm; evaluations of others as good or bad, and of their actions as appropriate or inappropriate; and so on. These processes, howsoever covert, are potentially important. Assuming that they are possible causal factors and that they can become known through reliable empirical indicators, the sociologist needs a new type of method. He needs techniques which help him become aware of the existence of these processes and which assist him in deciphering what we must assume to be the subtle signals through which they are manifest, whether those signals turn out to be linguistic, kinesic, physiological, or otherwise. At present, such techniques are in their infancy. In fact, their development is one of the frontiers of small-groups research (Birdwhistell, 1952; Mahl, 1959; Dittman and Wynne, 1961; Pittenger, Hockett, and Danehy, 1960; Barker, 1963).

Anticipating the time when such methods are available, we can appreciate not only the value of the clear distinction made by Bales, but the advantage of applying a number of observational methods simultaneously. This advantage accrues because the investigator may use a bank of observers, each employing a method that taps a separate dimension; one may classify content; another, problem-solving relevance; another, feelings; another, the relationship between activity and the rules; yet another, the relation between activity and group values. With independent but simultaneous readings on these analytically distinct dimensions, the investigator will be able to extend his study to an even more general sociological issue— namely, the dynamic principles that relate (1) interaction, (2) cultural content, (3) emotional processes, (4) rules and norms, and (5) beliefs and values. First, are there such principles? If so, are they uniform from one group to another, or are there different sets of principles for different types of groups? Are such principles constant throughout the life of a group, or do they alter as the group forms, develops, performs its purpose, and then disbands? This issue parallels major theoretical and empirical concerns of historians, sociologists, and anthropologists who study the dynamics of larger organizations, societies, and nations. Progress on the issue in the small-group setting depends heavily upon the development of systematic techniques for collecting empirical readings on the configurations of covert thoughts and feelings associated with overt action.

3

Methodological Issues in the Assessment of Total-Group Phenomena in Group Therapy

DOROTHY STOCK

MORTON A. LIEBERMAN

*I*n attempting to understand certain aspects of group functioning, investigators have found it useful to describe the group situation in terms which transcend the participation of individual members and capture some characteristic of the total group. Such theoretical constructs as "atmosphere," "mood," "cohesiveness," "morale," "group culture," and "common group tension" have been used to summarize and define various total-group characteristics. In our own work, we have used the term "group focal conflict" to refer to the shared, preconsciously maintained fantasies in the group. More specifically, the events of a particular

Reprinted from *International Journal of Group Psychotherapy* 1962, *12*, 312–325 with permission of the authors and American Group Psychotherapy Association, Inc. The work reported in this article was part of an ongoing research program on group therapy supported by a research grant (M-1048) from the National Institutes of Health, United States Public Health Service, therapy session are conceptualized in terms of a preconscious conflict between two opposing motives, together with various attempts to find a solution to the conflict. The construct "group focal conflict" appears useful in organizing the discrete, diverse, and often diffuse elements of the group interaction, and has been applied to such problems as therapeutic success and failure, deviancy, and shared concerns during the formative stages of therapy groups.

While convinced of its usefulness, we have found that the task of forming judgments about the character of the group focal conflict presents serious methodological difficulties. Additive approaches, usually more convenient, manageable, and reproducible, are inappropriate. Rather, one must adopt a holistic, clinical approach to the material of the group session. The high degree of inference which necessarily is involved leads to problems about procedures, agreement among independent analyzers, and the validity of formulations.

This paper describes the issues, considerations, and the successes and failures involved in an attempt to develop appropriate procedures for characterizing total-group phenomena in focal conflict terms. Our purpose is twofold. First, we would like to describe the procedures and spell out the considerations involved in this approach for those who might be interested in applying it themselves. Second, we would like to share some of our experiences with other investigators engaged in holistic, global, clinical analyses of therapeutic interaction.

Perhaps some further definition of "total-group phenomena" and the "group focal conflict" is in order. In the group therapy literature, Bion (1952) uses the term "group culture" to refer to total-group aspects of the interaction, and the term "basic assumption" to refer to the mechanism underlying the establishment of a common group culture. Ezriel (1950) sees the group members as sharing a "common group tension." He says: "The *manifest* content of discussions in groups may embrace practically any topic. They may talk about astronomy, philosophy, politics, or even psychology; but it is one of the essential assumptions for psychoanalytic work with groups that, whatever the manifest content may be, there always develops rapidly an *underlying* common group problem, a *common group tension* of which the group is not aware but which determines its behavior. This common group tension seems to represent what I should like to call the 'common denominator' of the dominant unconscious fantasies of all members."

Both Bion and Ezriel make it clear that they are referring not only to a phenomenon of the total group but to a level of experiencing which is not within the conscious awareness of the group members. Unconscious and preconscious levels of experiencing have, of course, long been understood as viable constructs in understanding individual personality and functioning. Thomas French (1954) uses the term "nuclear conflict" to refer to persistent, unconscious conflicts within the personality of the individual and the term "focal conflict" to refer to preconscious conflicts which derive from some nuclear conflict but are influenced in their special character and flavor by current life situations. The overt behavior of the individual, especially as it occurs in the dream life and in the free associations of psychoanalysis, provides the cues from which the character of the focal conflict is inferred. Although French developed his theories of the "focal conflict" in the context of individual therapy and dreams, we have found that with certain modifications and extensions, his concepts are applicable to group events. The assumption is the same whether one thinks of an individual therapy hour or a dream or a session in group therapy. With regard to the group interaction, we assume that there is an underlying coherence and relatedness in the diverse contributions of the patients, and that a group therapy session can be understood in terms of a slowly emerging, shared preconscious *conflict,* together with varying attempts to find an adequate *solution* to the conflict.

The "group focal conflict" can be schematized as follows:

disturbing motive   X   reactive motive

(in conflict with)

$\downarrow$

solution (s)

The group interaction flows from one focal conflict situation to another. As adequate solutions develop for one focal conflict, another

which has been "subfocal" may emerge. Or a solution may become
established which adequately deals with one conflict but which
generates another. Or one portion of the group may subscribe to a
solution which is unacceptable to the others, forcing the whole group
to deal with a derived "solutional conflict." The flow of interaction
within a single session can be traced in some detail in this manner.
It is also possible to formulate a single focal conflict with solution(s)
which summarizes the interaction for the entire session. For example,
one session was conceptualized in the following terms:

FC: sexual competitiveness   X   guilt

$$\downarrow$$

solution: express competitiveness in a displaced way:
            argue about who is sickest

A further example:

FC: angry feelings toward   fear of abandonment and
                    therapist   X   anger on part of therapist

$$\downarrow$$

solution: band together to express
            angry compliance

This approach has been described in detail in an earlier
theoretical paper (Whitman and Stock, 1958). Subsequent work
has utilized these concepts in exploring the issue of deviancy in
therapy groups with the associated problems of group standards and
conformity (Stock, Whitman, and Lieberman, 1958); in accounting
for the successful and unsuccessful utilization of the group situation
for therapeutic purposes on the part of various patients (Whitman,
Lieberman, and Stock, 1960); and in specifying the interpersonal
concerns typical of the formative stages of groups (Stock, 1962). In
the process of carrying out these investigations we have become
deeply involved in methodological issues involved in assessing this
level of group functioning.

Perhaps any investigator prefers an additive approach to data. Such an approach requires, first, adopting some principle by which the events of a session are divided into equivalent units; second, making judgments about the character of the units according to some schema; and finally, summing the judgments in order to arrive at characteristics of the group as a whole. Such an approach is attractive because it lends itself to concise definition, reproducibility, and statistical treatment.

Robert F. Bales (1950a) has developed such an approach in his interaction process analysis. Here, twelve major behavioral categories are utilized. Observers make judgments about the appropriate unit of interaction (a phrase, a sentence, several sentences, a bit of nonverbal behavior), and then characterize the unit in terms of one or another of the twelve categories. The present authors, together with Herbert A. Thelen and others (Stock and Thelen, 1958), developed a rating procedure based on the theories of Bion which characterize the work and emotionality aspects of group functioning. Each contribution is regarded as a unit, and judgments are made in terms of four work categories and six emotionality categories. Both these approaches are additive in that they require making a judgment about successive discrete units of the interaction and then summing these in order to arrive at a characterization of the session as a whole. The present authors have utilized an additive approach adapted from Leary (1957) in which raters make judgments about the affective meaning of the interpersonal message of each contribution. This procedure lends itself to the characterization of interpersonal patterns in the group.

With regard to the group focal conflict, however, we felt we were dealing with a phenomenon for which an additive approach was not appropriate. By definition, the "group focal conflict" is never expressed in direct, explicit, or succinct terms. The manifest content is a vehicle offering masked hints of the underlying issues. The preconscious themes and concerns are expressed in fragmented ways in distortions, partial revelations, displacements, denials, and symbolic representations. Important clues may not occur in the content at all but in the character of the interaction or in nonverbal behavior. Because the focal conflict characterizes the group rather than any single patient, individual expressions often bear only a tangential or partial relationship to the underlying conflict. The very notions of "unit," "category," or "summation" seem meaningless, and any attempt to force a systematic definition of units or a universe of categories would do violence to the phenomenon under consideration. By the nature of our task we seemed forced to resort to clinical, holistic, global approaches and to cope as best we could with the problems involved in such an approach.

During the initial period[1] when the usefulness of this theoretical approach was being explored, our procedure consisted of group discussion of verbatim protocols. Later we worked from summaries, again relying on group discussion in which issues were talked over until the group achieved some formulation which seemed "right" to all concerned. There was a continuing awareness that this approach was not entirely satisfactory. For one thing, it seemed reasonable to assume that our formulations were being influenced by the dynamics of the group doing the analyzing as well as by the dynamics of the group being analyzed. For another, we realized we were developing shared but unverbalized agreements which helped us to produce formulations but which also involved the danger of developing a private system which could not be reproduced easily by other investigators. At the same time, we realized that an analysis produced by a single individual might be influenced by individual biases and blind spots. While there were, of course, continuing attempts to make explicit the cues and criteria we were using in producing formulations, we recognized the need to investigate the analytic process more systematically.

Accordingly, a concerted effort was made to clarify the analytic steps involved in producing focal conflict analyses of group sessions. Five group therapy sessions were analyzed in focal conflict terms. In every case, two or more independent analyses were produced by an individual or a team of several persons. Composition of the teams as well as type of basic data (summary, verbatim, protocol, tape) was varied. Following each trial, the analyzers met, compared

---

[1] Our experiences with this approach cover a five-year span. At various points the following persons have contributed to developing theory and/or analyzing data in focal conflict terms: Thomas French, M.D., Phillip Seitz, M.D., Roy M. Whitman, M.D., Joanne Holden, M.A., Robert S. Daniels, M.D., and Andrew Mathis, Ph.D.

their formulations, attempted to define their thinking and rationale, and argued out differences. Procedural steps were clarified as we went along, and new variations in procedure were tried out as they occurred to us.

Rather than take the reader through each successive trial and the issues which came up in each, we shall attempt to summarize and discuss the major issues which we came to realize are involved in analyzing a group in focal conflict terms. Some of the points are specifically relevant to this kind of analysis; others are relevant to any holistic attempt to assess the underlying meaning of therapeutic interaction.

SOME ASSUMPTIONS AND CONSIDERATIONS

First of all, we realized we were operating on three assumptions: (1) that something akin to free association occurs in group therapy; (2) that the manifest content can be understood as the symbolic expression of feelings relevant to the here-and-now interaction; and (3) that all elements of the interaction are relevant to the shared, preconscious group focal conflict.

A process occurs in group therapy which for purposes of analysis we regard as analogous to the free associations which occur in individual analytic sessions. The group situation consists of a conversation; one comment followed by another and another in which a number of individuals participate. There is usually a surface coherence to these successive comments; that is, the patients can be described as having a conversation about some topic. However, the series of comments also can be understood as a sequence of associations which involve a subsurface implication with a coherence of its own. It was this level we were interested in tapping. In groups composed of sicker patients, the subsurface level is more apparent because it is not so obscured by a distracting surface coherence. However, both levels can be seen in groups composed of healthier individuals. Even in nontherapy groups, there are breaks and shifts in the surface coherence which can only be understood in terms of the underlying implications of the interaction.

Secondly, we assume that discussion about outside issues— whether it be baseball or architecture or food or someone's sister-in-law—has relevance for the here-and-now interaction within the group. For example, shared complaints about the inadequacy of the food in the hospital cafeteria might reflect some complaint that the therapists are not offering appropriate care; a long story about expecting to meet "decent" people at a club but being disappointed might reflect a concern about being disappointed if one expects too much from the group; or friendly sharing of tales about childhood mischief might constitute an exploration of whether the revelation of "badness" will be tolerated and accepted in the group. These are fairly direct inferences based on the assumption that underlying, preconscious concerns are expressed in the manifest content in displaced or symbolic terms.

Finally, we have adopted a working principle that *all* material of the session is relevant to the group focal conflict. Ideally, an adequate formulation accounts for *all* aspects of the session. If some bit of nonverbal behavior or detail of the interaction or content is inconsistent with the focal conflict formulation, then the latter needs to be modified.

Idiosyncratic versus Group-Relevant Material

One of the special problems related to defining preconscious concerns in group therapy as contrasted to individual therapy is the presence of a number of patients. The question arises as to whether all comments are relevant to the group focal conflict, or whether certain contributions may be regarded as truly idiosyncratic; that is, the property of the individual and not the group. We have come to feel that neither is strictly the case but, rather, that any comment has both a specific, personal meaning for the individual as well as some implication for the total group. *The clue for the group-level meaning lies in the manner in which the other patients react to the individual comment.* For example, a patient told a story about a man who had been misunderstood by using the word "intimate." It was known that this was a personal concern for this patient, since he was constantly apologizing to others for his sexual thoughts. However, the succeeding comments by other patients elaborated on the "misunderstood" aspect of his comment and ignored the "intimate" aspect. We therefore assume that for the group as a whole a concern about being misunderstood was of greater importance than a concern over intimacy. When three or four patients react to a topic or a story introduced by one individual, it is relatively easy to make this judgment. In other circumstances the judgment is more difficult. For example, if a patient tells a long story about a personal experience and elicits no response from others, it is difficult to tell which aspect of his story has group relevance or, indeed, whether the most relevant aspect might not be the fact that he has been permitted to hold forth at such length. Under such circumstances it is necessary to be far more cautious about making assumptions about the implications of individual comments for the total group.

Relevant Cues

While the verbal content is of major importance in providing cues about the underlying concerns, other relevant aspects include the character of the interpersonal interaction apart from the content, indications of mood derived from intonation, pacing, etc., nonverbal behavior, and the context of the session.

Occasionally, a group will permit or even encourage one patient to dominate the discussion. This fact in itself might be of greater importance than the details of the patient's comments. Or a therapist's intervention may be followed by a change in the topic or a shift toward a more general conversation. Again, the interactive characteristic might be more relevant than the content.

Nonverbal behavior is often very revealing. In one session the patients lined themselves in chairs along one wall and jokingly referred to this as the "line-up." This was the first indication that the major preoccupation of the session involved guilt. In another session, a wish for help was expressed behaviorally in that the patients consistently addressed themselves to the therapists rather than to one another. In an adolescent group, horseplay in which a boy pretended to snatch a purse from one of the girls expressed a preoccupation with sexual feelings.

The context in which a session occurs is often of such crucial importance that an adequate formulation cannot be made without taking this factor into account. For example, a particular session might be understood only if one knew that the therapist had changed the meeting time, or that this was the first session after an interruption, or that the previous session had ended on a note of severe frustration and unexpressed anger.

Sometimes the first few statements or the first bit of interaction provides extremely useful cues about the central issue of the session. Often this early interaction takes place in the chit-chat which occurs while the patients are assembling. In one session, mutual teasing about dirty pictures forecast the preoccupation with sex which emerged later. In another, the significant fact was that the patients had been talking freely before the therapist entered but then immediately subsided into an awkward silence.

For some time we attempted to define a hierarchy of cues, so that each analyzer would pay the appropriate amount of attention to content, interactive aspects, context, and nonverbal behavior. We came to feel, however, that no rules can be laid down. At times the content may seem to offer major cues. At other times the discrepancy between content and mood, or the interactive characteristics apart from the specific content, may seem relatively more significant. Therefore, we have found it best to encourage the investigator to *attend* to all these cues, and to be sensitive to relationships among them, but not to make an a priori assumption that one is necessarily of greater import than the others.

The Appropriate Level of the Formulation

Because the group focal conflict refers to preconscious aspects of interaction, we try to avoid, on the one hand, a mere summary of the manifest content, or, on the other hand, a formulation which deals with unconscious aspects. One way of specifying the appropriate level is to think in terms of material which is *almost* ready to enter the consciousness. That is to say, if one can imagine the patients accepting an interpretation but at the same time regarding it as something "new," then it is likely that one has hit on the preconscious level. Another check is to examine the specificity or generality of the formulation. If the formulation is couched in too general terms, it may be relevant to the underlying *nuclear* conflict but has probably missed the unique focal quality of its expression in the meeting under study. Such a formulation may not be "wrong" but it has lost its specific usefulness, since it may be equally applicable to any number of other group sessions.

THE ANALYTIC PROCEDURE

In general terms the analytic process involves building, testing, and revising hypotheses until a formulation is achieved which satisfactorily accounts for all aspects of the session. What occurs typically is that the early material suggests certain ideas about the character of the underlying group concern. Then, later material requires a successive modification, shifting, discarding, or subtle shading of the initial hypotheses. For example, early in one session the patients argued about whether or not the nurses might be hurt by the patients' talk about sex. Initially, this suggested a concern about the freedom with which the male patients could talk about sexual feelings in a group with two female therapists. Later material in this same session suggested that the major preoccupation had to do with a concern about dependency. On reviewing the earlier content, the material about sex seemed to have a displaced character, and the conclusion was drawn that the predominant shared concern was some feeling that the patients might endanger their dependent relationship with the therapist if they revealed their feelings frankly.

A major test of the adequacy of a focal conflict formulation is the extent to which it takes into account all the elements of the session. Sometimes, several alternative hypotheses must be examined in terms of the total character of the session in all its aspects. The hypothesis which can be accepted with the greatest confidence is the one which can account for and is supported by many elements and aspects of the session.

The Specific Procedure

In defining a step-by-step procedure, it was agreed that one could work best from a summary of a session supported by a tape. The first step is to listen to the tape while reading the summary. This provides the analyzer with a feeling for certain qualities of the interaction and corrects for the selection inevitably involved in a summary. A summary is most useful if it is set up as a part of a work sheet in which the summary is divided into a series of very brief paragraphs. This helps to force the rater to attend to every detail of the session. Room is left on the work sheet for comments, reactions, and tentative hypotheses. As the rater moves through the material, he formulates tentative hypotheses about the implications of the material. At this stage he may note down possible themes, or he may develop ideas about the various elements of the focal conflict pattern. He tries to keep in mind at each step the implications of interactive aspects, content, intonation and pacing, and context. We find that at times the material suggests something specific about the focal conflict pattern. More frequently the analyzer picks up successive themes but cannot immediately make a decision about implications for the focal conflict. Sometimes he merely notes some unusual or discrepant note in the interaction, or an individual reaction on the part of some patient. When the rater has completed this step, he has before him a running account of the successive themes and elements of the sessions. With this account available he proceeds to the next step, which is to translate the flow of the session into focal conflict terms. We have found it convenient to use a work sheet divided into three columns: "disturbing motive," "solution," and "reactive motive." The analyzer fills out this work sheet in some detail, indicating the movement which occurs within the meeting from a particular focal conflict, probably through several attempted solutions, perhaps through a solutional conflict, to a reemphasis or modification of the original focal conflict, further solutions, etc. This stage, in other words, is a rather detailed tracing out of the movement within the meeting of the elements of the focal conflict. In a final step, the analyzer produces a summary formulation in which he attempts to define the single focal conflict and solution which best describes the meeting as a whole. For such a summary he might, for example, ignore the initial expression of the focal conflict, since this tends to be a first approximation. His final formulation would, however, encompass within it the first approximation as well as succeeding approximations.

The utility of this procedure lies in its definition of intervening steps. Discrepancies between two analyzers can be pinpointed and differences argued out in a more specific and therefore more helpful fashion. As this implies, the final formulation is the product of two independent analyzers. If the two are in agreement, this step is simple and brief. But more typically the two have disagreed at least in some details. Through meeting together and reviewing the material and their own step-by-step thinking, they produce a final product which in their joint opinion is the most satisfactory analysis of the session.

Agreement Between Independent Analyses

Ideal agreement, which would involve correspondence at every step along the way, is not likely to occur. What happens more typically is that the analyzers agree about the final formulation but each of them has emphasized different aspects of the detailed development of the focal conflict, with certain elements ignored or missed by one or another of the analyzers. Another pattern is that there is agreement on several but not all aspects of the final formulation. For example, the raters may define the same disturbing motive and solution but formulate the reactive motive in different terms. Or the analyzers have identified the same themes but built them into the focal conflict pattern in somewhat different ways.[2] Occasionally disagreement occurs because the raters have expressed the focal conflict on different levels. For example, one formulation may be closer to the manifest level while the other may be approaching unconscious levels. Or one analyzer may be generalizing more than the other. Total disagreement, in which two analyzers have seen entirely different focal conflicts operating in the meeting, has never occurred. Independent formulations have always had some points in common.

It now appears to us that in making this type of analysis of complex interactive material, it is unrealistic to expect ideal agree-

[2] For example, in one trial, two independent teams saw sexual interest in the therapist as an important element in the session. However, one team saw the therapist as the primary object of the affect and therefore formulated a focal conflict in which the disturbing motive was "sexual interest in the therapist." The other team saw the therapist as the displaced object of the affect, assuming that the affect belonged primarily to the peers. Therefore, this team formulated a focal conflict in which the solution was "express interest in the therapist (displacement from peers)." Both teams saw the sexual interest in the therapist but built it into the focal conflict in different ways. In general, we have found greater agreement about affect than about the object of affect, perhaps because displacement is such a frequent mechanism.

ment. The analyses rely too heavily on clinical judgment for such a result. However, it is felt that the development of a step-by-step procedure which can be followed by any clinician permits a more adequate specification of points of disagreement between independent judges and facilitates resolution of disagreement and the production of a combined "final" analysis.

SOME GENERAL CONSIDERATIONS ABOUT RELIABILITY AND VALIDITY

In the type of analytic task described here, the essence of reliability is reproducibility by independent investigators. The major pitfall lies in developing a private system in which the criteria for making judgments have been communicated through extensive personal interaction and are effective for that small group of investigators but remain implicit and unverbalized and therefore difficult to communicate to others except by a similar process of personal contact and osmosis. While this was true of the earlier stages of our work, perhaps necessarily so, we hope we have now clarified the criteria and standards involved. We have tried to spell out procedures, identify cues, and make each step in the analytic procedure as explicit and public as possible. However, some remaining element of the analytic process may remain inevitably implicit and uncommunicable. While the procedure can be specified up to a point, the crux of the matter is the final integration of the elements of the session into a unitary whole. The achievement of a "Gestalt" is essentially a creative act, hard to specify in terms of procedure or ingredients. One can see the product but not the process.

We have presented no reliability figures, feeling that the absence of a true universe makes reliability impossible to assess meaningfully via statistics. A final formulation in focal conflict terms involves the integration of many elements of the meeting, including content, intonation, interactive aspects, pace and timing, context, etc. These are not equivalent elements, nor can one say (for example) that there are eighty or forty-two or thirty relevant elements in a particular session. Quantification becomes absurd, and any attempt to specify percentage of agreement or to correlate the formulations of two independent analyzers satisfies the letter of the law with regard to the assessment of reliability but violates its spirit. Another way in which a true universe is absent lies in the fact that we do not know how "many" distinguishable focal conflicts can be said to exist. On the one hand, there may be a limited number of *families* of focal conflicts, but on the other hand, every therapy session is unique. Our effort is to capture the unique flavor of each session in focal conflict terms and to discourage generalizations of the "wish vs. fear" sort. The effort toward uniqueness again makes comparisons difficult. If two analyzers produce formulations which clearly belong to the same family of focal conflicts but differ in certain details, should this be regarded as agreement or disagreement? Of course, the more generally stated the focal conflict, the more likely one is to achieve "agreement." However, such agreement may occur at the cost of meaningfulness. We have preferred to sacrifice agreement to some extent and to assume that the most useful formulation is the one which is most specific to the material and is the combined product of two independent analyzers whose formulations may have differed in certain details.

The references to meaningfulness lead directly into the issue of validity. Since we are dealing with a hypothetical construct, no direct measure of validity is possible. One becomes convinced of the validity of a focal conflict formulation to the extent that the formulation permits an accurate prediction of subsequent events in the group and facilitates the exploration and understanding of a variety of group issues.

Prediction can occur on several levels. In a general way, we now feel confident that we can predict the types of focal conflict patterns likely to emerge during the formative stages of a group. We cannot predict order, the particular form or content of the conflict, or the solution which will be characteristic of a particular group. We feel confident about assessing adequate as compared with inadequate solutions (the former deal with both aspects of the focal conflict and are consistent with external reality). This differentiation is relevant to prediction in that an adequate solution permits the group to loosen its preoccupation with a particular focal conflict, while an inadequate solution leads the group to further exploration and attempts at solution. Attempts to predict subsequent events based on this hypothesis have been most successful when they have been restricted to events within a single session. Predictive validity has not yet been put to a complete test. For example, one might be able to predict the effects of a therapist's intervention by assessing its relevance to the current group focal conflict. But a formal test of this must be preceded by careful descriptive studies.

Another criterion of validity of a hypothetical construct is its explanatory power. Thus far we have found the group focal conflict a useful construct for studying issues for which a delineation of group-level events is relevant. For example, in a series of therapy sessions the reactive motives of successive focal conflicts constitute shared preconscious concerns or group resistances. An analysis of the early sessions of several groups made it possible to identify the shared anxieties which appear to be typical of the formative stages of therapy groups. By tracing through the manner in which the groups dealt with successive conflicts, it was possible to identify the ways in which the patients "worked through" the early resistances. Thus far, such an analysis has been applied only to the early sessions (Stock, 1962), but further work may elucidate the character of "working through" on a group level during later phases of group development. Because individual personality can also be conceptualized in focal conflict terms, an understanding of the impact of group events on the individual patient is facilitated. Deviant behavior in therapy groups has occurred when the group was in a state of solutional conflict, in which most of the patients were pushing for the acceptance of a particular solution to some focal conflict, with one patient unable to accept this solution. The group's behavior toward the deviant could be understood as efforts on their part to protect their preferred solution in order to mitigate the anxieties involved in the associated focal conflict. The deviant's inability to accept the group's preferred solution could be seen in terms of the interaction between his personal dynamics and the group situation; the group's preferred solution violated some essential personal solution (= defense). This study has had implications beyond the functioning of therapy groups, since it suggested a way of viewing the development, maintenance, and dissolution of group standards (= solutions) (Stock, Whitman, and Lieberman, 1958). A study of two patients who respectively gained much and little from a group therapy experience again suggested the utility of specifying the relation between total-group events and individual dynamics. "Benefit" was defined in focal conflict terms as the individual's ability to modify certain maladaptive or disabling solutions to lifelong nuclear conflicts. The analyses suggested that conditions most likely to lead to change involve a combination of (1) high tension in the individual's nuclear conflict and (2) group conditions which activate a related focal conflict and which contribute toward an enhancement of hope and a diminution of fears (Whitman, Lieberman, and Stock, 1960). We also see an application to the investigation of the therapist's role, since each intervention can be studied from the point of view of its relation to the current focal conflict situation. That is, one might determine whether the intervention makes explicit the reactive motive, blocks a solution, misinterprets the disturbing motive, etc. Once having classified interventions in this manner, the effects on the flow of the group interaction might be specified.

SUMMARY

In order to understand certain aspects of group functioning, it is useful to hypothesize the existence of shared, preconscious fantasies which are the property of the total group, and to conceptualize these in "focal conflict" terms. This theoretical approach views the group interaction as involving a preconscious conflict between two opposing motives or impulses, together with various attempts to achieve a solution to the conflict. In analyzing group therapy sessions in these terms, additive methods are not appropriate and the investigator must rely on holistic, clinical approaches. Methodological problems arise concerning procedures, agreement among independent analyzers, and the validity of formulations.

In approaching the material of the therapy group in these terms, assumptions are made that something akin to free association occurs in group therapy; that the manifest content has a symbolic reference to the here-and-now interaction; and that all elements and aspects of the interaction are relevant to the group focal conflict. Theoretical issues and practical problems include the relevance of content, interaction, intonation, pacing, and nonverbal behavior to the underlying group concerns, "idiosyncratic" versus "group-relevant" material, and the appropriate level of the formulation.

The analytic steps involved in producing a focal conflict formulation have been clarified and a specific procedure is suggested. Special problems concerning reliability and validity are discussed.

4

Some Problems
Regarding Exemplification

PHILIP E. SLATER

*T*he examples appearing in my book
Microcosm are taken from my own notes and transcripts or from
personal communications with other group leaders unless references
are given. The use of examples presents many problems. In some
instances I have verbatim transcripts to draw upon, while in others
I have only notes written immediately following a session—notes
which often turn out to refer in broad conceptual terms to what was
recalled as a prize example of some process or other, rather than
presenting any data which could successfully convey the process to
someone else. One also has to make horrendous decisions about lift-
ing material from context. If one takes only the segment of a discussion which deals with the process under consideration, one may be
distorting the picture enormously and ignoring the very connections
that make the process understandable. On the other hand, if one

Reprinted from *Microcosm: Structural, Psychological and Religious
Evolution in Groups* by Philip E. Slater, pp. 259–265. Copyright © 1966 by
Philip E. Slater. Reprinted by permission of the author and John Wiley &
Sons, Inc.

tries to summarize the entire discussion and interpret all of its ramifications and thematic interrelationships and subplots, one becomes
bogged down in detail, loses sight of the central point, and seems
merely to be showing that everything is connected with everything
else. As will become evident, I have avoided neither of these pitfalls,
zigzagging into the mouths of Scylla and Charybdis alternately.
Finally, it may seem absurd that in my own groups I have referred
to myself always in the third person. This is done not merely to provide homogeneity, but also because the use of the first person is
highly distracting in reading reports of this kind: Bion's papers, I
feel, suffer from this defect, despite the candor of his reporting.
This may, however, be simply a matter of taste. Names of group
members are (with one necessary exception) fictitious.

Selection always involves a bias of some kind unless performed
with mechanical safeguards, and some consideration of the distortion
introduced by the selection of examples here is therefore appropriate.
First it should be emphasized that examples can only illustrate, not
demonstrate. Hypotheses are being developed rather than tested, and
the purpose of the examples is merely to provide an empirical re-
ferent for the ideas advanced. For it is from these experiences that
the ideas themselves emerged. Indeed, neither the theories nor the
empirical studies with which I was most impressed when I began
this enterprise have proved particularly useful, while on the other
hand those theoretical notions upon which ultimately I relied so
heavily were either unknown to me as in the case of Mills (1964),
Bennis and Shepard (1956), Neumann (1954, 1955) or objects of
disinterest as Piaget (1932) or disregard as Freud's *Totem and
Taboo* (1913).

This means that the examples chosen should not be viewed
as any sort of representative sample of group interaction. They are
selected to illustrate the points made and naturally leave out other
important preoccupations of groups. They are heavily weighted, for
example, on the member-leader as opposed to the member-member
relationship and on group rather than individual concerns.

Most of all, they necessarily exaggerate the importance of
the dramatic or symbolic event, at the expense of the real day-to-day
accomplishments for which these events are merely a kind of meta-
phorical representation. Unfortunately the human need to reduce

gradual change and development to sudden and violent transformations is a powerful one, as instanced by the universal use of ritual
and ceremony to mark transition. The sophisticated may recognize
that a boy does not change into a man all at once during a puberty
rite, or a neurotic individual into a healthy one during a dramatic catharsis-and-insight session in psychotherapy. But "working
through" is a profoundly dull and uninteresting process, and the tiny
increments derived from it, while of the greatest ultimate importance,
tell us nothing essentially new. While we must understand that the
individual (or group) is more changed before the event than he
thinks (otherwise the event could not take place) and less changed
after it than he thinks, some concession must nevertheless be made
to the frailty of author and reader: we must first look at what is
condensed, direct, and obvious, until it becomes familiar enough to
look beyond it.

The examples I have used are therefore not necessarily the
"best" ones. They are simply the most crudely condensed ones.

A corollary result is that the groups are portrayed in a somewhat unkindly light, highlighted when blindly acting out and
ignored when working and insightful. To construct a functioning
group in which all or most members are integrated without the aid
of social dishonesty is a painstaking task which proceeds in a block-
by-block fashion. Often I have presented a series of scattered meetings which revealed changing attitudes toward the leader but
omitted the intervening sessions in which the group was concentrating on building its own solidarity—providing the foundation for
such attitudinal change by partial mutual confrontations and so
forth. Yet it is these omitted sessions which usually inspire remarks
in my notes about how well they are working. They seem to occur in
"bursts" of five or six sessions and contain almost nothing in the way
of a briefly described incident which might illustrate the phenomenon.
Apparently, important things simply happen too gradually to be
thus exemplified.

I should also like to consider here the effect produced on
group members by their already having read or heard about group
revolts or other phenomena of the kind described in this volume.
Could it not be argued that much of the material presented is
merely a documentation of the effects of our own interpretations and

associations, faithfully reenacted by helpful group members? Can we treat as "evidence" cases which involve so much contamination?

I think I would answer no to both of these questions. Contrary to some versions of the experiment myth, these groups were not designed as experiments and satisfy none of the criteria for hypothesis testing. The examples are, as I have stated, merely illustrative. At the same time, it would be mendacious to pretend that I am not personally convinced of the validity of at least some of the generalizations I have presented, and these are typically distinguishable by the rather larger number of examples I have included in order to seduce the reader into sharing this obstinacy. Thus while I will try to show why I think the regurgitation interpretation of these phenomena is absurd, it is only fair to admit also that where there are several examples of the same phenomenon, a case could easily be made that they are not entirely independent of one another.

There are three related sources of contamination. The first is through hearing about other groups, the second through reading, and the third through the leader's interpretations. They correspond to situations familiar elsewhere in the social sciences, such as the problem of secrecy in experiments with student subjects, the problem of diffusion in cross-cultural analyses, and the problem of clinical evidence in psychotherapeutic situations.

Experimental "rigor" in the social sciences is often established by convention rather than logic. One such convention is that one is permitted to treat as independent cases subjects who are sworn to secrecy in the cooling-out period following an experiment in which foreknowledge of the experimental conditions is undesirable, provided that one includes in one's report the phrase that "so far as we know, this request was adhered to" or some equivalent. I doubt that many experimenters are so naïve as to believe that many of their subjects are so dedicated to social science as to withhold such information from the first person to ask, but since there is no practical alternative to such a procedure, it is accepted as a necessary expedient. Furthermore, although we know that students talk continually about experiments they have been in, it is my impression that those experimenters who have endeavored to discover after the fact how many subjects were actually forewarned have turned up very few cases. Perhaps curiosity is so important a motive for participation in experiments that forewarned prospects drop out altogether, or perhaps those subjects who were forewarned were ashamed to reveal it.

In our groups there is no attempt whatever at such control. Usually a number of the group members have heard a lot about previous groups from friends. I have always been impressed, however, with how little generalization proceeds from this information. In my experience, groups have an exaggerated concept of their own uniqueness, both in pride and in despair, and seem invariably to view their group as vastly different from whatever groups they have heard or read about. Their capacity to distort information about these other groups, furthermore, is impressive (as in the case of experimental subjects), and I often experience difficulty in reconstructing the factual kernel of events alleged to have happened before my eyes. In addition, any group which they read about is usually viewed as having been conducted in an entirely different manner, the other group's leader usually being seen as much more or much less active, or even nonexistent. It is difficult for me to imagine a group imitating the performance of a previous one because I am so used to these assumptions and protestations of group individuality. Nothing could be more of a cliché, for example, than bringing in food or drink or sitting in the leader's chair; yet I doubt that many individuals would be motivated to perform either act, or could muster such self-congratulatory expressions in doing so, if they did not think it was their own inspiration. Despite their dependent longings there is a strong reaction of embarrassment, anger, and futility when a group discovers it has been behaving in accordance with a known formula, and the argument that such would be the case has been enough to smother revolt behavior more than once.

While no effort is made to control intergroup communication, in most of the groups herein described reading bearing directly on these issues is assigned late in the group's career. Some students will already have encountered some of this material, however, so that it cannot be assumed that no "diffusion" of this type has taken place. Initially, of course, readings which discuss or analogically suggest the phenomena in this volume were assigned because we had been made aware of their relevance through events in our groups. Our subject matter thus resembles many primitive societies, which lost their uncontaminated state almost before professional anthropologists could bring sophisticated techniques and theories to bear on them.

An additional problem arises from the fact that our primary goal in the groups is a didactic one. Through interpretations and reading materials we attempt continually to deepen the student's understanding of the experiences he is undergoing. The moment we find reading material which might help the members understand group processes we add it to our repertory, without waiting for any research accumulation. (This does not mean, of course, that we could predict with any accuracy how a reading would be used. We were often surprised and enlightened at the uses to which a given reading was put.) This means our material is hopelessly inadequate for research purposes. Our position is analogous to the one Freud found himself in: as a doctor he felt obligated to apply his knowledge as fast as it was—or seemed to be—acquired, thus becoming vulnerable to the charge that the phenomena he observed had been implanted in his patients by his own interpretations.

There is no way out of these dilemmas, but we can at least strip them of their more absurd assumptions. The foremost of these is the notion that exposure to an idea leads automatically to its adoption. This is the essence of the cultural diffusion explanation of social change, which is a form of contiguity magic, the spatial version of *post hoc propter hoc* reasoning. An idea, or any item of a given culture, is not adopted by another unless it holds some meaning or value for the latter, and a group that has read *Totem and Taboo* is not under an automatic compulsion to attack the leader. The idea of revolt is not after all an unfamiliar one; it could be suggested by the morning newspaper. Group members are bombarded with information and ideas at all times, yet do not necessarily act them out in the group situation. They read Piaget without suggesting a marble game, they read Bettelheim without enacting mock initiation rites, they read Veblen without engaging in conspicuous consumption, *Street Corner Society* without inaugurating a bowling league, Lillian Smith without instituting segregation, and so forth. They also read Malinowski's *Sex and Repression in Savage Society,* which provides a convenient rationale for ignoring *Totem and Taboo* altogether.

It is indeed difficult to convey how far from automatic is the connection between an idea and its application to the immediate group. As can be seen from some of the examples included in *Microcosm,* even after students *have* read the Bennis and Shepard paper the idea of expelling the leader often does not occur to them. Occasionally the relevant passage seems not to have been perceived or remembered. A member will announce to the group what an interesting paper he has found and then give a summary which entirely omits this passage. Sometimes it is mentioned, but in rather abstract terms, so that one could not imagine exactly in what way the Bennis and Shepard groups "got along without" the leader. Sometimes the process is made clear but in the context of a description which assumes (as is usually the case) that the Bennis and Shepard groups were somehow of an entirely different order.

Finally, many things read, perceived, understood, associated to the group, and *told* to the group are not heard when the majority is not ready to deal with them. Bright counterdependent individuals often come up with the idea of group revolt, and if the group as a whole is not more or less "on the verge" it is as if they were speaking an unknown language. The individual who gets credit for the suggestion is usually the third or fourth person to mention it; his predecessors seem even to have forgotten it themselves.

Probably the best example of the way external ideas are utilized in a thoroughly "contaminated" revolt is the discussion of one particular group. Here the seriousness of the ambivalent striving toward independence seems clear and appears to antedate the playful manipulation of the "primal horde" theme. On the other hand, although the members talk vaguely and lengthily about "getting rid of" the leader, it is not until near the end of the second two-hour meeting that this is discussed in concrete and immediate terms. Even then it arouses some surprise and is ultimately dropped.

What is important and meaningful in the propulsion of this revolt, however, is the group's admiring anger at the leader and the intense and persistent desire to run the group "on their own." All of their exotic imagery expresses these feelings, and if we were to strip it all away they would still be visible. The theatrics and the dramatic incidents change from group to group, but the underlying feelings always appear in one form or another. In my experience, in fact, the "big events" of a group show a conspicuous incapacity for diffusion.

It almost seems as if knowledge that a dramatic incident had occurred in a former group establishes a kind of ownership, and if it should be mentioned in a subsequent group it is usually with a gloomy invidiousness. ("They had a really *exciting* group. *Nothing* ever happens here.") It cannot in any case be stated too often that the particular event or metaphor appearing in a group is the product of a great many factors, a large number of which are irrelevant to the issues I have raised.

It would certainly not be difficult to put together a dozen or so examples of deification or revolt which were free from any sort of contamination, and a few of the examples included here can be so regarded. My purpose, however, is not to demonstrate that some bit of behavior (or some specific set of words) can occur in a group (which I regard as long since demonstrated by others) or that it will always occur in groups such as these (which it most clearly will not) but rather to explore the feelings and ideas underlying them and the possible connections between them, and to pass on, for whatever purpose they may be put to, a group of observations which occasioned my surprise when I first came to make them.

PART TWO

GROUP PROCESS
AND DEVELOPMENT

Extending the historical analogy outlined in the introduction to Part One, we propose that the issue of group development is the small-group equivalent of historical change. In recent years small-group researchers have begun to identify, measure, and explain temporal change in several types of groups. Current writing in this area—despite vast differences in methodological approach, quite different findings, and varied explanations of observations and data—presents us with roughly three models of group development: the *linear-progressive* model, the *life-cycle* model, and the *pendular* model.

LINEAR-PROGRESSIVE MODELS

In his comprehensive review of research on group development, Tuckman (1965) concludes that groups in general (training groups, therapy groups, natural groups, laboratory groups) go through the following stages of development: (1) a stage of testing and dependence, the "forming" of the group; (2) a stage of intra-group conflict and emotional expression, the "storming" of the group; (3) a stage of group cohesion, the "norming" of the group; and (4) a stage of functional role-relatedness, the "performing" of

83

the group task. This scheme is consistent with reports of group development from a variety of sources, and has been given further support by a recent empirical study by Runkel and his associates (1971)'.

Tuckman's scheme can be termed a *linear-progressive* one in that he describes groups as moving from a hesitant, testing stage through conflict to cohesion and, in the last phase, to the accomplishment of the primary task of the group. This linear approach fits the reports of the groups he reviewed, and is apparent in two important studies which merit further attention.

Kaplan and Roman (1963) identified three major phases of development in an adult psychotherapy group. The first focused on dependency; the second on power; and the third on intimacy. Their implicit model has a progressive quality, though an alternative, more complex analogy is that of individual development. It fits to some extent the Freudian psychosexual sequence (oral, anal, and phallic) and certainly resembles Erikson's progression from trust to autonomy to initiative.

Bennis and Shepard (1956; this volume, Chapter 6), basing their conclusions about group development on their observations of training groups, propose a two-phase scheme with a number of subphases. The initial phase of group development, they postulate, is an authority phase, in which the problem of dependence holds the group's attention; the second phase is an interpersonal phase, in which the problem of interdependence predominates. The first subphase is marked by preoccupation with a submissive solution to the authority problem; the second subphase, by a hope that rebellion will provide a solution. The third subphase brings a compromise solution and a partial resolution of the dependency-authority issue. The second phase begins with a concern with intermember identification ("enchantment")', which gives way to a concern with individual identity ("disenchantment"), which is in turn followed by another subphase of resolution. This scheme reflects the assumption that a viable solution to the authority problem must be found before the group can move on to the interpersonal phase.

This model is in some respects a more elaborate statement of Kaplan and Roman's model, and is reasonably congruent with Tuckman's formulation. It is progressive in the sense that the group is portrayed as moving toward the resolution of two distinct issues, with dependence having a developmentally earlier connotation than interdependence. It is linear in the sense that the group moves onward and upward toward the implicit goals of the training group.

Two forces contribute, we believe, to the appeal of the linear-progressive model. The first is the fact that our society remains fundamentally committed to seventeenth- and eighteenth-century ideals of progress, so that our whole notion of change is inextricably tied up with progress. The goal of T-groups, therapy groups, self-analytic groups is to make people better—better able to function, to communicate, to learn. The second force operating to foster a linear-progressive view of groups is the ready and appealing possibility that individual development is replicated in the development of the group-as-a-whole. The sequence then becomes the transition from childhood (dependence) to adulthood (intimacy). We have already alluded to the fact that Kaplan and Roman's scheme for group development bears some similarities to the psychosexual and psychosocial schemes of Freud and Erikson. The group is treated as an organism which parallels the developmental progression of individuals.

LIFE-CYCLE MODELS

This notion of the group's replicating individual development omits one very important phase—decline and death. Whereas the linear model appears to assume that group activity reaches a peak of efficient work and then ends or continues at that level of development, the life-cycle model emphasizes the importance of a terminal phase for small groups. Mills (1964), for instance, defines five principal periods of group development: (1) the encounter, (2) testing boundaries and modeling roles, (3) negotiating an indigenous normative system, (4) production, and (5) separation. The first two are, in Tuckman's terms, "forming" with some "storming"; the third is clearly "norming"; and the fourth is "performing." But the last phase—the phase of separation, when the group begins to face and to cope with its own death, when members assess the success or failure of their experience—is a new contribution.

Mann (1966, 1967) also devotes considerable attention to

the terminal phase in self-analytic groups and actually delineates two terminal phases—"separation" and "terminal review." Dunphy (1964, 1968; this volume, Chapter 12), Schutz (1958), and Slater (1966) note the importance of coming to grips with the end of the group and the dissolution of group boundaries for return to the "outside world."

The life-cycle model is also influenced by the replication of certain issues of individual development in the group-as-a-whole. In one sense, the life-cycle model is merely an elaboration of the linear model, with greater weight given to an additional phase in which members are forced to deal with the finitude of group life. The life-cycle model places the period of maximum productivity near but not at the end. This model is progressive, however, and more accurate in replicating human development—moving from the dependence of childhood to the production of adulthood to the decline and taking stock of old age.

PENDULAR OR RECURRING-CYCLE MODELS

The third model of group development posits recurring cycles of issues or describes a pendular oscillation between issues. Bion (1959), for example, describes the basic-assumption activities of dependency, fight/flight, and pairing as recurring alternatives to work. Bion explicitly rejected the possibility of placing these assumptions in a developmental context, although others have tried to do so. It is apparent, for example, that dependency is more likely to occur earlier and pairing later, and that work becomes established only after the recognition and analysis of some initially covert agreements and fantasies. In Bion's work, however, one gets the sense of eternally enduring difficulties, which are not resolved once and for all and which need to be continually identified and addressed.

Schutz (1958) posits three areas of interpersonal need—inclusion, control, and affection. He describes cycles of recurring attention to these issues following a particular sequence. The sequence from the beginning to the final stages goes like this: inclusion-control-affection. The last stage of the group, however, triggers a reversal of this pattern: affection-control-inclusion. In effect, then, Schutz suggests an integration of the recurring-cycle and the life-cycle models. The earliest and last concern of the group is inclusion, which has to do with the establishment and dissolution of group boundaries. Further, Schutz's interpersonal needs approximate Freud's psychosexual and Erikson's psychosocial stages.

Slater (1966) has presented a more complicated model of group development. On the one hand, he assigns central importance to the role of the revolt in the establishment of group cohesion and an involvement in shared task activity. This is the progressive aspect of his model. On the other hand, he sees boundary evolution as the product of the wish/fear dilemma created by the group members' desire to merge with the group yet remain autonomous individuals. Although he discusses boundary establishment from a developmental, progressive perspective, he emphasizes the recurring quality of individual and boundary concerns throughout the life of the group, with the group constantly dealing with efforts to maintain equilibrium.

The notion that social change is a product of efforts to maintain a group equilibrium is anticipated in Bales' early work (1955) and has been elaborated by Mills (1964). Such a notion does not necessitate a total revision of theory, but does imply that, even in a developmental context with linear and progressive features, the dynamic issue of equilibrium is never surmounted once and for all. Group equilibrium is chronically unsteady, and efforts are constantly made both to undermine and to maintain that equilibrium.

Congruent with this essentially sociological argument is the work of Jaques (1955; this volume, Chapter 11), who asserts that social change can best be understood as an effort to deal with anxiety, the anxiety being a product of some psychic disequilibrium in the group. Change in social structure becomes an effort to modulate anxiety by a defensive operation involving the whole group.

This work has led us to formulate a model of group development which places primary emphasis on the structural features of groups and particularly on individual and group boundary issues (Hartman, 1969; Hartman and Gibbard, this volume, Chapter 7). In our view, group development is conceptualized as an accommodation to introjective and projective (individual) or inclusive and exclusive (group) processes in the development and maintenance of boundaries. This accommodation is described as a pendular process, which occurs and recurs as an issue throughout the life of the group but assumes quite different forms at different points in time. Anxiety, depression, and guilt can be employed as marker variables which signal strains and disequilibrium in individual or group boundaries.

It is obvious from this brief review that the linear-progressive model is incomplete. The implicit assumption is that groups are on a beeline for their soon-to-be-established goals and that only unfortunate interferences interrupt that progress. The life-cycle model provides a more accurate reflection of the fact that "close-ended" groups have as a major task an acceptance of their finitude and must resign themselves to the inevitability of imperfection. The recurring-cycle model reminds us that problems of dependency, intimacy, and boundary maintenance cannot be simply overcome, or achieved, and then never heard from again. Some conflicts and discomforts are too deeply rooted in the human condition to permit such total or permanent mastery.

We might conclude, then, that the most accurate model of group development should be based on an integration of the linear, the life-cycle, and the recurring-cycle models. This kind of synthesis is at least implicit in the work of Mann (1967), Mills (1964), Schutz (1958), Slater (1966), and to a lesser extent in many other studies. But there are serious conceptual obstacles to an integration of the three models. How, for example, can there be progress in the face of recurring patterns and cycles? The problem, as we see it, stems from the fact that groups operate at different levels, addressing several different issues simultaneously. Thus, no one model of group development is adequate. Let us explain this notion more fully in the context of our own theoretical scheme.

THE GROUP-AS-FAMILY; THE GROUP-AS-MOTHER

In a recent paper (Gibbard and Hartman, 1973c), we explored the hypothesis that group development reflects an essentially oedipal paradigm. We reviewed the theoretical and empirical evidence for this paradigm, which was introduced by Freud (1913, 1921) and which has been expanded to a variety of contexts. Holmes (1967), for example, found support for the primal horde hypothesis in his work with university seminars. Slater (1966) has offered a graphic and elaborate portrait of the revolt against the leader in self-analytic groups and has examined in great detail the oedipal implications of the revolt. Others have noted similar phenomena (Bennis and Shepard, 1956; Dunphy, 1964; Mann, 1967; Whitman, 1964). Lundgren's (1971) study of two ten-man training groups lends support to the notion that a hostile confrontation with the leader or trainer relatively early in the group serves to establish and maintain intermember solidarity and openness. O'Day's research on trainers (this volume, Chapter 16) confirms this finding. The reader will recall that the period of "storming" noted by Tuckman is in basic agreement with these studies.

We have labeled this hostile confrontation, coupled with member solidarity and increased sexuality, *oedipal;* and this terminology reflects our assumption that the group situation recreates the basic nuclear-family conditions that spawn the Oedipus complex. The leader is regarded as father, and some female member or the female subgroup or the group-as-a-whole is regarded as the mother (assuming the leader is male). The oedipal paradigm is also a progressive one in the sense that, just as in individual development, the resolution of the oedipal crisis leads to guilt and the internalization of the paternal superego, which is accompanied by a more stable identification and a period of work and task orientation. The paradigm also implies that, once the confrontation has taken place, group members begin to interact in a more mature and differentiated way. This sequence is a central feature of Bennis and Shepard's scheme and, as Tuckman's review demonstrates, in most other progressive models.

One additional view of the small group has provocative, but largely unexplored, developmental implications—the notion that the group is unconsciously experienced as a maternal entity. Bion (1959), Durkin (1964), Gibbard and Hartman (1973b), Jaques (1955), Ruiz (1972), and Scheidlinger (1964, 1968) see the group as a preoedipal mother. Slater (1966), too, adopts this point of view—particularly as it relates to boundary evolution. This notion points to a preoedipal paradigm, and it entails a completely different viewpoint. Instead of conceptualizing object relations in groups as involving differentiated whole objects, this point of view holds that ties between group members involve more "primitive" and less differentiated perceptions of self and others. The revolt, then, becomes less oedipal and more like the kind of anger that facilitates the establishment of a younger child's self and object boundaries. Ostensibly oedipal issues can be interpreted in part as efforts to establish and maintain personal and group integrity and to move from symbiosis to individuation. This paradigm is less exclusively linear in that the establishment and maintenance of boundaries are conceived as ever changing in response to threats to equilibrium. There is progression toward differentiation, but always a strong regressive pull as well.

The larger dilemma involves the individual versus the group. Group solidarity requires some loosening of individual boundaries, for in this way the group boundaries are enhanced and expanded. This sort of trade-off, with the inevitable conflict between individual autonomy and group loyalty, continues throughout the life of the group.

The preoedipal paradigm centers on a perception of the group as an ever waiting, potentially symbiotic mother. Although mature forms of relationship are certainly present in most groups, and quite sophisticated role differentiation and division of labor facilitated by them, one wonders if experiential groups are not utilized primarily for the kind of transitional experience that Winnicott (1953) describes. It may be precisely this maternal, preoedipal, psychoticlike quality about submersion into groups that gives them their great intrinsic appeal as well as their difficulties. As Bion has explicitly shown, groups provide a variety of temptations to avoid work, and individuals in groups are easily swayed into precisely such regressive behavior. Man needs to experience again and again the transition from symbiosis to individuation, and is capable of at least a partial recapitulation of the transition whenever he enters a new group.

It is our conclusion, then, that group development entails a *simultaneous* enactment of oedipal (relatively advanced) and pre-oedipal (relatively primitive) issues. A full-fledged revolt against authority involves a struggle for a forbidden sexual object (or objects), and incomplete revolts reflect a regressive flight from such a struggle. At the same time, the sequence of developmental stages is analogous to the preoedipal child's progress toward a clarification of self and object representations vis-à-vis a maternal entity. We believe that in most instances the group-as-a-whole represents the *preoedipal* mother, and the group leader the *oedipal* father, though there may be variations in these designations. We are suggesting that the group situation, unlike the dyadic situation in individual therapy, dictates that oedipal and preoedipal themes may influence group process at the same time and in ways that make it difficult to relate the two processes. It must be left to future work to unravel the interweaving of oedipal and predoedipal themes in the development of groups. Our experience so far, however, does not suggest a simple linear development as in the development of normal individuals. Rather, we believe that simultaneous processes analogous to oedipal *and* preoedipal paradigms have to be considered in any comprehensive theory of group development.

One explanation for the coexistence of a "mature" and a "primitive" group is that the beginning or infant group is composed (usually) of normal, individuated human beings with a variety of defensive options. Initially, however, and—in our view—throughout its existence, the group is composed of enough disparate and irreconcilable components to make it an imperfectly integrated entity. Thus, group members have available a continuum of alternative behaviors, ranging from the more regressed to the more mature, while the group-as-a-whole as it "matures" becomes more like a symbiotic mother with whom the members are ambivalently fused.

This leads us, then, to the nucleus of a theory of group development in which two separate issues must be considered in some depth. First, there is a historical dimension of development: the group recreates the nuclear-family situation, in which the resolution of oedipal conflict leads to cohesion and work. The second is a more dynamic one: here the group must contend with boundary problems and the eruption of disequilibrium signaled by disturbing affects; and part-objects and more primitive defense mechanisms such as introjection and projection play an important role. The fact that *both* issues are central to group development accounts for the seemingly incompatible theories of development which have been offered. We are not, however, in favor of an integration which simplifies the issues. We are now more than ever impressed with the complexity of group life. In our view, issues on different levels do occur simultaneously and must be seen that way.

This discussion serves as an introduction to the three studies presented in this section. These studies represent work from different kinds of groups, grow out of different theoretical perspectives, and offer different developmental schemes. Yet, when taken together, they can be viewed as quite complementary and *as a whole* representative of the complicated conceptualization of development we have outlined.

Kaplan's paper discusses the development of therapy and training groups and amplifies an earlier analysis of group formative processes (Kaplan and Roman, 1961, 1963). Describing phases of dependency, power, and intimacy in therapy and training groups, he discusses the role of myth in group development (see Part Four of this volume for further studies of this topic), emphasizing its ego-adaptive functions. While Kaplan's model is explicitly progressive, with analogies to individual psychosocial development (Erikson, 1950), his discussions of regression and object relations indicate a more complicated picture. He comes close to according object relations with the group-as-a-whole a crucial role in his theory, but does not pursue this feature systematically. While he recognizes the cyclical nature of many issues and the regressive pull of the group, he maintains a commitment to a progressive rather than a cyclical or pendular conception of group evolution. The other noteworthy aspect of this paper is the comparison between the two groups and the opportunity it affords to see differences in the developmental process in groups which meet for different lengths of time and for different purposes.

Bennis and Shepard's study of group development has already been discussed in some detail earlier in this introduction. It is an early and most influential work, an outstanding example of the linear-progressive point of view. We have already noted that this paper departs from the life-cycle model in that it ignores separation and implies that issues once dealt with are forever laid to rest. The stages described here are readily recognizable to anyone familiar with T-groups and self-analytic groups. Bennis and Shepard's outline of phases is both a confirmation and an extension of the phases found by Kaplan in therapy groups. Kaplan's dependency and power phases clearly have to do with authority, and the intimacy phase with member interdependence. The Bennis and Shepard study is noteworthy also in its description of the role of key subgroups in polarizing and resolving focal conflicts. Bennis and Shepard's work has influenced not only studies of development but also those of role differentiation (see Part Three of this volume). The function of the crucial group event is likewise described in this paper and provides the beginning of other more elaborate notions (see, for example, Slater, 1966) about the revolt against the leader.

The final contribution, by Hartman and Gibbard, is an attempt to integrate two previously isolated approaches to group development. The first, that development is a product of defense against primitive anxieties, has been articulated by Jaques (1955) among others. The second, that group development can be understood in terms of the establishment, maintenance, and dissolution of boundary awareness on a group basis, has been endorsed by Mills (1964) and Slater (1966). The model proposed by Hartman and Gibbard is a pendular one, with the group described as swinging between greater closeness to and greater distance from the maternal entity of the group. They focus primarily on the preoedipal paradigm and do not discuss in much detail the relationship between oedipal and preoedipal dynamics.

Thus, no single study offers a comprehensive theory of group development, one that demonstrates an integration of existing models. But, taken together, the studies offer complementary sets of observations and conceptualizations, which can provide a foundation for the integrating formulations that we are at least beginning to identify and work toward.

5

Therapy Groups and Training Groups: Similarities and Differences

Seymour R. Kaplan

With the marked growth in utilization of training groups within and outside the mental health field, their relationship to therapy groups has become a subject of increased interest. Most of the contributions on this theme to date (Frank, 1964; Zinberg and Friedman, 1967; Horwitz, 1964) have dealt with differences in goals, levels, and methodology. This paper focuses on the broader issue of covert group formative processes in the two approaches. In Part I, a training group of psychiatric residents utilized as a means of teaching group psychotherapy is described. This kind of group has common elements with the human relations or sensitivity group, often referred to as the "T-group," which has attained widespread popularity in the last fifteen years (Bradford, Gibb, and Benne, 1964). The developments in the training group for psychiatric residents are compared with parallel group processes within an adult therapy group (Kaplan and Roman, 1963). Part II of the paper addresses itself to the general

Reprinted from *International Journal of Group Psychotherapy*, 1967, *17*, 473–504, by permission of the author and the American Group Psychotherapy Association, Inc.

theoretical issues regarding group formative processes in therapy and training groups, with particular emphasis on the nature of transference and object relations.

I. OBSERVATIONS ON GROUP FORMATIVE PROCESSES

Setting and Format of the Training Group

The training group exercise to be described was a modification of the usual T-group in that the first half of each meeting consisted of observing a therapy group behind a one-way screen. Otherwise the meeting was unstructured. The agenda for the discussion period was left to any issue, whether related to observation of the therapy group or not. Two basic conditions were required of the residents: the first was agreement that every member of the training group, including the teacher, was completely free to participate or not in the discussion, and the second was that they must be willing to have the interactions within the training group brought up for discussion, whether by a fellow student or the teacher. It was explained that, although the emphasis within the training group was to be on group process, and particularly on the role of the leader in group process, individual emotional reactions of the members to the group events would often provide a necessary guideline for insight. Therefore, a degree of openness about personal feelings about group events was a necessary condition and would be instrumental in determining the productiveness of the meetings.

Sixteen residents were members of the training group, which was scheduled on a weekly basis for six months. The patients selected for the therapy group were persons who had come to, or had been referred to, the outpatient clinic of a large general hospital. A resident and a social worker, both of whom were members of the training group, were co-therapists of the therapy group. Most of the patients who were referred to the therapy group had been seen initially by one or another of the residents participating in the training group.

Observations of Behavior

Selected events that occurred during the training exercise will be summarized. The focus will be upon the training group, but highlights of some events in the therapy group will be noted. The central themes that appeared to characterize the events during a sequence of meetings—dependency, power, and intimacy—correspond to the outline of phases of development in an adult therapy group described elsewhere (Kaplan and Roman, 1963).

The Dependency Theme (Meetings 1–7). The residents had the reputation of being a close and cohesive unit. This appeared to be borne out in the first meeting, in which the discussion about the format of the seminar proceeded in a most cordial manner and with active participation on the part of the residents. They agreed to the conditions, which were stated above, and were enthusiastic about the format. At the third meeting, when four additional residents attended for the first time, they were treated by their fellows as interlopers. In fact, the "old" members talked in such a way as to imply that a special closeness existed between themselves and the teacher and that, in the short space of two meetings, a body of special knowledge had sprung up among them to which the "new" members could not be privy. The degree of basic good will that existed among the residents, however, was exemplified by the openness with which they were able to discuss the nuances of this interaction. They teased one another about the implied specialness of the "old group" and use of the teacher's first name by some of the residents as a means of implying a degree of familiarity that did not exist. It was suggested to the "old" residents that their reaction to the "newcomers" reflected a displacement to each other of feelings toward the teacher, who was in fact the only newcomer in the group.

In the first meeting of the therapy group, which was composed of seven adult females, one of the patients suddenly got up from her chair and moved to a seat next to the male therapist, an impulsive act of crucial significance for this patient, since she did not return to the group. In the following session this seat next to the therapist was left vacant. An identical sequence of events occurred in the training group. Attention was called to this, with particular emphasis placed upon the central role that the leader occupies in any group and the extent to which the members focus their feelings upon him.

Enthusiasm on the part of residents for the teacher and for the training group method continued to mount. "Why aren't all the seminars like this?" was a not infrequent expression of the residents' attitudes, and a similar type of enthusiasm for the treatment situation was evidenced by some of the patients in the therapy group. The residents' overvaluation of the teacher's role and the feelings of specialness they experienced in the training group were expressed in the fifth meeting by a request that the teacher intervene with the department in a dispute over financial arrangements. The residents not only incorrectly perceived the teacher's authority but it was implied that their relationship with him warranted his intervention on their behalf. In a similar way those patients who had problems with the Department of Welfare indicated in their expression of complaints that the therapists were empowered to alter the procedures of that agency and should do so on their behalf.

Such expectations of the teacher and the therapist not only represented dependent feelings but also reflected exaggerated feelings of helplessness. In the sixth session the residents brought up their dissatisfaction with another faculty member who supervised the work of some of them in group therapy. They requested the teacher's intervention, even though, after discussing the issues, it was evident that they had not yet made any remedial efforts of their own. As it turned out, they were able to manage the situation quite well. At this time the group therapist was asked by one of the patients to facilitate the hospitalization of her senile mother. This actually did not require any special intervention by the therapist, and the patient was able to expedite the arrangements on her own.

Their high opinion of the teacher and of the teaching method did not correspond to any degree of skill or knowledge that the residents had attained. Similarly, the enthusiasm of the patients for the treatment group did not correspond to any therapeutic benefits. Actually, it appeared that the high regard that the group members had for their respective group leaders and for the group method was in part influenced by their need to believe that significant advances in learning and treatment could be achieved in so short a time. It was as if their fondest hopes for the acquisition of knowledge or the attainment of a cure of their emotional problems by magic had been fulfilled.

The members' need to exaggerate the extent of their accomplishments in the group meetings was highlighted by their reactions to the leaders when they did not behave in a way to reinforce this

view. If the teacher or the therapist made observations that did not
provide a ready answer to a problem, these were often disregarded in
favor of a facile answer by another group member, and if there was
any delay by the leader in responding to a question, a group member would cut in with an answer. In this way, not only did the
groups maintain the illusion of their advanced accomplishments but
they also avoided the issue of whether or not the leader's behavior
corresponded with their view of events and their relationship to him.
Underlying ambivalence toward the leader was dissipated in bicker-
ings among the members. Overt expression of differences with the
teacher in the residents' group came in the sixth meeting, when he
was asked a technical question and did not respond. There was a
sufficient pause in the interaction in the group for his silence to
register, and the group's reaction was one of awkwardness and silence
followed by a marked sense of unease. After a few minutes the
teacher suggested they discuss this, and he pointed out that he was
acting upon his prerogatives as a member of the group. The fact that
they had not taken the teacher seriously was evident. One member
said that he was aware of a feeling of outrage and a sense that it was
within the group's prerogatives to force the teacher to talk as a
reflection of their right to control the behavior of a teacher in their
institution. That control over the teacher was an issue, not just frustration of the desire to learn, was indicated by the fact that the question originally posed had involved a vague, esoteric issue, while prior
to being asked this question, the teacher had ventured some observations about technical issues specific to the topic being discussed which
had gone unheeded. Since the patients in the therapy group had
been observed to ask questions of the therapists and then disregard
the replies, comparisons could be made and the meaning of this
type of interaction in terms of the underlying attitudes of members
of a group toward a leader explored.

Two unplanned-for events arose which brought the power
theme into sharp focus. In the fifth meeting the resident-therapist
announced to the patients that he would be away on vacation for a
month after the ninth meeting. At that time the only irritation expressed by the residents related to the resident-therapist's plans to
see the group the following week on an official holiday when most of
the other residents planned to stay at home. The second event was

that, by chance, another conference was scheduled which required the teacher's attendance at a time overlapping the training exercise. This meant that, every other week, the teacher would be about fifteen minutes late for the observation period. Although this change in schedule was announced in the fourth session, it did not come up for discussion until the eighth meeting.

The Power Theme (Meetings 8–14). The sharpest statement of a sense of outrage regarding the teacher's lateness and conflict of schedule came from the group in the eighth meeting. The residents claimed the right to control the conduct of the seminar and the teacher's time of attendance. It is relevant to keep in mind that, while the morale had been high up to this time, many of the residents themselves were given to coming late to the observation period. Furthermore, the teacher's lateness was brought up as unexplained and as implying a rather cavalier attitude on his part toward the teaching program. Upon reflection, the residents noted that their criticism was not made primarily in reference to the leader's role as a teacher, but, as in the instance of his silence in response to the question, seemed to be mediated by emotional reactions toward him personally. The residents did not complain that the teacher's lateness interfered with the teaching but that the teacher's absence appeared to affect their interest in watching the therapy group. When the teacher remarked that his schedule had to be altered to accommodate the schedule of the chairman of the department, who conducted the other conference, the residents became aware of the exaggerated authority which they had attributed to him. They had not only overvalued the teacher's power, but by their expectations that the teacher would submit to the group's demand, they had ascribed to themselves a position of power that rivaled the chairman's.

At this time the patients' reactions to the vacation of the resident-therapist were being observed. (The therapy group continued to meet with the social worker.) The patients tended not to be conscious of any emotional reaction to the therapist's absence and attempted to avoid any discussion of it, but it was evident by their behavior that there were strong feelings of helplessness, denial of any resentment, and compensatory self-inflating reactions. It was possible, in view of the similarity of events pertaining to the leaders of the two groups, for the residents to begin to appreciate the nature of the underlying feelings of the patients. Although the members of the training group had less recourse to the defense of denial and were able to verbalize some of their ambivalent feelings toward the teacher, this did not prevent an increase in anxiety and some avoidance reactions, although these may have been more marked at this time because the resident-therapist who was on vacation had a positive integrating role in the resident group as a whole. In any event, the "honeymoon period" of the training group was waning. With increasing awareness that there was much knowledge they had yet to acquire, their exaggerated view of the group's achievement leveled off and enthusiasm for the training method moderated.

Increased tension in the training group was reflected by waning interest in the exercise and a gradual decrease in attendance starting in the meeting one week prior to the resident-therapist's vacation and lasting until one week prior to his return. This first session that the resident-therapist was away, only two residents were present behind the screen for the first half hour. A low point was reached in the twelfth meeting, when only six members attended the exercise. By this time the therapy group, which had been attended by only two patients the first week of the therapist's vacation, had reconstituted itself, and on this day a key member was back after having missed three sessions. This patient's attendance was a response to a phone call from the social worker–therapist, whose active intervention had been decided upon because of the specific nature of the patient's problems. The discussion of this patient's absence and return led the training group members to discuss their own attendance. It was suggested that the sudden waning of interest in the seminar reflected in the absences and latenesses was a reaction to the emotionality of the group relationships. It was pointed out that since the residents were aware of the importance of the technical issues related to separation anxiety, rationally one would have expected that they would have looked upon these particular sessions as an especially valuable learning experience. The discussion about the meaning of absences was continued in subsequent meetings, and a renewed interest in the meetings emerged. While this interest continued for a majority of the residents for the remainder of the seminar, some members did not return and their absence became a significant issue in the group development.

Emergence of an awareness of shared group concerns, particularly conflicted feelings about the teacher, was preceded by bickering among the residents over relatively minor issues. For example, during the thirteenth meeting there was a rather bitter exchange between the social worker–therapist and some of the residents as to why the social worker had gone ten minutes overtime in the group therapy session. There had been discussion in the past about the relationship between the two therapists and the difficulties they experienced about their functions as co-therapists. It was felt that to some extent the tensions between them were a reaction to their status differences, the social worker having openly expressed her envy of the preferred status of the residents, and of psychiatrists in general, in the hierarchy of the hospital structure. During the thirteenth meeting, after the residents had expressed resentment toward the social worker for keeping them waiting ten minutes for the end of the therapy session, the teacher suggested that the members still felt some resentment about his lateness. It was suggested that the residents and social worker shared in common envious feelings toward the teacher because of his superior position in the hierarchy of the faculty and that these feelings may have contributed to the number of absences the previous week. With some difficulty several residents asknowledged that they had mixed feelings about their absence. On the one hand, they felt a sense of personal responsibility toward the teacher; on the other hand, they felt that the teacher might have a punitive response to their absence and make a negative evaluation of them to other members of the faculty. It was interesting that, during the therapy session that week, the patients had been preoccupied with fears of violence and had expressed criticism of the police for not providing sufficient protection.

In the fourteenth meeting the issue of absent members became more specific. This was the session in which the resident-therapist returned. Only one patient came to the therapy session (two others had explained that they might be absent). A strong reaction to the patients' absences in the training group members, most of whom were present, led the residents to discuss their response to cancellations by patients in individual as well as group therapy. They felt that cancellations reflected on their competence, and they experienced a lowered self-esteem and a sense of lack of professional worth. They were asked to consider to what extent similar motivations might be a factor in their own absences, particularly in view of what had been discussed about their ambivalent feelings toward the teacher.

It had become evident to the teacher at this time that the absence of one particular resident was of significance because of the nature of his role in the group. In the early meetings the residents, despite some bickering, had tended to interact as a unit, but in recent meetings dissension had split the members into conflicting subgroups, apparently around the pros and cons of the training method. Part of the underlying emotionality of this argument involved a covert overestimation of the teacher and, in more subtle fashion, of the group as a whole. The arguments between the contending subgroups had more of the tone of a political convention or a dispute over ideological beliefs than a scientific appraisal of a professional technique. The resident whose absence was considered significant was the most verbal antagonist of the training group as a teaching method, and for a time had marshaled the contending subgroup behind him. However, perhaps because he was somewhat too truculent in his criticism and because the group was not ready to deal with the common underlying issues, he recently had been alone in expressing his criticism. Although it had reached the point of his being covertly scapegoated for his intransigent position, particularly in social contacts outside the meeting, the group had not allowed this to emerge clearly enough for it to be dealt with during a meeting. Without being more specific about the absent members, it was apparent that this process could not be explored and dealt with.

In the fourteenth meeting, when some of the residents expressed concern about the social worker who was absent (due to illness), the teacher asked how they felt about talking about other members who were absent. There was some concern, as there had been in the previous meeting, that such a discussion, especially if there were to be a "naming of names," might result in a critical, even punitive, reaction on the teacher's part. However, since the fear that the teacher would abuse his power had diminished, some of the members came to realize that they were actually concerned about being labeled "tattletales." They associated this concern with personal experiences in adolescence when, under pressure of peer groups, they would often modify their behavior to conform to the norm. Actually, however, it was the residents who tended toward scapegoating. By attributing a superior ("holier than thou") value to their attendance, they implied an invidious comparison with their absent colleagues. It was suggested that this reaction of superiority might be a determining factor in explaining the meaning of some absences in the training group. An absence could be motivated to devalue the teacher's efforts or status, as the residents had speculated might be true of the patients in the therapy groups. To the extent that all members might be envious of the teacher's role, any one member through his absence could be a spokesman for the group as a whole. The discussion became more sharply focused when the resident who had been most opposed to the teaching method, and indirectly to the teacher, was mentioned by name. The history of his role in the group and the underlying emotionality of the conflict in which he had been involved were reviewed. There was more awareness of this process after clarification than had been evident at first, although some members felt that the dissenting resident was acting out of personal bias and that he did not represent their feelings.

The patients in the therapy group, because it was so early in its formation, were not confronted with their overvaluation of the therapists or their own compensating self-inflating reactions. There was dissension among the patients over the pros and cons of group versus individual treatment, and it had the same quality of an ideologic dispute as in the training group. Although the dissension was not as intense as in the training group, there was some scapegoating, and one of the two Negro patients was subtly isolated in the group, which resulted in her dropping out of therapy. By and large, the therapy group, by virtue of its composition and its goals, tended be more regressed, so that the ambivalent feelings toward the therapists were either acted out or expressed in symbolic terms. In the session following the therapist's departure on his vacation the two female patients who showed up were dressed in slacks. The content of the session revolved around the powerful role of their mothers in their families in comparison to the inadequacy of their fathers. In later sessions, as a manifestation of the ambivalence felt toward the male therapist, who was the dominant leader of the two therapists, the patients made inferences about the superior therapeutic skill of the female therapist and referred in general to the superior endowment of women. They attempted to cement a subgroup alliance of the women versus the dominant male in the group and men in general.

The Intimacy Theme (Meetings 15–24). Although fantasies of closeness to the teacher had been expressed earlier, the residents seemed freer to express their affectionate feelings at this time. This development occurred concomitantly with the return to the group of some members who had been absent for a number of meetings. Their return occurred on the same day that a patient who had been absent for some time returned to the therapy group. In both groups the members appeared pleased by these events and expressed their feelings warmly. There was some elaboration in the training group about anxieties attendant upon returning to the group, involving, on the one hand, a fantasy of finding the group bound together in a familiarity that would exclude the returning member and, on the other, a concern about their own attitudes toward the teacher. Because of the anxiety involved, the returning members chose not to explain this any further during that meeting. In the twentieth meeting one of the residents did discuss the efforts of a colleague some weeks before to induce him to return. These two members were close friends, and their quarreling over the value of the training group had jeopardized their friendship, although they subsequently resolved their feelings. In retrospect, it was possible for the members to see that the intrusion of personal feelings about the teacher and the underlying emotions of the group situation, rather than the pros and cons of the value of the training exercise, were the instigating factors.

At this point, two divergent trends expressed themselves in the training group in reaction to an increasing sense of involvement in the process. On the one hand, some members felt that more personal feelings should be expressed, which would have made the group more closely approximate a therapy group. This tendency to move the training group in the direction of a treatment process was reflected in a loss of interest in observation of the therapy group and in primary attention being given to the training group experience. On the other hand, some residents felt an increasing sense of "getting down to work" and tended to focus more specifically on the group therapists' technical procedures without as much effort to relate the issues to their own interactions. These differences were discussed more amicably than earlier disputes had been. However, by this time the group was cognizant of the nearness of the termination, and the pending separation influenced the group's development. For some individuals this termination period represented a pressure to be less defensive and more frank in discussion; for others it represented a time to close over emotionally and resume a more traditional, didactic student-teacher relationship.

The therapy group at this point might be viewed as having "settled in." The membership became stabilized. Those members who—because of the early group pressures or the composition of the group, or for idiosyncratic reasons—did not "fit in" had dropped out. The patients who were left were able to begin to talk more directly about their feelings since some measure of trust in the group had been established. However, the pace of the developments around the expression of personal feelings about one another, because of both the nature of the emotional problems of the patients and the goals of the group, was much slower than in the training group.

Discussion: The Role of the Group Formative Processes

Selected behavior of the members of a training group and a therapy group has been presented. The material is intended to high-light group formative processes. In this section, more specific implications of the role of the group formative processes will be outlined. It is hypothesized that the group formations occur in a sequence of developmental phases. The theme that appears to be specific to each phase has already been noted and will be reviewed. The specific role into which the formal leaders appeared to be cast as the central persons of the group formations, and the structural configurations which appear to be related to these formations, will be presented. The training group of residents and the therapy group they observed will be used as a model about which to focus this outline, with the primary emphasis on the training group. The inferences about the nature of group formative processes in small groups have been extra-polated from a number of therapy groups and training exercises with which the author has had direct experience. In addition, he has been influenced by the literature on group process and shares the views of those clinicians who approach the events in small groups in terms of processes involving the group as a whole. This approach is particularly espoused in the writings of English clinicians (Ezriel, 1950, 1957; Foulkes and Anthony, 1957; Bion, 1959). While clinicians in this country tend to eschew the group-process approach, studies along these lines have been published (Redl, 1942, 1945, 1959a; Stock and Thelen, 1958; Arsenian, Semrad, and Shapiro, 1962; Appelbaum, 1963; Kaplan and Roman, 1963; Whitaker and Lieberman, 1964; Whitman, 1964; Peck, Roman, Kaplan, and Bauman, 1965).

Dependency Phase. In the first meeting of the training group and the therapy group, the teacher and the therapist, respectively, by virtue of their formal roles were central to the transactions of the members, who related to one another in a loosely organized way. By the third meeting the interactions among the members had altered so that it appeared that they had changed from a collection of individuals into a "group." While the members continued to focus upon the formal leaders, it appeared that new emotional constellations involving the leaders had emerged. In Redl's (1942) terms, the formal leaders could be described as the central persons around whom group formative processes had coalesced, and the new emotional constellations reflected the group emotions generated by these processes. A characteristic aspect of these emotions was the exaggerated enthusiasm of the members, who, for the most part, behaved toward the teacher and the therapist as toward charismatic leaders. The leader's method of teaching or treatment, which early became the common focus of concern for both groups, was not evaluated objectively as a professional technique; rather, it appeared to be viewed by the group in a mystical light. With the exception of a minority of dissenters, the leaders were perceived by the group members as idealized figures and their ideas were accepted as a matter of faith.

As the meetings developed, it began to appear that this faith in the methodology of the leaders was motivated in part by the group members' need to believe in a magical process by which one learns or is cured quickly and without great effort. As was noted in the observations of the group behavior, this seemed to be indicated by the readiness with which members disregarded the leader's responses contradicting this belief and by their readiness to accept quick and facile answers from fellow group members. It seemed then that the group members not only tended to idealize the leaders but the group as a whole as well. An idealized group, such as the members appeared to be promoting, could readily produce substitute leaders in place of the formal leaders to meet the needs of the group for the type of charismatic leadership it required in this early phase.

The factors, then, which appeared to motivate the members to participate in the group formative processes had at least these two elements.[1] There were indications of interpersonal needs, which collectively can be described as dependency needs, expressed verbally or in behavior in the need for special attention from a person perceived to have exaggerated powers to teach or cure patients. The members appeared to be intensely involved in maintaining the assumption that these powers to teach or to cure patients had been readily absorbed and assimilated by the membership in the early meetings. The manifestations of the dependency needs were expressed in generic terms or implied by universal symbols and, with the exception of idiosyncratic reactions, did not seem to be specifically representative of the unique aspects of any one individual. Some theoretical implications for the nature of the transference and the object relationships in general of this generic or universal expression of needs of the collective group membership will be discussed in Part II of this paper.

A summary of hypothesized group formative process in the early phases of group development appeared in a paper based upon observations of an adult therapy group (Kaplan and Roman, 1963). With appropriate insertions for the training group, it represents the views being suggested here. "In summary, [the behavior was] characterized by a coalescence of the patients into a psychological unit based originally upon the medical model but later

---

[1] There are other determinants in group formative processes which will be developed in Part II. In particular, the necessity of a small group to give structure and a social organization to its interaction is omitted. However, the cause-and-effect relationship of these factors is of a different conceptual nature than the motivational determinants being considered here.

reinforced by a common conviction of the resources of the therapist to cure magically. The patients interacted as a unit and related to the therapist as a superior, and indeed godlike, person. The dependent needs of the patients were expressed not only by direct requests for advice or attention by some patients but by a common consensus that the reality of the group situation was more closely akin to a mythological construct than to a painstaking process of change over a period of time."

Power Phase. As the members of the training group during the middle phase of the meeting began to come to grips with the reality demands of the learning situation, their behavior seemed to indicate that the perception of the teacher had less of a myth-evoking, magical expectancy. However, the teacher continued as the major central person around whom group emotions coalesced, and the members ascribed exaggerated power to him.[2] Although the distorted perception of the teacher more clearly related to his realistic position as a member of the faculty, there was both an exaggerated view of his authority and an exaggerated concern that he would abuse this authority in punitive action against them. The emergence of these feelings corresponded with the beginning expressions of overt hostility toward the teacher. In the author's view, ambivalent attitudes toward the leader are a major determinant of hostility at this phase of the group's development. The hostility represents emergence of the denigration which, as Brierly (1951) observed, is regularly associated with the idealization process.

Although at this point the regression in the group had lessened, the members collectively were not ready to reckon with their underlying ambivalent emotions. Consequently, these emotions were displaced and enacted through the factional disputes of the subgroups. The members of the subgroups, in extolling their respective viewpoints, were unduly critical and behaved toward one another in the punitive manner that had been projected upon the teacher. It resulted, as was noted in the description of the group

[2] The group formations presented here, related to the shared themes of dependency and power, are similar to the hypothetical group formative processes that Redl (1942) describes coalescing around the central role of teachers of adolescent students, who either adore, idealize, or fear their teachers.

behavior, in the scapegoating of one of the residents. The extent of the scapegoating was more intense than in subsequent training groups, which may have been due to the idiosyncratic quality of the individual who was scapegoated but also may have been a result of the particular stress upon this group as the first resident group in which this innovative approach was attempted.

The emergence of subgroups, or the reinforcement of pre-existing, loosely organized subgroups, has been observed as a regular occurrence during this phase of a group's development in which, among other characteristics, concern with power is a predominant theme. The subgroup formations appear to have adaptive functions in that, for example, ambivalent attitudes toward the teacher were displaced upon the contending subgroups. Conscious awareness and expression of hostile, denigrating attitudes toward the teacher would not only be a potentially disrupting force threatening the group's existence but also would create unsettling conflictual feelings in the members. To some extent the latter were manifested in feelings of envy. However, strong differences among the members—for example, over the pros and cons of the training group as an educational method—provided a surface conflict which acted to disguise common anxieties about ambivalent attitudes toward the teacher. Freud (1921) commented upon "the narcissism of petty differences," which may be applicable to this type of reaction. When the resident who was the spokesman of the subgroup contesting the training method expressed a negative, denigrating attitude toward the teacher, it enabled the other members to feel unconflicted in experiencing these feelings as well as in expressing idealized attitudes toward the leader. This type of process is similar to that noted by Redl (1942), who referred to it as "exculpation magic through the initiatory act."

Apart from their adaptive functions, the motivational factors in this phase of the group formative processes were a continuation of the shared interpersonal needs that the members felt toward the leader, as well as their need to maintain the illusionary views of the learning or therapeutic situation. Shared interpersonal needs in the power theme appeared to involve the need to be protected and controlled by a powerful ally, especially in the face of the competitive nature of the group climate. Insofar as attainment of group goals is concerned, the power theme appeared to express the view that one is cured or attains knowledge by aligning oneself with, or perhaps controlling, a powerful central figure who can dispense the required knowledge or cure. One achieves this by a direct alliance either with the formal leader or with an equally powerful contending subgroup leader.

In the training group during the latter part of this phase, and until its termination, there was intermingling of immature and mature aspects of ego functioning in the challenges created by the learning process. On the one hand, the residents appeared to achieve their goal by submission to, or rebellion against, the perceived distorted authority of the teacher. To some extent, they identified with the teacher and imitated either the positive or negative components of this distorted perception. On the other hand, the members appeared to be striving for an expression of their professional and personal identity as a manifestation of their own unique style and identity. The importance of identification mechanisms as part of the normative and ego-enhancing aspects of the group formative processes will be discussed in Part II of this paper.

During this phase the group emotions in the therapy group appeared to diverge from the corresponding group emotions in the training group. The regressive elements were not interpreted or counteracted as actively in order to allow the emergence of pathological conflicts. Nevertheless, ambivalent feelings toward the therapists and displacement of these feelings into subgroup formations could be observed, although the intensity of this reaction did not become fully manifest until later meetings. The resident-therapist's vacation, which had a disruptive impact upon the group, did temporarily result in the emergence of conflicts around feelings of powerlessness which might not otherwise have become manifest at this stage. Some of the patients expressed this conflict in terms of its symbolic significance in their past life experiences. One of the reactions, which has been observed frequently in therapy groups in reaction to feelings of powerlessness, is the emergence of compensatory idealized subgroup formations. A characteristic pattern in groups whose composition includes men and women is alignment of the sexes into separate subgroups, with overvaluation of stereotyped attitudes about masculinity and femininity. In the therapy group the patients attempted to use overvaluation of the female co-therapist for this emotional constellation. Whitman (1964) has described what appears to be a similar subgroup pattern as a characteristic event in T-groups.

Intimacy Phase. The influence of the group formative processes in the training group began to diminish toward the later phases of the meetings, when the awareness of impending termination had its effect upon group behavior. However, to the extent that one might discern group formative processes at this point, concerns about feelings of intimacy seemed to characterize the behavior. The central role of the teacher could be inferred, but the interaction centered about group members, specifically those members of the group who might be referred to as "a pair," that is, as two people with a special affinity for one another.[3] The covert fantasy elaboration which appeared to motivate this group formation, either for those directly involved or for those who vicariously identified with the pair, was the assumption that one acquires knowledge or is cured through a close intimate relationship with another person. Although one could discern pairing relationships early in the group meetings, the significance of these as a group formative element did not seem to emerge until the dependent and power strivings had been clarified. Often, for example, group members seemed to "pair off" as an expression of the dependent phase of the group or as part of the subgroup alliances in which power strivings were foremost.

The impact of the group emotions upon the individual members was evidenced by the disruptive effect upon preexisting friendships and the threatened social ostracism of one of the residents. Zinberg and Friedman (1967) point out that the use of the sensi-

[3] Bion (1959) has formulated the nature of group emotions in terms of "basic assumptions" that underlie group behavior. The basic assumptions refer to the irrational elements of the group emotions in contrast to the "work group" emotionality. He has organized the former into three basic group emotional constellations, which are characterized by the themes of dependency, fight-flight, and pairing. The presentation in this paper of phases characterized by themes of dependency, power, and intimacy is an attempt to make the themes reflect congruent levels of reference. The fight-flight reaction tends to be associated with the concept of mechanisms of defense in psychoanalytic theory. The pairing reaction is a structural configuration as well as a thematic concept and has been placed in the context of other structural configurations observed to occur (i.e., group-as-a-unit, subgroup),

tivity or the "T-group" approach in settings in which the members
work together or socialize requires special caution. In this type of
setting it becomes particularly important to distinguish between the
therapeutic goals and techniques of a therapy group as compared to
the educational goals and techniques of the training group. This
issue will be discussed further in Part II of this paper. However, it is
noted here because the discussions about feelings of intimacy and the
nature of the pairing relationships present a point of departure between the therapeutic and training group approach. In the training
group the pairing relationships and the underlying feelings were
noted only insofar as they clarified the developments of the group
formative processes and affected the learning situation while, in the
therapy group, the pairing relationships were extensively explored
when sufficient trust and understanding among the members had
been established so that the potentiality for destructive acting out
after the sessions was not as great.

II. SOME THEORETICAL IMPLICATIONS OF GROUP FORMATIVE PROCESSES

In Part I observations of behavior in training groups and
therapy groups that were held to be manifestations of covert formative processes were described, and some inferences as to the preconscious significance of these phenomena were discussed. Part II will
address itself to some general theoretical views about group formative processes. In particular the nature of the transference and object
relationships in training groups and therapy groups during the group
formative phase will be considered. Although the primary frame of
reference for this discussion is based upon the psychoanalytic theory
of behavior, some attempts will be made to integrate theories of
social scientists who view the small group in nonclinical terms. In
particular, the small group as a social system will be considered.

The Therapy Group and the Training Group as a Social System

The social scientists who see the small group in terms of its
reference to society at large, as part of a social system interlocking
with larger social systems, have described aspects of the behavior of

members in training groups or similar groups in terms of the requirements for social organization in groups. It is their view that any
small group of individuals who have their formal relationship to
social structures temporarily suspended have as one of their primary
needs the reestablishment of a social structure, in order to communicate and to achieve agreed-upon tasks. "A T-group is a relatively
unstructured group in which individuals participate as learners. The
data for learning . . . are the transactions among members, their
own behavior in the group, as they struggle to create a productive
and viable organization, a miniature society; and as they work to
stimulate and support one another's learning within that society"
(Bradford, 1964).

Foulkes, whose experience with the small-group situation
comes from his work with therapy groups, observes, "This situation
is a miniature representation of the world at large, with which it is
coterminous, and . . . is analyzed in terms of structure, process,
and content. . . . Structure concerns patterns of relationships that
are relatively stable and continuous. . . . Process is the dynamic
component of the situation and can be defined as the interaction of
the elements of the situation in their reciprocal relationships and
communications, verbal and nonverbal. . . . Structure and process
are the channels through which content is transmitted . . . the
attitudes, ideas, values, sentiments, feelings. . . . Structure and
process also determine in what way the communication of content
takes place" (Foulkes and Anthony, 1957). The social scientist in
his laboratory study of small groups and the clinician in his therapeutic work with small groups often emphasize different aspects of
the same group phenomena.

*The Group-Evolved Mythology—Implications for Group
Process and Structure.* In Part I it was suggested that the group
members' need to believe in a magical process by which one learns
or is cured quickly and without great effort influenced their perception of the leaders and the group situation. The leaders were cast in
the image of deified or heroic figures as part of the shared mythology
about the nature of the group situation. The implications for the
small group of this group-evolved myth may be similar to the function of the cultural myths for society-at-large. Arlow (1961) comments about the functions of cultural myths, "The shared daydream

is a step toward group formation. . . . [Myths] are instruments of socialization." Freud (1921) speculated that civilized man emerged from primitive (primal horde) group formations through the use of the epic myth. "We have said that it would be possible to specify the point in the mental development of man at which the advance from group to individual psychology was also achieved by the individual members of the group. . . . He who did this was the first epic poet. . . . He invented the heroic myth. . . . The myth, then, is the step by which the individual emerges from group psychology." It is hypothecated that, apart from what the deified or heroic images projected upon the leaders represents in terms of individual psychology, the process reflects a method by which the members collectively attempt to define the reality of the situation and at the same time organize and give structure to the group. "The shared mythology seems to reflect the use [by group members] of earlier patterns of thinking and of learning to deal with the tensions created by the need to interpret and give meaning to a new and unfamiliar environment" (Kaplan and Roman, 1963).

In an earlier paper (Kaplan and Roman, 1961) the authors described what were considered to be characteristic responses in a number of ongoing adult therapy groups to the introduction of new members. It was suggested that one way of characterizing the events was in terms of a socialization process. "[The members acted as if] they had set up a therapy group of their own making, codified their activities [and as if] the new member was being indoctrinated into the codes of an established [social] group. . . . In order to avoid isolation, the new member then had to identify with the prevailing mores of the group, which had an identity apart from the therapist." While the focus in the paper was upon the symbolic significance of this behavior for the individuals involved, it was noted as a common element in all the groups that these events appeared to be similar to an initiation rite and that interactions around the events became ritualized. In retrospect, aspects of the ritualization appeared to involve means by which the members, albeit in an immature way, attempted to orient the newcomer to the prevailing social structure of the group. The possible relationship of "initiation rites" in these groups to such rituals in primitive societies and the mythology that underlies these rites might be worth exploration. However, what is suggested here is the manner in which a group-evolved myth may be used to structure and organize a group. "We may, then, summarize the complex character of myth in the following words: Myth is a form of poetry in that it proclaims a truth; a form of reasoning which transcends reasoning in that it wants to bring about the truth it proclaims; a form of action, of ritual behavior, which does not find its fulfillment in the act but must proclaim and elaborate a poetic form of truth" (Frankfort, Frankfort, Wilson, and Jacobson, 1949). The thesis presented by Frankfort has reference to the use of mythopoeic thinking in the development of earlier societies and its relationship to the evolution of the modern-day scientific thinking. However, his analysis of the function of the myth in society at large appears similar to the use of the myth in the early developmental phases of the unstructured small group.

Developmental Phases in Small Groups. A constellation of events in small groups which appears to be characteristic has been postulated for some time in both clinical and laboratory studies. That these phases are part of characteristic developmental sequences has been suggested (Bales, 1950a; Bennis and Shepard, 1956; Kaplan and Roman, 1963; Schutz, 1958; Stock and Thelen, 1958). There are several dimensions along which the developmental aspects of small-group behavior can be studied. One such approach, as noted, views the small group as a social system with structures, processes, and communication patterns similar to, and interlocking with, larger social systems. It has been hypothecated that, under the conditions in which training and therapy groups are established and conducted, these groups initially regress to structures and processes that resemble the social order of prescientific societies and then progress rapidly toward a more sophisticated social structure. In other words, a small group under certain conditions recapitulates the development of processes of thinking and of learning through which mankind has evolved.

Another but related dimension along which small-group development can be studied views the regression and progression as a recapitulation of aspects of early-childhood development. The common themes of the phases of development that have been used in these discussions—concerns with feelings of dependency, power, and intimacy—can be viewed as derivatives of the basic emotional needs for nurturing, security, and affection in early childhood. There appears to be a correspondence in the emergence of the group formations, with their related specific conflicts and resolutions, to the epigenetic model of psychosocial phases of development of children described by Erikson (1959). He states that there is a sequence of generic psychosocial tasks that the primary family group undertakes in child-rearing which reflect the confluence of the individual child's basic emotional needs, the collective resources of the family unit, and the expectations that society delegates to the family as part of its function in the socialization process. Appelbaum (1963) sees in the small group a direct recapitulation of early instinctual experiences and states that the phases of development are "a progression through infantile psychosexual stages." The relationship of childhood emotional developments to the observation of events in training groups is also suggested by Horwitz (1964): "Certain generic issues, like members' [shared] reactions to the trainer, the prototypes of dependency and counterdependency, the distorted attitudes toward authority figures, are observed by all writers of the Bethel School, though there is an assiduous avoidance of the term [transference]." While the author shares the views of these and other writers about the similarities of small-group development to early-childhood development, he feels that there are some important differences to be derived from these observations insofar as their implications for the use of psychoanalytic theory and, particularly, the concept of transference and object relations.

Implications of Small-Group Process for the Nature of Transference and Object Relations

In the foregoing, it has been held that the small-group situation, such as one observes in training and therapy groups, tends to produce characteristic phenomena which to some extent influence the behavior of all individuals participating in the group. While some aspects of these phenomena may also appear in the dyadic situation, the group situation appears to produce these effects regularly and in more observable dimensions. Bion (1959) has remarked: "I am impressed, as a practicing psychoanalyst, by the fact that the psychoanalytic approach, through the individual, and the approach these papers describe, through the group, are dealing with different facets of the same phenomena. The two methods provide the practitioner with a rudimentary binocular vision. The observations tend to fall into two categories, whose affinity is shown by phenomena which, when examined by one method, center on the oedipal situation, related to the pairing group, and when examined by the other, center on the sphinx, related to problems of knowledge and scientific method." Considerations of the significance for the individual member of the role of the leader in the group situation may help to clarify this distinction, particularly as it bears directly upon the nature of the transference and of object relations in general.

The Symbolic Significance of the Role of the Leader. It has been suggested that the role of the leader in therapy and training groups is overdetermined and encompasses at least several functions. The various symbolic images into which he is cast appear to be the result of coalescence of the wishes, fears, and conflicts of the imaginations of the group membership. The role of the leader as part of the mythological construction of the group-as-a-whole and the rituals that the group weaves about him is one facet of a process through which a social structure is achieved. Viewed from this context, the symbolic significance of the role of the leader is not as much a reflection of the individual teacher or therapist around whom the construction coalesces as it is a reflection of his position as the representative of a professional institution. Similarly, the individual member's contribution to the projected image of the leader does not necessarily represent the uniqueness of the individual's perception of the teacher or therapist but that aspect of the individual's group emotionality determined by the group formative processes specific to the phase of the group's development. The use of metaphors without qualifications tends to obscure this distinction, as when, for example, in analyzing the role of the central person, terms such as The Leader, The Father, The Group Deity are used interchangeably. The inference is that the individual member's projections are the result of unsolved oedipal conflicts that have been evoked by the therapist or teacher. Similar inferences of unresolved sibling conflicts are often drawn when a group member's response to a fellow member appears to be irrational and of a childish nature. These interpretations would suggest that the emotionality which the individual is experiencing in the group situation is similar to the transference neurosis in the dyadic situation, but this fails to take into account the influence upon the individual of group formative processes.

The use of metaphor is of course indispensable to the expression of human emotions, and the equation of leader, father, and deity may communicate aspects of the group emotions during specific phases of the group formative processes. However, the use of the father image in that phase of a group in which idealized emotions are projected upon a central person appears similar to the use of the expression Father of Our Country in reference to George Washington. In this context the father image appears to be used as an overdetermined symbol that includes references to historical traditions of a nation, to idealized human traits, as well as to aspects of the political and social structures of the country. In training and therapy groups, when the leader is cast in a deified image, this does not necessarily imply that the projected emotions emanate from the internalized father image of a member's unresolved infantile oedipal conflicts. In reference to the reactions of group members to the introduction of new members, the author noted: "It was very unusual for a member to respond to the introduction of a new member with any meaningful associations related to his early life history. The members' increased preoccupation with themselves in comparison to others and the implicit rivalries and jealousies with the new member could be incorrectly interpreted as a repetition of specific sibling transferences. Though they may have been sibling rivalries in the general descriptive sense, they were not necessarily repetitious of specific infantile conflicts in the transference. The increased narcissistic concerns in reaction to the new member may be a reflection of the basic libidinal configuration underlying group emotions" (Kaplan and Roman, 1961). This is not to say that unresolved infantile conflicts are not present in any of the group members but, rather, that the dynamic forces which generate the group emotions at certain stages appear to arise primarily from adaptive processes within the ego rather than as direct derivatives of instinctual conflicts.

The Importance of Ego Functions in Group Processes. The analysis of group behavior primarily in terms of id psychology without reference to ego psychology may be the result of what Arlow

(1961) refers to as a "cultural lag" in the understanding of psycho-analytic theory. He quotes Dorson's criticism of the arbitrary use of the "symbolism of the unconscious" in which, Dorson observes, "everything falls neatly into place, and dreams, myths, and fairy tales tell one common story, a genital-anal saga" (Dorson, 1960). Appel-baum (1963), who has suggested that small-group development be viewed in terms of a psychosexual saga, nevertheless observes else-where that group emotion "seems to have little in common with the infantile experiences of most people. . . . The emotional configura-tions may be activated not only because they are spurred by a per-son's early experience but also as if they were a tropism from antiquity" (Appelbaum, 1966). This latter observation refers to Freud's speculations about group formative processes. Freud (1921) hypothecated that "Both states, hypnosis and group formation, are an inherited deposit from the phylogenesis of human libido—hypnosis in the form of a predisposition, and the group, besides this, as a direct survival." However, it is to be remembered that these observa-tions predated Freud's development of ego psychology, and, in fact, it was partly as a result of his study of group behavior that he began to formulate his structural theories. The importance of ego psychology in group processes seems indicated by the impact of these processes upon individual ego functions.

One of the effects of group formative process upon the ego is the blurring of individual distinctiveness and a tendency for the indi-vidual to regress to an immature level of emotional and intellectual functioning. These phenomena seem to be most evident in the early phases of the groups and were suggested above as being characteristic of the group formative process that coalesced about the deified image of the teacher or therapist. The collective wishes of the group members to achieve immediate gratification appeared to be reflected in a group methodology based upon magical solutions. Freud (1921) described the behavior of individuals in relatively unstructured groups as having characteristics that "show an unmistakable picture of a regression of mental activity to an earlier stage such as we are not surprised to find among . . . children." While he generalized about the common occurrence of immature behavior in groups, Freud developed a specific concept about the nature of the emotional bonds between the group members and the leader of a group. He emphasized that the idealization of the leader of a group by all members is the basic motivating force in group formative processes and that, as a consequence of the members sharing a common idealized leader, they identify with one another. In some instances, Freud noted, an idea, actually an ideology, may become the force behind group formative processes. This tallies with the observation made of the two groups described herein that the idea of magical cure contributed to the initial motivations for the group formative processes.

Whatever may be the basic motivations for the group formations being discussed in this paper, identifications among the members and an idealization of the role of the leaders were a frequent observation. The common themes and the collective expression of shared emotions seem to indicate that the predominant emotional bond which the members experienced toward each other, at least during the early phases of the groups, was based upon identification relationships. These identification relationships, as the concept was developed by Freud, represent a special type of regression in object relationships which involved ego structures and functions that differentiate it from the instinctual, object-directed regression usually implied in transference relationships. Scheidlinger (1955), in a paper on the nature of identifications in therapy groups, comments: "There is almost always a failure [in the group therapy literature] to distinguish . . . its role in the group dynamic phenomena. . . . Furthermore, identifications are also apt to be lumped together with transference and object ties." In the broadest sense of the term, the collective regression to earlier modes of thinking and to identification types of object relationships in the group formative process could be referred to as transference reaction, although this tends to empty the concept of dynamic meaning. However, this type of identification relationship under the influence of group emotions is different in nature from a transference neurosis.[4] The fact that the symbolic expression of group emotions in mythopoeic form contains metaphors, the analysis of which shows obvious derivatives of indi-

[4] This is not meant to imply that a transference neurosis will not develop in a long-term therapy group, although its usefulness therapeutically is still unclear. These comments relate to the early phases of therapy groups and particularly to closed therapy groups with no individual sessions. Frequent individual sessions may significantly alter the nature of group processes described in this paper.

vidual unconscious instinctual drives, has led too readily to the direct application of id psychology to group process. Arlow (1961) discusses behavior in groups which is influenced by, or gives expression to, a shared myth. He stresses the importance of including in the analysis of the behavior assessment of the individual's level of ego integration and ego functioning in general.

The impact of group formative processes upon the ego appears to be manifested in other ego functions besides object relations. "In ego psychological terms, identification brings into play such functions as the adaptation to reality testing, sense of reality, the self concept (with its self and object representations), and the capacity to form object relationships" (Scheidlinger, 1964). There is a tendency toward a loosening of ego defenses and controls, toward externalization of aspects of the self and object representations, and toward the emergence of ambivalent feelings. The extent of the regression varies with the personality structure of the members, the setting and goals of the group, and the nature of the leadership. For an extensive survey of current views on these processes, the reader is referred to Scheidlinger (1955, 1960, 1964, 1968). One point about the particular types of group situations, the training and therapy groups, which are the subject of this discussion may be relevant to mention here. It was hypothecated that the roles of the central persons as deified or heroic figures involved projected, or externalized, idealized perceptions of these images. As was noted, the substitution of the leader for the individual member's ego ideal is Freud's formula for the motivation for group formative processes. He derived this view from his observations of crowds and large, loosely organized groups. With the additional factor of the role of an ideology as a group formative stimulus, Freud's formulation appears to correspond to the observations made about small training and therapy groups during the loosely organized, early phases of group development. However, apart from the style of leadership in these groups, the regressive group formations about the leaders might have been a special consequence of the professional institutions they represented. These institutions, the medical institutions and the institutions of higher learning, tend to be imbued with magical expectations by society at large.

Normative and Ego-Adaptive Functions of Group Process.

Although the emphasis in this paper has been upon the ego aspects of group process, the discussion of the regressive impact upon object relations and ego functions may tend to suggest that group emotions are perceived as derived from serious pathological conflicts. In part, this is a result of the emergence of psychoanalytic theory from the study of neurosis, and despite the recent developments in ego psychology, there is as yet no comprehensive psychoanalytic theory of normal behavior. Consequently, it is often necessary to use concepts to describe behavior which require supplementary comments to distinguish between normal and pathological inferences. The nature of the identifications in group process and the other regressive manifestations being discussed here are a case in point. In his description of identifications in groups, Scheidlinger (1964) remarked, "Contrary to the view prevalent among some writers, this kind of an indentification does not necessarily involve a pathological engulfment of the personality by another object . . . or a regressive replacement of an earlier object cathexis." Similarly, the immature aspects of the members' behavior described in these papers also are not necessarily meant to imply pathological conflicts and may subsume integrative and adaptive functions. The initial regressions and subsequent progression of group emotions often appear to be similar in function to the concept of "regression in the service of the ego" (Kris, 1952). While the utilization of mythopoeic thinking as the major methodology in the early meetings reflected a lower level of intellectual reasoning than the individual capacities of the members in the training group, and most of the members in the therapy group, it seemed to provide an opportunity for learning, for both students and patients, as a result of which the individual could achieve a higher level of integration of ego functioning than previously. Furthermore, the nature of group formations, even when they produced the most unsophisticated methods and magical solutions, included aspects of a social structure without which panic would have supervened. Although of lower order than the collective potential of the membership in the early phases, group processes even during this stage appeared to contain normative and adaptive components.

The members' emotional contributions to the shared group mythology and the related ritualistic behavior appear to serve the common task of the group, both in the evolving of a social structure and in providing the data from which the members may achieve their work goal. These goals or task-oriented identifications are of a "functional" nature as the result of the interdependency of group members upon one another, and they refer to mechanisms within the ego that have not been extensively considered in this context in analytic theory.

Other Differences in Therapy Groups and Training Groups

Since one of the major differences between training and therapy groups is individual personality factors, the emergence of similar phenomena in both group situations, at least in the early phases, is of interest. Perhaps one of the reasons for the similarities of process in groups composed of relatively normal individuals as compared to groups composed of patients with emotional problems is that group emotions include aspects of ego adaptation that are derived from the "conflict-free" areas of ego functioning. In some instances of group participation the impact of emotional conflict upon the ego diminishes. "On the other hand, it appears that where a powerful impetus has been given to group formation, neuroses may diminish and at all events temporarily disappear. Justifiable attempts have also been made to turn this antagonism between neuroses and group formation to therapeutic account" (Freud, 1921). Furthermore, the pressures on relatively normal individuals involved in training groups are not inconsiderable and may evoke immature reactions that exaggerate the regressive group emotions. As Zinberg and Friedman (1967) comment: "Other blocks against learning may arise from symbolic aspects of the learning process itself, e.g., learning resisted as seeming to be submission to the leader. . . . Another variation of this block depends on symbolic modes of thinking." However, it should be stressed that the similarities between group process in training and therapy groups is a relative one. Individual personality factors have a marked effect in determining the level of regression, the progression of the group's development, and the potential usefulness of the experience for learning or for therapy.

In a therapy group described previously (Kaplan and Roman, 1963), a level of development allowing analysis of concerns about feelings of intimacy was not achieved until between the sixtieth and eightieth meetings, suggesting that the time factor is also an important determinant. The time-limited span of a training group, which is considerably shorter than the usual life span of a therapy group, has a significant effect upon the emergence of regressive group emotions. If one uses long-term therapy groups of non-psychotic patients as a comparison, the training groups appear to progress rapidly through very similar group formative processes. The phenomena are sufficiently observable to most of the participants to allow for an effective learning experience about the nature of these processes. However, there is only limited opportunity for study of the processes in depth or for self-observations of individual determinants in these processes. Any proficiency in understanding and utilizing group process for therapy or training requires considerable supplementary reading and extended practice under supervision. As for the extent of self-awareness to be achieved, it naturally varies with the individual personality. The training group situation generally opens to view a circumscribed area of "self," limited for the most part to the context of the group emotions. This is not meant to minimize the possible results, since the aspect of self which is invested in the group process can be a very meaningful component of the total self. However, there has been a tendency recently to imply that the focus of change in training groups is the same as the therapeutic objectives that may result from the resolution of a transference neurosis. In part, this may have resulted from the type of misapplication of concepts of transference to the group situation that has been discussed above.

Another area in which differences between training and therapy groups can be noted relates to the nature of the leadership and the goals of meetings. The most obvious statement of goals is that the training group is used for educational purposes and a therapy group for therapeutic purposes. However, this distinction is not always easy to make, particularly in the dynamic approach to the use of the training groups being considered here. Zinberg and Friedman (1967) comment on this point in their article:

Mobilizing and working with these resistances against affect-laden, experiential learning demands something of the sort of clarification and interpretation which we usually think of as part of the curative process of therapy (Bibring, 1954). We find this conclusion inescapable although unwelcome, since it increases the difficulty in specifying the boundary between this teaching and psychotherapy. We expect no argument from others with comparable experience against the proposition that learning blocks are initially prominent when group participants confront data which stimulate unconscious conflicts and the defenses against them. The disputed region is at the border area between this teaching and psychotherapy—what and how to interpret, at what depth, with what intensity of affect mobilization and personal exposure—all very difficult territory to map.

The central area of difficulty is the delineation of the personal aspects of the individual's group emotionality. In the training group, interpretations of an individual's contributions to the group emotions are for the purpose of making the study of group process an effective experiential learning experience *for all the members*. In a sense, it is irrelevant to this purpose who the member is as a unique individual or what personal gains may accrue to him as an individual. The purpose is not to change the individual, other than to aid his growth as a student. The focus of change is a change in the group-as-a-whole toward its collective goal. This may be an oversimplification of the purpose of the "T-group" and may not represent the goals of some training group leaders. "There has been a steady trend toward deemphasizing the study of group process in T-groups in favor of enhanced personal insight. Some writers have referred to sensitivity training as 'psychotherapy for normals' (Wechsler, Massarik, and Tannenbaum, 1962) although many decry this therapeutic trend in T-groups" (Horwitz, 1964). In the therapy group the delineation of the individual's contribution to the group emotions also draws the attention of the therapist-leader. However, the relevance of the individual's group emotionality to his uniqueness as an individual is the foremost purpose of the interpretation. The subtle aspect of this purpose is that it may be necessary for some change to occur in the group as a whole to achieve this goal. The previous discussion about the importance of identification relationships in the group process has some bearing upon this issue; this, however, is a complex technical issue deserving considerably more elaboration than can be offered in this paper. The main point that is being presented is that while the area of the individual's group emotionality is a central area of development in both training and therapy groups, the manner, purpose, and goals for which this material is used ultimately differ considerably in the two situations.

A Theory
of Group Development

WARREN G. BENNIS
HERBERT A. SHEPARD

*I*f attention is focused on the organic properties of groups, criteria can be established by which phenomena of development, learning, or movement toward maturity can be identified. From this point of view, maturity for the group means something analogous to maturity for the person: a mature group knows very well what it is doing. The group can resolve its internal conflicts, mobilize its resources, and take intelligent action only if it has means for consensually validating its experience. The person can resolve his internal conflicts, mobilize his resources, and take intelligent action only if anxiety does not interfere with his ability to profit from his experience, to analyze, discriminate, and foresee. Anxiety prevents the person's internal communication system from functioning appropriately, and improvements in his ability to profit from experience hinge upon overcoming anxiety as

Reprinted in abridged form from *Human Relations,* 1956, *9,* 415–457 by permission of the authors. This theory is based for the most part on observations made over a five-year period of teaching graduate students "group dynamics." The main function of the seminar as it was set forth by the instructors was to improve the internal communication system of the group, hence a self-study group.

a source of distortion. Similarly, group development involves the overcoming of obstacles to valid communication among the members, or the development of methods for achieving and testing consensus. Extrapolating from Sullivan's definition of personal maturity, we can say a group has reached a state of valid communication when its members are armed with "referential tools for analyzing interpersonal experience, so that its significant differences from, as well as its resemblances to, past experience are discriminable, and the foresight of relatively near future events will be adequate and appropriate to maintaining one's security and securing one's satisfactions without useless or ultimately troublesome disturbance of self-esteem" (Sullivan, 1950, p. 111).

Relatively few investigations of the phenomena of group development have been undertaken. This paper outlines a theory of development in groups that have as their explicit goal improvement of their internal communication systems.

A group of strangers, meeting for the first time, has within it many obstacles to valid communication. The more heterogeneous the membership, the more accurately does the group become for each member a microcosm of the rest of his interpersonal experience. The problems of understanding the relationships that develop in any given group are from one aspect a unique product of the particular constellation of personalities assembled. But to construct a broadly useful theory of group development, it is necessary to identify major areas of internal uncertainty, or obstacles to valid communication, which are common to and important in all groups meeting under a given set of environmental conditions. These areas must be strategic in the sense that until the group has developed methods for reducing uncertainty in them, it cannot reduce uncertainty in other areas, and in its external relations.

THE TWO MAJOR AREAS OF INTERNAL UNCERTAINTY: DEPENDENCE (AUTHORITY RELATIONS) AND INTERDEPENDENCE (PERSONAL RELATIONS)

Two major areas of uncertainty can be identified by induction from common experience, at least within our own culture. The first of these is the area of group members' orientations toward authority, or more generally toward the handling and distribution of power in the group. The second is the area of members' orientations toward one another. These areas are not independent of each other: a particular set of intermember orientations will be associated with a particular authority structure. But the two sets of orientations are as distinct from each other as are the concepts of power and love. A number of authorities have used them as a starting point for the analysis of group behavior.

In his *Group Psychology and the Analysis of the Ego*, Freud noted that "each member is bound by libidinal ties on the one hand to the leader . . . and on the other hand to the other members of the group" (Freud, 1921, p. 95). Although he described both ties as libidinal, he was uncertain "how these two ties are related to each other, whether they are of the same kind and the same value, and how they are to be described psychologically." Without resolving this question, he noted that (for the Church and the Army) "one of these, the tie with the leader, seems . . . to be more of a ruling factor than the other, which holds between members of the group" (Freud, 1921, p. 100).

More recently, Schutz (1955) has made these two dimensions central to his theory of group compatibility. For him the strategic determinant of compatibility is the particular blend of orientations toward authority and orientations toward personal intimacy. Bion (1948a, 1948b) conceptualizes the major dimensions of the group somewhat differently. His "dependency" and "pairing" modalities correspond to our "dependence" and "interdependence" areas; to them he adds a "fight/flight" modality. For him these modalities are simply alternative modes of behavior; for us the fight/flight categorization has been useful for characterizing the means used by the group for maintaining a stereotyped orientation during a given subphase.

The core of the theory of group development is that the principal obstacles to the development of valid communication are to be found in the orientations toward authority and intimacy that members bring to the group. Rebelliousness, submissiveness, or withdrawal as the characteristic response to authority figures; destructive competitiveness, emotional exploitiveness, or withdrawal as the characteristic response to peers prevent consensual validation of experience. The behaviors determined by these orientations are directed toward enslavement of the other in the service of the self, enslavement of the self in the service of the other, or disintegration of the situation. Hence, they prevent the setting, clarification of, and movement toward group-shared goals.

In accord with Freud's observations, the orientations toward authority are regarded as being prior to, or partially determining of, orientations toward other members. In its development, the group moves from preoccupation with authority relations to preoccupation with personal relations. This movement defines the two major phases of group development. Within each phase are three subphases, determined by the ambivalence of orientations in each area. That is, during the authority ("dependence") phase, the group moves from a preoccupation with submission to a preoccupation with rebellion to a resolution of the dependence problem. Within the personal (or "interdependence") phase, the group moves from a preoccupation with intermember identification to a preoccupation with individual identity to a resolution of the interdependence problem.

THE RELEVANT ASPECTS OF PERSONALITY IN GROUP DEVELOPMENT

The aspects of member personality most heavily involved in group development are called, following Schutz, the dependence and personal aspects.

The dependence aspect is comprised by the member's characteristic patterns related to a leader or to a structure of rules. Members who find comfort in rules of procedure, an agenda, an expert, etc., are "dependent." Members who are discomfited by authoritative structures are called "counterdependent."

The personal aspect is comprised by the member's characteristic patterns with respect to interpersonal intimacy. Members who cannot rest until they have stabilized a relatively high degree of intimacy with all the others are called "overpersonal." Members who tend to avoid intimacy with any of the others are called "counterpersonal."

Psychodynamically, members who evidence some compulsiveness in the adoption of highly dependent, highly counterdependent, highly personal, or highly counterpersonal roles are regarded as "conflicted." Thus, the person who persists in being dependent upon any and all authorities thereby provides himself with ample evidence that authorities should not be so trustingly relied upon; yet he cannot profit from this experience in governing his future action. Hence, a deep, but unrecognized, distrust is likely to accompany the manifestly submissive behavior, and the highly dependent or highly counterdependent person is thus a person in conflict. The existence of the conflict accounts for the sometimes dramatic movement from extreme dependence to extreme rebelliousness. In this way counterdependence and dependence, while logically the extremes of a scale, are psychologically very close together.

The "unconflicted" person or "independent," who is better able to profit from his experience and assess the present situation more adequately, may of course act at times in rebellious or submissive ways. Psychodynamically, the difference between him and the conflicted is easy to understand. In terms of observable behavior, he lacks the compulsiveness and, significantly, does not create the communicative confusion so characteristic of, say, the conflicted dependent, who manifests submission in that part of his communication of which he is aware, and distrust or rebellion in that part of his communication of which he is unaware.[1]

Persons who are unconflicted with respect to the dependence or personal aspect are considered to be responsible for the major movements of the group toward valid communication. That is, the actions of members unconflicted with respect to the problems of a given phase of group development move the group to the next phase. Such actions are called barometric events, and the initiators are called catalysts. This part of the theory of group development is based on Redl's thesis concerning the "infectiousness of the unconflicted on the conflicted personality constellation" (Redl, 1942). The catalysts (Redl calls them "central persons") are the persons capable of reducing the uncertainty characterizing a given phase.

[1] Schutz has developed a test, Fundamental Interpersonal Relations Orientations (FIRO), which is capable of measuring "conflictedness" and "independence" with respect to each of the dimensions, dependency and intimacy, as well as a third, "assertiveness" or the degree to which an individual will make his views felt in a group. See Schutz (1958).

"Leadership" from the standpoint of group development can be defined in terms of catalysts responsible for group movement from one phase to the next. This consideration provides a basis for determining what membership roles are needed for group development. For example, it is expected that a group will have great difficulty in resolving problems of power and authority if it lacks members who are unconflicted with respect to dependence.

PHASE MOVEMENTS

The foregoing summary has introduced the major propositions in the theory of group development. While it is not possible to reproduce the concrete group experience from which the theory is drawn, we can take a step in this direction by discussing in more detail what seem to us to be the dominant features of each phase. The description given below is highly interpretive, and we emphasize what seem to us to be the major themes of each phase, even though many minor themes are present. In the process of abstracting, stereotyping, and interpreting, certain obvious facts about group process are lost. For example, each group meeting is to some extent a recapitulation of its past and a forecast of its future. This means that behavior that is "regressive" or "advanced" often appears.

Phase I: Dependence

Subphase 1: Dependence-Flight. The first days of group life are filled with behavior whose remote, as well as immediate, aim is to ward off anxiety. Much of the discussion content consists of fruitless searching for a common goal. Some of the security-seeking behavior is group-shared—for example, members may reassure one another by providing interesting and harmless facts about themselves. Some is idiosyncratic—for example, doodling, yawning, intellectualizing.

The search for a common goal is aimed at reducing the cause of anxiety, thus going beyond the satisfaction of immediate security needs. But just as evidencing boredom in this situation is a method of warding off anxiety by denying its proximity, so group goal-seeking is not quite what it is claimed to be. It can best be understood as a dependence plea. The trainer, not the lack of a goal, is the cause of insecurity. This interpretation is likely to be vigorously contested by the group, but it is probably valid. The characteristic expectations of group members are that the trainer will establish rules of the game and distribute rewards. He is presumed to know what the goals are or ought to be. Hence his behavior is regarded as a "technique"; he is merely playing hard to get. The pretense of a fruitless search for goals is a plea for him to tell the group what to do, by simultaneously demonstrating its helplessness without him and its willingness to work under his direction for his approval and protection.

We are here talking about the dominant theme in group life. Many minor themes are present, and even in connection with the major theme there are differences among members. For some, testing the power of the trainer to affect their futures is the major concern. In others, anxiety may be aroused through a sense of helplessness in a situation made threatening by the protector's desertion. These alternatives can be seen as the beginnings of the counterdependent and dependent adaptations. Those with a dependent orientation look vainly for cues from the trainer for procedure and direction; sometimes paradoxically they infer that the leader must want it that way. Those with a counterdependent orientation strive to detect in the trainer's action elements that would offer ground for rebellion, and may even paradoxically demand rules and leadership from him because he is failing to provide them.

The ambiguity of the situation at this stage quickly becomes intolerable for some, and a variety of ultimately unserviceable resolutions may be invented, many of them idiosyncratic. Alarm at the prospect of future meetings is likely to be group-shared, and at least a gesture may be made in the direction of formulating an agenda for subsequent meetings.

This phase is characterized by behavior that has gained approval from authorities in the past. Since the meetings are to be concerned with groups or with human relations, members offer information on these topics, to satisfy the presumed expectations of the trainer and to indicate expertise, interest, or achievement in these topics (ex-officers from the armed services, from fraternities, etc., have the floor). Topics such as business or political leadership, discrimination, and desegregation are likely to be discussed. During this phase the contributions made by members are designed to gain approval from the trainer, whose reaction to each comment is surreptitiously watched. If the trainer comments that this seems to be the case, or if he notes that the subject under discussion (say, discrimination) may be related to some concerns about membership in this group, he fails again to satisfy the needs of members. Not that the validity of this interpretation is held in much doubt. No one is misled by the "flight" behavior involved in discussing problems external to the group, least of all the group members. Discussion of these matters is filled with perilous uncertainties, however, and so the trainer's observation is politely ignored, as one would ignore a faux pas at a tea party. The attempts to gain approval based on implicit hypotheses about the potential power of the trainer for good and evil are continued until the active members have run through the repertoire of behaviors that have gained them favor in the past.

Subphase 2: Counterdependence-Fight. As the trainer continues to fail miserably in satisfying the needs of the group, discussion takes on a different tone, and counterdependent expressions begin to replace overt dependency. In many ways this subphase is the most stressful and unpleasant in the life of the group. It is marked by a paradoxical development of the trainer's role into one of omnipotence and powerlessness, and by division of the group into two warring subgroups. In subphase 1, feelings of hostility were strongly defended; if a slip were made that suggested hostility, particularly toward the trainer, the group members were embarrassed. Now expressions of hostility are more frequent, and are more likely to be supported by other members, or to be met with equally hostile responses. Power is much more overtly the concern of group members in this subphase. A topic such as leadership may again be discussed, but the undertones of the discussion are no longer dependence pleas. Discussion of leadership in subphase 2 is in part a vehicle for making explicit the trainer's failure as a leader. In part it is perceived by other members as a bid for leadership on the part of any member who participates in it.

The major themes of this subphase are as follows:

1. Two opposed subgroups emerge, together incorporating most of the group members. Characteristically, the subgroups are in

disagreement about the group's need for leadership or "structure." One subgroup attempts to elect a chairman, nominate working committees, establish agenda, or otherwise "structure" the meetings; the other subgroup opposes all such efforts. At first this appears to be merely an intellectual disagreement concerning the future organization of group activity. But soon it becomes the basis for destroying any semblance of group unity. Fragmentation is expressed and brought about in many ways: voting is a favorite way of dramatizing the schism; suggestions that the group is too large and should be divided into subgroups for the meetings are frequent; a chairman may be elected and then ignored as a demonstration of the group's ineffectualness. Although control mechanisms are sorely needed and desired, no one is willing to relinquish the rights of leadership and control to anyone else. The trainer's abdication has created a power gap, but no one is allowed to fill it.

2. Disenthrallment with the trainer proceeds rapidly. Group members see him as at best ineffectual, at worst damaging, to group progress. He is ignored and bullied almost simultaneously. His interventions are perceived by the counterdependents as an attempt to interrupt group progress; by the dependents as weak and incorrect statements. His silences are regarded by the dependents as desertion; by the counterdependents as manipulation. Much of the group activity is to be understood as punishment of the trainer, for his failure to meet needs and expectations, for getting the group into an unpleasant situation, for being the worst kind of authority figure—a weak and incompetent one, or a manipulative, insincere one. Misunderstanding or ignoring his comments, implying that his observations are paranoid fantasies, demonstrations that the group is cracking up, references to him in the past tense as though he were no longer present—these are the punishments for his failure.

As, in the first subphase, the trainer's wisdom, power, and competence were overtly unquestioned but secretly suspected, so, in the second subphase, the conviction that he is incompetent and helpless is clearly dramatized but secretly doubted. Out of this secret doubt arises the belief in the trainer's omnipotence. None of the punishments meted out to the trainer are recognized as such by the group members; in fact, if the trainer suggests that the members feel a need to punish him, they are most likely to respond in injured tones or in tones of contempt that what is going on has nothing to do with him and that he had best stay out of it. The trainer is still too imposing and threatening to challenge directly. There is a secret hope that the chaos in the group is in fact part of the master plan, that he is really leading them in the direction they should be going. That he may really be helpless as they imply, or that the failure may be theirs rather than his, are frightening possibilities. For this reason subphase 2 differs very little in the fundamental dynamics from subphase 1. There is still the secret wish that the trainer will stop all the bedlam which has replaced polite uncertainty, by taking his proper role (so that dependent members can cooperate with him and counterdependent can rebel in the usual ways).

Subphase 2 thus brings the group to the brink of catastrophe. The trainer has consistently failed to meet the group's needs. Not daring to turn directly on him, the group members engage in mutually destructive behavior; in fact, the group threatens suicide as the most extreme expression of dependence. The need to punish the trainer is so strong, however, that his act of salvation would have to be magical indeed.

Subphase 3: Resolution-Catharsis. No such magic is available to the trainer. Resolution of the group's difficulties at this point depends upon the presence in the group of other forces, which have until this time been inoperative, or ineffective. Only the degenerative aspects of the chain of events in subphases 1 and 2 have been presented up to this point and they are in fact the salient ones. But there has been a simultaneous, though less obvious, mobilization of constructive forces. First, within each of the warring subgroups bonds of mutual support have grown. The group member no longer feels helpless and isolated. Second, the trainer's role, seen as weak or manipulative in the dependence orientation, can also be perceived as permissive. Third, his interpretations, though openly ignored, have been secretly attended to. And, as the second and third points imply, some members of the group are less the prisoners of the dependence-counterdependence dilemma than others. These members, called the independents, have been relatively ineffective in the group for two reasons. First, they have not developed firm bonds with other members in either of the warring subgroups, because they have not identified with either cause. Typically, they have devoted their energies to an unsuccessful search for a compromise settlement of the disagreements in the group. Since their attitudes toward authority are less ambivalent than those of other members, they have accepted the alleged reason for disagreement in the group—for example, whether a chairman should be elected—at face value, and tried to mediate. Similarly, they have tended to accept the trainer's role and interpretations more nearly at face value. However, his interpretations have seemed inaccurate to them, since in fact the interpretations have applied much less to them than to the rest of the group.

Subphase 3 is the most crucial and fragile in group life up to this point. What occurs is a sudden shift in the whole basis of group action. It is truly a bridging phase; if it occurs at all, it is so rapid and mercurial that the end of subphase 2 appears to give way directly to the first subphase of Phase II. If it does not occur this rapidly and dramatically, a halting and arduous process of vacillation between Phases I and II is likely to persist for a long period, the total group movement being very gradual.

To summarize the state of affairs at the beginning of subphase 3: (1) The group is polarized into two competing groups, each unable to gain or relinquish power. (2) Those group members who are uncommitted to either subgroup are ineffective in their attempts to resolve the conflict. (3) The trainer's contributions only serve to deepen the cleavage in the group.

As the group enters subphase 3, it is moving rapidly toward extinction; that is, splintering into two or three subgroups. The independents, who have until now been passive or ineffectual, become the only hope for survival, since they have thus far avoided polarization and stereotypic behavior. The imminence of dissolution forces them to recognize the fruitlessness of their attempts at mediation. For this reason, the trainer's hypothesis that fighting one another is off-target behavior is likely to be acted upon at this point. A group member may openly express the opinion that the trainer's presence and comments are holding the group back, and suggest that "as an experiment" the trainer leave the group "to see how things go without him." When the trainer is thus directly challenged, the whole atmosphere of the meeting changes. There is a sudden increase in alertness and tension. Previously, there had been much acting out of the wish that the trainer were absent, but at the same time a conviction that he was the raison d'être of the group's existence—that it would fall apart without him. Previously, absence of the trainer would have constituted desertion, or defeat, fulfillment of the members' worst fears as to their own inadequacy or the trainer's. But now leaving the group can have a different meaning. General agreement that the trainer should leave is rarely achieved. However, after a little further discussion it becomes clear that he is at liberty to leave, with the understanding that he wishes to be a member of the group and will return if and when the group is willing to accept him.

The principal function of the symbolic removal of the trainer is in its effect of freeing the group to bring into awareness the hitherto carefully ignored feelings toward him as an authority figure, and toward the group activity as an off-target dramatization of the ambivalence toward authority. The leadership provided by the independents (whom the group sees as having no vested interest in power) leads to a new orientation toward membership in the group. In the discussion that follows the exit of the trainer, the dependents' assertion that the trainer deserted and the counterdependents' assertion that he was kicked out are soon replaced by consideration of whether his behavior was "responsible" or "irresponsible." The power problem is resolved by being defined in terms of member responsibilities, and the terms of the trainer's return to the group are settled by the requirement that he behave as "just another member of the group." This phrase is then explained as meaning that he should take neither more nor less responsibility for what happens in the group than any other member.

The above description of the process does not do justice to the excitement and involvement characteristic of this period. How much transferable insight ambivalent members acquire from it is difficult to assess. At least within the life of the group, later activity is rarely perceived in terms of submission and rebellion.

An interesting parallel, which throws light on the order of events in group development, is given in Freud's discussion of the myth of the primal horde. In his version: "These many individuals eventually banded themselves together, killed [the father], and cut him in pieces. . . . They then formed the totemistic community of brothers all with equal rights and were united by the totem prohibitions which were to preserve and to expiate the memory of the murder" (Freud, 1921, p. 135). The horde's act, according to Freud, was soon distorted into an heroic myth: instead of murder by the group, the myth held that the father had been overthrown single-handed by one person, usually the youngest son. In this attribution of the group act to one individual (the hero), Freud saw the "emergence of the individual from group psychology." His definition of a hero is ". . . a man who stands up manfully against his father and in the end victoriously overthrows him" (Freud, 1939, p. 112). (The heroic myth of Freud thus shares much in common with Sullivan's "delusion of unique individuality.")

In the training group, the member who initiates the events leading to the trainer's exit is sometimes referred to as a "hero" by the other members. Responsibility for the act is felt to be shared by the group, however, and out of their experience comes the first strong sense of group solidarity and involvement—a reversal of the original version, where the individual emerges from the group. This turn of events clarifies Freud's remark concerning the libidinal ties to the leader and to the other group members. Libidinal ties toward the other group members cannot be adequately developed until there is a resolution of the ties with the leader. In our terms, those components of group life having to do with intimacy and interdependence cannot be dealt with until those components having to do with authority and dependence have been resolved.

Other aspects of subphase 3 may be understood by investigating the dramatic significance of the revolt. The event is always marked in group history as "a turning point," "the time we became a group," "when I first got involved," etc. The mounting tension, followed by sometimes uproarious euphoria, cannot be entirely explained by the surface events. It may be that the revolt represents a realization of important fantasies individuals hold in all organizations, that the emotions involved are undercurrents wherever rebellious and submissive tendencies toward existing authorities must be controlled. These are the themes of some of our great dramas— *Antigone, Billy Budd, Hamlet,* and our most recent folk tale, *The Caine Mutiny.* But the event is more than the presentation of a drama, or an acting out of fantasies. For it can be argued that the moments of stress and catharsis, when emotions are labile and intense, are the times in the group life when there is readiness for change. Leighton's analysis of a minor revolution at a Japanese relocation camp is worth quoting in full on this point:

> While this [cathartic] situation is fraught with danger because of trends which may make the stress become worse before it gets better, there is also an opportunity for administrative action that is not likely to be found in more secure times. It is fairly well recognized in psychology that at periods of great emotional stir the individual human being can undergo far-reaching and permanent changes in his personality. It is as if the bone structure of his systems of belief and of his habitual patterns of behavior becomes soft, is fused into new shapes, and hardens there when the period of tension is over. . . . Possibly the same can be true of whole groups of people, and there are historical examples of social changes and movements occurring when there was widespread emotional tension, usually some form of anxiety. The Crusades, parts of the Reformation, the French Revolution, the change in Zulu life in the reign of Chaca, the Meiji Restoration, the Mormon movement, the Russian revolution, the rise of Fascism, and alterations in the social sentiments of the United States going on at present are all to some extent examples [Leighton, 1946, p. 360].

Observers of industrial relations have made similar observations. When strikes result from hostile labor-management relations (as contrasted to straight wage demands), there is a fluidity of relationships and a wide repertoire of structural changes during this period not available before the strike act (Gouldner, 1954; Park, 1955; Whyte, 1951a).

So it is, we believe, with the training group. But what are the new values and behavior patterns that emerge out of the emotional experience of Phase I? Principally, they are acceptance by each member of his full share of responsibility for what happens in the group. The outcome is autonomy for the group. After the events of subphase 3, there is no more attribution of magical powers to the trainer—either the dependent fantasy that he sees farther, knows better, is mysteriously guiding the group and protecting it from evil, or the very similar counterdependent fantasy that he is manipulating the group, exploiting it in his own interests, that the experience is one of "brainwashing." The criterion for evaluating a contribution is no longer who said it, but what is said. Thereafter, such power fantasies as the trainer himself may have present no different problem from the power fantasies of any other group member. At the same time, the illusion that there is a struggle for power in the group is suddenly dissipated, and the contributions of other members are evaluated in terms of their relevance to shared group goals.

Summary of Phase I

The very word *development* implies not only movement through time but also a definite order of progression. The group must traverse subphase 1 to reach subphase 2, and subphase 3 before it can move into Phase II. At the same time, lower levels of development coexist with more advanced levels. Blocking and regression occur frequently, and the group may be "stuck" at a certain phase of development. It would, of course, be difficult to imagine a group remaining long in subphase 3—the situation is too tense to be permanent. But the group may founder for some time in subphase 2 with little movement. In short, groups do not inevitably develop through the resolution of the dependence phase to Phase II. This movement may be retarded indefinitely. Obviously, much depends upon the trainer's role. In fact, the whole dependence modality may be submerged by certain styles of trainer behavior. The trainer has a certain range of choice as to whether dependency as a source of communication distortion is to be highlighted and made the subject of special experiential and conceptual consideration. The personality and training philosophy of the trainer determine his interest in introducing or avoiding explicit consideration of dependency.

There are other important forces in the group besides the trainer, and these may serve to facilitate or block the development that has been described as typical of Phase I. Occasionally there may be no strong independents capable of bringing about the barometric events that precipitate movement. Or the leaders of opposing subgroups may be the most assertive members of the group. In such cases the group may founder permanently in subphase 2. If a group has the misfortune to experience a "traumatic" event early in its existence—exceedingly schizoid behavior by some member during the first few meetings, for example—anxieties of other members may be aroused to such an extent that all culturally suspect behavior, particularly open expression of feelings, is strongly inhibited in subsequent meetings.

Table 1 summarizes the major events of Phase 1, as it typically proceeds. This phase has dealt primarily with the resolution of dependency needs. It ends with acceptance of mutual responsibility for the fate of the group and a sense of solidarity, but the implications of shared responsibility have yet to be explored. This exploration is reserved for Phase II, which we have chosen to call the Interdependence Phase.

Phase II: Interdependence

The resolution of dependence problems marks the transfer of group attention (and inattention) to the problems of shared responsibility.

Sullivan's description of the change from childhood to the juvenile era seems pertinent here: "The juvenile era is marked off from childhood by the appearance of an urgent need for compeers with whom to have one's existence. By 'compeers' I mean people who are on our level and have generically similar attitudes toward authoritative figures, activities, and the like. This marks the beginning of the juvenile era, the great developments in which are the talents for cooperation, competition, and compromise" (Sullivan, 1940, pp. 17–18).

The remaining barriers to valid communication are those associated with orientations toward interdependence: i.e., intimacy, friendship, identification. While the distribution of power was the cardinal issue during Phase I, the distribution of affection occupies the group during Phase II.

Subphase 4: Enchantment-Flight. At the outset of subphase 4, the group is happy, cohesive, relaxed. The atmosphere is one of "sweetness and light." Any slight increase in tension is instantly dissipated by joking and laughter. The fighting of Phase I is still fresh in the memory of the group, and the group's efforts are devoted to patching up differences, healing wounds, and maintaining a har-

Table 1: PHASE I: DEPENDENCE-POWER RELATIONS[a]

	Subphase 1 dependence-submission	Subphase 2 counterdependence	Subphase 3 resolution
1. Emotional Modality	Dependence-Flight	Counterdependence-Fight. Off-target fighting among members. Distrust of staff member. Ambivalence.	Pairing. Intense involvement in group task.
2. Content Themes	Discussion of interpersonal problems external to training groups.	Discussion of group organization; i.e., what degree of structuring devices is needed for "effective" group behavior?	Discussion and definition of trainer role.
3. Dominant Roles (Central Persons)	Assertive, aggressive members with rich previous organizational or social science experience.	Most assertive counterdependent and dependent members. Withdrawal of less assertive independents and dependents.	Assertive independents.
4. Group Structure	Organized mainly into multi-subgroups based on members' past experiences.	Two tight subcliques consisting of leaders and members, of counterdependents and dependents.	Group unified in pursuit of goal and develops internal authority system.
5. Group Activity	Self-oriented behavior reminiscent of most new social gatherings.	Search for consensus mechanism: voting, setting up chairman, search for "valid" content subjects	Group members take over leadership roles formerly perceived as held by trainer.
6. Group movement facilitated by:	Staff member abnegation of traditional role of structuring situation, setting up rules of fair play, regulation of participation.	Disenthrallment with staff member, coupled with absorption of uncertainty by most assertive counterdependent and dependent individuals. Subgroups form to ward off anxiety.	Revolt by assertive independents (catalysts), who fuse subgroups into unity by initiating and engineering trainer exit (barometric event).
7. Main Defenses	Projection. Denigration of authority.		Group moves into Phase II.

[a] Course terminates at the end of 17 weeks. It is not uncommon for groups to remain throughout the course in this phase.

monious atmosphere. Typically, this is a time of merrymaking and group minstrelsy. Coffee and cake may be served at the meetings. Hours may be passed in organizing a group party. Poetry or songs commemorating the important events and persons in the group's history may be composed by individuals or, more commonly, as a group project. All decisions must be unanimous during this period, since everyone must be happy, but the issues on which decisions are made are mostly ones about which group members have no strong feelings. At first the cathartic, healing function of these activities is clear; there is much spontaneity, playfulness, and pleasure. Soon the pleasures begin to wear thin.

The myth of mutual acceptance and universal harmony must eventually be recognized for what it is. From the beginning of this phase there are frequent evidences of underlying hostilities, unresolved issues in the group. But they are quickly, nervously smoothed over by laughter or misinterpretation. Subphase 4 begins with catharsis, but that is followed by the development of a rigid norm to which all members are forced to conform: "Nothing must be allowed to disturb our harmony in the future; we must avoid the mistakes of the painful past." Not that members have forgotten that the painful past was a necessary preliminary to the autonomous and (it is said) delightful present, though that fact is carefully overlooked. Rather, there is a dim realization that all members must have an experience somewhat analogous to the trainer's in subphase 3, before a mutually understood, accepted, and realistic definition of their own roles in the group can be arrived at.

Resistance of members to the requirement that harmony be maintained at all costs appears in subtle ways. In open group discussion the requirement is imperative: the member does not dare to endanger harmony with the group or to disturb the status quo by denying that all problems have been solved. Much as members may dislike the tedious work of maintaining the appearance of harmony, the alternative is worse. The house of cards would come tumbling down, and the painful and exacting work of building something more substantial would have to begin. The flight from these problems takes a number of forms. Group members may say, "We've had our fighting and are now a group. Thus, further self-study is unnecessary." Very commonly, the possibility of any change may be prevented by not coming together as a total group at all. Thus, the members may subgroup through an entire meeting. Those who would disturb the friendly subgroups are accused of "rocking the boat."

The solidarity and harmony become more and more illusory, but the group still clings to the illusion. This perseveration is in a way a consequence of the deprivation that members have experienced in maintaining the atmosphere of harmony. Maintaining it forces members to behave in ways alien to their own feelings; to go still further in group involvement would mean a complete loss of self. The group is therefore torn by a new ambivalence, which might be verbalized as follows: (1) "We all love one another and therefore we must maintain the solidarity of the group and give up whatever is necessary of our selfish desires." (2) "The group demands that I sacrifice my identity as a person; but the group is an evil mechanism which satisfies no dominant needs." As this subphase comes to a close, the happiness that marked its beginning is maintained only as a mask. The "innocent" splitting of the group into subgroups has gone so far that members will even walk around the meeting table to join in the conversation of a subgroup rather than speak across the table at the risk of bringing the whole group together. There is a certain uneasiness about the group; there is a feeling that "we should work together but cannot." There may be a tendency to regress to the orientation of subphase 1: group members would like the trainer to take over.

To recapitulate: subphase 4 begins with a happy sense of group belongingness. Individual identity is eclipsed by a "the group is bigger than all of us" sentiment. But this integration is short lived: it soon becomes perceived as a fake attempt to resolve interpersonal problems by denying their reality. In the later stages of this subphase, enchantment with the total group is replaced by enchantment with one's subgroup, and out of this breakdown of the group emerges a new organization based on the anxieties aroused out of this first, suffocating involvement.

Subphase 5: Disenchantment-Fight. This subphase is marked by a division into two subgroups—paralleling the experience of subphase 2—but this time based upon orientations toward the degree of intimacy required by group membership. Membership in the two subgroups is not necessarily the same as in subphase 2; for now the fragmentation occurs as a result of opposite and extreme attitudes toward the degree of intimacy desired in interpersonal relations. The counterpersonal members band together to resist further involvement. The overpersonal members band together in a demand for unconditional love. While these subgroups appear as divergent as possible, a common theme underlies them. For the one group, the only means seen for maintaining self-esteem is to avoid any real commitment to others; for the other group, the only way to maintain self-esteem is to obtain a commitment from others to forgive everything. The subgroups share in common the fear that intimacy breeds contempt.

This anxiety is reflected in many ways during subphase 5. For the first time, openly disparaging remarks are made about the group. Invidious comparisons are made between it and other groups. Similarly, psychology and social science may be attacked. The inadequacy of the group as a basis for self-esteem is dramatized in many ways—from stating "I don't care what you think," to boredom, to absenteeism. The overpersonals insist that they are happy and comfortable, while the counterpersonals complain about the lack of group morale. Intellectualization by the overpersonals frequently takes on religious overtones concerning Christian love, consideration for others, etc. In explanations of member behavior, the counterpersonal members account for all in terms of motives having nothing to do with the present group; the overpersonals explain all in terms of acceptance and rejection in the present group.

Subphase 5 belongs to the counterpersonals as subphase 4 belonged to the overpersonals. Subphase 4 might be caricatured as hiding in the womb of the group; subphase 5 as hiding out of sight of the group. It seems probable that both of these modalities serve to ward off anxieties associated with intimate interpersonal relations. A theme that links them together can be verbalized as follows: "If others really knew me, they would reject me." The overpersonal's formula for avoiding this rejection seems to be accepting all others so as to be protected by the others' guilt; the counterpersonal's way is by rejecting all others before they have a chance to reject him. Another way of characterizing the counterpersonal orientation is in the phrase "I would lose my identity as a member of the group."

The corresponding overpersonal orientation reads, "I have nothing to lose by identifying with the group." We can now look back on the past two subphases as countermeasures against loss of self-esteem; what Sullivan once referred to as the greatest inhibition to the understanding of what is distinctly human, "the overwhelming conviction of self-hood—this amounts to a delusion of unique individuality." The sharp swings and fluctuations that occurred between the enchantment and euphoria of subphase 4 and the disenchantment of subphase 5 can be seen as a struggle between the "institutionalization of complacency" on the one hand and anxiety associated with fantasy speculations about intimacy and involvement on the other. This dissociative behavior serves a purpose of its own: a generalized denial of the group and its meaning for individuals. For if the group is important and valid, then it has to be taken seriously. If it can wallow in the enchantment of subphase 4, it is safe; if it can continually vilify the goals and objectives of the group, it is also safe. The disenchantment theme in subphase 5 is perhaps a less skilful and more desperate security provision, with its elaborate wall of defenses, than the "group mind" theme of subphase 4. What should be stressed is that both subphase defenses were created almost entirely on fantastic expectations about the consequences of group involvement. These defenses are homologous to anxiety as it is experienced by the individual; i.e., the state of "anxiety arises as a response to a situation of danger and . . . will be reproduced thenceforward whenever such a situation recurs" (Freud, 1926, p. 134). In sum, the past two subphases were marked by a conviction that further group involvement would be injurious to members' self-esteem.

Subphase 6: Consensual Validation. In the groups of which we write, two forces combine to press the group toward a resolution of the interdependency problem. These are the approaching end of the training course, and the need to establish a method of evaluation (including course grades).

There are, of course, ways of denying or avoiding these realities. The group can agree to continue to meet after the course ends. It can extricate itself from evaluation activities by asking the trainer to perform the task, or by awarding a blanket grade. But turning this job over to the trainer is a regression to dependence;

and refusal to discriminate and reward is a failure to resolve the problems of interdependence. If the group has developed in general as we have described, the reality of termination and evaluation cannot be denied, and these regressive modes of adaptation cannot be tolerated.

The characteristic defenses of the two subgroups at first fuse to prevent any movement toward the accomplishment of the evaluation and grading task. The counterpersonals resist evaluation as an invasion of privacy; they foresee catastrophe if members begin to say what they think of one another. The overpersonals resist grading since it involves discriminating among the group members. At the same time, all members have a stake in the outcome of evaluation and grading. In avoiding the task, members of each subgroup are perceived by members of the other as "rationalizing," and the group becomes involved in a vicious circle of mutual disparagement. In this process, the fear of loss of self-esteem through group involvement is near to being realized. As in subphase 3, it is the independents—in this case those whose self-esteem is not threatened by the prospect of intimacy—who restore members' confidence in the group. Sometimes all that is required to reverse the vicious circle quite dramatically is a request by an independent for assessment of his own role. Or it may be an expression of confidence in the group's ability to accomplish the task.

The activity that follows group commitment to the evaluation task does not conform to the expectations of the overpersonal or counterpersonal members. Its chief characteristic is the willingness and ability of group members to validate their self-concepts with other members. The fear of rejection fades when tested against reality. The tensions that developed as a result of these fears diminish in the light of actual discussion of member roles. At the same time, there is revulsion against "capsule evaluations" and "curbstone psychoanalysis." Instead, what ensues is a serious attempt by each group member to verbalize his private conceptual scheme for understanding human behavior—his own and that of others. Bringing these assumptions into explicit communication is the main work of subphase 6. This activity demands a high level of work and of communicative skill. Some of the values that appear to underlie the group's work during this subphase are as follows:

(1) Members can accept one another's differences without associating "good" and "bad" with the differences. (2) Conflict exists but is over substantive issues rather than emotional issues. (3) Consensus is reached as a result of rational discussion rather than through a compulsive attempt at unanimity. (4) Members are aware of their own involvement, and of other aspects of group process, without being overwhelmed or alarmed. (5) Through the evaluation process, members take on greater personal meaning to each other. This facilitates communication and creates a deeper understanding of how the other person thinks, feels, behaves; it creates a series of personal expectations, as distinguished from the previous, more stereotyped, role expectations.

The above values, and some concomitant values, are of course very close to the authors' conception of a "good group." In actuality they are not always achieved by the end of the group life. The prospect of the death of the group, after much procrastination in the secret hope that it will be over before anything can be done, is likely to force the group into strenuous last-minute efforts to overcome the obstacles that have blocked its progress. As a result, the sixth subphase is too often hurried and incomplete. If the hurdles are not overcome in time, grading is likely to be an exercise that confirms members' worst suspicions about the group. And if role evaluation is attempted, either the initial evaluations contain so much hostile material as to block further efforts, or evaluations are so flowery and vacuous that no one, least of all the recipient, believes them.

In the resolution of interdependence problems, member personalities count for even more than they do in the resolution of dependence problems. The trainer's behavior is crucial in determining the group's ability to resolve the dependence issue, but in the interdependence issue the group is, so to speak, only as strong as its weakest link. The exceedingly dependent group member can ride through Phase I with a fixed belief in the existence of a private relationship between himself and the trainer; but the person whose anxieties are intense under the threats associated with intimacy can immobilize the group. (Table 2 summarizes the major events of Phase II.)

Table 2. PHASE II: INTERDEPENDENCE-PERSONAL RELATIONS

	Subphase 4 enchantment	Subphase 5 disenchantment	Subphase 6 consensual validation
1. Emotional Modality	Pairing-Flight. Group becomes a respected icon beyond further analysis.	Fight-Flight. Anxiety reactions. Distrust and suspicion of various group members.	Pairing, understanding, acceptance.
2. Content Themes	Discussion of "group history" and generally salutary aspects of course, group, and membership.	Revival of content themes used in subphase 1: What is a group? What are we doing here? What are the goals of the group? What do I have to give up—personally—to belong to this group? (How much intimacy and affection is required?) Invasion of privacy vs. "group giving." Setting up proper codes of social behavior.	Course grading system. Discussion and assessment of member roles.
3. Dominant Roles (Central Persons)	General distribution of participation for first time. Overpersonals have salience.	Most assertive counterpersonal and overpersonal individuals, with counterpersonals especially salient.	Assertive independents.
4. Group Structure	Solidarity, fusion. High degree of camaraderie and suggestibility. Le Bon's description of "group mind" would apply here.	Restructuring of membership into two competing predominant subgroups made up of individuals who share similar attitudes concerning degree of intimacy required in social interaction;	Diminishing of ties based on personal orientation. Group structure now presumably appropriate to needs of situation based on predominantly

5. Group Activity	Laughter, joking, humor. Planning out-of-class activities such as parties. The institutionalization of happiness to be accomplished by "fun" activities. High rate of interaction and participation.	Disparagement of group in a variety of ways: high rate of absenteeism, tardiness, balkiness in initiating total-group interaction, frequent statements concerning worthlessness of group, denial of importance of group. Occasional member asking for individual help finally rejected by the group.		substantive rather than emotional orientations. Consensus significantly easier on important issues.
6. Group movement facilitated by:	Independence and achievement attained by trainer rejection and its concomitant, deriving consensually some effective means for authority and control. (Subphase 3 rebellion bridges gap between subphases 2 and 4.)	Disenchantment of group as a result of fantasied expectations of group life. The perceived threat to self-esteem that further group involvement signifies creates schism of group according to amount of affection and intimacy desired. The counterpersonal and overpersonal assertive individuals alleviate source of anxiety by disparaging or abnegating further group involvement. Subgroups form to ward off anxiety.	i.e., the counterpersonal and overpersonal groups. The personal individuals remain uncommitted but act according to needs of situation.	Communication to others of self-system of interpersonal relations; i.e., making conscious to self, and others aware of, conceptual system one uses to predict consequences of personal behavior. Acceptance of group on reality terms.
7. Main Defenses	Denial, isolation, intellectualization, and alienation.			The external realities, group termination and the prescribed need for a course grading system, comprise the barometric event. Led by the personal individuals, the group tests reality and reduces autistic convictions concerning group involvement.

CONCLUSIONS

Dependence and interdependence—power and love, authority and intimacy—are regarded as the central problems of group life. In most organizations and societies, the rules governing the distribution of authority and the degree of intimacy among members are prescribed. In the human relations training group, they are major areas of uncertainty. While the choice of these matters as the focus of group attention and experience rests to some extent with the trainer, his choice is predicated on the belief that they are the core of interpersonal experience. As such, the principal obstacles to valid interpersonal communication lie in rigidities of interpretation and response carried over from the anxious experiences with particular love or power figures into new situations in which they are inappropriate. The existence of such autisms complicates all discussions unduly and in some instances makes an exchange of meanings impossible.

Stating the training goal as the establishment of valid communication means that the relevance of the autistic response to authority and intimacy on the part of any member can be explicitly examined, and at least a provisional alternative formulated by him. Whether this makes a lasting change in the member's flexibility, or whether he will return to his more restricted formula when confronted with a new situation, we do not know, but we expect that it varies with the success of his group experience—particularly his success in understanding it.

We have attempted to portray what we believe to be the typical pattern of group development, and to show the relationship of member orientations and changes in member orientations to the major movements of the group. In this connection, we have emphasized the catalytic role of persons unconflicted with respect to one or the other of the dependence and interdependence areas. This power to move the group lies mainly in his freedom from anxiety-based reactions to problems of authority (or intimacy): he has the freedom to be creative in searching for a way to reduce tension.

We have also emphasized the "barometric event" or event capable of moving the group from one phase to the next. The major events of this kind are the removal of the trainer, as part of the resolution of the dependence problem, and the evaluation-grading requirements at the termination of the course. Both these barometric events require a catalytic agent in the group to bring them about. That is to say, the trainer exit can take place only at the moment when it is capable of symbolizing the attainment of group autonomy, and it requires a catalytic agent in the group to give it this meaning. And the grading assignment can move the group forward only if the catalytic agent can reverse the vicious circle of disparagement that precedes it.

Whether the incorporation of these barometric events into the training design merely makes our picture of group development a self-fulfilling prophecy, or whether, as we wish to believe, these elements make dramatically clear the major forward movements of the group, and open the gate for a flood of new understanding and communication, can only be decided on the basis of more, and more varied, experience.

The evolution from Phase I to Phase II represents a change in emphasis not only from power to affection but also from role to personality. Phase I activity generally centers on broad role distinctions such as class, ethnic background, professional interests. Phase II activity involves a deeper concern with personality modalities, such as reaction to failure, warmth, retaliation, anxiety. This development presents an interesting paradox. For the group in Phase I emerged out of a heterogeneous collectivity of individuals; the individual in Phase II emerged out of the group. This suggests that group therapy, where attention is focused on individual movement, begins at the least enabling time. It is possible that, before group members are able to help each other, the barriers to communication must be partially understood.

7

Anxiety, Boundary Evolution, and Social Change

JOHN J. HARTMAN

GRAHAM S. GIBBARD

*T*he principal aim of this chapter is to bring together in an empirical study two related but previously isolated sets of observations and conceptualizations about group development. The first of these has to do with *ego-state distress*—painful affects which appear to be universal concomitants of social experience and which trigger both adaptive and defensive responses by individuals and groups. The second centers on *boundary evolution*—the struggle to develop and maintain personal and group identity by shifts in the psychological boundaries of the collectivity. These two sets of conceptualizations, while not synonymous, are closely related. In addition, different theoretical approaches have placed different emphases on these two issues. The importance of psychotic anxiety in the development of social structure has been explored by Kleinian theorists, particularly by Jaques (1955; this volume, Chapter 11). The concept of boundary awareness, though partly sociological and anthropological in origin, is based primarily on psychoanalytic ego psychology and has been given clearest articulation by Slater (1966).

We have attempted here to clarify these concepts and to suggest a broader scheme which integrates them more systematically. Boundaries are seen as the psychosocial basis of group structure, and shifting affects are seen as barometric indicators of the stability and effectiveness of that structure. This is also an empirical study in that our assessment of the usefulness of these conceptualizations is grounded in act-by-act coding of social interaction.

ANXIETY AND PHASE DEVELOPMENT

Bion (1959) has proposed that at various times in a group's life all of its members share a common assumption about the group —an assumption that has little basis in fact, obstructs the purpose for which the group meets, and springs from deep emotional sources. These unverbalized and largely unconscious "basic assumptions"— of "dependency," "fight/flight," or "pairing"—stand in the way of the more rational problem-solving agenda of the "work group." Despite the fruitfulness of this hypothesis, Bion believes that these assumptions are manifestations of more fundamental phenomena. Bion's notion is that the basic assumptions "appear far more to have the characteristics of defensive reactions to psychotic anxieties" (p. 189). He regards reactions to psychotic anxiety and the expression of primitive oedipal conflicts as the "ultimate source of all group behavior."

In related work Jaques (1953, 1955) presents a clearer exposition of a similar Kleinian hypothesis: "The specific hypothesis I shall consider is that *one* of the primary cohesive elements binding individuals into institutionalized human association is that of defense against psychotic anxiety. In this sense individuals may be thought of as externalizing those impulses and internal objects that would otherwise give rise to psychotic anxiety, and pooling them in the life of the social institutions in which they associate" (Jaques, 1955, p. 479). In Jaques' view, the nature of an institution or a group is determined not only by its rational and conscious functions but also by unconscious functions operating at the level of unconscious fantasy. In just these terms, he studied a factory and analyzed the relationships between the workers and management in a labor dispute. Jaques spells out Klein's notions of paranoid and depressive anxiety and shows how they operate in social systems.

Dunphy (1966, 1968; this volume, Chapter 12) explores these Kleinian concepts in his intensive study of self-analytic groups. He posits the existence of "nonrational role specialists," who represent elements of the internal fantasies of other group members: "This externalization of internal fantasies through their acting out in the group results in the development of a generalized group fantasy or 'mythology,' which exercises a controlling influence on the behavior of group members and on the evolution of the group" (1966, pp. 288–289). For Dunphy the development of the group proceeds by the emergence and working through of these "myths" shared by the group at large and portrayed by a few key members.

A major difficulty in small-group research has been the application of systematic observational techniques to the rich, evocative clinical material described in the studies of Bion and Jaques. Stock and Thelen (1958) attempted to test Bion's notions by combining clinical insights of some depth with the measurement techniques of the laboratory. Mann's (1966, 1967) "member-leader" scoring system is a method that combines psychological depth with the reliability and explicitness of systematic observation. Expression and denial of persecutory and depressive anxiety are fundamental parts of his scoring system. He terms these the "ego-state" categories. In a factor-analytic study of the development of the member-leader relationship in four self-analytic groups, these categories play an important role. One factor, "concern with inner distress," is composed entirely of ego-state categories. Mann's system allows for the act-by-act scoring of verbalizations that reflect a feeling of anxiety (fear of external object) or depression (feeling that self or internal objects are bad or empty), as well as denials of such feelings. In the groups he studied, the amount of anxiety and depression expressed showed regular peaks and troughs. This work, too, demonstrates that the ideas posited by clinical approaches could be subjected to systematic empirical scrutiny.

BOUNDARY AWARENESS AND GROUP DEVELOPMENT

Working from a sociological perspective, Bales has discussed adaptive and integrative changes in social systems: "The social system with its organization, we postulate, tends to swing or falter indeterminately back and forth between these two theoretical poles: optimum adaptation to the outer situation at the cost of internal malintegration or optimal internal integration at the cost of mal-adaptation to the outer situation" (Bales, 1955, pp. 127–128). Mills (1964) investigated this proposition, utilizing his systematic scoring of interaction, sign process analysis. He presents a theory of group development in small groups based on the creation and maintenance of group boundaries. The changes in the group coincide with atten-tion to internal and external concerns in a cyclical fashion. He con-cludes that boundary establishment plays a crucial part in the life-cycle model of group development.

Slater (1966) begins his analysis of developmental processes in self-analytic and various other small groups with an intensive examination of the group's relationship with its formal leader; he then moves into a more speculative discussion of the "evolution of boundary awareness" in various societal contexts.[1]

In most self-analytic groups the leader is at first relatively silent. Slater discusses in great detail the anxiety, the sense of abandonment, and the intense hostility stirred up by this silence. The group attempts to master this initial distress with the fantasy that the leader is omnipotent and omniscient ("deification as an antidote to deprivation"). The eventual "revolt" against this sacred figure, who mysteriously or cruelly withholds his brilliance and beneficence, actually reflects the "decay" of the deification. That is, since the leader is clearly not omniscient, it becomes increasingly difficult for the group to maintain this image of him; therefore, as the group progresses, he loses much of his transference-evoking ambiguity. The earlier the revolt, argues Slater, the more the mem-bers can imagine that they have captured the leader's *mana*.

Slater conceptualizes the revolt against the group leader as one facet of a more encompassing theory of group development. Slater has reformulated Bion's (1959) theory, arguing that the three basic assumptions must be understood as points on the same continuum and as quite different techniques or mechanisms for dealing with psychological conflict. He postulates "a continuum of group evolution, involving the increasing awareness of individual

[1] This discussion of Slater is based on Gibbard and Hartman (1973b).

and group identity and separateness." The basic assumptions (or mechanisms) can then be understood as ways of maintaining constant individual and group boundaries under various "cultural" conditions. This revised statement of what the assumptions entail suggests a progression from fight/flight to dependency to pairing. "Bion's fight/flight group is attempting to deal with the relation between the individual and the group at times when individuals find it difficult to differentiate between the two. The dependency group seems to be concerned with a somewhat more advanced stage, in which individuality is at once acknowledged and denied, through an attempt at symbiotic union with authority. . . . The pairing group is an attempt to make palatable individuation and separateness by maintaining a disembodied fantasy of mystical unity and immortality in the form of a distant future Messiah" (Slater, 1966, p. 181). Group development thus rests on the gradual substitution of "conscious" for "unconscious bonds." This substitution is reflected in "the emergence of awareness of a group as a group—a self-conscious and separate entity with differentiated parts and functions" (Slater, 1966, p. 237).

One implication of this argument is that there are moments, particularly early in the life of the group, when the relative absence of individuation and differentiation evokes fantasies of fusion with the group. Slater believes that the members focus on the group leader primarily to ward off envelopment by the group-as-mother. He makes extensive use of mythological parallels to support his interpretation that group development occurs through a series of fantasied confrontations (often sexualized and always ambivalent) between the group-as-mother and the leader-as-father. The dependency group is in part a defense against a more primitive, undifferentiated structure, in which fears of envelopment seem more real and fight/flight activity seems more necessary. At the same time, the group leader is imagined to have mastered the group-as-mother and thus to have gained some of her *mana* for himself. This makes him a threat as well as a protector, and the revolt against him is motivated partly by a need to reduce his power relative to that of the group.

It is through this alternation between leader and group orientations that conscious bonds grow stronger. In time, both the enveloping mother and the awesome father are reduced in importance and their "relationship" becomes more "secularized" and subdued.

CHANGE IN SMALL GROUPS

What emerges from this analysis is the possibility of making an integrated statement of social change based upon intrapsychic processes. Jaques has offered the following statement with regard to social change: "Change occurs where the fantasy social relations within an institution no longer serve to reinforce individual defenses against psychotic anxiety. The institution may be restructured at the manifest and fantasy level; or the manifest structure may be maintained, but the fantasy structure modified. Individuals may change roles or leave the institution altogether" (Jaques, 1955, p. 498). Jaques views the inertia toward change in many institutions as a manifestation of "resistances" of groups to change what has become a viable social defense against "psychotic" anxiety.

Slater's theory of change, as well as that of Mills, is based on a quite different, though potentially complementary, premise. For them change is more systemic and comes from strains and disequilibrium in the structural aspects of groups. Slater believes that the changes in boundary awareness cause the groups to shift to adapt to these changes. Mills has documented the cyclical shifts in attention to external and internal group concerns over time, and has traced their relationship to his phase changes.

This analysis of change in small groups suggests a potential integration of the theories that view change in social structure as a defense against distress and those theories that in view change primarily in structural terms. We believe that structural transformations are fundamental phenomena in the evolution of small groups. *Boundary concerns are cyclical and fluctuating in their attention to internal and external demands. The shifting equilibrium of group boundaries generates ego-state distress, which in turn must be dealt with by means of structural change.* Anxiety and depression, then, are signs or "symptoms" of strain or shift in the social equilibrium but also trigger defensive and adaptive maneuvers which lead to social change. But it is initial shifts in the structural properties of small groups which generate the distress. We shall now present briefly the act-by-act coding system which we utilized to explore the usefulness of this hypothesis.

PROCESS ANALYSIS SCORING SYSTEM

The member-leader scoring system developed by Mann and his associates (1966, 1967, 1970) proved to be a viable bridge between clinical and statistical approaches to the study of group interaction. We revised this system in several respects, most importantly in the extension of the scoring to include all interaction between *member* and *member*. The sixteen categories of the member-leader system have been retained, but they take on slightly different meanings in the context of member-member relations. Two new categories, expressing guilt and denying guilt, have been distinguished from expressing depression and denying depression. The categories are presented in Table 1. A fuller discussion of this scoring system can be found in Gibbard and Hartman (1973a).

Since the focus of this paper is on the ego-state area, only those categories will be discussed. The reader is referred to previous work for a more detailed discussion of the other categories, scoring conventions, and assessment of reliability. A brief description of each ego-state category is offered below.

Expressing Anxiety: Statements of tension, uneasiness, embarrassment, fear of criticism; feelings of being in danger or vulnerable.

Denying Anxiety: disavowals of one's own anxiety; minimizing or belittling the anxiety expressed by others.

Expressing Depression: demonstrating a sense of helplessness in relation to one's own competence, attractiveness, etc.; statements of sadness, loss, weakness, lack of understanding.

Denying Depression: disavowals of one's own depression; minimization of the impact of loss, sadness, failure, separation, etc.

Expressing Guilt: expressions of helplessness in relation to inner impulses felt to be "bad" or unacceptable; self-criticism, negative value judgments about the self.

Denying Guilt: disavowing one's own guilt; externalization of blame, disassociating oneself from the guilt of others.

Expressing Self-Esteem: statements of self-confidence, self-acceptance, pride, genuine freedom from anxiety, depression, and guilt.

Table 1. CATEGORIES IN PROCESS ANALYSIS SCORING SYSTEM

Category	Subarea	Area
1. Moving Against	Hostility	Impulse
2. Disagreeing		
3. Withdrawing		
4. Guilt-Inducing		
5. Making Reparation	Affection	
6. Identifying		
7. Agreeing		
8. Moving Toward		
9. Showing Submission		Power Relations
10. Showing Equality		
11. Showing Dominance		
12. Expressing Anxiety	Anxiety	Ego State
13. Denying Anxiety		
14. Expressing Depression	Depression	
15. Denying Depression		
16. Expressing Guilt	Guilt	
17. Denying Guilt		
18. Expressing Self-Esteem	Self-Esteem	

The evolution of these categories owes much to Klein's (1957) distinction between the paranoid and depressive positions. The understanding of the whole ego-state area owes as much to the work of Bibring (1953).

It is not hard to envision the difficulties of scoring inherent in this scheme. The distinction between denial and self-esteem necessitates a subtle clinical judgment, as well as a theoretical knowledge of mechanisms of defense. Likewise, distinguishing between depression and guilt is often difficult. Acceptable levels of interscorer agreement have been achieved (Mann, 1967; Gibbard and Hartman, 1973a; Mann and others, 1970), however, so that we believe the use of this system is warranted.

THE GROUP DATA

The two groups chosen for this study were sections of Psychology 454, Analysis of Interpersonal Behavior, an undergraduate course at the University of Michigan. This course is in most respects similar to Social Relations 120 at Harvard College (a course described by Bales, 1970; Dunphy, 1964, 1966, 1968; Gibbard and Hartman, 1973a; Mann, 1966, 1967; Mills, 1964; Slater, 1966). The instructors were the authors, who were of equivalent status. The classes met three times a week in one-hour sessions, for a total of forty sessions. The instructors generally assumed a quiet, inquiring, analytic stance toward the class. Much of the group's attention focused on its own behavior as a case study worthy of understanding. There was an extensive reading list, students were asked to keep weekly logs of the groups, and in addition there was a final examination. The membership of these particular groups was determined by the vagaries of the university bureaucracy. Those "preregistered" were admitted, and others were turned away. The size of the groups was around twenty-five, with an approximately equal number of males and females in each. All sessions were tape-recorded.

The primary data for this study consist of the interaction scores produced by the process analysis scoring system. Each group was scored by a trained scorer, who had in each case been a member of the group he scored. The scorers were trained over a three-week period devoted to joint scoring sessions, lengthy discussions of the scoring procedure, and independent practice scoring. The group data consist of about 15,000 lines of scored interactions for each group. Each speaker-object interaction was scored and punched on an IBM card identifying group and session. Data for each group were transferred to separate files on a magnetic computer tape. Data analysis was done from this tape.

DATA ANALYSIS

The first task was to determine whether developmental phases could be identified. In order to demarcate the phases, a method used previously by Mann (1966) was employed. Percentage profiles for each category for the sum of all of the speakers to all members in each session were used. These calculations yielded percentages of acts across the categories for each session. For example, a session might have 8 percent of its acts in "moving against," 4 percent in "agreeing," and so on. The data used were information yielded by median splits: a session was designated as above or below the median. The result of these computations was a series of phi coefficients describing the degree of association between a session and an adjacent session on all the categories. A positive phi coefficient would indicate that similar activity was going on for a pair of sessions; a negative phi would indicate a shift. The boundaries for subphases were defined by a very low positive or negative correlation between the last session of one phase and the first session of the next.

This analysis yielded four major phases (and seven major identifiable subphases) for each group. Each subphase was compared with all the other subphases combined, in order to specify the distinguishing characteristics of each subphase. Table 2 summarizes the phases and subphases for each group.

Table 2. PHASES AND SUBPHASES FOR EACH GROUP

GROUP 1		GROUP 2	
Phase	*Sessions*	*Phase*	*Sessions*
1	1–11[a]	1a	1–4
2a	13–20	1b	5–9
2b	21–22	1c	10–15
3a	23–26	2	16–20
3b	27–30	3a	21–26
4a	31–34	3b	27–34
4b	35–40	4	35–40

[a] Session 12 lost because of mechanical failure.

Given that four distinct periods in each group could be identified by statistical means, the task was then to discover the relationship, if any, between the demarcation of these phases and measures of ego-state distress. A factor analysis of these data yielded a bipolar factor which included all the ego-state categories. Because of the presence of other categories as well as the bipolar nature of the factor, however, we decided that a more precise measure of distress was needed for the present analysis. A new scale was constructed and labeled *Expression of Distress*. It consists of three ego-state categories—anxiety expressed, depression expressed, and guilt expressed —each equally weighted. (For more details concerning the construction of this scale, see Hartman, 1969.)

For each session in each group, all group speakers except the leader were scored on this scale. These scale scores were then standardized within groups, so that the mean was 50 and the standard deviation 10. Prior experience (Mann, 1967) had shown that to graph each session at this point would result in an erratic up-and-down picture, which would be difficult to describe and understand. A previously successful method, moving averages, was employed to highlight the peaks and valleys of group distress. Using the Expression of Distress scale for each session in each group, we computed four-session "moving averages"; that is, the average of sessions 1–4 was the first data point, sessions 2–5 the second data point, and so on.

To emphasize trends common to both groups, we further decided to present the pattern of group distress for both groups combined. The major differences between the two groups will be discussed later. Figure 1 shows the pattern of Expression of Distress in both groups combined, obtained by plotting the moving averages. The scores are standard scores, standardized within groups. The mean is 50, and the standard deviation is 10. The phases were demarcated by taking the average of the last set of sessions of a phase in each group and finding the statistical midpoint of that set of sessions. The last set of averages in phase 1 contained data from sessions 10–13. Thus, the demarcation point was between sessions 11 and 12, and so on.

Figure 1 shows three peaks of the Expression of Distress, marked A, B, and C. The first two appear at the beginning of a phase and the last toward the end. By returning to the original category data for each group separately, we can determine which kind of distress (anxiety, depression, or guilt) in which group is being reflected in the peaks. The greatest difference between the groups is that group 1 begins with the expression of depression and ends with

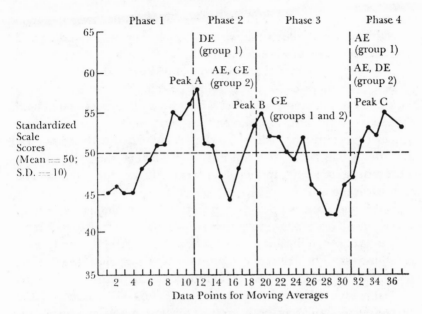

FIGURE 1. Moving averages for expression of distress by phase for groups 1 and 2. DE = depression expressed; AE = anxiety expressed; GE = guilt expressed.

the expression of anxiety. Group 2 begins with the expression of anxiety and guilt and ends with expression of anxiety and depression. These and other differences between the groups will be discussed in some detail shortly.

Previously reported work (Hartman, 1969) on these particular groups described the characteristics of the four phases of group development. Briefly, the first phase marks the group's reaction to a leader who does not lead in the customary manner. This reaction leads to a revolt against the authority of the leader and the structure of the course. The next phase involves an attempt to create what might be termed a "utopian group" by instituting new values of closeness and honesty not ordinarily associated with a classroom. (For a more detailed picture of this facet of group development, see Gibbard and Hartman, 1973b.) Competition, rivalry, and sexuality, and emerging disappointment at the breakdown of the new order, appear in the third phase. The last phase is concerned with the end of the group and the evaluation of previous performance, as well as the sadness associated with termination. These issues were common to both groups, although the ways in which they were handled and the reactions to them were different.

When we consider the patterns of distress in the light of these phases, it becomes clear that the first peak of distress is associated with the revolt against the leader. The second peak is associated with the failure of the utopian solution to group problems and the emergence of sexual rivalry. The third peak is associated with the sadness over the group's end, the concern over whether the group was a success or failure, and apprehension about the examination and the grading in the course.

These data support our hypothesis that changes in group development from phase to phase are signaled or anticipated by a shift in group equilibrium, which is signaled by an increase in ego-state distress. The collective solutions—revolt against the leader, attempts at utopian relations, sexual rivalry—can be seen as attempts to deal with feelings of distress in the group. The sources of the distress were similar in both groups: distress over the leader's inactive, ambiguous role; guilt over the group's treatment of the leader and scapegoats; concern about peer sexuality and rivalry; and distress over the end of the group.

HISTORIES OF THE GROUPS

Group 1

In group 1, as we have noted, the first peak of distress was created by the expression of depression. Anxiety was also present and contributed to the eventual attack on the leader; but since the leader's quiet, observing role in the group was unconsciously perceived as both an abandonment and a rebuke, the response was predominantly a depressive one. In addition, many group members had expected the leader to be Dr. M, older, more prestigious, and a popular campus figure. So the group experienced a double abandonment in Dr. M's absence and in the role behavior of the leader. The group evolved a complicated fantasy about Dr. M in these early sessions, a variant of the "experimenter myth" noted by Slater (1966). The fantasy centered on the notion that Dr. M was the "real leader" of the group and that he was providing the apparent leader with instructions on how to run the group. Because the leader refused to acknowledge this association and to reveal these plans from "above," the group felt mounting anger at the leader—with occasional shifts to feeling depressed and somewhat guilty about itself. As one member said: "He [the leader] is just going to sit there and make people feel guilty. You just get the feeling he thinks that you're not doing what you're supposed to be doing." Throughout the initial phase, group 1 struggled with this pervasive feeling of somehow not doing the correct thing in the group, as well as with a less conscious feeling of having been abandoned. The close of the first phase was marked by a verbal attack on the leader. He was told by several members that they were "furious" at him for being "vague," "obscure," and "incomprehensible." He was accused of being "selfish" and out to ruin the group experience by draining the group and never contributing. Finally, on one occasion when the leader refused to answer a question, a chant began which the entire group echoed: "Answer the question! Answer the question!"

After this attack on the leader, the expression of depression in group 1 virtually disappeared. The revolt against the leader can be seen as an attempt to deal with the depressive feelings. From Jaques' perspective one could argue that the group members' "bad self" was projected onto the leader and their "good self" onto Dr. M. The attack on the leader is really an attack on the members' own evilness, but they are relieved of responsibility in the process. The root of this evilness may be an unconscious fantasy that the group has destroyed the original "good leader" and thus is responsible for its perceived abandonment.

Group 1, having attacked and punished its bad leader (part of self), then sought to create a warm, open, noncompetitive, "utopian" group—in short, a new order, since the leader and the structure of the traditional class had been overthrown. The leader's comments, as well as the class readings, were more or less ignored. Group sessions were marked by attempts to assess allegiance and loyalty to the new way of doing things. Such allegiance was by no means universal. One member especially advocated "intimacy" and "closeness" as the new goals of the group, and the merits of this position were thoroughly debated. One problem with the establishment of the new order was the emergence of expressions of guilt. Manifestly, this guilt was associated with members' inability to achieve the desired closeness. The deeper significance of the guilt lies in the group's perception of itself as having excluded and hurt the leader during the revolt. This guilt may also be associated with the unconscious oedipal significance of the revolt (Gibbard and Hartman, 1973b, 1973c; Slater, 1966). This rising guilt peaks at the beginning of the third phase, when the collapse of the new order is most in evidence.

The emergence of guilt, and the realistic perception that the utopian group had not been achieved, ushered in a phase of peer competition, rivalry, and sexuality. The guilt that had built up, though, was markedly reduced during most of this phase. A great deal of male-female flirtation, as well as male-male confrontation, took place. The tension created by the rivalry and emerging sexuality was relieved by a group party, which the leader declined to attend. Following the party, there was more discussion of fathers and castration anxiety. The sexual rivalry was an expression of the oedipal significance of the original revolt against the leader, as well as an attempt to deal with the guilt associated with it. Indeed, although the party bears a strong resemblance to Slater's (1966) account of totemic feasts as celebrations of past revolts against the father, it was probably also an attempt to ward off feelings associated with the end of the group. Actually, the last phase began two sessions after the party.

The prominence of anxiety in the last phase of group 1 was somewhat unexpected. The anxiety was manifestly associated with the leader's evaluation of the group and the final examination and, less obviously, with the discussions of sexuality that had emerged in the third phase. One could argue that the intensity of the anxiety expressed in this phase points to an effort to defend against the depression that was prevalent in the beginning. Inspection of the scoring of the denial categories reveals that denial of depression was very high for group 1 during this phase. Discussions of the group's ending were left for the last three sessions and were filled more with manic-like denials than with expressions of sadness and loss.

Another way of dealing with the distress raised by the emergent sexuality, as well as a way of not dealing with the end of the group, was in "productive work," in Mann's (1967) sense of the term. One measure of the degree to which the group was taking on the leader's interpretive, inquisitive stance is the number of *observations* that members made about the group or themselves. An analysis of these observations reveals that the greatest period of this activity occurred in the last phase. (A more detailed explanation of the quantitative treatment of observations can be found in Hartman, 1969.) As one member commented, they were too busy getting things "straightened out" and understood to worry about the end of the group. All this work, as valuable as it was in accomplishing the goal of the group to understand itself, was also a defense against experiencing the loss of the group.

Group 2

In group 2 the revolt against the leader's authority was preceded by the expression of anxiety and followed by the expression of guilt. The leader's quiet, observing role was tolerated for the first several sessions, but this tolerance quickly gave way to discomfort and dissatisfaction. The class divided into those who wished for more "structure" and those who preferred "freedom" from authority. Gradually most of the group's complaints were about the leader. In the ninth session most members met in the campus cafeteria to map "revolutionary" plans to overthrow the leader and to force him to take on a more "useful" role. Those few members who chose to stay with the leader felt that they were "the faithful" and deserved the special attentions that the group-as-a-whole wished from the leader.

The next session saw a reuniting of the group and the emergence of guilt. In session 12 the leader handed back graded papers for the first time, and much distress was voiced about this. The group took the leader's evaluations of the logs as a punishment for the earlier revolt. Expressions of guilt built up during the second phase and were mostly concerned with the members' lack of worth.

In group 2 also there was an unsuccessful attempt to create a new order after the "revolution." This new order was to be based on equality and would have as its goal the creation of intimacy and friendliness in the group. Larry, a quiet but impressive member, was urged by many to become the leader. The revolt and the hope that

Larry's leadership would be effective in creating a friendly atmosphere succeeded in reducing the distress of the first phase. The failure of the utopian group to fulfill its mission resulted in the expression of guilt, which was in turn accompanied by themes relating to sexual rivalry.

Soon after the emergence of expressions of guilt, group 2 became obsessed with what its members called "the fear of analysis." Instead of acting out the conflicts concerning sexuality and rivalry, as the members of group 1 did, group 2 seemed to anticipate such issues by expressing a great deal of subjective distress. The fear of group analysis was best exemplified by Norm's announcement that his psychiatrist thought the group was "playing with" very dangerous matters. His announcement, as well as his removing himself from the group, resulted in more guilt and depression in other group members. His leaving, however, merely highlighted certain fears that other members harbored about the group.

This distress was followed by the introduction of a tape of a comedian's version of Noah and the Flood. A fuller analysis of the significance of this event has been presented elsewhere (Hartman and Gibbard, 1973). In the context of our present emphasis on distress, the tape can be viewed as an attempt to reduce stress through the use of fantasy. The playing of the story of Noah, with its theme of reproduction and rescue, was followed by an argument between two members over the relative merits of science and religion. The group seemed to make use of science and religion, as well as fantasy, when it was threatened with dissolution and great stress.

The fear of analysis can be interpreted as a fear of retaliation for sexual interest among the members. The story of Noah was appealing because it involved punishment for those who had sinned and rescue for those who had been favored by God. The pairing up of the animals was allowed, if not ordered by God for the preservation of life, and thus was to be distinguished from the "bad" sexuality that God had punished with the flood. It was on this fantasy level that group 2 tried to work through the issues of sexuality and competition—issues stated more explicitly in group 1.

The largest number of observations occurred in group 2 just after Norm's departure and the eruption of much distress. Indeed, just as in group 1, the percentage of observations rose just after a session high on the expression of depression. The percentage of observations stayed at a high level in group 2 until the termination.

The last phase of group 2 was quite high on Expression of Distress, primarily depression. Group 1 warded off feelings associated with the termination, whereas group 2 seemed to be preoccupied with them. These feelings reflected the perceived failure of the group members to express affection and achieve intimacy, with guilt over the past attacks on the leader and members, and with the sadness and loss that the experience would end.

DISCUSSION

The hypothesis that emergent group structures are products of attempts to deal with ego-state distress is supported by our data. The picture is, however, quite complicated, much more complicated than inspection of a single graph would indicate. What follows is an effort to synthesize our conceptualization of ego-state distress and our view of the evolution of boundary awareness in groups. We aim to develop a larger conceptual scheme of development encompassing both of these conceptualizations.

In all groups in which strangers meet for some collective purpose, there is uncertainty and discomfort. Certain questions are posed but not resolved: What will be the distribution of power in this group? How close or distant are the members to be? How much emotional expression can be or should be permitted? In experiential groups, in which lines of authority are ambiguous, the task problematic, and the usual structural anchors lifted, the initial situation causes anxiety and a concomitant regression. This regressive process in the initial phases of all groups has been insightfully discussed by Scheidlinger (1968). He distinguishes between a group formative regression, which is "normal" and usual in the initial phases of experiential groups, and an atypical, neurotic regression, which is characteristic of individual defensive maneuvers. This initial distress and regression sets in motion certain processes—splitting, introjection, and projection—which seem most characteristic of early ego development and of very disturbed individuals. In its initial phase the small group takes on a very paranoid cast. This is not to imply that the members of the group are psychotic. We would argue, however, that the group formative regression does involve mechanisms usually associated with early development. These mechanisms are employed by normal people to cope with the situation in which they find themselves.

In this initial situation of leaderlessness, strangeness, and high uncertainty, the group experiences chaos, violence, and abandonment, at least preconsciously and unconsciously, as distinct possibilities. The specific manifest concern varies depending upon the nature and primary task of the group and the concerns and capabilities of the members. The actual solution to this distress is quite similar from group to group. Whatever is experienced as bad (anxiety-producing, abandoning, depressing, destructive) is psychologically extruded, placed outside an emergent group boundary. Whatever is good (safe, supportive, productive) is held within that group boundary. Thus, the group boundary comes to be defined by what is outside it, by the bad aspects excluded from it. In an experiential group, the boundary is initially defined by the entire membership and leadership, meeting times, and other formal aspects of the situation. But the group formative regression and the initial uncertainty as to structure—where to proceed and how and under whose leadership— lead to splitting. The boundary is established by defining what is outside the group—the bad leader, the bad member (scapegoat)— or by the creation of two or more subgroups. In this way the group or subgroups attempt by exclusion and expulsion to create a good group entity.

In the early phase of these groups the most clearly extruded person is the leader. In intergroup exercises, such as those developed in the Tavistock tradition, the presence of similarly constituted outgroups provides an even simpler way of extrojecting badness onto an outside entity (cf. Howenstine and Miller, 1971). This is clearly what happens in the politics of the world's nations.

In small groups there is an effort to split good and bad and to put the good into the group and the bad into the leader or disorganizing subgroup. This effort culminates in the revolt against the leader. There is an attempt to force him into the group fully on the group's terms (make him good) or to exclude him fully by destroying him. The revolt is preceded by the expression of several components of distress. Whatever the antecedents, there is an effort to get back into the group anyone or anything (symbols, ideas) experienced as good. This situation occurs because members may at the same time have projected onto the leader good, "ideal" qualities which are then recaptured and introjected during the revolt. Although the leader is ostensibly excluded in the revolt, he is simultaneously included by the mechanism of introjection (Freud, 1921; Slater, 1966).

The revolt and the introjection of attributes of the leader lead inevitably to feelings of guilt because the leader has been ambivalently regarded. This guilt ushers in attempts to win the loyalty and allegiance of all group members, including deviants, to the establishment of a new egalitarian and utopian order. This is a process of assimilation, and inclusion, with boundaries becoming relatively permeable to assimilate all members and ideas which are endowed with goodness in the creation of this utopia (Gibbard and Hartman, 1973b; Hartman and Gibbard, this volume, Chapter 13).

The third phase, one in which competition and sexual rivalry emerge out of the failure to establish this utopia, involves another round of internal distinctions, exclusions, and boundary transformations. Here the issue is not simply power but the mixture of power and intimacy characteristic of the oedipal situation. In this phase the group boundaries again may shift because of the anxieties aroused around oedipal issues. Not only are there not enough women, power, territory to go around, but again the convenience of scapegoats provides an outgroup upon which to externalize sexual anxieties, unattractiveness, powerlessness, and the like.

The last phase, termination, would seem to be one involving dissolution of boundaries and the emergence of depression and guilt. There is an attempt to win back all the deviants in an effort to create for the last time the good group. These are again attempts at inclusion, at incorporating aspects (members) of the group so that it will be full of goodness at the end, so that it will last in memory if not in fact.

Our conclusion is that boundary evolution (reflected in a sense of we-ness, groupness, differentiation, autonomy) does not follow a linear course. Although most developmental studies have traced a linear-progressive course, our observations indicate a more complicated situation. That is, although there *is* an evolution toward a clearer sense of group boundaries and of each individual's relationship to that group entity, the oscillations and deviations from that path suggest a pendular pattern. The reaction to the uncertainty of the initial phase, with its regressive components, leads to an extreme reaction of exclusionary mechanisms. This process leads in turn to the inclusive preoccupation and the utopianism of the next phase. This phase denies and in a sense stimulates the competitive sexuality of the third phase, which brings with it more exclusive and differentiating mechanisms. This competition in turn threatens the solidarity needed to face termination and to deal with the sadness and regrets accompanying the end of the group.

This paradigm is consistent with Slater's theory of group development and is also complementary to Gibbard's conceptualization of role differentiation (see Gibbard, this volume, Chapter 10). In addition, Bales' polarity also would support a nonlinear view of development, although his scheme is not in the language we have used. Finally, Mills' (1964) thoughts on the life cycle of groups are very much akin to our notion of exclusive and inclusive mechanisms in boundary transformations.

What are the conceptual connections between boundary evolution and ego-state distress? Our conclusion is that the foundation of group development is boundary establishment, boundary maintenance, and boundary transformation. The intrapsychic processes of introjection and projection on a group-wide basis lead to the formation of psychic boundaries and other group structures— differentiated roles, hierarchies, ideologies. These processes and structures, in turn, can be viewed as ways of experiencing, expressing, containing, and neutralizing potentially disruptive and disorganizing affects. The primary affects that we explored in this study were anxiety, depression, and guilt. Ego-state distress emerges at those times when the equilibrium between inclusive and exclusive processes is breaking down or threatens to break down. Group solutions then have to be found to deal with this distress. The affects thus serve as *marker variables* to indicate that failures of equilibrium are occurring, and these affects point to the boundary activities which aim at correcting them. This conceptualization helps to tie together Slater's work and that of Jaques; psychotic anxiety in Jaques' terms or ego-state distress in ours is a sign or symptom of the larger issue of boundary maintenance, which we believe to be fundamental to group structure and to group process.

The analogy between this scheme of group development and early ego development is imperfect but provocative. Just as the object relations of the developing child move from an undifferentiated state in which self and object representations are fused, to a state of part-objects and partial fusions of self and other, to relatively permanent differentiation of self and object representations, groups evidence analogous processes. The child introjects and projects objects and part-objects, which eventually fuse into identifications and still later into identity. The group excludes members and then includes them in an evolving attempt at groupness. Just as the individual regresses to earlier states of object relations in sleep, in love, in altered states of consciousness—never entirely abandoning these earlier states—so the group goes through similar oscillations.

We do not mean to overdraw the analogy or to say that there is a one-to-one correspondence between individual ego development and group development. Even granting such a transsystemic analogy, the infant child and the infant group are by no means identical. The group composed of normal individuals begins with a far wider range of adaptive capacities than does the infant. The normal group does experience a group formative regression, which brings with it certain mechanisms that remind us of early ego functioning—splitting, projection, and introjection. But this normal regression does not make the group or its members truly psychotic. It does mean that groups do *by their very nature* pose problems of object relations, particularly the relationship of the individual to the group, which are reminiscent of the early mother-child object relationship.

Many studies have equated the group-as-a-whole with the preoedipal mother (Bion, 1959; Durkin, 1964; Ruiz, 1972; Scheidlinger, 1964, 1968; Slater, 1966). With this further analogy, group process can be viewed as an oscillation between a symbiotic relatedness with the group-as-a-whole and individuation. This symbiosis is desired in the form of inclusion in the group (mother) and is feared and defended against by the assertion of independence, individuality, and uniqueness.

If one looks not only backward from the self-analytic group to the developing individual but also forward to larger societal processes, further analogies present themselves. The universal social and political dilemma of man versus the state, of individualism versus group loyalty can be seen in a similar fashion. It may be that political evolution and system maintenance—particularly nation-building and the stabilizing of countries through time—replicate on a larger societal level both the small-group and the individual processes we have been discussing. If the nation (motherland) is analogous to the preoedipal mother (unconsciously shared fantasy of its members), then the formation of the state reflects the desire for individuation and the desire for and fear of fusion associated with early ego development. Just as we have noted splitting, projection, and a paranoid cast in the formation of small groups, so schisms, civil wars, and national wars all mark the political evolution of nations. Also, tendencies toward greater integration of races, religions, classes, and countries (fusion) have been opposed throughout history by forces advocating segregation, parochialism, ethnocentrism, and separateness (splitting). Dreams of universal harmony without national, racial, and class distinctions vie with fierce nationalisms and racial pride. These political phenomena are analogous to intrapsychic processes as well as to small-group phenomena.

Finally, we should note that the boundary oscillations and the solutions employed to bind the distress arising from this disequilibrium produce a chronically unstable situation. No solution is permanently successful because each solution violates some facet of reality by splitting the positive and negative sides of the ambivalence and, in most experiential groups, is undercut by interpretation. Presumably, solutions such as we have in mind can be and are institutionalized in many other settings. Some kinds of splits (for example, the infidels, the enemy, the other side) become stabilized in institutions and do not lead to such oscillations. The projection of evil, chaos, weakness rests on and necessitates the suppression of awareness of internal problems.

These observations are offered as a spur to further research into the connection between internal states such as affective distress and the formation and consolidation of group structure. At this juncture we must begin to explore with more sophistication and persistence the relationship between intrapsychic processes and the social structure of small groups and larger institutions.

PART THREE

THE INDIVIDUAL
AND THE GROUP

I t has often been noted that the
individual's fundamental attitudes toward group membership are
characterized by ambivalence. The seminal work of Bion (1959)
and the more recent contributions of Gibbard and Hartman
(1973b), Rice (1969), Slater (1966), and Turquet (1969; this
volume, Chapter 14) have identified some of the sources and vicissitudes of this ambivalence. Our own view is that the natural habitat
of man is the group. His adaptation to this habitat is imperfect, a state
of affairs reflected in his chronic dissatisfaction with groups. This
conflict is embedded in the psychic structure of human beings (and
is manifested in the social structure of human institutions) and can
be attenuated, but never eliminated, by successful compromise
formation.

The basic antagonism is between the individual's commitment to himself—to his own needs, beliefs, and ambitions—and his
yearning for psychological submersion in a group, for an obliteration
of those qualities that make him unique and thus distinct and
separate from others. Submersion brings a measure of security and a
sense of connectedness and belonging, but it also undermines individual autonomy, obstructs the attainment of any goal which is not
shared, and may in other respects demand a sacrifice of individual
wishes to those of the group.

In order to ensure his inclusion in the group and maximize the security which membership provides, the individual must overlook or deny the painful or frustrating aspects of the group experience. In his effort to maintain a view of the group as a source of gratification and protection, he must fix the blame for his own distress on something or someone other than the group—on a single member of the group, on the leader, or on an external person or group. The reluctance to allow good and bad to be brought together, the difficulty in tolerating a genuinely ambivalent position vis-à-vis the group, gives rise to a variety of denials, projections, and defensive splittings. A more realistic stance is attained only when the ambivalence is seen as unresolvable. At this point, splitting, projection, and denial can be replaced by an accurate appraisal of and a greater tolerance for ambivalence.

Among Bion's most compelling clinical observations are his portraits of this ambivalent bond between the individual and the group. He argues that this ambivalence can be endured only because of the operation of a "group mentality," a process of unconscious collusion through which some individual "contributions" are made openly while others can remain "anonymous." In this way ambivalent feelings can be split, and individuals can be lured into the acting out of unacceptable impulses. The locus of responsibility is ambiguous, and the individual is shielded from guilt and retribution by the contract of anonymity. The "culture" or manifest structure of the group reflects a collective compromise formation. The conscious aims of individual members and the unconscious and disavowed aims which group members have "pooled" by means of the group mentality are brought together, however tenuously, into an equilibrium.

Bion's notions of group mentality and group culture offer one way of describing and understanding the impact of unconscious fantasy[1] on individual and group behavior. The group culture represents the intersection of individual and group psychology. By beginning with the content and process of the manifest culture, one can to some extent determine the relative strength of conscious, idiosyncratic motives and unconscious, shared motives. But despite the

[1] See our introduction to Part Four for a fuller explanation of unconscious fantasy and its role in group theory.

originality and the heuristic value of Bion's work, the ambiguities and clear contradictions in his discussions of the group mentality and the basic assumptions (see Gibbard, 1972) make it very difficult to apply his model of unconscious collusion to a wider range of settings. The more familiar concept of *role* can be employed with greater precision and flexibility to examine relations between the individual and the group.

As Levinson (1959) has pointed out, the general concept of role must, in any careful analysis, be separated into its major components. Without such a separation one loses sight of the fact that there is often not an exact or even a close fit between societal or institutional prescription and individual adaptation. Levinson identifies three aspects of any complex role: (1) structurally given demands (norms, expectations) associated with a given social position; (2) the individual's conception of his role; and (3) the actual behavior of the individual in a particular social position. Levinson observes that the role demands of the organization vary widely in several respects—explicitness, clarity, integration, coherence, rationality. When the demands on a given position are ambiguous or inconsistent, individual members have some choice among existing role definitions and some opportunity to develop new definitions, but may also find themselves paralyzed by the absence of clear norms. Levinson argues that role definition is an "ego achievement," an indication of the individual's ability to compromise between conflicting pressures, to adapt to existing opportunities and create new ones, and to forge a balance between stability and innovation.

Students of group dynamics and participant-observers of psychotherapy and sensitivity training groups have long sought to identify and explain the distinctive individual roles which emerge in such groups. One of the most intriguing characteristics of relatively unstructured and ego-involving small groups is the evolution of a constellation of informal roles that serve important social and psychological functions for the group. Most small-group research has addressed itself to groups that do not have formal statuses and ascribed social positions. The roles that emerge are usually described as "behavior patterns," "individual roles," or "interpersonal styles." Under relatively unstructured conditions psychological factors, conscious and unconscious, become increasingly important as determinants of role structure. A wider range of individual styles and adaptations is possible. Explicit and formal social prescriptions are replaced by fantasy conceptions of norms and sanctions. At the same time, it is assumed that such roles are not simply expressive of idiosyncratic needs but perform necessary and recurrent psychological functions for the social system—such functions as impulse expression, group maintenance, tension release. Some writers have been most interested in delineating the casts of characters which emerge in specific types of groups, in specifying the thematic content of role structures. Others have attempted to formulate a more inclusive conceptualization of group roles, to explore the bases and mechanisms of role differentiation, and to identify the developmental processes which govern the evolution of role structures. This overview encompasses both emphases, and for this reason we shall review studies of laboratory as well as experiential groups.

The systematic examination of interaction process and role differentiation began, in fact, with the work of Bales (1950a), who focused almost exclusively on short-term laboratory groups with predetermined problem-solving tasks. Bales' interaction process analysis (IPA) represents the first comprehensive effort to record and quantify interaction in small groups. The most impressive empirical specification of group roles to date is that generated by the application of the interaction process method to the study of small task-oriented groups. Two kinds of peer leaders tend to emerge in these groups—an "instrumental" (task) leader and an "expressive" (social-emotional) leader. Members selected as task leaders on peer ratings tend to rank high on interaction categories such as "giving suggestions" and "showing disagreement." Social-emotional leaders are more inclined to rank high on categories such as "showing solidarity" and "asking for suggestions."

This differentiation of function or division of labor corresponds to a split between the internal and external tasks of the social system. It is usually assumed that instrumental and expressive leaders are mutually supportive and complementary. From this assumption it follows that task groups will be most effective and productive and group members most satisfied when both styles of leadership are available and when the occupants of these role positions are clearly identified. In theory, each role specialist helps the group to solve certain problems but in the process ignores or exacerbates others. The task specialist, in forcing the group to meet its problem-solving commitments and to delay gratification, contributes to increased tension and resentment. The expressive specialist soothes tempers, encourages tension release, and attempts to restore a more harmonious atmosphere. If this type of complementarity is consistently present, the dual leaders are able to maintain a coalition characterized by mutual cooperation and a high level of status consensus (agreement about the relative positions of key members in the hierarchy of informal statuses). But when specialists do not emerge or are unable to cooperate with one another, the group's equilibrium is threatened, status agreement declines, and negative affect increases. If this frustrating state continues, further differentiation, including development of a scapegoat role, is likely to occur. The beginnings of this kind of differentiation under varying conditions in triads have been observed by Mills (1953, 1954).

This conception of dual, complementary leadership conflicts with the more popular and intuitively appealing notion that a single person assumes all leadership functions for the group. Borgatta, Couch, and Bales (1954) advanced the notion that under some conditions a "great-man" leader—a member who takes on both task and social-emotional functions—may emerge. Slater's (1955, 1961) discussions of this issue suggest that a group will try, if forced to choose (on a sociometric questionnaire) an "overall" leader, to establish a certain balance of task and social-emotional activity. The result is that the member chosen as overall leader is one whose ratings approximate the entire group's average position on the task and social-emotional dimensions. But most often this is at best an approximation, apparently less reliable than a clear differentiation of roles. In addition, most people appear to be socialized to specialize in one of the two functions. More recently, Bales (1970) has proposed a model of group structure and a constellation of "group role types" based on a three-dimensional "evaluative space." This model is, however, too elaborate, and its theoretical and empirical implications are too complex, to be dealt with here.

The division of labor along instrumental and expressive lines occurs primarily in groups whose principal goal is the accomplishment of a specific task, but the general model of differentiation is of considerable heuristic value in a consideration of other kinds of groups. In experimental groups, role differentiation can be understood as an adaptive response to a variety of threats to group equilibrium—threats such as intragroup frustration and conflict, increases in group size, and complexity of the task. Beyond a certain point, however, such differentiation might produce new frustrations and conflicts, as well as increase the psychological distance between group members. In addition, intense and unmanageable conflict could lead not to an adaptive increase in differentiation but to disorganization and complete dedifferentiation. Finally, the concept of the great-man leader suggests that at some level of awareness there is a psychological pull toward the establishment of a single leader, though the characteristics of this phenomenon have not been studied.

To explore these questions and to investigate the further course of role differentiation, we shall review research on larger groups with complex tasks and goals as well as initially ambiguous role structures. In unstructured situations such as psychotherapy groups, sensitivity training groups, and self-analytic classrooms, the relatively inactive and nondirective role of the therapist or consultant allows high and intense participation but lowers status consensus and usually provides no explicit index of movement toward a goal. Lewin, Lippitt, and White (1939) and White and Lippitt (1960) have commented on the lowered satisfaction and productivity of groups with "laissez-faire" as opposed to "democratic" leadership. The groups discussed in these studies are not comparable in every respect, but they do share a certain degree of structural ambiguity, and all tend to include in their definition of the task some analysis of the group interaction.

Freud's (1921) major contribution to group psychology focused on the organizational function of leadership. The leader is portrayed as the emotional hub of the collectivity, as the primary basis for the formation and maintenance of a psychological group. Redl (1942) subsequently expanded Freud's conceptualization by introducing the broader notion of a "central person" who serves as a "crystallization point" for other members. Redl described several paths to centrality—for instance, the "tryant," the "good influence," and the "central person as love object." Though he did not explore the process of role differentiation or spell out the relationships among central persons, he did offer a more complex and flexible psychodynamic model of leadership than had any of the early psychoanalytic writers. Miller's (1972) more recent reconsideration of Freud's paradigm stresses the ambivalence aroused by the exercise of authority. Miller argues that all social systems organize around a task, and that a task implies and requires leadership of some type. Restating Freud's formulation, he suggests that when initially faced with a complex, novel situation, the members of a nascent group project (or externalize) their ego ideals onto the group leader, whom they attempt to view as a strong, resourceful, and potentially nurturant figure. This view is from the beginning complicated, however, by a central paradox of leadership and group formation: once the ego ideal is externalized and objectified, attaining it means overcoming the group leader. In this sense, then, the conditions for group formation and for group conflict and dissolution are identical. In addition, the leader's visibility makes him the most likely target for a variety of other feelings, positive and negative. Miller concludes that many of the irrational efforts to deal with authority and leadership reflect an inability to tolerate, understand, and compromise the disorganizing ambivalence toward authority which is the direct result of the leader's becoming the externalized ego ideal of the group.

Bion's group psychology provides an alternative, though complementary, way of thinking about leadership and role specialization. Moving beyond the concept of group mentality, Bion distinguishes between "work" and "basic-assumption" activity. The concepts of basic assumption and work refer to modes of thought and action which are fundamentally antithetical. Basic-assumption activity is grounded in magical thinking and is directed toward the immediate reduction of tension and the avoidance of effective distress. A group that is working is, on the other hand, committed to sound reality testing and to the tolerance of frustration and delay. The working group requires and fosters rationality, adaptive and flexible structure, and creative collaboration. To the extent that basic-assumption thinking prevails, interpersonal relationships are governed by unconscious collusion among group members, and the criteria for acceptable leadership are determined by the demands and limitations of the basic assumption which is salient at that particular time. Bion thus describes the basic-assumption leader as "an individual whose personality renders him peculiarly susceptible to the obliteration of individuality by the basic assumption's leadership requirements" (1959, p. 177). In the work group, the criteria for leadership are rational and are reasonably congruent with the actual needs of the group. Formal and informal leaders may be replaced if the task requirements of the group shift.

Bion observes that work and basic-assumption activity are seldom, if ever, found in pure form. The group that is functioning most effectively has succeeded in mobilizing and mastering the basic assumption most appropriate to its aims and has blended work and basic-assumption goals into a successful compromise formation. A viable balance between work and basic-assumption orientations also entails a compromise between strictly rational qualifications for leadership and the irrational characteristics of basic-assumption leadership. A "dependency" group can, for example, come to depend on a leader who is perceived as reliable but not infallible. The "fight/flight" leader is no longer likely to be *indiscriminately* aggressive or suspicious. The messiah of the "pairing group" can take on more realistic and human form and can offer enthusiastic and creative leadership without being subjected to excessive idealization or derogation.

In recent years leadership has been equated with a constellation of functions, essentially invariant from group to group, which may be performed by several members or by different members at different periods in the group's history. Arsenian, Semrad, and Shapiro (1962) have made the most general statement of this point of view. They identify "cohesion" and "dispersion" as the "integral functions" in small groups and argue that any number of interchangeable "billets" may discharge these functions.

Stock, Whitman, and Lieberman (1958) and Whitaker and Lieberman (1964) have gone a step further to develop a well-articulated interactional explanation of individual centrality in psychotherapy groups. Drawing on French's notion of "focal conflict," they have offered many illustrations of the interrelationships among the individual "nuclear conflict" and the "group focal conflict." The "deviant member," for example, is a person who is unable or unwilling to endorse existing group "solutions" to focal conflicts. His deviance necessitates further compromise measures in order to maintain some sense of solidarity.

All of these psychodynamic models of role differentiation assume that specialized roles, especially the more visible leadership roles, are reflections of and attempts to resolve the basic polarities of group life: positive versus negative feelings, especially toward authority; rational versus irrational responses to conflict and complexity; solidarity versus fragmentation. What all of them overlook or ignore is the question of commonalities in development. To what extent can comparable role structures be identified across groups? Is it possible to describe similar developmental processes and patterns which lead to the consolidation of relatively stable role structures?

Bennis and Shepard (1956; this volume, Chapter 6) were the first to advance a theory of development in experiential groups in which phase movement and shifts in role structure are closely interwoven. They postulate two principal "areas of internal uncertainty." The first centers on the members' ambivalently dependent tie to the group leader ("the distribution of power in the group"); the second concerns the relationships among group members ("the distribution of affection in the group"). The first (authority-centered) issue must, in their view, be more or less resolved before the conflicts associated with intermember involvement can be fully engaged and worked through. Each of these areas (which constitute the two major phases of group development) are worked through in three subphases. In the first two subphases the "conflicted" (for example, "dependent" and "counterdependent") members alternate dominance in the group. In the third subphase the issue is resolved primarily by the less conflicted members, who are able to forge some compromise between opposing factions. In the interdependence phase, for example, the group is first dominated by the "overpersonals," who deny all disagreement and hostility within the group. In the second subphase the "counterpersonals" are more in control, and interpersonal disengagement is more in evidence. Finally, the relatively less conflicted "personals" gain more influence and establish a viable balance of revelation and concealment, positive feelings and negative reactions, and the like.

Here again, the specific content of this typology is less important than the implicit conceptualization of role differentiation. Gibbard (this volume, Chapter Ten) suggests an *epigenetic* model; that is, although the potential for certain kinds of informal leadership is always present, each becomes salient only at a certain point in the life of the group. Also of interest is the notion that group conflict is resolved by members whose personal problems are not stirred up by that particular conflict. Similarly, Herbert and Trist (1953) have spoken of members who bring together "seemingly incompatible opposites." Stock and Thelen (1958) have noted something very similar, and Stock (1964) has added a fuller description of these "bridging members."

The epigenetic scheme of Bennis and Shepard, in which role specialists emerge sequentially throughout the development of the group, is not the only general model proposed. Bales and Slater (1955) have discussed the alternatives for differentiation beyond the instrumental-expressive polarity. They tentatively suggest an "evolutionary tree" paradigm—a "branching process of development, in which certain divisions or differentiations are not only more primary in time for a given group but also functionally more fundamental, and so likely to be similar from one type of group to another" (1955, pp. 259–260). They discuss in some detail the ways in which the "functionally diffuse" role of social-emotional leader might become more differentiated. Another possibility is that the process is actually the opposite of an evolutionary tree; that is, all the major roles are differentiated early, but some of these roles atrophy and become insignificant as the group begins to solve internal conflicts and to achieve a higher level of satisfaction.

Dunphy (1964, 1968; this volume, Chapter 12) has studied role structures in two self-analytic college classroom groups with the aim of clarifying the differentiation process and extending the repertory of documented roles to include those that he terms "nonrational." He concludes that these nonrational role specialists play a crucial part in integrating the preconscious and unconscious fantasies of group members in a group "mythology" which serves as an "overarching symbol system" unifying group interaction. Dunphy begins with the following assumption:

The nonrational role specialists who emerge in groups [facilitate] projective identification by playing roles which represent important elements in the internal fantasies of group members. This externalization of internal fantasies through their acting out in the group results in the development of a generalized group fantasy, or "mythology," which exercises a controlling influence on the behavior of group members and on the evolution of the group. . . . Group integration occurs through the "matching" of similar internalized objects with externalized objects so that a delimited range of modes of relating is established; i.e., the group arrives at a consensus about the class of internal objects to which links will be brought into play. . . . The group roles represent the externalization and dramatization of conflicts centering around the handling of primary processes in the relative absence of external restraints and the breakdown of traditional normative expectations. Thus, the role specialists become symbols of the major alternatives which the group faces in the evolution of its culture; and through the interaction of the specialists in the context of group response, patterns of action evolve which resolve these basic dilemmas [1964, pp. 55, 67, 257].

Dunphy approaches this problem somewhat indirectly, relying primarily on the periodic written descriptions of self and others by group members (role images or role perceptions) rather than on transcripts or accounts of the group interaction. These descriptive reports were content analyzed by the General Inquirer technique (see Stone, Dunphy, Smith, and Ogilvie, 1966).

Selecting groups that met throughout the regular academic year, three times a week for about seventy sessions, Dunphy found that the groups did in fact develop a more extensive repertory of roles than did the Bales laboratory groups. Dunphy identifies two of the five major roles as the self-analytic group's equivalents of task and social-emotional specialists. Observing that the "common image of the instructor is of a distant and judging authority figure," he concludes that members perceived the instructor as the instrumental specialist. In both groups a fairly active female member played the role of a social-emotional leader who accepted and supported the instructor's authority and attempted to resolve interpersonal difficulties within the group. Dunphy also describes a "seducer," an "aggressor," and a "scapegoat." The seducer attempts to weaken defenses against personal exposure and self-revelation. He challenges the instructor's authority, threatens both internal and external normative controls, and pushes the group toward intimacy. The aggressor strives to maintain rigid personal control and reacts strongly against the introduction of personal feelings and values. Other members describe him as overly dependent on the instructor and as unable to cope with the ambiguity of the group situation. He is quickly attacked and disposed of. Dunphy attributes this scapegoat phenomenon to the group members' repudiation and denial of their own anxiety and dependency and the projection of these feelings onto the scapegoat.

In tying this role structure to phases in group development, Dunphy argues that the dynamic basis of the role system is essentially oedipal: "The derivation of this constellation of roles from focal conflicts experienced in socialization is evident. The roles include a clearly defined father figure, a rather shadowy mother figure, two dominant siblings who stand respectively for the free expression of libidinal drives and for their repression. . . . Finally a resolution of the problem is worked out, which for most members again follows the pattern established in the family—identification with the authority figure and the sublimation of impulses in the interests of achievement and rationality" (1964, pp. 259–260). Dunphy thus concludes that the group eventually settles the impulse-expression struggle in favor of suppression and sublimation and the acceptance of the instructor's authority in the service of the group's self-analytic tasks.

Mann (1967) employed a very different methodology in his intensive study of four self-analytic groups. He coded the interaction with an act-by-act scoring system designed to assess and record the members' feelings toward the formal leader (the instructor) and thus based his analyses on observers' ratings of individual behavior rather than, as in Dunphy's study, on the content analysis of other members' perceptions of individual behavior. Despite this major and several minor methodological differences, the Dunphy and Mann studies appear to have come to similar conclusions about the nature of role differentiation in self-analytic groups.

A parellel between Dunphy's seducer and aggressor and three of Mann's major types is the most apparent correspondence. Mann identifies a male figure whom he describes as a "hero." The hero presses for increased impulse expression, "complete honesty and candor" even at the expense of "sensitivity," and the muffling of all expressions of anxiety, depression, and dependency. The two "resisters," on the other hand, are adamantly opposed to precisely those aspects of the group task which the hero endorses so enthusiastically —self-revelation, impulse expression, and an active involvement in the here-and-now events of the group. Mann also notes the emergence of a scapegoat who, like Dunphy's scapegoat, is seen as representing unacceptable and projected facets of the group members' personalities—in this instance, fears of sexual inadequacy.

Unlike Dunphy, Mann found a significant number of "enactors," both male and female, whose principal function is to modify the hero's demands for total self-exposure and the resister's defensiveness in the face of these demands. Mann's conclusions on this score are more in line with Bennis and Shepard's than with Dunphy's. He found it necessary to look closely at changes over time in order to understand either subgroup formation or the evolution of individual roles. The hero and the resisters, for example, can be identified early in the group. Many of the early sessions are devoted to a conflict between demands for involvement and exposure and a defensive reliance on sensitivity, compassion, and tact. But the enactors, who seem similar in many respects to Bennis and Shepard's independents, are able to synthesize interpretation and sensitivity after this initial conflict has continued for some time, even though in the early stages of this battle they are inconspicuous. The scapegoat's centrality may be limited to a single phase, and before this point it is impossible to identify any such role.

Both Dunphy and Mann conceptualize the major roles as serving integrative functions of a "nonrational" nature. Both argue that the impulse-expression/impulse-suppression polarity is central in the entire role-differentiation process. Some members represent the forces for more "personal" involvement and a freer display of hostile and affectionate feelings. Others plead for a minimum of personal involvement and a maximum of impulse control.

There are two principal differences. First, Dunphy has found no evidence for differentiation of either the "evolutionary tree" or the epigenetic variety. Mann's findings are in partial agreement with Dunphy's, though they also, as we have noted, provide some support for the epigenetic notion first considered by Bennis and Shepard. His findings do not, however, support Bennis and Shepard's two-phase, six-subphase developmental model, in which a particular subgroup tends to dominate a given subphase. Instead, he has offered a more complex view in that the principal roles and subgroups are described as evolving and shifting over time. This more detailed examination of interpersonal self-presentation is made possible by act-by-act scoring and session-by-session summaries. Second, Dunphy argues that the resolution of group conflicts is facilitated by and reflected in the group's eventual acceptance of the normative structure (embodied in the instructor and the female social-emotional specialist). Mann has emphasized the forces of moderation and compromise inherent in the peer group: a redefinition of "work" on the part of the enactors incorporates some of the instructor's expectations, rejects some of his demands, and modifies still others.

The three new contributions in this section attempt in different ways to extend our understanding of role differentiation in small groups. Winter's paper deals primarily with the dynamics of interracial classroom groups with a white female consultant, offering a valuable departure from the more typical self-analytic group with an all-white (or virtually all-white) membership and a male consultant. Her work raises important questions about the relevance of our evolving theory of group process and role structure to small study groups with more variable memberships and with female consultants or co-consultants. Ringwald's cluster-analytic study of two groups combines Mann's act-by-act scoring system (as subsequently revised by Gibbard and Hartman) and Dunphy's focus on shared role images. Ringwald presents a typology of group roles derived from a clinical and statistical analysis of group members' reactions to individuals, and suggests that these roles represent facets of the individual's struggle to formulate and maintain a sense of purpose and identity congruent with his ego ideals. Gibbard's paper, which includes a case study of a central figure in one of the two groups studied by Ringwald, is an effort to move toward a more general theory of role differentiation, drawing both on the clinical observations of Bion, Slater, and others and the more quantitative work of Dunphy and Mann.

Winter describes an intriguing constellation of roles in her sample of three interracial groups. The most salient figure is the "black male leader," who insists on maintaining an extremely provocative position on the boundary of the group. His commitment to the group is marginal; he demands and acts out the fantasy of an intense and special relationship with the leader; he urges the open expression of sexual and aggressive feelings; his response to threatening situations is consistently counterphobic. Winter portrays the other black members as loyal to the black male leader, though not without some ambivalence. The white women are alternately enthralled and repelled, and the white men are for the most part frustrated, sullen, and impotent. She suggests that the recurrence of this patterning of informal roles is a manifestation of the interaction between cultural myth and the immediate reality of the interracial study group. Black males in society and in the self-analytic group often come to be viewed (and allow themselves to be viewed) as the repository of the sexual and aggressive impulses of the collectivity. The black members are at times seen as strongly united in their hostility to all whites, and the white members (particularly the men) are seen as intellectually superior and malevolent, yet inferior vis-à-vis black male sexual potency.

One shortcoming of this line of analysis is that the focus on the dynamic and technical problems specific to a group with an interracial composition obscures the possibility that the impact of racial differences and racial myths can be understood as a reflection of more basic and universal group processes. The black male leader is, for example, strikingly similar to the heroic member discussed by Mann (1967) and Gibbard (this volume, Chapter 10) and has much in common with Dunphy's seducer. This degree of correspondence suggests that the essential dynamics of role differentiation in Winter's interracial groups are not significantly different from those documented by Dunphy, Gibbard, and Mann. Clearly, they differ in that racial issues serve to dramatize a variety of other themes. The question is whether racial themes constitute a crucial reality in these three groups or a metaphor through which group members attempt to work through other problems. To the extent that the second explanation is valid, it is understandable that racial myths and splits should prove so refractory to analysis. The acceptance of race as *the* issue, rather than as a more complex representation of many issues, vitiates an examination of the multiple determinants of racial concerns. One set of determinants, which Winter does explore in some detail, centers on the regulation of intrapsychic and group boundaries and the conflict between individuation and fusion. Another set of determinants—more visible and usually more easily interpreted—stems from the sexual differences in the group. If one can generalize from the dynamics of the all-white groups studied previously (see Gibbard and Hartman, 1973a; Hartman and Gibbard, 1973; Hartman and Gibbard, this volume, Chapter 13), it is apparent that in Winter's groups racial concerns supplant or subsume a concern with sexual differences and sexual identity. In the three interracial groups utopian fantasies are stated in racial terms—as a wish for racial harmony, solidarity, and integration. In all-white groups the analogous fantasy is stated in sexual terms—as a wish for a blending of the sexes, an escape from the tension of heterosexual attraction and competition and from the anxiety and guilt associated with intragroup sexuality.

This does not imply that the racial myths identified by Winter are merely a screen for sexual concerns. It is debatable, in fact, whether race or sex is the more "fundamental" issue. But it is important to be aware that racial concerns are, at least in this context, overdetermined and that race, once established as a primary manifest theme, provides a convenient stage for the dramatization of a number of other themes. The major implication for role theory is that the dynamic processes and the role structure in interracial self-analytic groups are remarkably similar to those in groups with an all-white composition.

Ringwald's work demonstrates the strength of a methodology attuned to both the interpersonal styles of individual members and the impact of group process and structure. Others have dealt theoretically and clinically with this interaction, but most quantitative research with groups of this type has stressed either the group's conception of the individual's role (Dunphy) or the actual behavior of individuals (Mann). A thorough assessment of role structure requires, as Levinson (1959) argues, an investigation of the three components of role—the structural demands and pressures on the individual, his conception of his role, and his manifest behavior. Ringwald deals systematically with two of the three components (role image and interpersonal behavior). As he points out, an immediate advantage of this strategy is that one can begin to explore the interweaving of structural demands and idiosyncratic responses to those demands. He concludes that the initial absence of normative structure, reflected in the consultant's refusal to prescribe solutions to the problems facing the group, sets in motion a search for peer leadership. This search entails a process of recruitment and an effort to identify and forge tacit agreements with potential task leaders, idealized role models, sexual objects, and pariahs.

The original cast of characters to be recruited seems to vary little from group to group. The "anxious participators" are, for example, reminiscent of the "distressed females" discussed by Mann. The "respected enactors" are very similar to Mann's "enactors." The role of the "sexual idols" has been discussed by Dunphy and by Gibbard (1969). The "outsiders" appear to overlap with other variants of the scapegoat role, and the "prophets" include a heroic member (Mann, 1967; Gibbard, Chapter 10) and two other active males. What is more noteworthy is the range of individual responses to the recruitment process. Without some collusion on the part of individuals, no recruitment can occur, which means that under some circumstances major roles remain unoccupied despite persistent efforts at recruitment. Moreover, group members' attitudes toward individuals who do move into salient roles vary as a function of two dimensions: the extent to which the role is seen as enhancing group solidarity and the extent to which individuals are willing to stay within the boundaries of the roles assigned to them. The sexual idols, for example, are courted and pursued, and their detachment creates problems in boundary maintenance. The outsiders, by contrast, refuse to collude with the group's image of them, and even idealized and respected members of this cluster do not receive the reparative overtures which are directed toward the sexual idols.

Ringwald's formulation remains ambiguous in one important respect: the study of the recruitment process must at some point include a consideration of other developmental questions. Do all the major roles emerge simultaneously? How much do individual and group perceptions of roles change over time? With what degree of precision can we specify the characteristics of the recruitment process? These kinds of questions are not addressed, and it may be that a more detailed analysis of such developmental phenomena will ultimately rely on naturalistic observation over relatively short time spans.

Gibbard's paper offers a systematic statement of the developmental process and the dynamic significance of role differentiation. He believes that the primary function of differentiation is to counter the disruption of individual and group functioning precipitated by anomie and internal conflict. Viewed from this perspective, role differentiation becomes a special case of the general rule that internal conflict and the threat of chaos give rise to splitting, externalization, and compartmentalization. He comments at some length on the advantages and disadvantages of this response to conflict and distress.

Gibbard contends that structural differentiation must be defined not simply as the emergence of a few vividly differentiated roles but as the gradual development of more differentiated roles for all group members. He stresses the importance of the conflict between individuation and fusion and proposes a general model of the differentiation process. As an intrapsychic phenomenon, the focus is on individuation, a covert and largely unconscious process of self-definition. Gibbard endorses Slater's argument that the developmental course of individuation is linear. At the more observable level of group structure the focus is on the differentiation of group roles. He believes that role differentiation follows a pendular course, but that within this basic framework the differentiation which occurs in response to more circumscribed conflicts may follow an epigenetic pattern. The difficulty with this model is that almost all of the empirical research on role differentiation (Bennis and Shepard, Dunphy, Mann, Ringwald, Winter) has implicitly or explicitly emphasized the interlocking functions of central figures in the acting out and resolution of manifest and relatively delimited focal conflicts. Only Slater's recent work and the much earlier sociological contributions of Bales and his collaborators have dealt with structural differentiation as a broader, fundamental phenomenon. Gibbard, despite his argument that we should move beyond an assessment of the roles of a handful of central figures, presents a case study of a single member (the hero) as a paradigm of the differentiation process. Thus while the conceptual clarification which his paper offers is essential, he does not deal with the more specific empirical questions which he raises.

By way of summary, it is important to ask how distinctions which are obviously of some importance theoretically can be made more accessible to empirical investigation. Perhaps the intrapsychic phenomenon of individuation can be explored only through introspection and the clinical interview. We assume that the individual entering an experiential group must undergo a partial disorganization and eventual reorganization of his internal world. He experiences becoming a member of the group as an assault on his way of thinking about himself in relation to others. There is considerable agreement (see Gibbard, 1972; Scheidlinger, 1964, 1968) that the early phase of group development is marked by a group formative regression and that intrapsychic and interpersonal tensions trigger reparative efforts to master the phenomenologically real possibility of psychic disruption and the objectively real difficulties of creating a new social system. Our understanding of this experience for the individual is limited, and demands more persistent and systematic scrutiny.

Moving to the level of group structure, it seems reasonable to conclude, as Gibbard, Slater, and others have suggested, that we should begin to focus our empirical efforts on the evolution of intragroup and intergroup boundaries. Mills (1964), for example, has devoted considerable attention to the phenomena of group boundary creation, maintenance, and dissolution. He has developed an act-by-act coding system (sign process analysis) which makes possible a careful longitudinal analysis of positive, negative, and neutral references to internal and external objects. Hartman and Gibbard (Chapter 7) have employed a scoring system to trace developmental shifts in self-analytic groups. They suggest that much of group development can be understood as an alternation between "introjective" and "extrojective" processes, which are in turn indicative of individual and collective efforts to reorganize internal and external boundaries. Though neither of these studies comes close to providing a direct and reliable measure of group boundaries, they do demonstrate that such an undertaking may be much more realistic than one might imagine.

Finally, we should not overlook the fact that all these phenomena are extremely subtle and that the developmental processes through which group structures are consolidated can be captured only by the most careful and fine-grained observation. Some developmental changes (for instance, the emergence of relatively differentiated roles for all group members) may be so gradual that they are visible only from a distance and over a relatively long time span. Other shifts (for instance, the early recruiting of central figures) may occur so quickly and be compressed into so short a period of time that only an act-by-act analysis of process can provide a detailed picture. Certainly no single methodology can serve all these functions, and we must learn to move more fluently, conceptually and methodologically, from one level of analysis to another.

8

Interracial Dynamics
in Self-Analytic Groups

SARA K. WINTER

*R*ole differentiation is a basic process in self-analytic groups. Leadership emerges, further differentiated into instrumental and expressive types; individuals, on the basis of the match between their personal qualities and the group's needs, assume and are acknowledged as assuming differing roles. The process is affected by the fact that such ascribed characteristics as age, social class, sex, and physical attractiveness influence the assignment of individuals to particular roles. For example, the instrumental leadership of a group is likely to be provided by an older male. Working with several interracial study groups in college classrooms, I have been struck by the fact that race, like sex, is a powerful element affecting the selection of individuals for particular roles. Blacks and whites assume, or are assigned, distinctive positions within

This chapter is based in part on material presented in a paper which appeared in *Psychology Today* (September 1971). The author, while taking full responsibility for the interpretations presented here, wishes to acknowledge the contributions of many group members and observers. Chris Palames, Heath Millinger, Harold Davis, and especially Dwight Greene originally suggested many of the ideas included in this paper.

197

the social structure of the group—not surprisingly, since the realities and the shared fantasies of racial differences are so pervasive in American culture.

The theories presented here are based on participant observation in three self-analytic groups (each with fifteen to twenty-two members), sections of a class entitled Analysis of Interpersonal Behavior, taught at Wesleyan University in three successive semesters. Each section met for three hour-long sessions weekly, about forty meetings in all, with the primary purpose of learning about group process through studying its own interaction.[1] I was the instructor for groups I and II; two male undergraduates, one black and one white, were instructors for group III while I observed from behind the one-way mirror. The groups were not established with any special interest in interracial issues, but the presence of three to five black students in each section inevitably set in motion the race-related dynamics which are the subject of this chapter.

BASIC PATTERNS

The most striking recurring pattern in the groups was the emergence of the initially most active black male as unquestioned group leader. It seems extremely unlikely that in three successive groups leadership would be granted to one of the two or three black male members on the basis of chance alone. The black male leadership, acknowledged in group discussion, was confirmed by results from a sociometric questionnaire completed by members late in each semester. Each of the three black male leaders (Harmon in group I, Lester in group II, Ralph in group III) received the greatest number of nominations as "most influential" within his group. Members and observers of the groups also rated all group members both early and late in the term, using Bales' (1970) "interpersonal rating system."[2] In each group the black male leader received the

---

[1] For descriptions of readings, leadership style, and the observation room with one-way mirror, see Bales (1970), Mann (1967), and Slater (1966).

[2] Bales' scheme assigns each member a rating on three dimensions: Upward-Downward (status and power), Positive-Negative (likeability), and Forward-Backward (task commitment). In the groups described by Bales, *overall* leadership is most often attributed by group members to the member or members typed Upward-Positive-Forward (UPF). Such a member or

highest Upward rating early in the term, and by the end of the semester had increased his ascendancy over other group members.

The black leaders, late in their respective groups, received the following ratings: Harmon (group I): 9 Upward, 5 Negative, 1 Backward; Lester (group II): 9 Upward, 1 Negative, 1 Backward; Ralph (group III): 13 Upward, 1 Negative, 6 Backward. These black leaders, then, were perceived very similarly by their groups: as very powerful, slightly disliked, and not especially valuable in leading the group toward its collective goal of self-understanding. The black leaders' ratings fit Bales' "Upward-Negative-Backward" type, described as "advocating rugged individualism and gratification, the power to defy authority." This description captures something of the way in which the black leaders differed from the Upward-Positive-Forward leaders described as more common by Bales.

Each black male's ascendancy began early in his group, when in the first few meetings he rather dramatically laid the groundwork for his future role. Each of the three black leaders presented himself, very early in the group, as *aggressive,* as *marginally committed to the group enterprise,* and as *in some special relationship to the course instructor(s).*

> In the first meeting of group I, the usual awkward silence was broken by Harmon, who challenged the instructor assertively about the absence of certain black-related readings from the reading list. Harmon stated that he would provide a list of books that the other students might read. Harmon was absent, or observed from the observation room, for three of the first five meetings.
>
> In group II's initial meeting, Lester and the three black female members "happened" to sit together—Lester in the middle, with his arms over the backs of two of the girls' chairs. The other black male in this group, an African student, sat with a white acquaintance on the other side of the circle. Lester joked with and about "his women," addressed a number of direct questions to the instructor in a familiar tone, talked a

members are perceived as active and assertive in the group, as friendly and well liked, and as committed to the group task. The UPF member "advocates social solidarity and progress; the group as a whole."

great deal, questioned the group purposes. He asserted that he planned to bring beer to the next meeting, and he urged everyone to sit back, relax, and have a good time, not taking it all too seriously.

In the initial meeting of group III—after a long period of silence and some uncomfortable general discussion by others about doubts of the leaders' willingness to protect members "in case something erupts," and feelings of being in an experiment—Ralph stated firmly that *he* did not feel like a guinea pig. He described the course as "a great opportunity." Later in the first meeting, he turned to a white male who had spoken at length, accusing him of triviality and alleging that the distinctions made were all artificial. In the second session, Ralph amplified and clarified some of the black instructor's remarks, which others had found incomprehensible, and interpreted the behavior of several white members as indicating dependency or fear. Twice during these meetings, Ralph lay down on the floor and closed his eyes during the discussions, feigning sleep.

In each case, it seemed to me and to the observers that the black male was, like other members, actually quite apprehensive about the impression he was making, anxious about the possible danger of future attack, and unsure about what the group was supposed to do in the absence of direction by the instructor. While most members dealt with initial anxieties through silence, through expressing discomfort, or through introducing extremely abstract topics unrelated to the group, the black leader took the alternative approach of devaluing the whole enterprise while demonstrating with bravado his ability to confront the situation and the instructor.

As group development continued, the black male leader's role emerged with greater clarity. The role common to the three black leaders had the following characteristics: (1) demonstrating aggressive potential vis-à-vis whites (for example, launching at least one strong verbal attack on one or more white members, usually for their racism or white liberalism); (2) displaying ease about sexuality (joking sexual references, casual physical contact with the black girls, bringing records and suggesting that the group dance); (3) anti-intellectualism (attacks on the group discussions as "trivial, abstract bullshit"); (4) marginality (frequent unexplained ab-

sences, sitting outside the group circle, sleeping during sessions);
(5) presuming unilaterally a special relationship with the instructor
(Ralph took the black instructor's chair during his absence, addressed in-jokes to the black instructor, and characteristically served
as interpreter of both instructors' enigmatic remarks; Lester was
much more familiar, seductive, and casual with me than were other
members; Harmon persisted in attempts to engage me in one-to-one
conversation, and was more direct than other members in expres-
ing criticisms of me and the course.) While the black male leaders
were similar to other members in their desire to establish a close and
special relationship to the instructor(s), they approached the in-
structor(s) with an atypical directness and confidence early in the
group. The black leaders were also alike in that they refrained from
attacking or disagreeing with other black members of the groups.

These similarities in the behavior of the three black leaders
were especially striking for two reasons: (1) The three individuals
involved were different from one another in personality, academic
interests, and ideology as manifested outside the group. In social
situations and in other classes, Harmon was a "straight," upwardly
mobile, hard-working student. Lester might be described as a soci-
able, conservative, somewhat anxious playboy. Ralph was a creative, intellectual, and well-organized individual, more involved than
the other two with the ideology of Black Power. In the light of these
differences, it was surprising that these three young men assumed
such similar roles in their respective groups. (2) The black male
leader role appeared to be played only intermittently, and with a
good deal of ambivalence, by the three individuals. In line with his
particular personality characteristics and personal goals in the
group, each of the three displayed characteristics that frequently
conflicted directly with the role of black male leader. For example,
Harmon in several sessions confessed directly his feelings of weakness and vulnerability, and stressed his intense desire for close personal relations with other group members. Lester attempted to lead
several discussions on course readings, urging that the group take
the intellectual aims of the course more seriously; he also consistently
disavowed any interest in leadership, and seemed dismayed when
members emphasized his leadership role. Within group III, Ralph
was often the major advocate of group analysis and commitment to

the group, and was the most candid member regarding emotions experienced during meetings. When a white group member expresses this much discomfort with, and behavior discrepant with, his initial leadership role, his role is generally modified with the passage of time. What was striking was the persistence of the black male leader role, even in the face of such ambivalence on the part of its occupants.

Before we speculate on the reasons for this persistence, it is essential to consider the equally striking similarities in the three groups in the roles assumed by the other black men, the black women, the white women, and the white men.

The most salient reaction of the other black male group members was loyalty to the black leader. In group I, the other two black male members (there were no black women in this group) seldom directly questioned, interrupted, or disagreed with Harmon during the entire semester, although his obstructionism frequently appeared to irritate them as much as it did others, and although they did not particularly respect or agree with Harmon outside the group. In this case, the black males chose a path of somewhat withdrawn autonomy within the group, participating unconflictedly on issues of personal interest to them but leaving to Harmon the task of dealing directly with the white members. In groups II and III, the single other black male member took a definitely subordinate role on occasions when the black male leader was present in the group, becoming more vocal in his absence though never in opposition to the black male leader's ideas. In summary, it appeared that the other black male members in these groups felt constrained to be loyal to the black male leader but within this context experienced little pressure from the group to behave in any particular way.

Tentatively (since there were no black women in group I, three in group II, and only one in group III), I would describe the black women as ambivalently loyal to the black male leader. On one hand, they gave many indications of direct support, especially early and very late in the group: sitting beside the black leader, exchanging jokes and whispers during group sessions, directly defending his views. At the same time, however, and in contrast to the behavior of the black men as described above, the black women seemed interested in establishing closer relationships with white members. Especially when the black male leader was absent, black girls expressed a desire for greater openness in the group or engaged in personal interchange with individual white members. Occasionally, the black women even undercut the black male leader's position more directly, as if to express to whites that the group was taking the black leader more seriously than it should. In group II, for example, Arlette, the most active black girl, on several occasions asked Lester whether he was actually as self-confident as he seemed. It appeared that the black women leaned in two possibly conflicting directions within the group. On the one hand, they supported the black male leader, presumably to retain his protection against possible danger from whites. As one of the girls stated to me later, "I always felt safe in the group, knowing that Lester was there to take the heat off if necessary." Other motives for supporting the black male leader were perhaps to affirm black solidarity and to protect the black male leader at points where they accurately sensed that his bravado concealed underlying vulnerability. On the other hand, at times the black women seemed to seek to detach themselves temporarily from the black male leader (whose weaknesses they sensed more perceptively than did most whites), in order to seek friendly or even sexualized relationships with other group members.

The primary reaction of the white females to the black male leader was ambivalent fascination. Although the white girls, in agreement with the rest of the group, rated the black leaders slightly negatively on the Bales ratings, they were striking in the amount of attention and positive interaction they addressed to the black male leaders. In group I, four of the five white girls chose as one of their topics for course papers Harmon's role in the group. (The only male who chose to write on Harmon's role was Harmon himself.) In group III, one of the white girls was virtually silent, but the other, Marilyn, addressed many of her remarks to Ralph directly.

> In one early session, Marilyn told a long story about her sleeping with a boy on the first date and being subsequently rejected. Ralph avowed that a girl who was so easy deserved to be dropped. Marilyn subsequently alternated between attacking Ralph for his heartlessness and unresponsiveness to women, and sympathizing with him as a victim of white racism. "I can understand why you are so bitter, in the light of what you have

suffered," she said—over Ralph's protests that she did not understand him at all. Ralph insisted that Marilyn really wanted to "lay with a black man," which Marilyn vehemently denied. The two established a pattern of excited hostile interchange, evoked whenever sexuality was a topic of discussion in the group.

In group II, Cathy, the most active white girl, expressed great liking and admiration for Lester.

In session 20, the group arranged the chairs in two parallel rows facing one another, but with Ms. Winter at the head of the line. Members held hands, looked directly at one another, and joked about sex and about "expressing our true feelings." After one male shook hands with all those members he said he respected, Cathy got up and kissed Lester. There was much giggling and confusion; Cathy insisted that she felt nothing special for Lester, but wanted to express her love for the entire group. A little later, Lester moved his chair to the head of the line to sit beside Ms. Winter, and made personal joking remarks until she visibly reacted, in contrast to her usual impassiveness in the group. The group joked that a marriage between Lester and Ms. W. had taken place.

As can be inferred from the last example, I was also involved as a white woman in the patterns of reaction to the black male leader. Despite attempts to be scrupulously impassive, I found that my greatest difficulties in remaining objective and uninvolved were in relation to the black male leaders of the respective groups. I confronted Harmon's obstructionism directly on several occasions in group I; at the same time, I reacted overpositively to his written work. I found it almost impossible to deal impassively with Lester's friendly approaches outside sessions of group II; and I realized, while observing group III, that I was gratified by the frequent indications of Ralph's awareness of me as an audience. Awareness of my own reactions was one of the first salient clues for the eventual recognition of the reaction patterns being described here.

It can be readily inferred from the foregoing material that sexual attraction was a prominent element in the white female reaction to the black male leader. In all three groups, however, this element was consistently denied by all participants in the interactions. My own sometimes exaggerated attention to the black male leaders in the respective groups was never commented on by group members, although in other contexts members were highly sensitive to possible favoritism. Denial of white female sexuality was seen most directly in group I, where a lovely, childish-looking, extremely reticent married girl was the white female acknowledged by the group as most involved with the black male leader, while the roles played vis-à-vis Harmon by the four other more active or openly sexual female members were ignored. In groups II and III, none of the female members lent themselves so appropriately to this "pure white female" role (Smith, 1963); yet denial of the white girls' sexuality in relation to the black leader was equally prominent.

The dominant reaction of the white male group members to the black male leader was frustrated impotence, although white men were in a strong numerical majority in all three groups. In each group, one or two white men assumed the loyal role previously described as characteristic of the other black members, agreeing with the black male leader and even defending his right to attack white members, including themselves. The more typical white male reaction, however, was a somewhat unwilling but helpless acceptance of the black male's sexual and aggressive primacy in the group. In groups I and II, the white males' impotence was expressed primarily through their confessions of continued and extreme sexualized dependency on me (it should be noted that I was visibly pregnant during group I). The men took the role of little boys still so tied to the mother figure that assertive independent action seemed impossible. In contrast, the black male leaders in these two groups, as noted earlier, demonstrated their concern with my reaction through more direct approaches and confrontations. (It is an interesting question whether the black male leaders were actually as dependent as the white men but merely expressed it differently or whether they actually experienced less sexualized dependency toward me, possibly because of a less direct generalization to me of their feelings toward their own black mothers.) In group III, with the two male leaders, the white males' impotence was expressed less in relation to dependency issues but was prominent in other ways. White males persisted in endless abstract discussions, even though they agreed with

Ralph (and the instructors) that this talk accomplished little. They found it difficult to propose definite courses of action for the group. Although there were signs that they found the female members, and especially the black girls, attractive, they expressed the opinion that sexualized relationships between male and female members would cause great problems within the group.

Gradually, in each of the three groups, a type of white male leadership did emerge in contrast to the black male's anti-intellectual sexual and aggressive primacy. The three groups' white male leaders (sometimes more than one individual within a group) achieved their influence through their ability to give support to other members, to create a climate within which intimacy might be possible, and, especially, to express and analyze whatever anxieties and concerns were salient at a particular phase in group life but were difficult for members to reveal. For example, the white male leader in each group was most dependent during the group's early phase, most articulate about fears of aggression during the subsequent leadership struggle, and most direct in revealing sexual fears when intimacy was the group concern. In Bion's terms, the typical white male leader possessed great valency for the group, serving to embody and articulate the group's current irrational concerns (Bion, 1959, pp. 116–117). In stereotype, the white male leader was gentle, intelligent, unassertive, sympathetic, and sensitive.

In all three groups, the white males and especially the white male leaders were under a good deal of pressure from some of the women to assert themselves more directly. As Slater (1966) notes, women in self-analytic college groups typically talk more directly about sex and appear more interested in sexually related interaction than do the more inhibited men. In the groups described here, female pressure for more direct expression of sexuality was directed particularly toward the white men. Both black and white women urged the white men to break their dependency on me and to "fight back" against the preeminence of the black male leader. In groups II and III, incidents occurred in which an individual white male did not defend himself when challenged or criticized by the black male leader; the women referred to such passivity as "pitiful" or "disgusting." As suggested above, the white women seemed uncomfortable with their sexual feelings for the black leader; stronger actions by the white men would presumably have made it easier for them to focus their attentions on the white men instead. The black women's overtures to the white men were more subtle and restrained but equally noticeable within the group.

The frustrated impotence associated with the white male roles is well communicated in the following transcribed conversation from group III. Chuck, one of the white male leaders, began by defending Marilyn against one of Ralph's disparaging attacks.

CHUCK: You're talking about Marilyn's fear and Marilyn's desire in an animal kind of way—I think you're seeing too much aggressiveness in the sex, too much competitiveness.

RALPH: I think it *is*. I think it's a competitive thing.

CHUCK: Well, you're putting it in extremes. When I said I felt some kind of sexual attraction for Karen [the black girl], by that I didn't mean—I realize now that I'm trying to elevate my own feelings—but I didn't see it as a carnal, lascivious kind of thing, but rather just sort of masculine-feminine, the niceties of it. You can appreciate a girl because of her femininity, not really because she is a carnal, sexual object. Do you know what I mean?

RALPH: Yes, but . . .

CHUCK: Well, like I say, there's a possibility that I'm covering up my real feelings. But I think you're seeing sex as too competitive. I just sort of accept my own level of sexual performance, because, you know, you're only going to be able to run the hundred so fast no matter how hard you train; you might as well accept it. Your abilities to make one woman happy aren't entirely limited to that one aspect, so what you lack in one place you make up in another. . . . What I'm saying is that I have to accept me at a certain level of performance, whatever that may be, because, like I say, you can only be so good. Then, for my own ego, what I try to do is fulfill myself in other areas. So that you don't go around worrying, "Am I as good as somebody else?"

RALPH: I'm not saying that you're consciously worried . . .

The situation of the white men can be described from another perspective, using Bales' typology. In all-white groups at Harvard and Wesleyan, a differentiation of leadership into instrumental
(UF and UPF) and expressive (UP and UPB) types is typical;
male leaders of both types are likely to emerge. In the interracial
groups, as we have seen, the black male leader tends to occupy the
Backward leadership position and tends to be rated Negative (a
feature not common in all-white groups). The white men, in the
interracial groups, take on the Forward leadership; but their ratings
are more Positive and somewhat less Upward than in all-white
groups. A white male leader coexisting in a group with a UNB
black male leader appears to assume a less dominant, and more
softened, version of the forward leadership role.

DISCUSSION

Having described the ways that race functioned in relation
to role differentiation in this series of groups, I will consider two
more general questions: Why did blacks and whites assume these
particular roles? Why did the groups find the race-linked structure
difficult to examine and to change?

We can first speculate on the reasons the black male leaders
as individuals acted, early in each group, to present themselves as
aggressive, sexually free, and marginally committed to the group
enterprise. One interesting possibility here is that behavior which
would not be seen as strikingly aggressive or sexualized within the
black ghetto subculture (from which all three of these black males
came) was simply perceived as such by the white members (and
by me), in the context of white middle-class norms for "appropriate
behavior in classroom groups." Another possibility is that the black
males, feeling unsafe early in group life, had available to them a
different repertory of defensive and self-protective behavior than
did the white students faced with the same threatening situation.
The whites dealt with their initial fears through anxious withdrawal, yea-saying, and abstract intellectualism; the black male
leaders, equally threatened, chose to defend themselves by assertion,
aggression, and sexual openness of a kind known to be intimidating
to white college students. The black leaders' disparagement of "intellectual bullshit" perhaps reflected their special feelings of vul-

nerability within the white university. As Ralph put it, in a later meeting of group III: "In certain situations, when you have a bunch of intellectuals standing around with that mentality—how does a black dude proceed, baby? He has to be pretty careful."

The black male leaders' initial tentativeness of commitment to the group can similarly be viewed as an effective defensive and controlling posture within the potentially threatening group situation. In the groups described here, "liberal" whites made up the majority, yet were dependent on the blacks in one important way: the whites could not establish the close, trusting interracial relationships they desired (and which would alleviate their guilt) without the cooperation of black members. It seems possible that the black male leaders accurately sensed that they possessed as a powerful resource the power to withhold their trust, keeping whites waiting until such time as blacks might choose to establish relationships on their own terms. Levy (1968) suggests similar dynamics among black and white workers in the southern civil rights movement.

So the black male leaders, for these or other personal reasons, acted early in their groups in a way which invited group members to cast them in the black male leader role. Later in group life, as has been noted, these leaders displayed ambivalence, discomfort, and behavior discrepant with the roles; yet the members' perceptions of them, and the assumption by other members of roles complementary to theirs, worked to stabilize the group structure and maintain the black male leaders in their roles. Redl's concept of "group psychological role suction" applies: "Under certain conditions a specific group situation seems to have an amazing power to 'suck' individuals into performing certain tasks, even though they may not have been strongly inclined in that direction; these are tasks which are important for the comfort, or which respond to the motivational or organizational needs, of the group" (Redl, 1959b, p. 83).

What possible motives exist within the *group* for locking the black male leader into his role and consolidating the other role patterns that have been described? We can first note the simple fact that in a group with a white middle-class majority, sexuality and aggression are likely to be experienced as bad, dangerous, and ego-alien, generating a collective pressure to deny such qualities or to project them away. In all-white groups, the leader is sometimes the object of such projections (being seen as overbearing, dangerous, preoccupied with sex, and the like). In a racially mixed group, the behavior of the black male leader prevents the group from denying the existence of sex and aggression early in its life. As an alternative, projection may be especially strongly employed; the black male is perceived as strikingly "other" and is assigned all the bad, dangerous qualities that members do not wish to acknowledge in themselves.

It is at this point that the group becomes involved with a network of racial stereotypes and shared myths about blackness and whiteness—myths consciously rejected by most group members yet evidently present as models to which the actual events of the group are fitted as members construct their interpretations of what is going on. These myths, though consciously denied, appear as important as the actual group events in determining members' interpretations of one another's roles (see Dunphy, 1968).

Ralph, groping for an understanding of the ways that such myths had constrained his own actions and the reactions to him in group III, attempted to articulate some of the underlying themes:

RALPH: Like I came in here looking like the average black dude, and you have the average white dude's conceptions of how I'm supposed to be. And you came in with the average white hang-ups in terms of physical aggressiveness . . . I don't know about verbal aggressiveness. And I like represented a totally different thing; I represented more or less a supermasculine thing, which I haven't understood yet. . . . You admired my aggressiveness, even though you didn't want to, it wasn't like a comfortable thing for you.

JOHN: Are you talking to me specifically? [John is a white member who had been under attack by Ralph earlier.]

RALPH: I'm talking to you and the rest of the white cats with you. At the same time that you were accepting what you saw in me consciously, unconsciously you were rejecting it. Because to really truly accept it meant to reject what *you* probably were, what you probably see yourself as being, which is a white person. And you were looking at me in the same way that every white cat looked at a black dude, in terms of physical aggressive-

ness and stuff like this. I don't think that you ever saw
me in terms of mental type things, in terms of my mind,
I don't think you looked at me in those terms at all. I
think that as a result you went to Chuck [a white leader,
actually much less active and insightful in intellectual
analysis than Ralph] for that particular type thing. I
kinda like noticed that, and sort of consciously tried to
explore the thing in more depth by slanting things I
said in terms of the way I thought you perceived me.
Then I stopped, and it kept on anyway.

Ralph went on to recall accurately the group's earlier discussions of
sexuality, in which members had focused their analysis around differences between Ralph's reactions and their own. He concluded:
"It's really like I'm a part of the group, but yet I'm not a part of
the group . . . that the white populace make up one part, and I
make up, and probably Karen [the black woman], a distinct different part of the group."

The myths operating in these groups, tangled and frequently
contradictory, can be tentatively identified as follows: (1) the myth
of the black male "supermasculine menial" (Cleaver, 1967)—aggressive, sexually powerful, intellectually inadequate; (2) the myth
of black unity in hostile opposition to whites; (3) the myth of whites
as impotent except through a sterile, abstract intellectualism; and
(4) the myth of white power to destroy, with the accompanying
myth that each white malevolently wishes to humiliate blacks and
perpetuate his dominant position. That these myths contradict one
another only increases the complexity of their influence, and their
resistance to change. White reaction to the black leader, for example, is based simultaneously upon two opposing perceptions.
Most of the time, whites relate to the black leader as the supermasculine menial, so strong and powerful that submission to him is the
only possible response. At other times, however, the group seems
covertly to be protecting and supporting the black leader in his
position, as though he were so weak and vulnerable that he would
be destroyed if his role were challenged. Behavior by the black
leader which suggests strength *or* weakness is used in the group to
strengthen one or the other of the mythic interpretations.

Such myths, once activated, were distressingly self-perpetuating within these groups. Members' actions reinforced their distorted perception of situations, even when this was the last thing consciously desired, as in the following example from group II.

When three of the five black members, including Lester, happened to be absent on the day after an incident of campus racial tension, the white members wildly and unquestioningly assumed that all five blacks had explicitly agreed to boycott the group. In fact, Arlette, the black woman who did attend, was in tears for the first half of the meeting, directly expressing at one point her despair at the lack of communication between black and white members as all sat in virtual silence. When her communication was ignored, and the whites continued to act as if the blacks were in collusion against them, Arlette abruptly left the room. White members gave no overt reaction to the departure, despite the instructor's comment that feelings about it were surely present; finally the remaining black member left too.

Through these events, this group's myths of black unity, of black hostility to whites, and of white impotence in the face of strong emotion took on even greater subsequent power. In any group, of course, inaccurate and irrational expectations are present, shaping and constraining ongoing behavior; clear perception of what is actually going on in the here-and-now is always hindered by expectations brought in from the past. Yet the myths described here take on an unusual degree of power because, having been formed in America over centuries, they are *shared* in similar form by blacks and whites alike. They take on reality as a collective, mutually assented-to network of projections by all members upon all others.

Why are these racially related myths so resistant to change? The purpose of a self-analytic group is to examine the data of its own interaction, to bring just such shared irrational assumptions to light, in order to mitigate against the distortions they create in the ongoing interaction. Members of the groups described here made considerable progress in recognizing and examining their collective projections in areas of dependency, authority, and sexuality. Yet the myths related to race seemed especially difficult to face squarely, especially for whites. Only in group III, in the session from which

Ralph's remarks are quoted above, did the racially related material become an extended topic of analysis; even here, most white members seemed to find Ralph's ideas obscure and incomprehensible. The myths about black male leadership were accepted as real. Countervailing data were ignored, suppressed, forgotten.

Several rather simple sources of the difficulty may be mentioned initially. First, and perhaps most important, the course instructors—because of their preference for interpretations involving the whole group rather than the actions of, or reactions to, specific individuals—gave members little help in analyzing race-related dynamics. And, as has been suggested, I participated unknowingly in some of the same projections as the members, further contributing to the influence of these projections in the group. Second, both blacks and whites would have suffered in tangible though different ways had the racial myths come to light. Whites would have been called on to give up their positive self-perceptions as tolerant and unprejudiced, while blacks would have been more individually vulnerable within the group once the irrational attributions to them of power had been dispelled. The white men would have had to face the fact that white female attentions were directed mainly to blacks. White women would have had to acknowledge the sexual element in their supposedly altruistic and protective interest in the black men. The black men would have been called on to recognize their own participation in sexualized interaction with the white women, in contrast to their consciously held "black is beautiful" values and their consciously stated disavowal of attraction to anything white. The black women would have had to risk rejection in revealing more directly their interest in closeness to the white members.

In addition, the race-related issues posed threats to group solidarity. As the semester progressed and increasingly anxiety-arousing material emerged in the group sessions, concern for group stability and mutual solidarity was expressed more and more by the majority of group members. As was noted above, the black male leaders in the groups indicated from time to time, through absences and withdrawal, the possible tentativeness of their commitment to the group. Subtle threats to leave, or actual absences, were especially prominent when the black male leaders felt that their personal security in the group was being threatened. Members seemed to fear that examination of "the race issue" would uncover the mythic white malevolence, putting unbearable pressure on the black male leader (here seen as helpless against the all-powerful whites). The collective fear seemed to be that the group's tenuously achieved solidarity was insufficient to assure the black male leader's commitment; as pressure mounted, he would leave, and the group would "fall apart" once and for all. Insight into race-related dynamics was surely not worth the price of loss of group solidarity.

Another allied source of resistance can be mentioned, based on the fact that solidarity of blacks and whites within the group appeared to be deeply desired by many members as an expression of the pairing assumption (Bion, 1959)—the unconscious fantasy that the purpose of the group was for the races to come together, be friends, and achieve intimacy. In this fantasy, the group would "succeed" only if the divisions and tensions in outside society could be overcome and some new form of racial understanding could be born. Some white members and some black female members seemed strongly committed to this only partially articulated hope for the group. To the extent that the hope for racial utopia was maintained, the group found it discouraging and depressing to look directly at the fears, distortions, and differences which did in fact characterize actual interracial relationships in the group. Of course, the pairing hope for interracial understanding would not necessarily preclude examination of racial fears and irrationalities. But in the groups described here, members seemed to hope for a more magical coming together, in which divisive tensions would simply disappear if they were kept out of awareness.

Finally, it seems possible that the race-related myths described here could not readily be examined by group members because they implied a radical threat to the members' sense of existence as autonomous individuals. Slater (1966, pp. 169–181) has persuasively characterized group interaction as involving a continuing tension between the opposing processes of personal boundary maintenance and personal boundary loss. Experienced fully, each of these two processes is infinitely attractive and infinitely terrifying: boundary maintenance implies autonomy and self-possession, yet isolation; boundary loss implies intimacy and communion, yet a potentially frightening loss of the sense of individual self. Slater further proposes that Bion's three basic assumptions (Bion, 1959) represent members' experiences at different points on the continuum between boundary maintenance and boundary loss. In a pairing group, individual members' boundaries are experienced as relatively intact; in a dependency group, members' boundaries are more deeply threatened by the pull toward dependent union with the instructor. Slater conceives of Bion's fight/flight group as posing (or expressing) the most radical degree of threat to individual boundary maintenance. The group operates with the basic assumptions of fight and/or flight when individual identity is threatened so completely that members feel in danger of being overwhelmed, being swept away within the group, losing themselves.

It has been my observation that the abortive race-related discussions which *did* occur in the groups described here invariably took place within Bion's modalities of fight or flight. As has been noted several times, flight was the black male leaders' most consistent style of coping with tension. The group II session described above, involving black absences, provides further examples of the group's use of flight when "the race issue" was made unavoidably salient (here, by events on the campus). In this session, some black members were in flight through physical absence, while the white members fled from attending to or reacting to Arlette's despair. Equally prominent, in these groups' primitive efforts to deal with race, were exceptionally tension-filled "fight" sessions. Typically the black male leaders, confronting one or more whites, would become increasingly aggressive, evoking in turn all members' flight from the topic with expressions of fear about attack, injury, or destruction of the group.

The regularity with which these groups expressed interracial concerns in the fight/flight modality may possibly reflect the members' sense that this issue threatened in especially primitive ways their existence as distinct individuals. Corroborating evidence comes from group II, during the extremely painful and depressed period in which campus-wide racial concern forced consciousness of "the race issue" upon the group for several sessions, including and subsequent to the one described above. Black and white members expressed feelings of inability even to consider the implications of the racial differences present in the group (despite, in this case, the

continued efforts of the instructor to draw attention to the issue).
Members' expressed anxiety seemed to center on the fact that, as
one girl put it, "What I am as a person doesn't count for anything
now. I am *nothing but* a white—I can't break out of it, no matter
what I say or do."

An even more vivid example occurred in group I. Manifestly
in reaction to a remark by a white member (but actually, probably,
in an effort to reestablish his position in the group after a series of
absences), Harmon launched an extended black-militant ideological
tirade. Instead of countering with arguments in their defense, as he
had evidently expected, the whites reacted with expressions of guilt.
Brian, the white leader of the group, unquestioningly accepted Harmon's remarks as justly critical of himself (ignoring completely a
number of past incidents of expressed solidarity between Harmon
and himself, within and outside the group). Brian went on and on
in mournful recital of his blindness and insensitivity, ending with
a request to Harmon to deliver the final blow.

BRIAN: I *am* a racist, Harmon, aren't I?

HARMON: Don't ask *me*, man! You're a man, you can speak for
          yourself. You know who you are. *Are* you a racist?

BRIAN: Well, I never really thought so . . .

HARMON: Well, then, don't just take what I say. Someone calls
          me a motherfucker, I think, "Have I fucked any
          mothers? No, I haven't!" So I say to that guy, "You're
          full of shit. I'm no motherfucker." But you're letting
          me lay anything on you. You know yourself, man.
          . . . Stand up for yourself.

Here Harmon, appalled at the boundary loss that his remarks have
engendered in Brian, attempts to restore for Brian his temporarily
lost frame of reference as an autonomous individual.

Thus, the vivid sense of individual boundary loss due to
being subsumed into the "white" group evoked intense depression
and anxiety. At other times in group life, of course, members had
operated with a similar though less disturbing sense of boundary loss
due to felt identification with other groupings—as males or females,

as children vis-à-vis the instructor, or as nearly anonymous parts of the group as a whole. It seemed, however, that sensed loss of individuality within either the "black" or the "white" group was notably more painful than were these other identifications. For sensitive Americans in this period of history, both blackness and whiteness can easily be felt as profoundly *bad*. To be "nothing but" black is to be lost within a group that has been oppressed and hated by the majority, powerless to act in its own defense. To be "nothing but" white is to be the guilty agent of past and present racial injustices.[3] Each instance of heightened consciousness of race within the group seemed to sweep away, for the individual, a sense of his *individuality*. The resulting sense of powerlessness was too great to tolerate except through frenzied fighting or terrified flight. These groups continued to work together as well as they did through the eventual reestablishment of collective defenses against recognizing or talking about race as an ongoing factor in their midst. This solution, of course, left the myths largely intact.

CONCLUSIONS

Finally, two remaining issues will be considered: possible limitations of the generality of the dynamics described here; and the implications of these findings for furthering effective work in interracial groups.

A number of possible limitations should be briefly mentioned. First, members of the groups described here came largely from the "white liberal" upper middle class; other group leaders (Lane K. Conn, personal communication; Marvin Fraenkel, personal communication) have suggested to me that lower-class whites might behave more assertively in relation to blacks. Second, it seems likely that the dynamics outlined here are visible only in groups in which whites do not outnumber blacks too markedly. In similar groups with only one or two black members, the blacks' greater

---

[3] See also Levy's (1968) description of the effort of whites to maintain a sense of "personal exemption" as they became increasingly aware of blacks' negative feelings about whites in southern settings. Whites went to extreme lengths to maintain the idea that they as individuals were not perceived negatively. When this notion could no longer be maintained, whites typically fled from the situation.

guardedness in interaction allows whites to gloss over the presence of the uncomfortable interracial issues. Third, in all the groups described here, I played an important role either as leader or observer. One cannot overlook the possibility that the patterns described are unique to white-female-led groups, or even perhaps to my groups alone. Fourth, members enter self-analytic college groups with few if any initial differences in ascribed status and potential for group power. In this regard, the self-analytic group represents a very imperfect analogy to groups in the larger society, where whites often possess disproportionate resources and potential for influence. Finally, the phenomena described here may represent merely a fulfillment of the instructors' increasingly well-formulated expectations about racial dynamics within groups.

If the findings described here prove valid despite these possible objections, it is important to ask whether the material presented has implications for increasing the effectiveness of other interracial work groups. The intense resistance experienced as the self-analytic groups struggled to examine their own internal racial dynamics is not encouraging in this respect. But despite the group's recurring collusion to keep painful race-related awareness from consciousness and to perpetuate interaction based on myth, some individual group members did gain liberating insight into the operation of the myths in their own behavior. Many of the black members, in particular, became sensitive to the ways in which their own actions were constrained by these irrationalities in others and in themselves. Such awareness, although seldom elaborated in the group meetings, was prominent in the course papers written by most black and some white members late in each group's life. To the extent, then, that individuals became conscious of the racial myths in themselves, and of the operation of these myths in the group, perceptions did become less stereotyped and freedom of individual action was increased. As in an individual psychoanalysis, insight led to no magic dissolution of the force of the irrational in behavior; but some slight and gradual changes were apparent as awareness was worked through. For example, Ralph in group III was able, through his articulation of some of the mythic material, to help other group members regard him in a more complex and accurate light.

The precondition for such insight appeared to be, not surprisingly, the existence of a sufficient degree of trust and group solidarity to give members support as the painful insights were worked through. Sufficient support for the black members appeared especially crucial in this regard within the groups described here, perhaps because blacks were in an initial position of disadvantage as a minority within a primarily white course in a primarily white university. For example, the presence of Don, the black instructor in group III, seemed helpful in two specific ways in allowing Ralph to move beyond the black male role to a greater extent than had Harmon and Lester in earlier groups. First, the black instructor was perceived as a direct source of support: Ralph was less defensive and marginal than the other two black male leaders, probably because, as he said early in the group, "Don would be loyal to the blacks in the group if need be." Second, the black instructor represented for all group members a model of black male ability to function in other than the supermasculine menial role. The presence of the intellectually effective black instructor as a central figure undoubtedly made possible Ralph's commitment to the intellectual and analytical goals of the group, and the other members' at least partial willingness to acknowledge him in this role.

If conditions for trust and solidarity can be established to an even greater degree in future groups, members may feel safe enough to examine and partly overcome their myth-laden fearful initial perceptions of one another. In groups in the future, it may be possible to explore further the extent to which the paralyzing race-related myths can be brought to full awareness, and group members liberated from their constraints.

9

An Investigation of Group Reaction
to Central Figures

JOHN W. RINGWALD

*T*his chapter offers a typology of roles based on a statistical analysis of group reaction to central figures in two self-analytic classroom groups. The present study is in many respects similar in theoretical perspective and methodology to earlier investigations by Dunphy (1964; this volume, Chapter 12) and by Mann and his colleagues (Mann, 1967; Mann and others, 1970; B. Ringwald and others, 1971; Gibbard, this volume, Chapter 10). The most important theoretical assumption in the current study is derived from Melanie Klein's work, particularly the following statements: "The need to control others can to some extent be explained by a deflected drive to control parts of the self. When these parts have been projected excessively into another person, they can only be controlled by controlling the other person" (Klein, 1946). Throughout this study, I have assumed that role differentia-

The present study analyzes data originally collected by Graham Gibbard and John Hartman. I am also grateful to Richard Mann and to Richard Cabot, who, working with Gibbard, Hartman, and Mann, wrote a series of computer programs which made it possible to reduce the original 30,000 lines of data to manageable proportions.

tion in groups is in part an attempt by group members to resolve internal conflicts by projecting those conflicts onto central persons whose behavior is influenced by role pressures. In other words, I view role differentiation partly as an external dramatization of widely shared internal conflicts, with actors and actresses accepting the roles assigned them with greater or lesser enthusiasm.

The methodological focus in this study is on similarities in *what was actually said to central figures,* rather than on what active individuals said (as in the previous studies by Mann and his colleagues) or on role images derived from retrospective written impressions of participating members (as in Dunphy's work). In so doing, I have attempted to develop a better understanding of the group forces which influenced the group's perception of and reaction to individuals, and of the forces leading to nonrational role specialization.

GENERAL METHODOLOGY

The raw data for this research were generated by the act-by-act scoring of the ongoing interaction of two self-analytic classroom groups, described in more detail elsewhere in this collection (see Chapters 7, 10, 13; for descriptions of similar self-analytic groups, see Mills, 1964; Slater, 1966; Mann, 1967).

The scoring system used to score the group interaction was the process analysis scoring system (or PASS), Gibbard and Hartman's (1973a) modification of Mann's (1966, 1967) member-leader scoring system. Twelve of the eighteen categories of PASS were used in the data analyses for this study: four categories recording different expressions of hostility (moving against, disagreeing, withdrawing, guilt-inducing); four noting expressions of affection (making reparation, identifying, agreeing, moving toward); two noting power concerns (showing submission, showing dominance); and two focusing on the ego state of the speaker (expressing distress, denying distress). Space does not permit a thorough presentation of this system or a discussion of the statistical components of the methodology. The interested reader can find extended discussions of the categories, scorer reliability, and other details elsewhere (Gibbard and Hartman, 1973a; Hartman and Gibbard, this volume, Chapter 7; Mann, 1966, 1967; Mann and others, 1970).

My strategy was to utilize the process analysis scoring system to achieve statistical summaries of the scores that individuals received as the objects of expression by other group participants. Several statistical procedures were used to identify individuals who were the objects of similar group reactions. First, the phi coefficient (see Hays, 1963, pp. 604–606; Mann, 1967; Hartman, 1969) was used to identify phases—that is, points in each group's development when the focus of attention tended to shift from one subset of individuals to another. Four such phases were delineated in each group. Phase summaries were then computed for all individuals who were the objects of at least fifteen "acts" in any phase.

The "acts" directed to the ten most central members in each group, plus the scores directed to the two leaders, comprised over 90 percent of the expressions directed to the twenty-two individuals in the groups. The standard scores of the phase summaries for each of the individuals in the groups were then collated to form the input for a cluster-analysis procedure developed by Kulik, Revelle, and Kulik (1970). For our purposes here, the most important thing to note is that two individuals are clustered together only if their profiles as objects of affective expression are similar for each of the four phases. In other words, to be included in the same cluster two individuals must be *the objects of the same feelings at the same point in the group's development*. To identify the distinguishing characteristics of each cluster, a cluster profile was constructed for each phase. Then the transcripts of the two groups were reread in order to determine what was actually said to the individuals whose session scores were similar to the cluster profiles for that phase.

This statistical treatment yielded six distinct clusters of participants who were objects of similar kinds of affective expression by other group members. They did not necessarily have similar interpersonal styles; in fact, some members included in the same cluster had interpersonal styles that appeared to be polar opposites. The clusters and the PASS categories which characterized the group's reaction to them are as follows: (1) *the anxious participators* (ranked first[1] as the object of disagreeing; last as the object of withdrawing, moving toward, showing submission, expressing distress,

[1] Rankings are based on summaries of acts directed to members of the cluster over all sessions.

denying distress); (2) *the respected enactors* (ranked first as the object of agreeing; last as the object of moving against, disagreeing, showing dominance); (3) *the sexual idols* (ranked first as the object of reparation, moving toward; last as the object of withdrawing); (4) *the leaders and the fall guy* (ranked first as the object of withdrawing, identifying, showing dominance, expressing distress, denying distress; last as the object of disagreeing, agreeing); (5) *the outsiders* (ranked first on no category; last as the object of reparation, identifying); (6) *the prophets* (ranked first as the object of moving against, guilt-inducing, showing submission; last on no category).

The question I have tried to answer with each cluster is: What dimensions help one to understand why this group of individuals elicited a similar reaction from the group as a whole? Thus, discussions of what individuals said and the functions they served for the group focus primarily on those features which elicited a reaction from the group characteristic of the cluster profile. The picture presented here is consequently a distilled one, intended to capture the essence of the *cluster pattern* rather than the individuals who comprise the cluster. In fact, no individual "belongs" exclusively to one cluster pattern. With the exception of the leaders, most individuals also show a similarity to one or more other cluster patterns in addition to the cluster to which they were assigned. It is as if each individual could and did play a number of roles in the group, with the primary focus being placed on the role which led to his or her inclusion in the cluster. Finally, for most clusters I have used member logs, written as part of the course requirements, as well as statements in class, to illustrate some of the problems created for individuals by the group's role image of them. Pseudonyms are used for all group members.

THE CLUSTERS

The Anxious Participators

The four women who comprised this cluster all took an active part in ensuring that group discussions kept moving. Two of the four members stated in their logs that their idea of a successful group was one in which members carried on stimulating discussions each week. But for the most part, they did not express or generate much excitement or sense of purpose within the group, and the predominant reaction to them was one of bland distance. The only category on which they are ranked first over all sessions is disagreeing, the most indirect and least personal expression of hostility scored in PASS. In fact, few strong feelings were expressed to them, and they rank last on five of the twelve categories used in the present study.

On the most general level, the somewhat distant reaction to them mirrored their own distance and ambivalence about involvement in the group. Vickie, the most active member in group 2, wrote in her log: "Either I feel the need to bounce my personality off of the group reflectors or I don't; either I am intellectually and, most importantly, emotionally drawn to a person or I am not; either a person makes me want to be a responsible listener and speaker or he doesn't."

Several component issues seemed to underlie their ambivalence about involvement in the group, and led to the high scores they received as objects of disagreement. First, they were more distressed than other group members by the lack of structure and by the leader's nondirective stance. One large block of expressions scored "disagreeing" occurred when more counterdependent group members objected to their expressions of distress about the unstructured situation and their preference for a more dependent relationship with the leader. Second, members of this cluster tended not to contribute concepts that pulled things together. They focused on small details; and, in attempting to raise relevant issues for group discussion, they often asked questions that invited disagreement—questions such as "Maybe you feel like . . ." or "Isn't it true that . . ." Reactions to such questions were frequently scored "disagreeing" as other members attempted to clarify themselves.

Members of this cluster were all quite ambivalent about the expression of feelings and the process of analyzing group interaction. They expressed concern about their vulnerability in the face of turbulent emotions, and commented on their fears that the "lid will blow off" the group. Although some of them wrote insightful, articulate analyses of the group interaction in their logs, all expressed an inability to comprehend underlying group forces, and related this sense of intellectual inefficacy to their fear that things would get out of control. Many reactions to them which were scored as "disagreeing" occurred in discussions of how deeply one should look at one's self and others. The following discussion involving Beatrice and Vickie, two members of this cluster, is one example:

BEATRICE: Lots of people grow up with no knowledge of psychology and live very well.

JOAN: They live and die, in other words.

AL: Like plants and mice.

BEATRICE: No, no, no.

VICKIE: They can be very happy.

AL: So can mice.

Hannah, the strongest opponent of expression and analysis in group 1, wrote in her log that she was opposed to the expression of personal feelings, that interpretation was "overdone" in the group, and that "maybe a little variety would change this." Many disagreements expressed to members of this cluster came from the leader and group members as they defended the analytic perspective or the validity of specific interpretations.

Finally, it should be noted that three of the four women who comprised this cluster were or had been married (one woman was separated from her husband). All announced this early in the group; and Vickie, in particular, stressed that she did not share the need for personal involvement that unmarried members might feel. The matronly image thus created eventually became an oppressive one, and the three married women attempted to shed the more constricting aspects of the role as they became more comfortable with other members. Vickie put it this way: "Being referred to as a mother bothered me. . . . I wanted to be referred to more as a girl . . . someone that was nice to talk to, nice to be with." Beatrice quickly noted that she felt the same way. Eileen, whose divorce was pending, had already asked Al if he had a girl friend, and said she was interested in a relationship with him. The reaction to this shift in their behavior can be seen in their scores in phase III (where the cluster received high scores on three affection categories—reparation, agreeing, and moving toward—and did not receive a high score on disagreeing); together, these scores comprise a profile indicative of flirtatiousness and support.

In summary, although their apprehensions kept them from making a more significant contribution to the group's sense of purpose and its definition of work, the anxious participators performed important group functions in raising issues, keeping the discussion moving, and expressing the distress experienced by a substantial number of the less vocal group members. Except for the drawbacks of being regarded as "matrons," their role in the group seemed to be consistent with their own image of themselves, and for the most part they did not seem to feel pressured by the group to be something they were not or to deny any aspect of themselves. The group's reaction to them was predominantly one of distance, except in phase III, when a more explicitly affectionate profile occurred.

The Respected Enactors

Although they spoke less frequently than the anxious participators, the members of this cluster (a woman and two men) tended to raise issues more directly and contributed more to a resolution of conflict and sense of purpose within the group. The group's reaction to them also lacked intensity, but the profile of scores for this cluster was more affectionate.

In general, they gave the impression of being more involved, more enthusiastic about their participation in the group, and less distressed than members of the previous cluster. Rather than stressing the need to have a stimulating discussion, they tended to emphasize their involvement in the group and their excitement about the intellectual tasks of observing and understanding group events. Nonetheless, they, too, tended to hold back. Although they were respected for their contributions and urged by other group members to take a more active leadership role, they restricted their participation to commentary on group events. Their leadership efforts rarely went beyond the point of demanding that group members stop to examine their assumptions.

Members of this cluster, in contrast to the anxious participators, tended to be accurate in their assessment of the feelings of others in the group. They were frequently blunt, and many of the expressions scored "agreeing" were little more than grudging acknowledgment that one's position had been correctly stated. In fact, in phase I their high scores on withdrawing occurred mainly as other members and the leader attempted to elude the main thrust of questions which were all too relevant. On the whole, however, the group seemed to appreciate this cluster's interpretations of group events, which frequently made the group seem more comprehensible and less frightening to the members. Their analyses were frequently turning points of sorts, in which other group members seemed to see the group in a new light, feel somewhat reassured, and move on. Several of the sessions in which they were the objects of high scores on agreeing involved such turning points. For example, Jeffrey, at a particularly difficult time in the group's history, brought in a tape recording of Bill Cosby's account of Noah and the Flood. The comic relief and Jeffrey's later comment that he viewed the leader more as Noah than as God allowed the group members to acknowledge their dependency on and gratitude to the leader. At the same time, they were able to assert that he was not a god, but a benevolent caretaker who shared their human foibles (for an extended discussion of this incident, see Hartman and Gibbard, Chapter 13).

Members of this cluster also offered a compromise position to many polarized debates, and their high scores on agreeing occurred partly because many times both protagonists agreed with the compromise position. This was particularly true at one point in group 2, when Vickie and Beatrice (two members of the anxious participators cluster) were arguing with Al about the desirability of defenses. Al contended that all defenses should be stripped away in the group, and Vickie and Beatrice both maintained that defenses are necessary to life and that people cannot cope with self-awareness. Joan took the position that although people could be hurt by questioning which threatened them, an exaggerated concern with hurting people might immobilize the group. Her compromise, supported by both sides, was to suggest that individuals who felt anxious should say so, and not be forced to submit to questions which increased their anxiety.

The ability of members of this cluster to contribute insightful conceptualizations of group events without denying the concerns of more anxious and dependent group members served an important function in that it added a sense of cohesiveness and coherence to the group. Although their function in the group was essentially similar to that attributed to the independent enactors by Mann (1967), members of this cluster were not necessarily independent of authority concerns. Joan, in particular, was extremely counterdependent, and questioned the legitimacy of the leader's authority as vehemently as any member of group 2. It would therefore be more accurate to say that members of this cluster, being comparatively uninvolved in leadership struggles within the group, were able to maintain some distance, which allowed them to use their conflict creatively. They were less likely than other members to deny one or another side of their ambivalence, and their ability to see both sides of group focal conflicts elicited agreement and support.

The Sexual Idols

By serving as the objects of pleasant fantasies and daydreams, members of this cluster (one man and three women) played a major part in group myths. As Dunphy (1964) has noted, the fact that many group members entertain the same fantasy and promulgate the same myth serves as an integrating force for the group. The fantasies also offer group members a respite from the frustrations of real interpersonal interaction.

There was no hint of blandness in the expressions directed to members of this cluster. They were the objects of more strong expressions of affection than any other cluster. This affection could not, however, be attributed to their friendliness. In fact, over all sessions members of this cluster expressed more direct, personal hostility than any other cluster. It would be more accurate to say that the group was drawn to the members of this cluster because each possessed some air of mystery stemming from involvement in some activity outside the group situation.

They set themselves apart from the group almost as soon as the course began. Kathleen would have been set apart in any case as the only black person in the group and because of her beauty; her statement in phase I that she was engaged to a professional football player and her subsequent election as homecoming queen only added to her allure. Becky was also quite attractive. As early as the third session, other group members noticed her; the leader commented that she tended to sit outside the group and encouraged her to be more revealing. The group's fascination with her was further enhanced by discussions of her career as a concert cellist. The following discussion about an upcoming concert in Flint is typical of the flirtatious interactions which contributed to high scores on moving toward and served to add to the idols' mystery.

> ELI: The concert hall is new and ready in Flint.
>
> BECKY: It's one of the most beautiful things.
>
> ELI: It's nice from the outside.
>
> BECKY: It's like a house of ill repute—all red velvet—very beautiful; acoustically good, too.
>
> ELI: All ready to be played in.

Examples involving the other two members of this cluster are somewhat less striking, but involve a similar dynamic. Rolfe was a handsome antiwar activist whose discussions of teach-ins and protests captured the group's attention. Josephine was not as strikingly attractive as the other three members of the cluster and was in some respects—particularly her active interest in being a better observer and analyst—similar to the respected enactors. But she tended to be more flirtatious than Joan, and established her mystery by revealing in session 20 (the same session in which the group learned that Kathleen had been elected homecoming queen) that she had fantasies about the leader. Upon subsequent questioning she declined to reveal exactly what the fantasies were, but described them as "oedipal." Following that session she was referred to as "the mysterious lady" and later as "the epitome of girlness."

All members of this cluster tended to be flirtatious and coy, dropping a hint and then leaving other members to pursue it; and the reaction to them was similar. Particularly in phase I, when they received many expressions scored "moving toward" and "withdrawing," there were interactions characterized on both sides by approach and followed by teasing withdrawal.

Both the sexual idols and other group members seemed to enjoy the air of excitement and mystery which surrounded them. However, the mystery and excitement were predicated to a large extent upon the idols' distance from the group, and this fact created a particular problem in the area of boundary maintenance. Because of their detachment, members of this cluster frequently expressed concern as to whether they were "really" a part of the group. The group's consistent reaction was to reassure the sexual idols that they were indeed an integral part of the group, and such reactions accounted for their high scores on reparation. Usually, reparative acts involve incidents in which apologies are rendered for an earlier attack. The sexual idols were rarely the object of direct attack but were higher than any other cluster as objects of reparation.

Their feeling that they were playing a part in a myth was so strong that members of this cluster frequently expressed feelings about the unreality of their role. Becky discussed in her log the allure of certain fantasies, such as the idea that she was able to "control the situation . . . [by her] indirect and subtle control of the men," and her difficulty in distinguishing fact from fantasy in her relationship to the group. Similarly, Kathleen stated in the group that it was difficult for her to distinguish what she put on as an act and what she really felt. In other words, the pull of the myth was often so strong for members of this cluster that they found it difficult to maintain a coherent sense of self-identity independent of the myth.

The idols were aware that their detachment was a central aspect of their role. Josephine and Becky discussed the nature of this detachment during one of the last sessions of the group; and Rolfe wrote in his log: "All semester I have been wondering why people have been attributing a great deal of leadership to me, especially when I have done so little talking. . . . I guess that because I have kept so much to myself, and only revealed dribs and drabs, people think I have much below."

In sum, the sexual idols added an air of mystery and excite-

ment to the group, and were the object of more expressions of affection than any other cluster. But their detachment from the group
and feelings that there was something "unreal" about their role led
them to seek reassurance from the group that their participation
was important.

The Leaders and the Fall Guy

Members of this cluster included the leaders of the two
groups and one male member. Group reaction to them was rarely
mild and frequently included some expression or denial of distress.
The members of this cluster rank last as objects of agreeing and
disagreeing, and first on five of the twelve affective categories (withdrawing, identifying, showing dominance, expressing distress, and
denying distress)'.

The fact that members of this cluster were the objects of so
many varied expressions (five times as many as the next most central cluster)' makes it even more difficult than usual to render a brief
summary. In the discussion that follows, I have focused on several
selected aspects of the groups' reactions to the leaders and then discussed briefly how a member came to be included in this leader
cluster. A more comprehensive discussion of the development of the
member-leader relationship can be found elsewhere in this volume
(see Hartman and Gibbard, Chapter 7, and in Mann, 1967)'.

The most striking aspect of the groups' reaction to the
leaders is that the leaders were the main focal point for the members' distress. No other cluster begins to approach their score as objects of the expression and denial of distress, and much of the expression and denial of distress to the leaders occurred as members
attempted to come to grips with the problem of developing a coherent sense of purpose within the group. Particularly in the first
phase, the distress was precipitated by the fact that the leaders did
not tell the members what pathways they should follow in order to
learn how to observe and understand group events. One member
put it this way: "You're cheating us. We've been trying to learn
how to analyze, and unless we get a report on how to do it, there's
no way we can." The fantasies underlying this complaint were that

the leader had a plan or blueprint for the group which could have provided a sense of purpose, but that he had chosen to withhold it from the group.

Some members were also quite concerned about being evaluated. Their distress is understandable. Grades received on their logs were based on the leader's assessment of their perceptiveness and analytic ability, and represented a more personal evaluation than grades on a multiple-choice examination. Most members did not see, however, that the intensity of their distress came partly from the fact that in exaggerating the leader's skills and competence they had minimized their own. In the process of idealizing him, members projected their own sense of competence onto the leader, and this resulted in an exaggerated estimate of the discrepancy between the leader's competence and their own. Much of the early resentment expressed to the leaders occurred because members felt that they had been forced to cope with problems which the leader could have solved at a time when the difference between their competence and his seemed enormous. In other words, many members resented having to forge a sense of purpose within the group when they felt so inadequate, and would have preferred that the leader foreclose the issue by prescribing the purpose and the pathways to his prescribed goals.

Some members seemed to sense that the feeling of inadequacy within the group stemmed in large part from the idealization of the leader, and these members frequently challenged and belittled the leader in an attempt to bring him down to the group's level. For example, Josephine and Abe (in group 1) and Joan (in group 2)ʹ challenged the leader's right to give grades and suggested that the group was "owned" by the members. Abe constantly mocked the leader, particularly when distress expressed by other group members was high. At different times he told the group that the leader was silent because he had had "a disabling accident," that he (Abe) had poked the leader in the stomach, and that the leader's friends called him "Tex" (all these statements were untrue). However, as members developed greater confidence in their own competence and strength, they became more willing to struggle with the issue of the group's purpose on their own. Consequently, both the resentment expressed toward the leader for not foreclosing the issue and the expressions of extreme incompetence in relation to him waned. Expressions (and denials) of distress were still frequently directed to both leaders, but the content of the expressions was more often that the problems being confronted by members in the group were complex and difficult; there were fewer requests that the designated leader take complete control.

Harvey, the fall guy, was frequently referred to as a "caricature" of the leader of group 2 and as "a plastic doll" you hit "instead of your parents." He became the object of expressions that otherwise might have been directed to the leader. The scores suggest a process of splitting in group 2: the leader became the good object, the object of affection and indentification; and Harvey, his fall guy, bore the brunt of the group's hostility. This did not occur in group 1. The leader in that group was directly attacked early in the group by Abe, and there is no member of group 1 with a profile of scores comparable to Harvey's. It is interesting to note that the leader of group 1 tends to fall midway between the scores of Harvey and the leader of group 2 for moving against and identifying. In the absence of a fall guy, there was apparently less idealization and thus a more manifestly ambivalent relationship to the leader throughout the group.

The main indictments of Harvey were that he intruded on the group and that he caused confusion because he did not present a consistent image to the group. In fact, both statements accurately described Harvey. Only one person in group 2 talked more (Vickie), and it was thus difficult for the group to ignore Harvey. His rambling comments often verged on the incoherent. He used words inappropriately (for example, he would say "nutrients" when he seemed to mean "nuturance," "strings" instead of "strains," "fractions" when he meant "factions"), and his comments often disrupted an attempt by the group to focus on another member. The following example is typical of many of Harvey's comments:

> Well, of course, I mean different people. Larry has certain characteristics. And Mr. Hartman has certain characteristics. But overall Natalie gave the qualifications of the leader. She was also in fact saying that Hartman possibly didn't have these qualifications to lead the class, and therefore someone else must

take over. And she's imposing some of these qualifications to Larry. Now, in fact, what you have said, this is what Natalie has said, this is what I more or less consider a leader of this class to be. This is what you, Vickie, have also said when you're agreeing with Natalie. Now, if this is the truth, if this is the case, why can't you pose some of the questions you have thought about Hartman to Larry? Some of the qualifications of what makes him think the way he does, possibly. What is his format, and he must obviously have one in order to understand the group because understanding implies structure.

Harvey, therefore, was viewed by the group as an irritant who caused confusion, could not be ignored, but had to be silenced or removed. Although the leader's comments were quite a bit more articulate than Harvey's, they, too, were regarded as intrusive and confusing (following one interpretation, one member remarked, "Why does he say these things?") and his nondirective, analytic stance was also regarded as a source of confusion and distress by many members. Harvey and the leader were both felt to be obstacles to the development of a coherent sense of the group's purpose.

The other point to be noted is that Harvey was very involved in the group, and other group members regarded him as an integral part of the group. He was the object of many reparative expressions (which typically constituted attempts to reintegrate an individual into the group), and his average scores on identifying are an indication that group members were willing to be more or less empathic in examining their own feelings in relation to Harvey. They may have wished that it were not so, but the group was frequently involved and preoccupied with Harvey. The group was never able to react to him with neutrality (his phase scores on agreeing and disagreeing are invariably low), and he elicited a reaction similar in its intensity and ambivalence to the reaction to the leader's.

The Outsiders

This cluster includes two men who were clearly scapegoats in their respective groups (Percy and Norman), and one member (Larry) whose idealized image was regarded as one to be emulated in group 2. As a cluster they had three things in common: (1) All announced their detachment from the group, and all three stopped coming to the group for at least three consecutive sessions. (2) In their respective groups, a role image of each emerged which was inconsistent with their own self-images. (3) In contrast to the sexual idols, the group made few attempts to implement their integration within the group or to understand what they were feeling.

It is interesting to contrast this cluster with the sexual idols. Both clusters expressed detachment and were on the boundary of the group. In expressing their detachment, the sexual idols tended to imply that they were involved with something more exciting than the ongoing interaction, and the group frequently reacted with explicit attempts to entice them to rejoin the group. The Outsiders, on the other hand, tended either to say little in the early sessions or to express disinterest, unqualified by excitement about other areas of their lives. For example, in the second session Percy stated that he was taking the course only to fulfill distribution requirements and implied that he did not expect to get anything out of it. Norman implied that the course was below him, since he was a senior psychology major and many members of the group were not psychology majors.

The group's reaction was anything but friendly. Whereas the sexual idols were the object of reparation in the absence of expressed hostility, members of this cluster (except for Larry) were the object of hostility untempered by any reparation or apology. When the leader of group 1 observed that the group appeared to be blaming Percy for the group's use of him as a scapegoat, Eli replied: "You can see it as scapegoating. I don't. I see it as normal expression." The predominant mood seemed to be that the outsiders had it coming, and expressions of apology or guilt concerning attacks on them were rare.

The fact that the outsiders were the object of so few expressions of reparation implies that the group as a whole had little commitment to maintaining interpersonal contact with them. Two facts support this hypothesis. It has already been noted that acts scored "reparation" frequently involved reassurances to central members that they were still considered an integral part of the group, and that the outsiders rarely received such reassurance. The absence of stable relationships in the group was also manifest in the pattern of activity directed to the outsiders. As a cluster, they tended to be the focus of intense attention for a relatively brief period of time, and were subsequently ignored. For example, 48 percent of all the expressions directed to Larry occurred in sessions 18 and 19. The remainder were distributed among the other thirty-eight sessions.

Contributing to the group's tendency to focus on these members and then ignore them was the fact that each member of this cluster was unwilling to accept the group's image of himself. Norman, for example, attempted to adopt the kind of leadership position that would emphasize his sense of superiority to other group members. He often referred to his previous course work in psychology and to his leadership position in campus organizations, and finally attempted to lecture the group on the theories of Kurt Lewin. The following dialogue illustrates the conflict between his perception of himself as a leader and the group's image of him as an irritant to be removed. It also illustrates the harshness of the attack on the scapegoats.

EILEEN: Can I say something hostile? Well, I feel like you're the old Harvey, the thorn in the side of the group.

NORMAN: I feel we do need a leader.

LARRY: I don't think that's what she said. She didn't call you a leader. She called you a thorn in the side.

NORMAN: [Somewhat later in the session] Lewin did start group dynamics.

LARRY: What does that mean? Not a thing. Why should we rely on theories to find things out? Why can't we rely on ourselves?

Even Larry, who in group 2 was pictured as the ideal combination of strength, tenderness, and wisdom, felt constrained by the role pressures upon him. The following are two excerpts from his log: "My role in class seems a desirable one, yet within this role there is little flexibility. It is not possible for me to fail for the class, except that I know that this isn't true. Alhough I enjoyed the role I was given and assumed in the class, I disliked being compelled to be in that position. I was used as much for the class as was Harvey. Staying in my role symbolized for me a certain impotency in spite of the role itself."

Finally, the group's reaction to the outsiders represented an attempt to transcend its fantasy that nothing good could occur in the group unless the leader reverted to a traditional structure. Both the attack on the scapegoats and the idealization of Larry served to assert that individuals had strengths within themselves and that the group was capable of generating its own excitement. This sense of self-esteem produced was somewhat fragile, however. Each group was unwilling to examine its use of any of the members of this cluster or group pressures on them, and there seemed to be little interest in understanding how the outsiders felt.

Although reactions to the outsiders were related to reactions to the leader, they were not as closely identified with the leader as Harvey, the fall guy, was. Both Harvey and the leaders were attacked for creating ambiguity and confusion, but their obvious involvement in the group led to expressions of guilt following the attack, reparation, and identification. The outsiders were the object of few such expressions, and were regarded with little ambivalence. The outsiders were either attacked or idealized as other group members asserted the strength that existed within the group membership. When they did not accept the image assigned to them, the group tended to ignore them and focus on other individuals in the group.

The Prophets

The three members of this all-male cluster were prophets in the sense that each seemed to have some individual vision of what the group should be, and the vision was compelling enough that he worked to create such a group. These members emerged from the group itself (unlike the leader, who seemed to offer a purpose from "above") and, as a result, received the gratifications and tribulations of being prophets in their own land.

The prophets were the three most active members of group 1, and as speakers they tended to be assertive, intense, and affectionate. By their attempts to define what goals the group should pursue, they added excitement to the group and evoked the involve-

ment of the others in the ongoing group interaction. But the fact
that their individual conceptions of the group's purpose were in conflict created factions and divisions within the group. Many of the
expressions scored "moving against" and "showing dominance"
occurred in fights among the prophets when their visions were at
odds. Dave's need to build a group which emphasized warmth and
unconditional acceptance was in conflict with Abe and Eli's emphasis on the importance of candor in expressing hostility; and Eli's
conception of the group as a situation in which to learn the clinical
skills of the leader sacrificed too much autonomy for Abe. At times
the conflict among the members of this cluster had an air of sexual
rivalry, but the following interaction between Abe and Eli illustrates
the extent to which they were also fighting to determine the values
and sense of purpose within the group.

ELI: Wanna lock horns?

ABE: Yeah.

ELI: Which one [of the women] do you want?

ABE: I don't care; it's OK . . . You pick yours and I'll take the
       leavings. [Group laughter] . . . I don't think it has to do
       with specific people at all . . . it has to do with other
       stuff—sort of has to do with the whole group . . . I see
       one of the group norms as honesty. You're a person who
       along with me and Dave have certain power which can
       establish group norms. That's where I see competition . . .

ELI: You have certain values you want to establish in the group
       and I'm opposed to them?

ABE: Not exactly. Not opposed to them consciously, but in the
       group you act as if you wouldn't work for them. That's the
       whole thing . . . I see certain good things that you're
       counterposed to. Unless you change I'll keep picking on
       you in the group. I think that's the nature of competition.

The prophets, then, were willing to state explicitly what
their sense of the group's purpose was and to challenge those who
stood in their way. That the overall reaction to them is high on
showing submission is in part an indication that the group accepted

their leadership and used them as spokesmen for widely shared feelings. But the fact that they also are the objects of more direct hostility and guilt-inducing than any other cluster indicates the extent to which they were regarded as prophets "in their own land." Other members were willing to accept their leadership when they felt anxious and without direction; but as they developed their own sense of competence and purpose, they increasingly came to feel that the prophets had been using the group for their own selfish ends and did not always place the best interests of the group foremost in their thoughts. All members of this cluster were eventually indicted for allowing their egocentrism and narcissism to interfere with the good of the group. Rolfe, for example, stated that Abe's motives in attempting to lead the group were 70 percent selfish and 30 percent in the group's interest; and Kathleen, after including Eli in the indictment, revised the figure to 85–15.

Similarly, Dave was attacked in a later session for not getting to know other people in the group (his stated goal). As Josephine said, "I think you're just going around the world looking at yourself. You can only see people as they relate to you." And Eli was attacked by Rolfe for attempting to understand people on his "own terms" rather than theirs.

The intensity of the attack on members of this cluster created a problem for the group. Subsequent to the attack on the prophets, no one else felt confident enough in their altruism to accept leadership in the group. Clyde (one of the respected enactors) was pressed on several occasions to be more assertive in his leadership, but he always declined, saying at one point that the group seemed to want a computer for a leader rather than a person with human foibles. Only the designated leader (who did not emerge from the group membership) seemed beyond reproach, and the group turned increasingly to him for leadership after the prophets were attacked.

It is interesting to note that all three members of this cluster accepted personal responsibility for the group's failure to achieve utopian goals. All seemed to believe that the group would have been successful if they had only been better leaders. Abe said that he believed he had "wrecked" the group's good mood and that he was not "good" for the group. Eli expressed his disillusionment with himself and related this to the group's limited success, and Dave also expressed the sense that he had been inadequate as a leader and had contributed to the group's failures.

Although the attack on the prophets was strong, the group nonetheless was willing to express its gratitude to members of the cluster for their leadership, and to acknowledge the ways in which the group had used them. Group discussions of their roles were often warm and empathic (in contrast to discussions involving th: outsiders), and often served to reduce the intensity of role pressure; upon them.

SUMMARY AND CONCLUSIONS

The clustering procedure used in this study to identify central figures who were the objects of similar group reactions has generated a typology similar in several respects to earlier studies of role differentiation and interpersonal style which employed different methodologies.

The anxious participators identified in the present study are essentially similar to the distressed females discussed by Mann (1967) and the anxious dependent students identified in the study of college classrooms (Mann and others, 1970; B. Ringwald and others, 1971). In the two groups studied here, these members served to keep the discussion moving and expressed the distress experienced by a substantial number of less vocal members. Although the group's reaction was not generally affectionate (it was usually characterized by blandness and distance), they were not subjected to intense role pressures and seemed to feel that the group's image of them was reasonably accurate.

The respected enactors were in most respects similar to the independent enactors identified by Mann (1967), and to the discouraged workers portrayed by Mann and others (Mann and others, 1970; B. Ringwald and others, 1971). They offered compromises which depolarized debates within the group, and they contributed to the group's sense of intellectual accomplishment by their incisive, integrating commentary. Nonetheless, they offered little active leadership or charisma, and the responses to them tended to be affectionate but bland.

Two of the clusters suggest that several members in a given group can serve functions previously discussed in the literature in relation to a single member. For example, Dunphy (1968; this volume, Chapter 12) and Gibbard (1969) both noted that a female member linked in some way to the leader often contributed to the evolution of cohesiveness by serving as the object of widely shared sexual fantasies. The analysis presented here of the sexual idols demonstrates that more than one member in the group can serve such a function, and that the curiosity and mystery surrounding the role need not be reserved exclusively for females. Members of this cluster were the objects of much affection (even though as a cluster they expressed more hostility than any other) and of repeated efforts to reassure them that they played an integral role in the group.

Similarly, examination of the group's reaction to the prophets reveals that it is not only the hero who comes to represent the conflict between desires for individuation and fusion (see Gibbard, this volume, Chapter 10). Each of the three members who attempted to influence the group in the direction of his own unique vision was attacked for selfishly asserting his individuality and egocentricity in opposition to the best interest of the group, and this was true whether he adopted a counterdependent, heroic stance (Abe) or was dependent (Dave).

Finally, the linking of an idealized member and two scapegoats to form the cluster of outsiders reminds us that even a positively regarded member may be ignored and extruded when he is unwilling to accept the group's role image of him.

The clusters thus delineated can be viewed from at least two perspectives: (a) as attempts by participants in the group to represent and control aspects of the self by projecting certain parts of the self onto others and then controlling (through the group's reaction) the external representation thus created; and (b) as an attempt to deal with the conflict generated by contradictory wishes to be a unique and distinctive figure in the group and to remain an anonymous contributor in the group indistinguishable from any other member.

Viewed from the former perspective, Larry (the idealized outsider), the sexual idols, and the leaders were regarded as ideal aspects of the self (or ego ideal). However, in order to maintain the idealized image, they had to be kept at some distance, since closer scrutiny would inevitably have revealed the discrepancies between their idealized images and the facts. As long as the images could be maintained, they helped to preserve the hope that an ideal sense of self-identity, shorn of frustration and the awareness of one's inadequacies, could be attained.

Harvey (the fall guy) and the two scapegoats (the outsiders who were attacked) represented the opposite extreme—the aspects of the self felt to be devoid of any redeeming goodness or worth. The attacks on these members were in large part an effort to control and/or eliminate the painful fantasy that the discrepancy between one's actual self and one's ideals is infinitely great—that one's ideals would always remain hopelessly beyond reach.

The anxious participators and the respected enactors both can be viewed as personifications of the ego-syntonic parts of the self, those parts that seem neither ideal nor worthless; as such, they are representations of the aspects of the self not actively engaged in the struggle to attain one's ideals. Consequently, they correspond to independent ego functioning—the ego functions that protect the self from the intrusion of unacceptable impulses, and the synthesizing functions that contribute to a sense of efficacy and competence.

Finally, the prophets from this perspective become the personification of the actual struggle to attain ego identity. All expressed a sense of what their purpose was in relation to the group as a whole, and in the process repudiated some ideals in favor of those which seemed most important. This willingness to assert their own individuality led to accusations that they were selfishly concerned with their own interests rather than the best interests of the group.

With regard to the problem of individuation, Gibbard's discussion (this volume, Chapter 10) of the hero as the personification of conflicts surrounding individuation applies as well to other aspects of the nonrational role structure of the group. Gibbard argues that individuals in groups wish that they could be distinctive, with their idiosyncratic needs acknowledged, and at the same time maintain a sense of unity and sameness with other group members. He goes on to discuss the extent to which Abe, the hero in group 1, attempted to create a synthesis of such contradictory wishes. In other words, individuals wish to maintain a group mentality that allows anonymous (and often unconscious) gratification of needs while simultaneously asserting their distinctiveness.[2]

In fact, the sexual idols came close to approximating just such a magical solution. Mysterious and apparently inaccessible, they stood out as the "beautiful people" of the group, and their participation in the group was actively courted. Yet, by acting as the common object of shared fantasies, they served the function of maintaining an atmosphere conducive to the group mentality. The pleasant fantasies entertained about them and curiosity about their lives outside the group offered a respite from conflicts generated by differences among the individual members and tended to fuse the group into a cohesive, amorphous whole. They consequently can be viewed as one reflection of a wider effort to resolve frustration and conflict through fantasy and withdrawal. Their detachment from the group and their low participation support this notion.

The role of the sexual idols appeared to be satisfying in many respects for the group as well as the members who comprised the cluster, and they rarely challenged the group myths surrounding their role. Their collusion in supporting the group mentality may account in part for the strength of the group's affectionate reaction to them. The prophets, on the other hand, challenged the spirit of unanimity by asserting their unique conception of what the group ought to be; and in renouncing some goals they challenged a key assumption of the group mentality—the fantasy that contradictory wishes can be gratified simultaneously. The notion that the sexual idols represented the facilitation of the group mentality receives further support from the fact that the members of his cluster were the ones who led the attack on the prophets for asserting their individual interests in opposition to the (unspecified) interests of the group. Rolfe and Kathleen were the main prosecutors of Abe and Eli; and Josephine was most outspoken in noting that Dave had really not become close to anyone in the group. In such confrontations one can see the conflict between the desire for uniqueness and

---

[2] Bion (1959, p. 65) defines the group mentality as "the unanimous expression of the will of the group, contributed to by the individual in ways of which he is unaware, influencing him disagreeably whenever he thinks or behaves in a manner at variance with the basic assumptions."

the desire for group solidarity acted out by the two opposing sub-groups. In fact, the strength of the attack on the prophets comes not only because they are held responsible for the failure of group goals but also because they disrupt the spirit of sameness and unanimity within the group.

Similarly, the attacks on the two leaders for not providing a more structured situation can be viewed as a reaction to the perceived disruption of a sense of uniformity which might have been expressed in the statement "We are all here for the same purpose— to learn from the leader how to observe and analyze interpersonal behavior." The lack of structure created by the leaders' analytic stance encouraged members to examine their own individual goals and expectations. Since these goals were often in conflict, the sense of uniformity of purpose was threatened.

The outsiders contributed to a sense of uniformity (and hence the group mentality) by serving as the objects of group reaction which approached consensus; that is, nearly unanimous hostility was expressed to the scapegoats and nearly universal adulation to Larry. When all three refused to accept the group's reaction to them, thus challenging the unanimity, they tended to be ignored. In fact, Larry's refusal to accept the group's idealization of him (which would have supported the group mentality) is probably the main factor leading to his inclusion in the outsiders rather than the sexual idols.

In sum, the greatest affection in these two groups was reserved for the sexual idols, who contributed an atmosphere of excitement and mystery which facilitated rather than challenged the group mentality. They appeared to be aware that their contribution to the group was more magical and rooted in unconscious fantasy than the substantive product of conscious collaboration, as is evidenced in their continuing concern with the "unreality" of their role. The most intense hostility, conversely, was focused on the three clusters which were perceived as posing direct challenges to a sense of unanimity of purpose and the anonymous gratification of unconscious impulses.

Finally, it should be clear that group reaction to central figures is not a simple matter of the group's responding to the expressions of its individuals. In fact, groups appear to have their own dynamic needs, which influence the manner in which central figures are perceived and reacted to. Consequently, individuals with different interpersonal styles (for instance, Abe, the hero of group 1, and Dave, a staunch advocate of warmth and dependency) came to represent similar issues and conflicts for the group as a whole, and were included in the same cluster because the group reacted to them in similar fashion.

There is no reason to assume that the typology proposed here will necessarily occur in other groups. In fact, although the course structure, group composition, and leadership styles of the course instructors were similar for the two groups studied, two clusters (the sexual idols and the prophets) appeared only in group 1. However, there were structural pressures (that is, pressures from the needs of the group) on members of group 2 to accept an image of themselves consistent with the images of the sexual idols and the prophets. For example, Larry was referred to as the epitome of nonverbal sexuality, and at other times was urged to lead the group toward more meaningful goals. But, unlike the sexual idols, Larry was unwilling to tolerate the idealization of his characteristics; and, unlike the prophets, he had no goal which seemed compelling enough to fight for. Consequently, although he was the object of as much direct affection as the mean score of the sexual idols, there were never the attempts to reintegrate him into the group; and since he did not argue or accept responsibility for a definition of the group's purpose, he was never the object of as much direct hostility or guilt-inducing as the prophets. Similarly, Clyde and Joan refused to adopt a more active leadership stance in spite of encouragement by the group, because they feared disillusionment and had no compelling vision of what the group should be. Consequently, they were never subjected to the scrutiny and attack reserved for the prophets.

One implication is that individual members of groups should not be surprised if it seems that the group's reaction to them is based on a role image which is a caricature of their own image of themselves. The group reaction might be thought of as being like a funhouse mirror—the group sends back a reflection to the individual, but in the process adds its own distortions to the original image presented. The present study does provide some estimate of the reactions which individuals might expect, depending on their relationship to the group (and the group mentality); (a) Individuals who do not accept the image for which the group recruits them (for example, the outsiders) are more likely to be ignored if not vehemently attacked by the group. (b) Those who contribute an atmosphere of mystery and excitement by the combination of their detachment and involvement outside the everyday interaction of the group (for example, the sexual idols) might expect considerable expressions of affection and solicitousness, but an accompanying suspicion that their role is somehow lacking in substance. (c) Those who actively challenge the unanimity of the group mentality by asserting that certain values should guide the conduct of the group's interaction (for example, the prophets) should be prepared for intense scrutiny of their motives and the accusation that they are raising disruptive issues because of their own selfish interests. (d) Finally, those who do not challenge the prevailing assumptions might expect a somewhat bland reaction characterized by distance or approval, depending on their contribution to the group's sense of competence in relation to its task.

10

Individuation, Fusion,
and Role Specialization

GRAHAM S. GIBBARD

*R*ecent studies of informal role differentiation in self-analytic groups[1] have made an important contribution to our understanding of the functions and vicissitudes of role differentiation. Dunphy (1964; 1968; this volume, chapter 12), Mann (1967, 1970), Slater (1966), and Winter (this volume, chapter 8) have moved considerably beyond the earlier formulations of Freud, Redl, Bales, and others. Their theoretical and empirical efforts provide a foundation for the primary task of this chapter— the development of a systematic conceptualization of the process and the dynamic significance of role differentiation.

It is not surprising that the self-analytic classroom group has proved to be a particularly rewarding setting for the study of role differentiation. These are large (fifteen to twenty-five person)

[1] The term *self-analytic group* here refers to a specific kind of experiential group conducted in a college classroom. Such groups were introduced at Harvard (originally in the business school and subsequently in the college) and have been offered at Brandeis, Michigan, North Carolina, Wesleyan, and Yale.

247

groups which present their membership with relatively little structure and with complex and inherently frustrating tasks. The nondirective, interpretive style of the instructor[2] provides no clear index of accomplishment. The aims and structure of the course make it difficult to avoid emotional involvement. This combination of conditions (size, task complexity, frustration, and emotional engagement) fosters a rapid emergence of differentiated roles in a setting where they can be studied in some depth. In addition, a major goal of the course is to analyze group process and structure, including the process which leads to the formation and maintenance of a structure of informal roles. This is less true in therapy groups, where many of the same phenomena probably occur, since in therapy groups such analysis is usually considered a secondary or even an irrelevant task. The study group conducted in the Tavistock tradition has much in common with the self-analytic group. The main difference is that study groups are typically offered as one part of a group-relations conference, which makes it very difficult to compare self-analytic and study groups. The self-analytic classroom, while not a closed system, does have reasonably stable and distinct psychological boundaries. In the conference setting the study group is small (eight to twelve members), lasts for no more than six or eight sessions, and is only one of several events. As the conference evolves, it becomes virtually impossible to demarcate the boundaries of study group life; that is, small-group dynamics are inextricably bound up with intergroup and large-group dynamics.

The self-analytic group is, in my estimation, the only setting that promotes rapid and extensive role differentiation and permits a careful examination of the process of differentiation. Moreover, self-analytic groups tend, because of their academic roots and affiliations, to be reasonably similar in composition, organizational context, and primary task. This similarity engenders a certain parochialism, but it also facilitates a comparative assessment of observations and data from different studies.

The principal aim of this chapter is conceptual. I hope to move toward a general theory of role differentiation in relatively unstructured groups. I shall begin with a brief statement of what I

[2] The formal leader of a self-analytic classroom group is the course instructor. The terms *instructor* and *consultant* are here used interchangeably.

believe previous work in this area tells us about the bases and mechanisms of role differentiation. I shall then focus on a case study of a particularly salient role which emerges quite often in self-analytic groups and which appears to be paradigmatic of the entire process of role differentiation. The concluding section proposes a broader conceptualization of this process.

ROLE DIFFERENTIATION: A GENERAL FRAMEWORK

In early psychoanalytic discussions of group roles and leadership (see Freud, 1921), the group formative function of group leaders was emphasized: the leader becomes a shared ego ideal; group members identify with one another on the basis of this shared attitude toward the leader, and such identification serves to organize and reinforce intragroup bonds. Redl (1942), in his amplification of Freud's model of leadership, specified several ways in which central figures can serve an organizing function for groups: as role models, as objects of libidinal or aggressive drives, as facilitators of other members' efforts to resolve conflicts. These initial formulations were, however, tied too closely to traditional conceptions of leadership and social structure to provide a foundation for a more general view of structural differentiation in small social systems. Subsequent contributions representing a variety of traditions—among them, Bales' interaction process analysis (1950a, 1970), Whitaker and Lieberman's (1964) focal conflict paradigm, Bennis and Shepard's (1956) theory of group development, and the research on self-analytic groups cited above—have at least raised the possibility of an integration of intrapsychic, interpersonal, and group dynamics. What follows is my own synthesis of current thinking about role differentiation in small groups. It is intended to provide a conceptual framework for the clinical material and the theoretical propositions in later sections of the paper. This synthesis reflects two assumptions about structural differentiation in small groups: first, that intrapsychic, interpersonal, and group processes are closely related to one another; second, that structural differentiation, whether psychological or sociological, can be understood only in a developmental context.

The evolution of small, relatively unstructured groups is best characterized in terms of the group-wide concerns, the conflicts and divisive issues, that inevitably arise in any group. These unsettled issues create disequilibrium, within each group member and within the group-as-a-whole. This disruption catalyzes the differentiation of specialized roles, a process that facilitates the recovery of intra-psychic and group equilibrium. There appears to be a good deal of correspondence among explanations of this process.

The most common response of a group faced with frustration, ambivalence, or internal conflict is splitting and compartment-alization. From a developmental point of view, one would predict that unstructured experiential groups are particularly vulnerable to conflict and further disorganization in the early sessions, and that this initial intragroup conflict would lead to a specialization of roles. This differentiation should become less necessary as the group dis-covers alternative ways of dealing with conflict. Role differentiation, then, is in part a defensive and restitutive effort; and the cost of such differentiation, to the individual and the group, is that split-ting, projection, and compartmentalization all entail some distor-tion and simplification of emotional life.

Any specialization limits the individual's range of possibilities —a limitation often compounded by group pressures, which seduce or lock the individual into roles that do not meet his emotional re-quirements. Scapegoating is only the most dramatic manifestation of the group's tendency to exploit the individual. To some degree all group membership is contingent on a conscious or unconscious contract which obligates the individual to sacrifice or suppress some aspects of himself in order to express or develop others. Thus, the individual often finds that groups do not permit him to "be himself." An additional, less obvious, cost of specialization is that differences reflect and create distance between people. It is this distance, and the accompanying sense of isolation and loneliness, that sets in motion a move toward closeness, fusion, and a dedifferentiation of roles.

On the other side of the coin, role differentiation may serve primarily adaptive functions for the individual and the group. A division of labor, for example, frequently makes it possible to deal with conflicts that are counterproductive. Rather than becoming flooded with conflict, the group can make use of individuals (or of dyads or subgroups) to circumscribe, localize, and isolate conflict. Through projective identification a group is divided into actors and audience. Members are recruited to dramatize the central conflicts of the collectivity, and other members are able to participate vicariously in this dramatization. Compressed into a smaller arena, conflict can often be worked through, which in turn makes possible a reintegration of the group. Implicit in this view is the notion that mechanisms and structures which are adaptive when employed as temporary measures become maladaptive unless discarded or modified.

There is, however, one fundamental difficulty with this line of reasoning: its tendency to focus on a few key individuals or peer leaders and to portray other group members as vicarious participants or silent supporters. This emphasis on the salience of a few individuals obscures the fact that the differentiation of individual roles is a more general phenomenon, one that affects all members of a group. In stressing the emergence of a small number of central figures, researchers have tended to overlook some more elemental and less easily discerned aspects of the differentiation process. At the same time, as Dunphy and others have observed, the most visible role specialists *do* dramatize the major conflicts of the group. What is lacking in most studies is a clear articulation of the relationship between the "actors" and the "audience." While the central figures may serve as symbols of the principal polarities in the group, they do not provide a precise reflection, a mirror image, of those polarities. We should not lose sight of the distinction between the emergence of one or more highly distinct and differentiated roles and the gradual evolution of more idiosyncratic styles for all of the members of a group. The first type of differentiation is often dramatic. The second, assuming that it does occur with some regularity, is more subtle.

Slater's (1966) discussion of the relationship between individuation and role differentiation may help to clarify these distinctions. He argues that individuation is an *intrapsychic process* through which the individual crystallizes an increasingly firm sense of his own personal distinctiveness, coherence, and independence. Role differentiation, on the other hand, refers primarily to *group structure*. From a developmental point of view, the difference is crucial. Slater points out that individuation increases in a linear fashion, whereas role differentiation is more likely to follow a pendular pattern. The initial absence of structure is quickly replaced by role specialization; but once a certain degree of differentiation has been reached, the boundaries between roles begin to become more permeable—a manifestation of a process of dedifferentiation which may continue throughout the life of the group.

Role specialization is a reflection of an intermediate form of individuation. The differentiation of individual roles serves as a defense against subjectively experienced threats to individuation. But once the individual has succeeded in consolidating a reliable sense of identity in a relatively unstructured situation, role specialization becomes less necessary and is gradually replaced by behavioral flexibility. Slater does not extend this model to include a consideration of specific roles. Instead, he focuses on the role of the formal leader. The formal leader, in Slater's view, becomes the principal focus of members' transference fantasies.

> There is a point, both in the group and in the individual, at which individuation seems to be enormously facilitated by identification with some central person. . . . By focusing one's attention and libido on some prominent individual who appears to have achieved a clear separateness from mother, group, unconscious, or whatever; by magnifying and glorifying the individual's power and invulnerability, and identifying with him, one feels strengthened in one's own individuation (although the identification itself makes this individuation somewhat illusory). . . . Later, of course, when this identification has been achieved, it too must be relinquished. The ego must be separated from the leader or authority which helped to build it up, since this also is a part of individuation [Slater, 1966, pp. 240–241].

Slater's formulations are provocative, but they fall short of a comprehensive theory of informal role differentiation. His emphasis on the position of the consultant precludes a consideration of alternative responses to the initial absence of group structure. The case study which follows demonstrates one way in which *a group mem-*

ber can come to play a pivotal role in the dramatization and eventual resolution of the conflict between individuation and fusion.

The member whose role in a self-analytic group is explored in some detail here corresponds in most respects to the role type identified by Mann (1967, 1970) as the "hero." Mann's detailed studies of interpersonal styles point to several key features of the heroic style: The hero initially presents himself as an exceptional person. He is scornful of those who are manifestly anxious about the lack of structure in the group, denies any personal experience of distress, and endorses impulse expression as a primary goal of the group. He alternately rebels against and identifies with the consultant. Toward his peers he is aloof, patronizing, and self-absorbed. Despite the hero's hostility toward the consultant, they are perceived by other group members as quite similar to one another. Both seem to pursue their own personal agendas; both appear to be relatively untroubled, unconcerned with what others think of them, and in this sense above the group. One common fantasy is that the hero is acting out aspects of the consultant's personality which the constraints of his formal position hold in check.

Dunphy (1968; this volume, Chapter 12) describes a similar role type, which he terms "the seducer." The seducer attempts to move the group toward self-revelation, to mount a rebellion against the instructor's authority, and to break through defenses against personal exposure. Winter's (chapter 8) analysis of the "black male leader" role in self-analytic groups with an interracial composition points to some remarkable correspondences between the black male leader and the hero. Winter identifies three cardinal features of the black male leader's self-presentation—aggressiveness, marginality, and a demand to be viewed as special, particularly by and in relation to the consultant.

The work of Dunphy, Mann, and Winter suggests that the heroic role may be of particular relevance to the development of a more general understanding of role differentiation. The case presented here does support the hypothesis that the centrality of the hero can be attributed primarily to the group members' profound ambivalence with respect to the establishment and maintenance of differentiation and individuation.

THE HERO: A CLINICAL STUDY

A brief description of the self-analytic classroom group which was studied in some detail will help place this case study in context. The group was a section of a course entitled Analysis of Interpersonal Behavior, an advanced undergraduate course at the University of Michigan. The group met three times a week for a total of forty sessions (each session lasting fifty minutes) throughout one academic trimester. Each student was required to write a weekly log based on the sessions of the previous week and to take a final examination. Several case studies of small-group phenomena were assigned, and the group members were free to discuss or to ignore them. The grade in the course was based only on the student's work on the weekly logs and the final examination. There were twenty-six members in the group, fourteen women and twelve men. The group leader (the author) was relatively nondirective and analytic, particularly in the early meetings, and he tended to focus his interventions on whole-group dynamics. (For discussions of other aspects of this group, see Chapters 7, 9, and 13.)

The hero in this group was Abe (pseudonyms are used for all group members). Predictably, he was the first member to confront authority. In the third meeting he asked whether it was appropriate for the students to address the instructor by his first name and even pursued the matter when the instructor parried the question. A little later, in fact, he announced that the question had been settled—the consultant was to be referred to by his first name. He explained that *he* had already done so when he had telephoned the consultant to ask whether he could take the course (this was true) and attributed the consultant's silence to a "disabling accident," which he claimed to have observed and implied that he had caused (which was quite untrue). During the next few sessions, he frequently reminded his fellow members that the instructor had no special ability to analyze group behavior and that he might just as well be "forgotten." At the same time, he said that he could "intuitively" read the consultant's mind and appeared keenly interested in trying to understand what the consultant was thinking and feeling. He scoffed at most of the instructor's interventions; yet when the consultant did not comment on some aspect of the group, Abe would himself offer "the interpretation." His intuitive guesses were often remarkably accurate. He thus identified himself as both the professional and the personal equal of the instructor. Early in the semester he was the most sexually expressive and the most openly hostile member of the group. It was his consistent mockery of the consultant that led, in the eleventh session, to the group's most intense and prolonged confrontation with the consultant.

Toward his peers he was often hostile and condescending, particularly when others t̥ ·eatened to challenge his position in the group. He was much more intensely involved with the consultant than with the other members of the group. At the same time, he complained that he was being "used" by the group and that through him the group was acting out its rebelliousness toward the consultant. He would at times become angry and irritable, refusing to say anything, and would turn aside repeated expressions of affection. Still, the support of other members was important to him, and he was obviously hurt when that support was withdrawn. He saw himself as exploited by the group, but also as guilty of having "manipulated" the group.

Following the confrontation with the consultant, Abe appeared to withdraw even more into what one member described as a "private world." Throughout this phase of the group, he was one of the staunchest supporters of Kevin, who was at this point endorsing a move toward "warmth" and "closeness." He even encouraged Kevin to call Kathleen, one of the most attractive women in the group, though he maintained his control of the situation by supplying her telephone number from memory. He commented on the increasingly flirtatious atmosphere in the group but did not actively participate, though he was a frequent recipient of female flirtation. He continued to "intuit" and "relay" the interpretations and unspoken wishes of the consultant. On several occasions during this phase, Abe visited the instructor in his office. He was the first and for some time the only member who took the initiative to approach the instructor privately. The content of these conversations varied from current events to Abe's more personal problems, but the latent goal of all of these meetings was to gain some assurance that he was what he termed the "favorite son" and that he was still more attuned to the consultant's thoughts and feelings than were any of the other members. In the group he described himself as a "matchmaker" and consistently refused to "lock horns" with other males, implying that he was above such petty squabbling.

Near the end of the group, Abe pressed for a more explicit and public recognition of his favorite-son status. A small subgroup asked to meet with the consultant to discuss the entire question of favoritism. This caucus appeared to develop spontaneously when Clyde, Eli, and Josephine—all active members of the group—came to the instructor's office on the same day. Abe had already come to the instructor, and Eli immediately demanded a clarification of the favorite-son issue. Abe asserted that he was the favorite son by virtue of his special "understanding" of the consultant, an explanation which left the consultant both guiltless and helpless to alter the situation. Favoritism was something which Abe had both forced upon and taken from the consultant—not a gift which the consultant was free to bestow. Josephine agreed with Abe, saying that he was simply "too cocky" to be defeated in this particular competition. This discussion ended Eli's active participation in the competition and was followed a few days later by a group-wide review of the issue. Josephine stated that Abe was the favorite son. Suzy called attention to Abe's "uncanny rapport" with the consultant. Becky described the consultant as "Apollo" and Abe as "a priest of Apollo, a messenger of the prophet."

Several intriguing themes emerge from this material. In Abe's relationship with the consultant, we find an interweaving of intensely rebellious and intensely affectionate and even submissive behavior. His rebelliousness is quite personalized and appears to be directed toward the creation of a deep and unique relationship with the consultant. He is almost always closely attuned to the instructor's thoughts and feelings, particularly those which are largely preconscious; and he employs this empathy to protect the instructor and, at the same time, to ridicule and expose the instructor's shortcomings.

Toward his peers Abe appears contemptuous and intent on maintaining an attitude which combines aloofness and depressive isolation. He strikes others as very much aware of sexual feelings and imagery in group discussions and yet as quite uninterested in any erotic involvement with the women in the group. He is, in fact, particularly hostile toward his female peers. But despite his emphasis on uniqueness and disengagement, he feels very much a part of the group; at times he feels that he is being "used" as a spokesman for the group and that he himself has brought about this state of affairs. Other group members find themselves caught up in an ambivalent fascination with him. His deviance is both exciting and unacceptable. His intense involvement with the consultant arouses similarly mixed feelings.

Much of this behavior becomes more understandable when we review Abe's weekly logs, which provide us with a richer subjective report of his group experience. Not surprisingly, we find that from the very beginning Abe portrays himself as more knowledgeable, experienced, and poised than the other members. He regards himself as an ally and even a confederate of the consultant. He suggests that he is writing the weekly logs—an important assignment in the course—simply to keep up appearances and to share his own rather unsystematic ruminations with a colleague who happens to be sitting in on the same group. He is less attentive to the analytic tasks which the log assignments entail than to noting group events that he finds particularly "interesting" or "amusing"—an observational stance in which he imagines himself closely identified with the instructor. Much of the latent significance of this identification is revealed in Abe's third log, an abridged version of which is presented below:

> Last week was weird.
> From the opening comment on Monday to the end on Friday.
> Weird.
> The first thing I noticed was that the group called on me to start things off Monday morning. Joe asked about my weekend and immediately thereafter a red-haired chick asked about the button [Impeach Johnson] I was wearing. I took this to be a recognition by them of the power I had in the group but I wanted to bring this out into the open.
> That wasn't hard. You [the consultant] gave me the chance. During a silence you asked the group why they let me

interpret your comments. Kathleen and Kevin defended me actively and the subject fell. More likely than not a depressed silence followed. I broke the silence by returning to your comment. I interpreted it as an attack, the first real rise anyone had gotten from you up to then, and asked the group why they defended me from attack but they wouldn't defend you in a similar situation. In effect, I wanted them to admit that they liked me more than you. Or if that wasn't the case to see what kinds of hostility people bore toward me.

People responded a little and I learned some, but no one really wanted to talk about us and another depression followed. . . .

Monday afternoon I thought a lot about Monday morning. I realized that the group and I had worked out an arrangement whereby I satisfied my needs of combatting authority and they satisfied their need of having an authority figure. I got mad at all of us and decided to undermine my authority by first identifying it and then renouncing it.

Wednesday I came in determined that someone else would break the silence. You almost wrecked it by making some announcements about class cards and logs at the outset, which could have gotten the session going; but your comments were taken as merely parenthetical. The usual chaotic early rambling drifted into a prolonged silence which I relished and some people found most uncomfortable. In some ways it made me feel more powerful than ever. Arthur was called on for help, but he couldn't maintain nonsilence for very long and shortly it settled back on the group. . . .

After about twenty minutes of on again off again I exposed my ruse and the silence ended. I think later, if anyone has the inclination to reflect, this moment will be looked upon as the birth of the group. Everything up until then had been gestation. First in your womb and then in mine. But from that moment on, it was out in the world bare and struggling.

No one wanted to believe that I could manipulate the group, so they refused to talk about it at that time. Not surprisingly though, the topic blended easily into power and powerlessness. This was pushed by Peggy mostly and the group resisted, but I asked her to go on and she did. Also expectedly the question of responsibility to the group came up. They were pissed off.

And rightly so. From now on they will be more careful about letting me exercise authority.

Abe's preoccupation with the consultant and with his own centrality in the group is abundantly clear. He works hard to maximize his own "power" and is both closely identified with and fiercely competitive toward the consultant. He alternately accentuates and disclaims his "authority," though each disclaimer leads to further demonstrations of that authority. The fantasy of giving birth to the group is especially revealing and deserves more detailed consideration.

The fantasy involves the definition of both the consultant and Abe as hermaphrodites. Each possesses a womb and is capable of giving birth. At the same time, the consultant's procreative activity precedes Abe's and entails, we may infer, an impregnation of the hero by the consultant. Such an impregnation implies a distinctly homosexual submission and places the consultant in the dominant position in the relationship. Yet it is this very submission which enables Abe to imagine himself as having defeated and replaced the consultant. Interestingly, the manifest content of the fantasy involves a fusion of consultant and hero, both of whom are seen as hermaphrodites and as giving birth to the group. The latent content points, however, to more differentiated roles and functions. The consultant does not give birth to the group. It is the hero who gives birth after having been impregnated, behind the scenes as it were, by the consultant. (The hero's bisexual involvement with the consultant may have more general implications as well. For a discussion of the significance of bisexual fantasies shared on a group-wide basis, see Chapter 13.)

Abe's impregnation and group-birth fantasy is paradigmatic of his position vis-à-vis the consultant. The fantasied relationship is one characterized by an ambivalent merging, a confusion of sexual and perhaps personal identities, and an envelopment that is both feared and desired. With respect to the issue of sexual identity, the clear danger is that the hero will be emasculated. Perhaps less obviously, there is also the promise of gaining the characteristics of both sexes and thus the capacity both to impregnate and to give birth. Even more fundamental, however, is the conflict between total fusion and total individuation, a conflict which can be conceptualized most concretely in terms of sexual identity but which is by no means exclusively sexual.

To return to the small-group context, we are now more able to explain the hero's extraordinary involvement with the consultant. He is, on the one hand, intensely "wrapped up" with the consultant —claiming the ability to read his mind and demonstrating an almost uncanny sensitivity to his unspoken thoughts. This kind of closeness is, on the other hand, neutralized by a rebellious stance which serves to distance him from the consultant, even though it also moves him closer to imagining that he has grasped the interpretive power and the charisma of the consultant. A similar paradox is at the heart of the hero/group relationship. He is aloof, alone, consistently deviant; but despite this dramatization of uniqueness he is very much a part of the group and feels, in fact, angry and confused because he finds himself hopelessly entangled in a quasi-symbiotic relationship with his group, each "using" or "manipulating" the other.

Our analysis of the role of the hero confirms our initial impression that a central concern in unstructured small groups such as these is the resolution of a profoundly ambivalent preoccupation with the whole issue of individuation. The hero's importance in the self-analytic group, particularly in the initial phases of the group's development, is clearly tied to *his* concern with the issue of individuation. He acts out both sides of all the major polarities facing the group, attempting to establish a more inclusive synthesis of opposing and often contradictory alternatives. He is not able to maintain such a synthesis, but what is heroic in his performance is this very *effort* to balance fusion and separation, dependency and rebellion, male and female, uniqueness and identity with the group.

Slater (1966) has speculated that the nascent group is unconsciously experienced by its members as a dangerous and enveloping mass. The leader of the group is viewed as struggling to differentiate himself from this mass. The successful outcome of this struggle demonstrates the possibility of survival and growth even after the painful separation from the primal state of unity with the mother. Our study of the peer hero has made possible an exploration of this developmental sequence at a less inferential level of analysis. As we have seen, the hero recapitulates the consultant's struggle to differentiate himself from the group. At the same time, he acts out a conflict between a desire for and a flight from fusion with (blending into submission to) the consultant. The hero attempts to compromise between capitulation to and revolt against the consultant and, at a less conscious level of awareness, between fusion with and differentiation from the group-as-a-whole.

To carry this argument a step further, it may well be that in groups with an actively heroic figure the dramatization of the conflict between individuation and fusion is more compelling than in groups in which the consultant's centrality and power are not challenged in the early sessions. The consultant does not, after all, experience an actual process of differentiation. In the very beginning he establishes a differentiated position for himself and has access to a variety of formal role prescriptions which help to ward off dedifferentiation and envelopment. His struggle is largely imaginary, crystallized out of the common elements in the members' transference fantasies. The hero, on the other hand, is from the very beginning in and of the group, and he must simultaneously assert his independence from the consultant and his separateness from the group. Both struggles are genuine, albeit qualified by ambivalence, and both are played out in the group. It may also be that the presence of a heroic member permits a more thorough and less protracted working through of the conflict. By making the hero the most salient (differentiated) deviant, the group both accentuates and isolates the deviance and can use the hero as a target for the full range of the members' ambivalence about differentiation.

I cautioned earlier, however, against too exclusive a focus on the most visible group roles. Role specialists such as the hero (and the consultant) do appear to express and facilitate the settling of widely shared conflicts, but the analysis of one or two key roles does not provide a reliable foundation for a theory of role differentiation. While the individuation/fusion polarity is crucial early in the group, it is eventually eclipsed by other issues. Other group roles become important.

A PSYCHOANALYTIC THEORY OF
ROLE DIFFERENTIATION

It is reasonable to postulate, given the evidence reviewed, that there is in all social systems a fundamental ambivalence with respect to the differentiation of specialized roles. This observation may, in fact, have been made originally by Bales (1950a, 1953), who noted the chronic tension between an optimal adaptation to the requirements of the group task and a consistent commitment to the social-emotional integration of the group. Work necessitates shifts in the division of labor and differential distributions of power and status—differences inevitably accompanied by envy, invidious competition, and increased social distance. The integration of the social system moves the group in the opposite direction, toward the modulation or dissolution of all such distinctions. Bales argued that in any social system faced with recurrent tasks, problem-solving challenges, and the like, there is always an "indeterminate oscillation" between an accommodation to the demands of the task and an accommodation to the integrative needs of the group. The modal response to this dilemma is role differentiation. The system is dependent on both task and integrative activity, which means that both types of leadership (presumably reflecting different personality styles) must be available. Ideally, the task and social-emotional leaders are able to establish a relationship based on mutual respect and cooperation, an arrangement which suppresses at least the most extreme and disruptive manifestations of the antagonism. This initial view of differentiation was, however, more sociological than psychological. The social system requires certain kinds of leadership; the appropriate roles are differentiated. The psychodynamic bases of differentiation were not explored.

The work of Bion (1959) and Slater (1966) calls our attention to the operation of another polarity, which is best understood as an intrapsychic conflict between individuation and fusion. To extrapolate from their arguments, the essence of the dichotomy is this: Individuation offers the individual the opportunity to move toward greater autonomy and self-awareness, to attain a genuine, though not unlimited self-sufficiency, and to actualize his idiosyncratic potential. But individuation also entails the sacrifice of some potential in the interest of more specialized, focused development. Such development is contingent on the renunciation of wishes for an all-inclusive completeness and *total* self-sufficiency. Through individuation one becomes more distinctive and particularized and consequently more distant from others, more isolated and lonely. Unconsciously, the process of individuation reflects the gradual surrendering of the fantasy of fusion with the mother. It follows, then, that the magical solution-in-fantasy would center on the wish that *unity* and *uniqueness* could coexist without contradiction. This is, of course, the unconscious significance of the hero's ambivalent entanglements with the consultant and the collectivity.

It can be argued, with considerable justification, that the opposition of individuation and fusion is not always a crucial issue in group development. It is often not an overt issue at all, as there are a wide range of institutionalized defenses against the unsettling effects of the conflict. Many psychotherapy and sensitivity training groups provide (appropriately)' enough initial structure to muffle and obscure the conflict. The combination of personal involvement and ambiguity which characterizes many self-analytic classroom groups offers the most fertile setting for a preoccupation with individuation and envelopment. In such a setting, intrapsychic and interpersonal tensions trigger reparative efforts to master the phenomenologically real threat of psychic disruption and the objectively real challenge of creating a new social system.

It is under such conditions that role differentiation becomes essential for survival. Both individual and institutional anchors of identity are temporarily lost, and only a rapid differentiation of some type can hold in check intense fears of deindividuation. Slater's portrait of the consultant as the conqueror of the maternal mass is consistent with this interpretation. The consultant presents himself as a lodestar, which the members first follow, then turn away from. The position of the peer hero is more ambivalent, in that his role encapsulates all facets of the conflict and thus reduces it to manageable proportions. There is a third possibility which we have not considered—the differentiation of an entire constellation of distinctive roles. This may well occur, but it does not appear to provide a viable alternative in the initial sessions, primarily because such a generalized process of differentiation proceeds too slowly to ward off the more immediate danger of group envelopment. The group's first and most pressing need is for a central figure who can be utilized as a point of orientation. Predictably, both the consultant (see Slater, 1966, pp. 234–252) and the peer hero (see Gibbard, 1969, pp. 196–208) become less important to the group once the initial anxiety about deindividuation has diminished.

From a developmental perspective, the process of differentiation of the leader and/or hero can be described as pendular: the initial absence of role structure evokes a widely shared fantasy of fusion and engulfment; the anxiety aroused by this fantasy is countered by a rapid and dramatic differentiation of roles which facilitate the working through of the anxiety; the fears subside and a partial dedifferentiation occurs.

Slater's speculative discussion of the relationship between individuation and differentiation concludes, as we have noted, with the suggestion that *all* role differentiation in self-analytic groups follows a pendular pattern. He offers little evidence in support of this proposition, though it is an interesting idea, certainly worthy of further exploration.

It is possible, for example, that there are really two waves of differentiation in the opening sessions of an unstructured group. The first wave—the emergence of the consultant/hero role—has been considered in some detail. The second wave may entail the more gradual emergence of an array of differentiated roles which includes all or almost all of the group members. This conceptualization is consistent with our analysis of the consultant/hero phenomenon as a stopgap response to fears of fusion. The focus on the central figure has obvious advantages, but it also binds the group to an ambivalent and often stifling fascination with one or two central figures. Perhaps as other members regain their psychic bearings they begin to establish more distinctive roles, to replace fantasied fusions with more realistic and partial identifications and object ties, and thus to formulate a more sophisticated and flexible adaptation to the individuation/fusion dilemma.

This gain in flexibility is not, however, apparent for some time. If the developmental sequence as we have described it is reasonably accurate, we should find an initial flight from the dangers of role diffusion. Early efforts to differentiate individual roles should lead not to behavioral plasticity but to a defensive rigidity, a reliance on stereotypy, and an overstatement of individual and subgroup differences. Once the most intense fears of envelopment have passed, this buttressing of individuation should become less necessary. This shift should be reflected in a generalized reduction of role pressures on specialists and a redistribution of special functions. Personal attributes and affects previously assigned to central figures through projective identification can be reclaimed by group members.

This paradigm has received support from naturalistic observers of small groups (for example, Bennis and Shepard, 1956; Gibbard and Hartman, 1973b; Slater, 1966), though it is exceedingly difficult to specify the kinds of quantitative recordings of observations or the experimental conditions which would enable us to treat these phenomena with more precision. Clearly, one task of future research in this area is to develop a style of investigation which will make possible a systematic developmental study of the differentiation process as it affects all members of a group. The central issues in such a study seem to be fairly well established—the rigidity/flexibility dimension, the degree of stereotypy in the group, the relative permeability of subgroup boundaries. The principal challenge is the identification of the most reliable and informative behavioral manifestations of these developmental shifts.

This leaves unresolved, however, one issue raised by previous research—the assessment of the relative merit of the two general models of role differentiation which have been proposed. Bales and Slater (1955) have offered their endorsement of an *evolutionary* model in which the most basic, relatively diffuse roles become more differentiated over time. Bennis and Shepard's (1956) observations appear to support an alternative model; they argue that while the potential for certain kinds of leadership is always present, each kind becomes salient only at a certain point in the life of the group. Following Erikson's (1950) developmental theory of the human life cycle, I have termed this model an *epigenetic* one.

One implication of the preceding discussion is that the two models should not be taken as alternative, opposing interpretations of the same data but rather as complementary paradigms referring to different levels of abstraction. The evolution of individuation is, at the most abstract level of conceptualization, the central issue in group development. Moreover, the individuation/fusion polarity must be confronted in some fashion by every group. Groups with a minimum of prescribed structure often devote a great deal of time and energy to the resolution of this conflict. In other settings initial structures and less ambiguous styles of leadership provide institutional supports for both individual and group identity. But even in these groups the maintenance of individuation is somewhat problematic; what is missing are the most intense anxieties about engulfment and the most dramatic defenses against dedifferentiation. This view suggests that the pendular movement from diffusion to specialization to role flexibility is characteristic of all relatively unstructured groups. Within this broad framework, other issues may influence the differentiation of individual roles. As the group members progress gradually, almost imperceptibly, toward individuation, they must confront a variety of other, more circumscribed conflicts. Previously peripheral roles become salient; the central conflict is dramatized and resolved; the group turns to another issue and another set of salient roles. If this distinction between general and specific determinants of differentiation is valid, it may help us to resolve some of the apparent contradictions between theories and to avoid the confounding of different levels of abstraction which seems to have clouded our view of these phenomena.

I have proposed that the process of informal role differentiation should be studied from three separable levels of conceptualization, since previous theoretical and empirical work points to the operation of quite different determinants at each of these levels. From an intrapsychic point of view, the central issue is individuation, and the course of development is linear. From another perspective, the focus is on the differentiation of roles, and the developmental pattern is pendular. At a much less abstract—and probably more observable—level of conceptualization, the concern is with the patterning of the group roles which are most closely tied to the focal conflicts in the group, and the developmental paradigm here may well be epigenetic rather than evolutionary. This proposition and the preceding discussion will, I hope, prove heuristically valuable and provide a solid foundation for future investigations of the process of informal role differentiation.

PART FOUR

SHARED FANTASY
AND MYTH

Fantasy in small groups is a subject not often studied with the same intensity or persistence as other facets of group life. Yet it is clear that myth, ideology, ritual, and other forms of irrational belief play a crucial role in the establishment and maintenance of social structure and culture, and even of nation-building. We speak of the American Dream, we salute the flag, we feel that the nation's ideals, if not its soul, reside in certain "hallowed" places in Washington, D.C. Our recounting of history is, in part, based on a fantastical reworking of actual historical events. Small groups, particularly those with relatively open-ended agenda, often produce active and elaborate collective fantasies which have provided some observers an excellent opportunity to study the relationship between fantasy and group process and group structure.

The notion of fantasy has been used in a number of different ways. In psychoanalytic work, the term *fantasy* has taken on so many meanings that a firm distinction between different meanings is difficult to maintain. It is therefore important to clarify some of the different uses to which the term has been put.

The most common usage of the term in psychoanalytic writ-

267

ing (and in the literature on small groups) should be called *unconscious fantasy*. An unconscious fantasy is a set of assumptions, feelings, attitudes, or beliefs usually involving childhood events—experiences, real or imagined, which have come under repression and remain unconscious but continue to exert influence into adulthood. The oedipus complex is the most obvious and famous unconscious fantasy. Most oedipal thoughts, feelings, and attitudes are unconscious but may exert an unseen influence in our adult relationships and work life. In contrast, such fantasy activities as dreams, daydreams, and other imaginative productions are quite conscious or nearly so, and these have been confused with unconscious fantasy. It is misleading to equate unconscious fantasy with *all* fantasy activity.

The night dream is a form of fantasy that serves various functions. The interpretation of night dreams has been used in traditional psychoanalysis to plumb the depths of the unconscious. Although a dream is not a direct expression of unconscious fantasy, it has been understood as a manifestation of such. Recent studies (for instance, Jones, 1970) have concentrated on the manifest content of dreams and on structural and biological factors in dream production and have paid less attention to unconscious fantasy as a motivator of dreams. Daydreams and various forms of imaginative thought are *conscious fantasy activity* in which may be discovered traces of unconscious fantasy if one takes the time through free association to pursue that goal. However, daydreams in particular have been found to arise from other than unconscious sources, although they may contain traces of such motivation. Singer (1966) especially has stressed the adaptive and information-processing role of daydreams. Daydreams, for example, have been found to play a role in active problem solving of various kinds.

For purposes of understanding fantasy in groups, it may be said that belief, ideology, various kinds of ritual, and artistic productions are forms of fantasy activity as well. These, in turn, may contain traces of unconscious fantasy, as various psychoanalytic studies of rituals and artistic productions have shown (see Reik, 1946). However, it can also be demonstrated that unconscious fantasy may not be the primary determinant of ideology and belief; relatively conscious group structural and group process factors may play an even stronger role.

Not all fantasy, then, has the same function; not all forms of fantasy derive their sole importance from unconscious infantile conflict. For instance, fantasy activity in groups has been traced to two quite separate sources. The first is intrapsychic and psychological in nature. The importance of this source is stressed by the proponents of the kind of determinism that views social structure or group-wide events as the product of the inner workings of the individual's psychic apparatus, drive dynamics, and (often) unconscious wishes. The second is group-based and sociological in nature. This source is emphasized by the group-functional approach that views individual functioning as related primarily to the needs of the social system; that is, the intrapsychic manifestations that find group-wide acceptance do so because they fill some need in the collectivity's functioning at that time. This latter view is also exemplified by the more recent efforts toward integrating systems theory with small-group theory (Astrachan, 1970; Durkin, 1972).

Let us turn now to the question of why shared fantasy has been so little studied and why the subject of fantasy continues to be a debated one within social science as a whole. There is nothing that raises the ire of "hard-nosed" traditional social scientists more than the subject of fantasy. In the minds of these "scientists," fantasy, psychoanalysis, and the unconscious fit into the same boat, which to them should be cast adrift from the main body of scientific psychology and let out to sea. On the other hand, fantasy—particularly the notion of unconscious fantasy, and the use of dreams and conscious fantasy as sources of understanding the unconscious—has formed a cornerstone of psychodynamic theories almost from their inception. This controversy is also at the heart of the methodological controversy explored in Part One of this volume. The more clinically minded tend to utilize fantasy in their theory building and in their observational techniques, and have woven it into their way of understanding groups. The more statistically, quantitatively, or scientifically minded have tended to shy away from fantasy because they cannot readily quantify or concretize the irrational, the illusive, and the unconscious. Even though Freud sought to bring this irrational side of man into the scientific mainstream, to make logical and rational sense of otherwise inexplicable phenomena, the study of fantasy remains suspect and risky. The risk involves (as

Mann points out in Chapter 1) the fact that one's sense of reality can be threatened with the possibility of "going crazy." That is one important reason, we believe, that fantasy has not been more studied and has not reached a significant stature in social science research.

We have implied that for many researchers the risk of entering the world of the irrational and the fantastic or the whimsical may be unsettling. They prefer to stay with concrete, logical, rational methodology and study the cognitive problem-solving aspects of group life. But clinicians, especially the psychoanalysts, have adopted another assumption, which has in a quite different way hampered research: the orthodox assumption that all fantasy activity is a "compromise formation" between unconscious wishes and defensive operations. In this view fantasy—as well as dreams and symptoms—is primarily an expression of infantile sexual and aggressive urges. Fantasy, in particular, has been linked with masturbation, with the implication that all fantasy activity is at its roots masturbatory and as such is a manifestation of these repressed urges.

More recent research on individual fantasy, especially the work of Singer (1966), has stressed the adaptive role of fantasy and daydreaming in individual functioning. In Singer's view daydreaming is part of an ongoing stream of consciousness; and, although the entrance of the daydream into conscious awareness may be motivated by internal conflicts and psychodynamic forces, this inner stream of consciousness has its own motivational sources. He has argued persuasively that fantasy activity is an alternative form of planning and imaginative thought; as such, it often plays an important role in problem solving of various kinds. Fantasy has been utilized in the solving of creative problems in science and mathematics, it has been used in everyday planning of activity and in the improvement of interpersonal relations. This view of fantasy stresses less its use as a defense against infantile wishes and more its adaptive role in human problem solving.

Our own view of fantasy is somewhat different from either Freud's or Singer's, but we think it has relevance both for empirical research and for a general theory of shared fantasy. Winnicott (1953), in his remarkable paper on transitional objects in infancy, refers to an "intermediate area" in child development—a period that demarcates activity between "primary creativity" and "objective perception based on reality testing." This is a transitional period —a middle area of "illusion" on the way to differentiating reality from hallucination, a step toward the development of a feeling of separateness and individuation. In this connection, Winnicott makes a statement that has great relevance for fantasy in groups: "It is assumed here that the task of reality acceptance is never completed, that no human being is free from the strain of relating inner and outer reality, and that relief from this strain is provided by an intermediate area of experience which is not challenged (arts, religion, etc.). This intermediate area of experience, unchallenged in respect of its belonging to inner or external shared reality, constitutes the greater part of the infant's experience and throughout life is retained in the intense experiencing that belongs to the arts and to religion and to imaginative living, and to creative scientific work. A positive value of illusion can therefore be stated" (Winnicott, 1953, p. 97).

We can regard group fantasy activity—as well as daydreaming and creative and adaptive fantasy—as just this type of intermediate phenomenon. As such, it is not a true apprehension, a completely veridical perception of reality; at the same time, it is not the kind of distortion that is associated with hallucination, delusion, and other such images. Much of the fantasy activity that has been discussed in small-group research is, in our view, just this kind of intermediate phenomenon. If Winnicott's view is correct, and likewise our application of his views to myth, ritual, and shared conscious fantasies in groups, then such activity can be regarded as adaptive if not crucial to group process and structure. In this sense, Winnicott is in agreement with Arlow (1961) and his view of the adaptive function of group mythology. Winnicott's view, however, remains within the framework of intrapsychic determinism. He does not deal with the function of such intermediate phenomena for the group itself, for its creation, maintenance, and structure.

Psychoanalytic research in groups has stressed the role of unconscious fantasy in group structure. Bion (1959), for example, describes the group-as-a-whole as an object of the members' fantasy. He believes that the group-as-a-whole is regarded unconsciously as a maternal entity. This notion is first of all based on the theoretical assumptions of Melanie Klein, and second on the assumption that members project their inner unconscious fantasies onto the group-as-a-whole. Working in the same tradition, Jaques (this volume, Chapter 11) regards social structure or group structure as a product of depressive and persecutory anxiety stemming from just such unconscious fantasy. Group development, then, is seen as a shift in these "psychotic anxieties" and the institutionalized defenses against them. In this view the group-as-a-whole is like a blank screen upon which members project deep infantile wishes and conflicts; group process, then, really involves a sharing of unconscious fantasies at a deep level. Bion in particular assumes the formation of a group culture; that is, the unconscious sharing of certain basic assumptions about the nature of the group. These basic assumptions really involve unconscious fantasies about dependency, fight/flight, and pairing.

Slater (1966) portrays group development as an accommodation to wishes for individuation, on the one hand, and fusion with the group entity, on the other. In elaborating this theory, he utilizes the conscious fantasy productions of group members, infers certain deeply unconscious fantasies about the maternal entity, and draws parallels between phenomena in small groups and mythological and religious beliefs and customs. For example, in discussing what he calls the "deification" of the leader in the early phases of self-analytic classroom groups, he notes various references to the inanimate or stonelike qualities of the leader. He then marshals evidence from biblical references as well as mythological sources which make similar allusions to inanimate objects and begins to draw his parallels between processes in small groups and theories of religious evolution. In Slater's work we see something of the notion that Winnicott describes. That is, transitional phenomena involve illusion and fantasy, which are an intimate part of religious ideas and which play a surprising role in everyday adult life as well. Also, we can begin to see that the religious notions described by Slater come to have a purpose and a function on a societal level larger than individual theories of intrapsychic determinism would seem to suggest.

An understanding of these dynamics necessitates the spelling out of distinctions along several dimensions. The first is the distinction between conscious fantasy and unconscious fantasy. The second involves the identification of fantasy along a continuum of autistic-interpersonal-collective. There is no necessary connection between these two dimensions, although one may glimpse some correspondences from time to time. That is, an individual can easily maintain unconscious fantasies in isolation; as more verbal communication comes into play, however, he may find it less easy to maintain the necessary repression, and the derivatives of unconscious elements come to the fore. These elements are still edited and transformed as the fantasies become shared. They may have adaptive functions as well.

Dunphy (1964, 1966, 1968; this volume, Chapter 12) has come as close as anyone to synthesizing the individual and the social approaches to fantasy in groups. Dunphy explains group development as a shift in assumptions (myths) about the group and the group leader. These myths are group-shared, although not always consciously articulated, attitudes toward, perceptions of, and feelings about the group and leader. These ideas are sometimes unconscious, or preconscious, and can only be inferred from the group behavior. At other times, myths can be detected in certain conscious fantasies, which may be elaborated later in the group. These shared myths allow for the integration of the group on unconscious levels. On the other hand, since these myths are often irrational and unrealistic, they may serve as hindrances to the more rational problem-solving activities of groups. Dunphy's theory is an attempt to integrate the *intrapsychic unconscious* projections of internal concerns and the *social-functional* needs of the group-as-a-whole. He sees the elaboration of myth as the coming together of individual and group needs on a fantasy basis.

Bales (1970) has attempted to come to grips with some of the methodological problems involved in fantasy research. As part of his systematic approach to group observations, he has developed a series of quantifiable questions which allow the interested group observer to score observations about fantasy in a way that can be integrated into a general theory of role types in small groups.

In all this research there is evidence of the difficulties alluded to earlier. There is little distinction between unconscious fantasy, conscious fantasy, daydream activity, and myth, ideology, and ritual. There is some confusion between unconscious and conscious; and between intrapsychic, interpersonal, and group-wide phenomena. What is needed in future research on group fantasy is, first of all, a clarification of these different types of phenomena, and second, a coherent theory which can order the relationships between these quite different sets of phenomena.

Despite the difficulties inherent in such research and the shortcomings of the studies we have cited, it is clear that groups are a wellspring for the types of transitional phenomena that Winnicott describes. Groups are replete with mythological or mythlike assumptions about themselves. Members and leaders make use of conscious fantasy productions, involve their fellows in issues of political faith and ideology, have rituals and ritualistic activity, and invent religiouslike beliefs as well. Fantasy in diverse and varied form would seem to play an important role in the creation and maintenance of groups. The three papers presented in this section illustrate different but related facets of this subject of fantasy in groups. In addition, Winter (Chapter 8) refers to myths about racial issues in groups; and Gibbard (Chapter 10) demonstrates that a particular group member can become the object of many unconscious fantasies on the part of other group members. Similarly, Ringwald (Chapter 9) shows that certain members come to occupy roles by playing out different facets of shared conflicts which have many fantasy overtones; and finally, Kaplan (Chapter 5) makes reference to shared myths in therapy and training groups and relates these to group formative process.

Jaques begins this section with his study of the ways in which "psychotic anxieties" influence institutional and social structural characteristics of groups. His thesis is that social structure provides a way of defending against these persecutory and depressive anxieties. As mentioned, this study is based on a Kleinian theoretical perspective. The Kleinians posit very early and very primitive fantasies about the mother and the mother's body as being at the root of individual personality development. These attitudes about the mother and her body form the core of unconscious fantasies that are projected and introjected by individuals in their transactions with the world. The notion of projective identification, referred to by Ringwald (Chapter 9), is especially important to this theoretical perspective. Introjective identification, as Jaques mentions, entails the taking in of the attributes of another person as one's own.

Projective identification involves, first, the attribution of certain of one's own characteristics to another person, and second, an acting toward that person on the basis of those projections. Although this is a complicated and controversial psychological notion, it is a theoretical construct that provides a link between intrapsychic and interpersonal transactions (Zinner and Shapiro, 1972). In addition, the Kleinian perspective allows for an explanation of the fragmentation of the group into different roles and members. Jaques' article is a good example of a psychoanalytic study in which intrapsychic variables are seen as projected and writ large upon the group-as-a-whole.

Dunphy's article is a shortened version of his previous work on self-analytic groups. Dunphy himself makes use of the notion of projective identification in delineating his theory of role differentiation in small groups. His contribution is included in the section on fantasy because of his emphasis on the establishment of what he calls myths in the course of the group's development. Dunphy, too, sees these myths as a collective solution and a collective portrayal of intrapsychic issues. However, he is able to combine these psychological notions with a more sophisticated understanding of the needs of the group-as-a-whole. These might be called the group-functional aspects of the development of the group myth. Dunphy's study, then, is somewhat of an integration of psychoanalytic and sociological notions about fantasy in groups.

Hartman and Gibbard attempt a similar integration of psychological and group-wide approaches to fantasy in groups. Their focus is on utopianism, bisexuality, and messianism in self-analytic groups. Utopianism and messianism are certainly manifestations of widely shared myths, hopes, and assumptions that go beyond the fantasies or daydreams of particular individuals. They are daydreams that are shared by many, if not most, group members at different times in groups. Here, Hartman and Gibbard have tried to point out the connections between intrapsychic issues, phenomena in small groups, and myths and ideologies that are manifest in larger societal systems. Their thesis is that daydreams, group-wide fantasies in small groups, and belief systems in large groups all can be analyzed from the same perspective. This perspective is one largely of defense: in the individual case, a defense against lowered self-esteem and depression; in small groups, a defense against a variety of group issues that would cause distress; and in large groups, a defense against the threatened dissolution of group ties. The role of group fantasy is presented in a developmental context.

The principal correspondence among these studies is their reliance on theoretical notions about ego processes in early childhood. They regard the group entity as a reflection of both the omnipotent self and a maternal entity. The clearest developmental analogy is the symbiotic state of very early childhood. These three studies differ, though, in the relative weight given to intrapsychic factors as causative in group phenomena, and thus on the weight given to the group functional aspects of fantasy as well.

11

Social Systems as a Defense Against Persecutory and Depressive Anxiety

ELLIOT JAQUES

*I*t has often been noted that many social phenomena show a strikingly close correspondence with psychotic processes in individuals. Melitta Schmideberg (1930), for instance, has pointed to the psychotic content of many primitive ceremonies and rites. And Bion (1952) has suggested that the emotional life of the group is only understandable in terms of psychotic mechanisms. My own recent experience (Jaques, 1951) has impressed upon me how much institutions are used by their individual members to reinforce individual mechanisms of defense against anxiety, and in particular against recurrence of the early paranoid and depressive anxieties first described by Melanie Klein (1932, 1946, 1948a, 1948b, 1948c). In connecting social behavior with defense against psychotic anxiety, I do not wish in any way to suggest that social relationships serve none other than a defensive func-

Reprinted from Melanie Klein, Paula Heimann, and R. E. Money-Kyrle (Eds.), *New Directions in Psychoanalysis* (London: Tavistock Publications, 1955), pp. 478–498, by permission of the author and Basic Books, Inc.

tion of this kind. Instances of other functions include the equally important expression and gratification of libidinal impulses in constructive social activities, as well as social cooperation in institutions providing creative, sublimatory opportunities. In the present chapter, however, I propose to limit myself to a consideration of certain defensive functions, and in so doing I hope to illustrate and define how the mechanisms of projective and introjective identification operate in linking individual and social behavior.

The specific hypothesis I shall consider is that *one* of the primary cohesive elements binding individuals into institutionalized human association is that of defense against psychotic anxiety. In this sense individuals may be thought of as externalizing those impulses and internal objects that would otherwise give rise to psychotic anxiety and pooling them in the life of the social institutions in which they associate. This is not to say that the institutions so used thereby become "psychotic." But it does imply that we would expect to find in group relationships manifestations of unreality, splitting, hostility, suspicion, and other forms of maladaptive behavior. These would be the social counterpart of—although not identical with—what would appear as psychotic symptoms in individuals who have not developed the ability to use the mechanism of association in social groups to avoid psychotic anxiety.

If the above hypothesis holds true, then observation of social process is likely to provide a magnified view of the psychotic mechanisms observable in individuals, while also providing a setting in which more than one observer can share. Moreover, many social problems—economic and political—which are often laid at the door of human ignorance, stupidity, wrong attitudes, selfishness, or power seeking may become more understandable if seen as containing unconsciously motivated attempts by human beings to defend themselves in the best way available at the moment against the experience of anxieties whose sources could not be consciously controlled. And the reasons for the intractability to change of many social stresses and group tensions may be more clearly appreciated if seen as the "resistances" of groups of people unconsciously clinging to the institutions that they have, because changes in social relationships threaten to disturb existing social defenses against psychotic anxiety.

Social institutions, as I shall here use the term, are social structures with the cultural mechanisms governing relationships within them. Social structures are systems of roles, or positions, which may be taken up and occupied by persons. Cultural mechanisms are conventions, customs, taboos, rules, etc., which are used in regulating the relations among members of a society. For purposes of analysis, institutions can be defined independently of the particular individuals occupying roles and operating a culture. But the actual working of institutions takes place through real people using cultural mechanisms within a social structure; and the unconscious or implicit functions of an institution are specifically determined by the particular individuals associated in the instituton, occupying roles within a structure and operating the culture. Changes may occur in the unconscious functions of an institution through change in personnel, without there necessarily being any apparent change in manifest structure of functions. And conversely, as is so often noted, the imposition of a change in manifest structure or culture for the purpose of resolving a problem may often leave the problem unsolved because the unconscious relationships remain unchanged.

PROJECTION, INTROJECTION, AND IDENTIFICATION IN SOCIAL RELATIONSHIPS

In *Group Psychology and the Analysis of the Ego* (1921), Freud takes as his starting point in group psychology the relationship between the group and its leader. The essence of this relationship he sees in the mechanisms of identifications of the members of the group with the leader and with each other.[1] Group processes in this sense can be linked to earlier forms of behavior, since "identification is known to psychoanalysis as the earliest expression of an emotional tie with another person" (1921, p. 105). But Freud did not explicitly develop the concept of identification beyond that of identification by introjection, a conception deriving from his work on the retention of lost objects through introjection (Freud, 1917). In his analysis of group life, he does, however, differentiate between

[1] He states, "A primary group . . . is a number of individuals who have substituted one and the same object for their ego ideal and have consequently identified themselves with one another in their ego" (1921, p. 116).

identification of the ego with an object (or identification by intro-jection)` and what he terms replacement of the ego ideal by an external object (Freud, 1921, p. 129). Thus, in the two cases he describes, the army and the church, he points out that the soldier replaces his ego ideal by the leader who becomes his ideal, whereas the Christian takes Christ into himself as his ideal and identifies himself with Him.

Like Freud, Melanie Klein sees introjection as one of the primary processes whereby the infant makes emotional relationships with its objects. But she considers that introjection interacts with the process of projection in the making of these relationships.[2] Such a formulation seems to me to be consistent with, although not ex-plicit in, the views of Freud expressed above. That is to say, identi-fication of the ego with an object is identification by introjection; this is explicit in Freud. But replacement of the ego ideal by an external object seems to me implicitly to contain the conception of identification by projection. Thus, the soldiers who take their leader for their ego ideal are in effect projectively identifying with him or putting part of themselves into him. It is this common or shared projective identification which enables the soldiers to identify with each other. In the extreme form of projective identification of this kind, the followers become totally dependent on the leader, because each has given up a part of himself to the leader.[3] Indeed, it is just such an extreme of projective identification which might explain the case of panic described by Freud (1921, p. 97), where the Assyrians take to flight on learning that Holofernes, their leader, has

[2] "I have often expressed my view that object relations exist from the beginning of life. . . . I have further suggested that the relation to the first object implies its introjection and projection, and that from the beginning object relations are molded by an interaction between introjection and projec-tion, between internal and external objects and situations" (Klein [1946], 1952, p. 293).

[3] "The projection of good feelings and good parts of the self into the mother is essential for the infant's ability to develop good object relations and to integrate his ego. However, if this projective process is carried out exces-sively, good parts of the personality are felt to be lost, and in this way the mother becomes the ego ideal; this process too results in weakening and im-poverishing the ego. Very soon such processes extend to other people, and the result may be an overstrong dependence on these external representatives of one's own good parts" (Klein [1946], 1952, p. 301).

had his head cut off by Judith. For not only has the commonly shared external object (the figurehead) binding them all together been lost, but the leader having lost his head, every soldier has lost his head through being inside the leader by projective identification.

I shall take as the basis of my analysis of group processes the conception of identification in group formation, as described by Freud, but with particular reference to the processes of introjective and projective identification, as elaborated by Melanie Klein. Such a form of analysis has been suggested in another context by Paula Heimann,[4] who puts forward the notion that introjection and projection may be at the bottom of even the most complex social processes. I shall try to show how individuals make unconscious use of institutions by associating in these institutions and unconsciously cooperating to reinforce internal defenses against anxiety and guilt. These social defenses bear a reciprocal relationship with the internal defense mechanisms. For instance, the schizoid and manic defenses against anxiety and guilt both involve splitting and projection mechanisms, and, through projection, a link with the outside world. When external objects are shared with others and used in common for purposes of projection, fantasy social relationships may be established through projective identification with the common object. These fantasy relationships are further elaborated by introjection; and the two-way character of social relationships is mediated by virtue of the two-way play of projective and introjective identification.

I shall speak of the "fantasy social form and content of an institution" to refer to the form and content of social relationships at the level of the common individual fantasies which the members of an institution share by projective and introjective identification. Fantasy is used in the sense of completely unconscious intrapsychic activity as defined by Susan Isaacs (1952). From this point of view the character of institutions is determined and colored not only by

---

[4] "Such taking in and expelling consists of an active interplay between the organism and the outer world; on this primordial pattern rests all intercourse between subject and object, no matter how complex and sophisticated such intercourse appears. (I believe that in the last analysis we may find it at the bottom of all our complicated dealings with one another.) The patterns Nature uses seem to be few, but she is inexhaustible in their variation" (Heimann, 1952a, p. 129).

their explicit or consciously agreed and accepted functions but also by their manifold unrecognized functions at the fantasy level.

ILLUSTRATIONS OF SOCIALLY STRUCTURED DEFENSE MECHANISMS

It is not my intention to explore either systematically or comprehensively the manner in which social defense mechanisms operate. I shall first examine certain paranoid anxieties and defenses, and then depressive anxieties and defenses, keeping them to some extent separate for purposes of explication and giving illustrations from everyday experience. Then I shall present case material from a social study in industry, which may make clearer some of the theoretical considerations by showing the interaction of paranoid and depressive phenomena.

Defenses Against Paranoid Anxiety

One example of social mechanisms of defense against paranoid anxieties is that of putting bad internal objects[5] and impulses into particular members of an institution who, whatever their explicit function in a society, are unconsciously selected, or themselves choose to introject these projected objects and impulses and either to *absorb* them or *deflect* them. By absorption is meant the process of introjecting the objects and impulses and containing them, whereas in deflection they are again projected but not into the same members from whom they were introjected.

The fantasy social structuring of the process of absorption may be seen, for example, in the case of a first officer in a ship, who, in addition to his normal duty, is held responsible for many things

[5] The nature of the objects projected and introjected (e.g., feces, penis, breast), the medium of introjection and projection (e.g., anal, urethral, oral), and the sensory mechanism of introjection and projection (kinesthetic, visual, auditory, etc.) are variables of fundamental importance in the analysis of group relationships. I shall not, however, consider these variables to any extent here, but I hope to show in subsequent publications that their introduction makes possible a systematic explanation of differences between many types of institution.

that go wrong, but for which he was not actually responsible. Everyone's bad objects and impulses may unconsciously be put into the first officer, who is consciously regarded by common consent as the source of the trouble. By this mechanism the members of the crew can unconsciously find relief from their own internal persecutors. And the ship's captain can thereby be more readily idealized and identified with as a good protective figure. The anal content of the fantasy attack on the first officer is indicated in the colloquialism that "the first officer must take all the shit; and he must be prepared to be a shit." Naval officers in the normal course of promotion are expected to accept this masochistic role; and the norm is to accept it without demurring.

The process of deflection may be seen in certain aspects of the complex situation of nations at war. The manifest social structure is that of two opposing armies, each backed and supported by its community. At the fantasy level, however, we may consider the following possibility. The members of each community put their bad objects and sadistic impulses into the commonly shared and accepted external enemy. They rid themselves. of their hostile, destructive impulses by projecting them into their armies for deflection against the enemy. Paranoid anxiety in the total community, army and civilian alike, may be alleviated, or at least transmuted into fear of known and identifiable enemies, since the bad impulses and objects projected into the enemy return not in the form of introjected fantastic persecutors but of actual physical attack, which can be experienced in reality. Under appropriate conditions, objective fear may be more readily coped with than fantasy persecution. The bad sadistic enemy is fought against, not in the solitary isolation of the unconscious inner world but in cooperation with comrades-in-arms in real life. Individuals not only rid themselves of fantastic persecution in this way; but further, the members of the army are temporarily freed from depressive anxiety because their own sadistic impulses can be denied by attributing their aggressiveness to doing their duty; that is, expressing the aggressive impulses collected and introjected from all the community. And members of the community may also avoid guilt by introjecting the socially sanctioned hatred of the enemy. Such introjected sanction reinforces the denial of unconscious hatred and destructive impulses against good objects by allowing for conscious expression of these impulses against a commonly shared and publicly hated real external enemy.

Social cooperation at the reality level may thus allow for a redistribution of the bad objects and impulses in the fantasy relations obtaining among the members of a society.[6] In conjunction with such a redistribution, introjective identification makes it possible for individuals to take in social sanction and support. The primitive aim of the absorption and deflection mechanisms is to achieve a nonreturn at the fantasy level of the projected fantasy bad objects and impulses.

But even where absorption and deflection are not entirely successful (and mechanisms at the fantasy level can never be completely controlled), the social defense mechanisms provide some gain. Paula Heimann (1952b) has described the introjection of projected bad objects, and their related impulses, into the ego, where they are maintained in a split-off state, subjected to intrapsychic projection, and kept under attack. In the cases described above, the ego receives support from the social sanctions which are introjected, and which legitimize the intrapsychic projection and aggression. The first officer, for example, may be introjected, and the impulses projected into him introjected as well. But in the fantasy social situation other members of the crew who also attack the first officer are identified with by introjection, partly into the ego and partly into the superego. Hence the ego is reinforced by possession of the internalized members of the crew, all of whom take part in the attack on the segregated bad objects within the ego. And there is an alleviation of the harshness of the superego by adding to it objects that socially sanction and legitimize the attack.

These illustrations are obviously not completely elaborated; nor are they intended to be so. They are abstractions from real-life situations in which a fuller analysis would show defenses against persecutory and depressive anxiety interacting with each other and with other more explicit functions of the group. But perhaps they suffice to indicate how the use of the concepts of introjective and projective identifications, regarded as interacting mechanisms, may

[6] Cf. Freud's description of the redistribution of libido in the group (Freud, 1921, p. 90).

serve to add further dimensions to Freud's analysis of the army and the church. We may also note that the social mechanisms described contain in their most primitive aspects features which may be related to the earliest attempts of the infant, described by Melanie Klein (1946, 1948a), to deal with persecutory anxiety in relation to part objects by means of splitting and projection and introjection of both the good and bad objects and impulses. If we now turn to the question of social defenses against depressive anxieties, we shall be able to illustrate further some of the general points.

Defenses Against Depressive Anxiety

Let us consider first certain aspects of the problems of the scapegoating of a minority group. As seen from the viewpoint of the community at large, the community is split into a good majority and a bad minority—a split consistent with the splitting of internal objects into good and bad, and the creation of a good and bad internal world. The persecuting group's belief in its own good is preserved by heaping contempt upon and attacking the scapegoated group. The internal splitting mechanisms and preservation of the internal good objects of individuals, and the attack upon, and contempt for, internal bad persecutory objects, are reinforced by introjective identification of individuals with other members taking part in the group-sanctioned attack upon the scapegoat.[7]

If we now turn to the minority groups, we may ask why only some minorities are selected for persecution while others are not. Here a feature often overlooked in consideration of minority problems may be of help. The members of the persecuted minority commonly entertain a precise and defined hatred and contempt for their persecutors, matching in intensity the contempt and aggression to which they are themselves subjected. That this should be so is perhaps not surprising. But in view of the selective factor in choice of persecuted minorities, we must consider the possibility that one of the operative factors in this selection is the consensus in the minority group, at the fantasy level, to seek contempt and suffering in order to alleviate unconscious guilt. That is to say, there is an un-

[7] Cf. Melanie Klein's description of the operation of splitting mechanisms in the depressive position (1948b).

conscious cooperation (or collusion) at the fantasy level between persecutor and persecuted. For the members of the minority group, such a collusion reinforces their own defenses against depressive anxiety—by such mechanisms as social justification for feelings of contempt and hatred for an external persecutor, with consequent alleviation of guilt and reinforcement of denial in the protection of internal good objects.

Another way in which depressive anxiety may be alleviated by social mechanisms is through manic denial of destructive impulses, and destroyed good objects, and the reinforcement of good impulses and good objects, by participation in group idealization. These social mechanisms are the reflection in the group of mechanisms of denial and idealization shown by Melanie Klein to be important mechanisms of defense against depressive anxiety (Klein, 1948c).

The operation of these social mechanisms may be seen in mourning ceremonies. The bereaved are joined by others in common display of grief and public reiteration of the good qualities of the deceased. There is a common sharing of guilt, through comparison of the shortcomings of the survivors with the good qualities of the deceased. Bad objects and impulses are gotten rid of by unconscious projection into the corpse, disguised by the decoration of the corpse, and safely put out of the way through projective identification with the dead during the burial ceremony; such mechanisms are unconsciously aimed at the avoidance of persecution by demonic figures. At the same time good objects and impulses are also projected into the dead person. Public and socially sanctioned idealization of the deceased then reinforces the sense that the good object has after all not been destroyed, for "his good works" are held to live on in the memory of the community as well as the surviving family, a memory which is reified in the tombstone. These mechanisms are unconsciously aimed at the avoidance of haunting by guilt-provoking ghosts. Hence, through mourning ceremonies, the community and the bereaved are provided with the opportunity of unconsciously cooperating in splitting the destroyed bad part of the loved object from the loved part, of burying the destroyed bad object and impulses, and of protecting the good loved part as an eternal memory.

One general feature of each of the instances cited is that the fantasy social systems established have survival value for the group as well as affording protection against anxiety in the individual. Thus, for example, in the case of the mourning ceremony the social idealizing and manic denial make it possible for a bereaved person to reduce the internal chaos, to weather the immediate and intense impact of death, and to undertake the process of mature internal mourning at his own time and his own pace (Klein 1948c, p. 329). But there is a general social gain as well, in that all those associated in the mourning ceremony can further their internal mourning and continue the lifelong process of working through the unresolved conflicts of the infantile depressive position. As Melanie Klein has described the process, "It seems that every advance in the process of mourning results in a deepening in the individual's relation to his inner objects, in the happiness of regaining them after they were felt to be lost ('Paradise Lost and Regained'), in an increased trust in them and love for them because they proved to be good and helpful after all" (1948c, p. 328). Hence, through the mourning ceremony, the toleration of ambivalence is increased and friendship in the community can be strengthened. Or again, in the case of the first officer, the ship's crew, in a situation made difficult by close confinement and isolation from other groups, is enabled to cooperate with the captain in carrying out the required and consciously planned tasks by isolating and concentrating their bad objects and impulses within an available human receptacle.

CASE STUDY

I shall now turn to a more detailed and precise examination of fantasy social systems as defense mechanisms for the individual and as mechanisms allowing the group to proceed with its sophisticated or survival tasks, by examining a case study from industry. It may be noted that the conception of sophisticated tasks derives from Bion's (1952) conception of the sophisticated task of the work or W group. I am refraining from using Bion's more elaborate conceptual scheme defining what he terms the "basic assumptions" of groups, since the relationship between the operation of basic assumptions and of depressive and persecutory phenomena remains to be worked out.

The case to be presented is one part of a larger study carried out in a light engineering factory, the Glacier Metal Company, between June 1948 and the present time. The relationship with the firm is a therapeutic one; work is done only on request, from groups or individuals within the firm, for assistance in working through intragroup stresses or in dealing with organizational problems. The relationship between the social consultant (or therapist) and the people with whom he works is a confidential one; and the only reports published are those which have been worked through with the people concerned and agreed by them for publication. Within these terms of reference, I have published a detailed report on the first three years of the project (Jaques, 1951).

The illustration I shall use is taken from work done with one department in the factory.[8] The department employs roughly sixty people. It was organized with a departmental manager as head. Under him was a superintendent, who was in turn responsible for four foremen, each of whom had a working group of ten to sixteen operatives. The operatives had elected five representatives, two of whom were shop stewards, to negotiate with the departmental manager on matters affecting the department. One such matter had to do with a change in methods of wage payments. The shop had been on piece rates (i.e., the operatives were paid a basic wage, plus a bonus dependent on their output). This method of payment had, for a number of years, been felt to be unsatisfactory. From the workers' point of view it meant uncertainty about the amount of their weekly wage, and for the management it meant complicated rate fixing and administrative arrangements. For all concerned, the not infrequent wrangling about rates that took place was felt to be unnecessarily disturbing. The possibility of changing over to a flat-rate method of payment had been discussed for over a year before the project began. In spite of the fact that the change was commonly desired, they had not been able to come to a decision.

[8] This case material is a condensation of material which is given in much greater detail in two published articles: Jaques (1950) and Jaques, Rice, and Hill (1951).

A Period of Negotiation

Work with the department began in January 1949, by attendance at discussions of a subcommittee composed of the departmental manager, the superintendent, and three workers' representatives. The general tone of the discussions was friendly. The committee members laid stress upon the fact that good relationships existed in the department and that they all wanted to strive for further improvement. From time to time, however, there was sharp disagreement over specific points, and these disagreements led the workers' representatives to state that there were many matters on which they felt they could not trust the management. This statement of suspicion was answered by the management members, who emphasized that they for their part had great trust in the workers' sense of responsibility.

The workers' suspicion of management also revealed itself in discussions held at shop floor level between the elected representatives and their worker constituents. The purpose of these discussions was to elicit in a detailed and concrete manner the views of the workers about the proposed changeover. The workers were on the whole in favor of the changeover, but they had some doubt as to whether they could trust the management to implement and to administer the changeover in a fair manner. What guarantees did they have, they asked, that management had nothing up its sleeve? At the same time, the workers showed an ambivalent attitude toward their own representatives. They urged and trusted them to carry on negotiations with management, but at the same time suspected that the representatives were management "stooges" and did not take the workers' views sufficiently into account. This negative attitude toward their representatives came out more clearly in interviews with the workers alone, in which opinions were expressed that although the elected representatives were known as militant trade unionists, nevertheless they were seen as liable to be outwitted by the management and as not carrying their representative role as effectively as they might.

The day-to-day working relationships between supervisors and workers were quite different from what would be expected as the consequence of these views. Work in the shop was carried out with good morale, and the supervisors were felt to do their best for the workers. A high proportion of the shop had been employed in the company for five years or more, and genuinely good personal relationships had been established.

The discussions in the committee composed of the managers and elected representatives went on for seven months, between January and July 1949. They had a great deal of difficulty in working toward a decision, becoming embroiled in arguments that were sometimes quite heated and had no obvious cause—other than the workers' suspicion of the management, counterbalanced by the management's idealization of the workers. Much of the suspicion and idealization, however, was autistic, in the sense that although consciously experienced it was not expressed openly as between managers and workers. These attitudes came out much more sharply when the elected representatives and the managers were meeting separately. The workers expressed deep suspicion and mistrust, while the managers expressed some of their anxieties about how responsible the workers could be—anxieties which existed alongside their strong sense of the workers' responsibility and of their faith in them.

Analysis of the Negotiation Phase

I now wish to apply certain of our theoretical formulations to the above data. This is in no sense intended to be a complete analysis of the material. Many important factors, such as changes in the executive organization of the shop, personal attitudes, changes in personnel, and variations in the economic and production situation, all played a part in determining the changes which occurred. I do wish, however, to demonstrate how, if we assume the operation of defenses against paranoid and depressive anxiety at the fantasy social level, we may be able to explain some of the very great difficulties encountered by the members of the department. And I would emphasize here that these difficulties were encountered in spite of the high morale implied in the willingness of those concerned to face, and to work through in a serious manner, the group stresses they experienced in trying to arrive at a commonly desired goal.

The degree of inhibition of the autistic suspicion and idealization becomes understandable, I think, if we make the following assumptions about unconscious attitudes at the fantasy level. The workers in the shop had split the managers into good and bad—the good managers being the ones with whom they worked and the bad being the same managers but in the negotiation situation. They had unconsciously projected their hostile destructive impulses into their elected representatives so that the representatives could deflect, or redirect, these impulses against the bad "management" with whom negotiations were carried on, while the good objects and impulses could be put into individual real managers in the day-to-day work situation. This splitting of the management into good and bad and the projective identification with the elected representatives against the bad management served two purposes. At the reality level it allowed the good relations necessary to the work task of the department to be maintained; at the fantasy level it provided a system of social relationships reinforcing individual defenses against paranoid and depressive anxiety.

Putting their good impulses into managers in the work situation allowed the workers to reintroject the good relations with management, and hence to preserve an undamaged good object and alleviate depressive anxiety. This depressive anxiety was further avoided by reversion to the paranoid position in the negotiating situation.[9] During the negotiations paranoid anxiety was partially avoided by the workers by putting their bad impulses into their elected representatives. The representatives, while consciously the negotiating representatives of the workers, became unconsciously the representatives of their bad impulses. These split-off bad impulses were partially dealt with and avoided because they were directed against the bad objects put into management in the negotiation situation by the workers and their representatives.

Another mechanism for dealing with the workers' own pro-

[9] Melanie Klein has described how paranoid fears and suspicions are often used as a defense against the depressive position. See for instance, Klein (1948b, p. 293).

jected bad objects and impulses was to attack their representatives, with an accompanying despair that not much good would come of the negotiations. These feelings tended to be expressed privately by individuals. The workers who felt like this had introjected their representatives as bad objects and maintained them as a segregated part of the ego. Intrapsychic projection and aggression against these internal bad objects were supported by introjective identification with other workers, who held that the representatives were not doing their job properly. That is to say, other members of the department were introjected to reinforce the intrapsychic projection and as protection against the internal bad representatives striking back. In addition to defense against internal persecution, the introjection of the other workers provided social sanction for considering the internalized representatives as bad, offsetting the harshness of superego recrimination for attacking objects containing a good as well as a persecuting component.

From the point of view of the elected representatives, anxiety about bad impulses was diminished by unconsciously accepting the bad impulses and objects of all the workers they represented. They could feel that their own hostile and aggressive impulses did not belong to them but belonged to the people on whose behalf they were acting. They were thus able to derive external social sanction for their aggression and hostile suspicion. But the mechanism did not operate with complete success, for there still remained their own unconscious suspicion and hostility to be dealt with, and the reality of what they considered to be the good external management. Hence, there was some anxiety and guilt about damaging the good managers. The primary defense mechanism against the onset of depressive anxiety was that of retreat to the paranoid position. This came out as a rigid clinging to attitudes of suspicion and hostility even in circumstances where they consciously felt that some of this suspicion was not justified by the situation they were actually experiencing.

From the management side, the paranoid attitude of the elected representatives was countered by the reiteration of the view that the workers could be trusted to do their part. This positive attitude unconsciously contained both idealization of the workers and placation of the hostile representatives. The idealization can be understood as an unconscious mechanism for diminishing guilt, stimulated by fears of injuring or destroying workers in the day-to-day work situation through the exercise of managerial authority—an authority which there is good reason to believe is, at least to some extent, felt unconsciously to be uncontrolled and omnipotent. To the extent that managers unconsciously felt their authority to be bad, they feared retaliation by the operatives. This in turn led to a reinforcement of the idealization of the elected representatives, so that reality mechanisms could operate in the relationships with workers in the work situation, less encumbered with the content of uncontrolled fantasy.

It can thus be seen that the unconscious use of paranoid attitudes by the workers and idealizing and placatory attitudes by the management were complementary and reinforced each other. A circular process was set in motion. The more the workers' representatives attacked the managers, the more the managers idealized them in order to placate them. The greater the concessions given by management to the workers, the greater was the guilt and fear of depressive anxiety in the workers and hence the greater the retreat to paranoid attitudes as a means of avoiding depressive anxiety.

Description and Analysis of the Post-Negotiation Phase

In June, six months after the discussions began, these attitudes, rather than the wages problem, were for a time taken as the main focus of consideration. A partial resolution occurred,[10] and the workers decided, after a ballot in the whole department, to try out a flat-rate method of payment. The condition for the changeover, however, was the setting up of a council, composed of managers and elected representatives, which would have the authority to determine departmental policy—a procedure for which the principles had already been established in the company. The prime principle was that of unanimous agreement on all decisions, and the agree-

---

[10] The work-through process is in part described in the articles referred to above, and includes an account of the manner in which transference phenomena were handled in the face-to-face group situation. An analysis of the work-through process is outside the scope of the present paper, and hence there is only passing reference to it in the text.

ment to work through all obstacles to unanimous decision by discovering sources of disagreement so that they could be resolved.

It appeared as though the open discussion of autistic attitudes facilitated a restructuring of the fantasy social relations in the department—a restructuring which brought with it a greater degree of conscious or ego control over their relationships. The fact, however, that there was only a partial restructuring of social relations at the fantasy level showed itself in the subsequent history of the shop council. For, following the changeover to a flat-rate method of payment, the council came up against the major question of reassessing the times in which given jobs ought to be done.

Under piece rates such assessment of times was necessary, both for calculation of the bonus to operatives and for giving estimated prices to customers. On the flat rates, it was required only for estimating to customers, but the times thus set inevitably constituted targets for the workers. Under piece rates, if a worker did not achieve the target, it meant that he lost his bonus; in other words, he himself paid for any drop in effort. Under flat rates, however, a drop below the target meant that the worker was getting paid for work that he was not doing. A detailed exploration of workers' attitudes (Jaques, Rice, and Hill, 1951) showed that the changeover from piece rates to flat rates had in no way altered their personal targets and personal rate of work. They felt guilty whenever they fell below their estimated targets, because they were no longer paying for the difference. In order to avoid this guilt, the workers applied strong pressure to keep the estimated times on jobs as high as possible, as well as pressure to get the so-called tight times (times on jobs that were difficult to achieve) reassessed. There were strong resistances to any changes in job assessment methods which the workers suspected might set difficult targets for them.

On the management side, the changeover to flat rates inevitably stirred whatever unconscious anxieties they might have about authority. For under piece rates the bonus payment itself acted as an impersonal and independent disciplinarian, ensuring that workers put in the necessary effort. Under flat rates it was up to managers to see that a reasonable rate of work was carried on. This forced upon them more direct responsibility for the supervision of their subordinates and brought them more directly into contact with the authority that they held.

The newly constituted council, with its managers and elected representatives, had great difficulty in coping with the more manifest depressive anxiety both in the managers and in the workers. This showed in managers' views that the council might possibly turn out to be a bad thing because it slowed down administrative developments in the department. Similar opinions that the council would not work and might not prove worthwhile played some part in the decision of five out of six of the elected representatives not to stand for reelection in the shop elections which occurred sixteen months after the setting up of the council. These five were replaced by five newly elected representatives, who in turn brought with them a considerable amount of suspicion. That is, there was again a retreat to the paranoid position while the managers' depressive anxiety continued to show to some extent in the form of depressive feelings that the council would not work. It has only been slowly, over a period of two years, that the council has been able to operate in the new situation as a constitutional mechanism for getting agreement on policy and at the same time intuitively to be used for the containment of the fantasy social relationships. An exploration of the rerating problem has been agreed upon and is being carried on with the assistance of an outside industrial consultant.

This case study, then, illustrates the development of an explicit social institution, that of meetings between management and elected representatives, which allowed for the establishment of unconscious mechanisms at the fantasy level for dealing with paranoid and depressive anxieties. The main mechanisms were those of management idealizing the hostile workers and the workers maintaining an attitude of suspicion toward the idealizing management. To the extent that splitting and projective identification operated successfully, these unconscious mechanisms helped individuals to deal with anxiety, by getting their anxieties into the fantasy social relations structured in the management–elected-representative group. In this way the anxieties were eliminated from the day-to-day work situation and allowed for the efficient operation of the sophisticated work task and the achievement of good working relationships.

However, it will be noted that the elected-representative–management group was also charged with a sophisticated work task —that of negotiating new methods of wages payment. They found it difficult to get on with the sophisticated task itself. In terms of the theory here propounded, these difficulties have been explained as arising from the manner in which the predominant unconscious fantasy relations in the negotiating group ran counter to the requirements of the sophisticated task. In other words, an essentially constitutional procedure, that of elected representatives meeting with an executive body, was difficult to operate because it was being used in an unrecognized fashion at the fantasy level to help deal with the depressive and paranoid anxieties of the members of the department as a whole.

SOME OBSERVATIONS ON SOCIAL CHANGE

In the above case study, it might be said that social change was sought when the structure and culture no longer met the requirements of the individual members of the department and in particular of the managers and the elected representatives. Manifest changes were brought about and in turn appeared to lead to a considerable restructuring of the fantasy social form and content of the institution. Change having taken place, however, the individual members found themselves in the grip of new relationships, to which they had to conform because they were self-made. But they had brought about more than they had bargained for, in the sense that the new relationships under flat rates and the policy-making council had to be experienced before their implications could be fully appreciated.

The effects of the change on individuals were different according to the roles they occupied. The elected representatives were able to change roles by the simple expedient of not standing for reelection. And this expedient, it will be noted, was resorted to by five of the six representatives. The managers, however, were in a very different position. They could not relinquish or change their roles without in a major sense changing their positions, and possibly status, in the organization as a whole. They had, therefore, individually to bear considerable personal stress in adjusting themselves to the new situation.

It is unlikely that members of an institution can ever bring about social changes that suit perfectly the needs of each individual. Once change is undertaken, it is more than likely that individuals will have to adjust and change personally in order to catch up with the changes they have produced. And until some readjustment is made at the fantasy level, the individual's social defenses against psychotic anxiety are likely to be weakened. It may well be because of the effects on the unconscious defense systems of individuals against psychotic anxiety that social change is resisted—and in particular, imposed social change. For it is one thing to readjust to changes that the individual has himself helped to bring about. It is quite another to be required to adjust one's internal defense systems in order to conform to changes brought about by some outside agency.

SUMMARY AND CONCLUSIONS

Freud has argued that two main processes operate in the formation of what he calls artificial groups, like the army and the church; one is identification by introjection, and the other is replacement of the ego ideal by an object. I have suggested that this latter process implicitly contains the concept, formulated by Melanie Klein, of identification by projection. Further, Melanie Klein states explicitly that in the interaction between introjective and projective identification lies the basis of the infant's earliest relations with its objects. The character of these early relations is determined by the way in which the infant attempts to deal with its paranoid and depressive anxieties and by the intensity of these anxieties.

Taking these conceptions of Freud and Melanie Klein, the view has here been advanced that one of the primary dynamic forces pulling individuals into institutionalized human association is that of defense against paranoid and depressive anxiety, and, conversely, that all institutions are unconsciously used by their members as mechanisms of defense against these psychotic anxieties. Individuals may put their internal conflicts into persons in the external world, unconsciously follow the course of the conflict by means of projective identification, and reinternalize the course and outcome of the externally perceived conflict by means of introjective identification. Societies provide institutionalized roles whose occu-

pants are sanctioned, or required, to take into themselves the projected objects or impulses of other members. The occupants of such
roles may absorb the objects and impulses—take them into themselves and become either the good or bad object with corresponding impulses; or they may deflect the objects and impulses—put
them into an externally perceived ally, or enemy, who is then loved,
or attacked. The gain for the individual in projecting objects and
impulses and introjecting their careers in the external world lies in
the unconscious cooperation with other members of the institution
or group who are using similar projection mechanisms. Introjective
identification then allows more than the return of projected objects
and impulses. The other members are also taken inside and legitimize and reinforce attacks upon internal persecutors or support
manic idealization of loved objects, thereby reinforcing the denial of
destructive impulses against them.

The unconscious cooperation at the fantasy level among
members of an institution is structured in terms of what is here
called the fantasy social form and content of institutions. The form
and content of institutions may thus be considered from two distinct
levels: that of the manifest and consciously agreed form and content (including structure and function, which, although possibly
unrecognized, are nevertheless in the preconscious of members of
the institution, and hence are relatively accessible to identification
by means of conscious study); and that of the fantasy form and
content, which are unconsciously avoided and denied, and, because
they are totally unconscious, remain unidentified by members of
the institution.

A case study is presented to illustrate how within one department in a factory a subinstitution, a committee of managers
and elected workers' representatives, was used at the fantasy level
for segregating hostile relations from good relations, which were
maintained in the day-to-day production work of the department.
When, however, the committee was charged with a serious and conscious negotiating task, its members encountered great difficulties
because of the socially sanctioned fantasy content of their relationships with each other.

Some observations are made on the dynamics of social
change. Change occurs where the fantasy social relations within an

institution no longer serve to reinforce individual defenses against psychotic anxiety. The institution may be restructured at the manifest and fantasy level; or the manifest structure may be maintained, but the fantasy structure modified. Individuals may change roles or leave the institution altogether. Or apparent change at the manifest level may often conceal the fact that no real change has taken place, the fantasy social form and content of the institution being left untouched. Imposed social change which does not take account of the use of institutions by individuals, to cope with unconscious psychotic anxieties, is likely to be resisted.

Finally, if the mechanisms herein described have any validity, then at least two consequences may follow. First, observation of social processes may provide one means of studying, as through a magnifying glass, the operation of paranoid and depressive anxieties and the defenses built up against them. Unlike the psychoanalytical situation, such observations can be made by more than one person at the same time. And second, it may become more clear why social change is so difficult to achieve, and why many social problems are so intractable. For from the point of view here elaborated, changes in social relationships and procedures call for a restructuring of relationships at the fantasy level, with a consequent demand upon individuals to accept and tolerate changes in their existing pattern of defenses against psychotic anxiety. Effective social change is likely to require analysis of the common anxieties and unconscious collusions underlying the social defenses determining fantasy social relationships.

12

Phases, Roles, and Myths
in Self-Analytic Groups

Dexter C. Dunphy

*T*his chapter reports a study of social change in small groups. The study arose out of an extensive review of previous theory and empirical research relating to this subject, which indicated that two general problems have been of continuing importance: first, the problem of establishing the existence and nature of generalized *phase movements* which are hypothesized to characterize the development of groups of many kinds; second, the problem of identifying and describing characteristic *role types* which emerge in groups and their relationship to such phase movements. Information relevant to these two problems requires the study of change in long-term groups where members

Reprinted in abridged form from *Journal of Applied Behavioral Science,* 1968, *4,* 195–225, by special permission from the author and the publisher, NTL Institute for Applied Behavioral Science. The interested reader is referred to the original article for a fuller description of methodology used in this study. Self-analytic groups are groups such as therapy and T-groups, where a major part of the group task is the development of a greater sensitivity to and understanding of the motivations, emotions, and defenses of the group members (including oneself) and to interpersonal and group processes within the group itself.

are emotionally involved in group goals and processes. Self-analytic groups are groups of this kind.

It seems fairly obvious that further empirical studies of long-term self-analytic groups should provide real insight into the question of whether or not there are predictable phase movements and patterns of role differentiation and into the conditions which induce and modify these patterns. The new research presented in this paper is an empirical study of developmental processes in two such groups and focuses on the two issues of phase sequence and role differentiation.

The empirical investigation is concerned specifically with two sections of a Harvard undergraduate course, Social Relations 120: Analysis of Interpersonal Behavior, which met for a full academic year. These groups are self-analytic groups since, like therapy and sensitivity training or T-Groups, a major part of the group task is the study of behavior within the group itself.

The instructors for the two sections were Professor R. F. Bales, Director, Laboratory of Social Relations, Harvard University, and myself. The role of instructor in the course is analogous to that of a trainer in a training group: i.e., no formal teaching is undertaken; the instructor deliberately refrains, while in the classroom, from assuming the role of teacher and, in particular, from giving direct encouragement, discipline, or direction.

The primary focus of the investigation is change in the content of weekly reports written by individual group members. The reports describe and comment upon group interaction within the group. The use of written reports, rather than verbal interaction within the group, reduced the amount of verbal data to be processed, ensured contributions from all members, and focused the study on those aspects of the group interaction which members themselves regarded as important.

The method used to analyze the reports was a computer system of content analysis called the General Inquirer. This automated system of content analysis has been developed at Harvard by a research group involving P. J. Stone, R. F. Bales, myself, and others (Dunphy, Stone, and Smith, 1965; Stone, Dunphy, Smith, and Ogilvie, 1966). Briefly, the method proceeds in the following way: The text to be processed is key-punched in verbal (i.e., nonnumerical) form on IBM cards and fed into a series of programs using IBM 7094 and 1401 computers. These programs "translate" the numerous words and phrases of the text into a simpler social science language consisting in this case of 83 terms[1] representing variables in the investigator's theory. The frequencies with which these terms are applied in each document are then calculated and may be compared using statistical programs.

The weekly reports submitted by group members were processed in sets of four consecutive notes; i.e., reports submitted by each member over a four-week period were combined into a single document, which then became the basic data unit for analysis. Each four-week period was referred to as a phase. There were six phase periods in the year.

In order to test for the existence, extent, and nature of common phase movements, use was made of the entire text of the written reports produced by members of the two groups (approximately 300,000 words). Two major statistical techniques were used to identify changes in content: (a) an analysis of variance to test for the relative amount of variance on each content variable explained by *groups,* by *phases,* or by an interaction of these effects; (b) a factor analysis to reduce the complexity of using 83 variables and to establish patterns of change in content of important common factors over the year.

HYPOTHESES

The particular hypotheses being tested by this method were as follows: (1) The content of the written reports from the two self-analytic groups will show similar quantitative and qualitative changes over time; i.e., common "phase movements." (2) These phase movements will explain more variance in the data than will differences between the two groups. (3) The characteristics of consecutive phase movements will reflect an emerging group unity and an increasing emotional involvement on the part of the group members.[2]

In terms of the *analysis of variance* design, trends which are

---

[1] See Stone, Dunphy, Smith, and Ogilvie (1966) for elaboration of the tag names and their description.

[2] Hypotheses relating to role differentiation are discussed later in this paper.

common to both groups are represented by content variables (tags) for which "phases" make a significant contribution to total variance, while particular group characteristics are represented by variables (tags) for which "group" makes a significant contribution.

All significant tag patterns were investigated in this way, and a detailed account of the procedure is to be found in the larger work from which this article is derived (Dunphy, 1964). Here we can only summarize the major shifts in theme in the analyses from both groups over the year. The analysis of variance shows that in his initial view of the group, the individual member differentiates himself ("self"), the instructor, and other individuals who are able to gain the attention of the group ("leaders" = neuter role), and an undifferentiated collection of others ("people" = neuter role). At this time little coordination of group activity is perceived and members appear to be striving at cross-purposes. The group is viewed primarily in terms of categories of structure and power and, after a short period of trying to maintain a traditional normative pattern, action takes on a strongly manipulative character (action-norm, ought, political). Behavior is seen as increasingly directed toward the satisfaction of aggressive and sexual drives (attack, sex theme), with men being particularly active and women largely withdrawn from active participation (male role). The viewpoint taken by members in the analysis is that of "detached observer"— descriptions deal primarily with external objects and concrete behavior (space references). Early attempts to achieve interpersonal closeness are resisted, emotional involvement in the group is avoided, and, with the aid of the superego, ego boundaries are maintained with increasing rigidity. It is as if the disintegraton of the external normative system is reacted to as a threat to the internalized normative system, so that a barrier is thrown up around the ego for its protection and stability.

In the first part of the second semester (Phase 4), a major change in this pattern becomes evident. Rigid ego boundaries are undermined as involvement in the group increases markedly. There is a consequent feeling of personal weakness and of threat, as some sense of individual identity is lost in the "oceanic" experience of merging with the group (attack, sign-weak, natural object). At this time there seems to be an increased sensitivity to the qualities of external objects which is complemented by a new concern with internal objects, emotions, and cognitive processes (arousal, affection, thought form). Both depression and anxiety increase markedly (danger theme, death theme). Libidinal drives are sublimated in the interest of stronger affective ties within the group, and increased efforts are devoted to the realization of group goals (small group). The primary concerns in interpersonal relationships are with personal involvement with others and affection. Women play a relatively more active role at this time—a role with considerable significance in working through problems of acceptance and the expression of affection (female role). Toward the end of the course a view develops of the group as an evolving communal entity with coordinated emotional states and persistent patterns of behavior (small group). In referring to the group, members attribute human qualities to it as if, in "giving themselves" to the group, the group had in their minds acquired some of their own human qualities. Thus loss of individual identity contributes in some way to a sense of group identity, and the common extension of personality boundaries leads to greater coordination of the emotions and actions of the individual members of the group. An elementary set of symbols derived from readings and from fantasy develops toward the end of the year, and these symbols are employed to give a deeper level of meaning to the group experience (natural world, natural object). This process is accompanied by the development of an indigenous set of group norms (action-norm). The interiorization of the group is responded to, however, by a deeper set of defenses. The earlier defense of noninvolvement, which found its active expression in aggression, gives way to the deeper defenses of resistance and denial, actively expressed in avoidance (avoid, overstate, understate). Considerable concern about these reactions is exhibited in the group reports, for they are seen as detracting from an idealized form of group life toward which many group members are now consciously striving (ascend theme). As the group ends, concern is expressed for the loss of the group and for its relative state of unity and achievement.

FACTOR ANALYSIS

A second technique used to summarize common trends was a *factor analysis* of the same basic data units as were used for the analysis of variance. The advantage of performing a factor analysis is that it yields a measure of co-occurrence of tags, unlike the analysis of variance which examines ᴄach tag separately.

The first three factors, derived from a principal components factor analysis, were named as follows:

I. *Expressed negativity versus denied negativity.* The positive end of this factor is concerned with aggression, the anxiety underlying aggressive acts, and the effects of aggression. The negative end of this factor shows high loadings for a number of tags which in other studies have been found to indicate defensiveness. Presumably the vague style of language represented here indicates defensiveness about discussing aggression.

II. *Normative structure versus anomie.* The tags clustered about the positive end of this factor are related to the institutional structure of the course and the patterned behavior resulting from this structure; e.g., references to the instructors, the assigned cases, the group itself, processes of guiding and following. Clustered about the negative end of the factor is a mixed group of tags which have as a unifying theme an awareness of lack of controls and structure; e.g., words relating to stress, deviance, and sexuality.

III. *Strength versus weakness.* The notion of strength characterizes tags on the positive end of this factor and references to male roles are closely associated with it. On the other hand, the negative end is characterized by tags indicating indecision and weakness, particularly references to silence, avoidance, and ending (of the group).[3]

In order to study change on the factor structure, the three factors are treated as three variables. A univariate analysis of variance, applied separately to each of the three factors, tests for change in exactly the same way as was done for each individual tag.

The results of this analysis show no significant change over time occurring on Factor I. Negativity remains an element of con-

---

[3] Fusion factors lying midway between the main factors were also identified but will not be discussed here.

tinuing importance in the way that members view the group. For Factors II and III phase effects are both significant at the .001 level. The mean of each group on each of the two factors was plotted by phase, so that their relative positions may be compared.

The general course of change distinguished by the General Inquirer may be summarized briefly as follows: An early period may be distinguished (Phases 1-3) where relationships were primarily counterpersonal and negativity predominated. The first phase of these three had certain distinguishing characteristics which marked it off from the other two which followed; those characteristics indicated that an attempt was being made to maintain external normative standards. Phases 2 and 3 were characterized by individualistic rivalry and aggression—"the war of all against all." Phase 4 was another transitional period marked by continued concern with negativity coupled with a new concern with absenteeism and communication. Finally, the last two phases showed clear qualitative differences from those preceding, with emotional concerns, particularly affection, seen as relatively high. There is a general correspondence between these phases and those identified in previous studies of self-analytic groups. In addition, the detailed and systematic character of the method and the large number of content categories yield a more detailed picture of these changes.

It will be remembered that, besides being interested in developmental phases within groups, we posed the problem of identifying common role types, if any such existed, and of determining their relationships to the common phase movement.

Two hypotheses relating to role differentiation were made, based on a previous review of the literature (Dunphy, 1964). These were stated as follows: (1) Analysis of the "role images" of the most psychologically salient members will reflect a process of role differentiation in the group; i.e., a movement from functionally diffuse to functionally specialized roles with a consistent rather than random order in the division of major functions. (2) The process of role differentiation bears a clear relationship to the identifiable common phase movement, with the role specialists functioning as important symbols of alternative responses to the focal conflicts of each major stage in group development.

In order to test for the emergence of common role types, a

new selection was made from the data used for the analysis of group trends. A measure of the psychological saliency or centrality of each member was made by counting the number of references to each group member in each phase. The five most "central" persons in each group were chosen and a role description was compiled for each central person by retrieving all sentences referring to him. These "group portraits" of the central persons were now used as basic data units and summarized, using General Inquirer procedures. The resulting summary profiles were compared across the two groups and, when pairs were matched up, showed remarkable consistency and continuity rather than, as hypothesized, change. These consistencies demonstrated the existence of five role types appearing in each group. These role types were named to correspond with their distinguishing characteristics: *instructor, aggressor, scapegoat, seducer, idol.*[4] Table 1 lists the tags which characterized these role types.

There is insufficient space to examine each of these roles in detail, but we may attempt to indicate how this was done by examining some of the characteristics of the aggressor. *Attack,* for example, is one of the tags most strongly emphasized in the descriptions of occupants of this role. Reading the retrieved sentences tagged in this way indicates that the member concerned is the group specialist in aggression. (In the examples below, the italicized word is the one tagged *attack.*)

> He showed himself to be inflexible and at times *hostile.*
> Wednesday, again Noel opened with an *attack.*
> Keith Monk *attacked* the two Jewish leaders for their
> poses.

In describing the actions of the aggressor, group members also recognize the danger (*danger theme*) to individuals and to the group in the exercise of overt aggression.

> His dumping on others is *dangerous.*

[4] The four member roles may correspond to some extent to Bennis and Shepard's conflicted leader roles, a possible correspondence being as follows: aggressor = counterpersonal; scapegoat = overdependent; seducer = overpersonal; and perhaps the idol = counterpersonal.

Table 1.

Summary of the Characteristics of the Common Role Images*

Instructor	*Aggressor*	*Scapegoat*	*Seducer*	*Idol*
selves	self	*self*	other	female role
neuter role	other	*male role*	*sensory ref.*	time ref.
job role	time ref.	action-norm	message form	if
ideal value	spatial ref.	*guide*	*equal*	cause
action-norm	*quantity ref.*	control	approach	communicate
message form	arousal	attack	follow	attempt
ought	distress	get	work	sex theme
guide	ought	community	get	ascend theme
control	*attack*	overstate	community	
academic	*military*	sign-weak	*legal*	
family	recreational	sign-reject	recreational	
political	overstate	authority	*sex theme*	
technological	*sign-reject*	theme		
higher status	danger theme			
sign-accept				
authority				
theme				

* The common characteristics listed are those tags on which both in-
cumbents ranked first or second for at least three of the six phases.
Italicized tags indicate those tags on which both specialists were consistently high for four or more of the six phases.

They also express guilt and anxiety (*distress*) about the
extent to which they may be responsible for encouraging the actions
of the aggressor.

In fact several, notably Yolande, felt *guilty* about having
provoked Keith into making observations which they felt had
embarrassed him.

The examples above illustrate the procedure by which the
nature of these roles was deduced from the data. We cannot pursue
this analysis in such detail here for all roles, but we shall attempt to

summarize the part played by these nonrational role specialists in group development. In doing this, we shall draw on the content of these role images and on the observed behavior of the specialists and group members in the group situations. The role specialists are, above all else, the symbols of the predominant emotional states of the group members. Thus the *scapegoat* represents anxiety about personal weakness stemming from frustration of dependency needs by the instructor. Judging by the extreme reactions of male members to this role, it may also represent, at a deeper level, sexual impotence. It is the overreaction of the scapegoat to the frustrating role of the *instructor* and the scapegoat's futile attempts to organize the group which crystallize the anxieties of group members and lead to projection of images of weak authority figures. The scapegoating of this member represents, at the individual level, a way of handling fears about insufficiency, and, at the group level, a short-term way of uniting the majority of group members into a cohesive group. It is as if members were denying their own weakness by projecting it onto the scapegoat and, by implication, onto the instructor whom the scapegoat represents.

The role of *seducer* is another form of denial of the same fears. The seducer tries to represent strong, potent, compulsive masculinity. He attempts to capitalize on the developing anomie and to act out deviant fantasies, particularly in relationship to the *idol*. The idol is typically an attractive female group member who supports the authority of the instructor and overtly rejects the sexual fantasies of the men in the group. To unify the group around a common love object is a time-tested way of unifying groups, just as is unification through aggression against a common object of hate. However, they are both methods which create anxiety and guilt. Both methods unify the group in the short run but create divisive problems in the long run.

The threats to group unity and self-control which are posed by the scapegoat and the seducer are handled in the first semester by the *aggressor,* who represents harsh and repressive superego functions. The aggressor acts out the fears of punishment for forbidden wishes. (Both occupants of the seducer role spontaneously told stories expressive of fears of harsh punishment by authority figures.) Thus it is the buildup of tension in the group in response to the actions of the scapegoat and the seducer which leads to the aggressor's response—the release of this tension through rejection of both of these members. However, the developmentally tested method of maintaining order through repression results in the loss of mutual trust within the group and a consequent lack of progress on the group task. Instead of finding themselves growing more appreciative of the motives of others and more sensitive in their reactions, members find themselves feeling increasingly shut off from others—frustrated both intellectually and emotionally. When in Phase 4 the group seems on the verge of disintegration, members sense that a choice has to be made between the preservation of individual defenses and group goal attainment. Slowly a few members begin sacrificing some of their defenses in the interest of furthering group progress. This process is aided by the fact that guilt is felt for the fantasies, expressed and unexpressed, of destroying others and the group itself.

From this point fantasies of the utopian group and the idealized instructor begin to emerge. At the same time, the progress made toward intimacy and trust revives earlier fears of betrayal and of direct sexual expression. The laying of these "shades of the past" is a slow and difficult process. At this point there must be a reworking of relationships with both the aggressor and seducer if this is to be accomplished to any extent. The solution which these groups worked out consisted of a kind of uneasy acceptance of the roles by recognizing their meaning in relation to internal fantasies, while depriving them of power by destroying their charismatic qualities. The latter is accomplished mainly by members recognizing in themselves the unacceptable fantasies which these group members act out. The actions of the "idol" are of significance at the final stages of group development. In standing for the sublimation of drives in the service of goal attainment and group cohesion, the attractive female group member helps the group accept the role of the instructor and work toward a new integration among drives, emotions, and ideal images.

Thus our first hypothesis about the evolution of role images was not borne out. The major significant roles apparently emerged early, and the psychological image of them remained largely constant throughout the year. However, our second hypothesis did appear to hold up. The role specialists functioned as important symbols of focal conflicts, but change was indicated by the relative salience attributed to the specialist at any stage rather than by a change in the role image itself. The role specialists are important reference points for members as they work out the developing direction of the group culture.

GROUP MYTHOLOGY AS A UNIFYING CONCEPT

Finally I should like to propose a view of process in self-analytic groups which does not derive directly from the content analysis described above, but which I think orders and makes sense of the results. In my view, the common phase movements and differentiated roles may be seen as a reflection of the evolution of an elementary group mythology centering about the formal authority figure, the instructor, and the group. Over the course of the year it is possible to distinguish major shifts in the character of the prevailing group mythology by tracing consistencies in the individual fantasies brought before the group and in consistent responses to these fantasies. They are more easily identified in the content of the spontaneous group interaction than in the written reports. In understanding them we would do well to keep in mind Malinowski's (1948) words concerning the role of mythology in cultural life: "Myth . . . is a vital ingredient of human civilization; it is not idle talk, but a hard-worked active force, it is not an intellectual explanation or an artistic imagery but a pragmatic charter of primitive faith and moral wisdom" (p. 3). In my view, a myth is a shared, rather than an individual, fantasy, built up over time out of events in the history of groups and incorporating elements of the individual fantasies of members.

In examining the development of group mythology, I will try to answer two questions: (1) To what extent does a mythology develop to justify each period of group development, and in what way is the mythology modified as major changes occur in the emotional climate of the group? (2) What part do role specialists play in the development and change of the group mythology?

The first myth centers about the role of the instructor and derives from the relatively inactive role which he adopts. In this myth the instructor is the central character, and he is seen as a weak and impotent authority figure unable to control the activities of those in his charge. This period culminates in the scapegoating of a weak member of the group who has attempted to play the trainer's role. This dramatic destruction in effigy of the instructor occurred in the Dunphy group on October 29 and in the Bales group on November 30. (In part, my own lesser status characteristics precipitated earlier attention to the problem of anomie in my group.) Thus this early myth is dominant during the first phase, where an attempt was being made to maintain external norms, and persists into the next phase. At the same time the group is also felt to be confused and unable to control its actions.

The second myth evolves some time after the first, but the two coexist for a period of time despite the fact that they are logically contradictory. In this myth the instructor is seen as a secretly strong but malicious and manipulative figure. This period is characterized by the clear differentiation of the roles of aggressor and seducer and the dramatization of the tension between them. The aggressor and seducer seem to stand respectively for (1) emotional concealment and rigid control of deviant impulses: the embodiment of the punitive, judging superego and restrictive social norms; (2) emotional exposure and gratification of deviant, especially sexual, impulses: the embodiment of the id and social anomie. During this time, action in the group swings from one pole to the other, as a symbolic dialectic discussion of these two alternatives takes place. Some members polarize around one or the other of these figures, while the majority of the group members are progressively immobilized by their inability to resolve the "pull" between the two extremes. However, as the conflict develops through the first semester, the seducer gradually appears as weak while the aggressor appears as strong. As the aggressor emerges as victor in this struggle, defenses against emotional exposure and gratification of impulses become deeply entrenched. The myth culminates in February-March with the expression of fantasies which portray the instructor as a cold, rejecting, evil authority figure, the group members as betraying and hurting one another, and consequent fears of individual and group disintegration. This myth covers the period where direct discussion of sexuality and aggression is highest and climaxes in Phase 4, the stage of transition.

Finally in March new fantasies begin to emerge which express wishes for a warmer, more personal, and trusting emotional climate in the groups. Through these fantasies a third myth is constructed of a utopian group in which members are engaged in creative work, communicate emotions honestly, and act with understanding and compassion for others. Wishes are expressed for an apocalyptic arrival of this "new dawn," and there are fantasies of a messiah or hero who will arise within the group, overthrowing the old patterns and ushering in the new. This represents the reconstruction of the image of the instructor into an ego ideal or heroic figure, who can then be internalized to "harness" the motivations of members to this goal. In April the aggressor is overthrown; he is shown as weak and foolish rather than strong, and so the image of the "evil instructor" is disposed of. This act is followed by identification with the ideal image of the instructor, increased expression of affection for others in the group, and the emergence of religious symbolism in discussing the group experience. In the final phases the group members face the problem of reconciling themselves to the fact that the change in the group emotional climate has been only relative, that utopian wishes have not been and cannot be fully realized, and that the group must disband as the course ends.

It appears therefore that the chief elements in each of these myths are prototypical images of the group and of the instructor and that these images derive primarily from the inner emotional experiences of the group members at successive stages in the cultural evolution of the group. What is exemplified in the major shifts in the character of the group mythology are: (1) the ego anxieties developed through the unstructured nature of the situation; (2) the exercise of rigid superego functions to control fantasies of deviance, maintain threatened ego boundaries, and at the same time create group solidarity in aggressing against a common object, establishing common fantasies of sexual fulfillment; (3) the abandonment of rigid ego boundaries, renunciation of deviant wishes by the majority of members, and the internalization of an idealized image of the group and the instructor as the basis for a group solidarity marked by a level of trust which makes cooperative pursuance of the course goals feasible—i.e., a phase of sublimation in the service of greater understanding and group unity.

It seems therefore that each of the major periods in the evolution of the group is accompanied by a myth which represents an ideal-typical image of group relationships and of the instructor and that the role specialists function as important symbols in these myths.

CONCLUSION

This study must be regarded as tentative in its establishment of phase movements and role differentiation in self-analytic groups. We have no way of knowing how representative these two groups are of self-analytic groups in general. The study is suggestive, however; and its findings are generally in accord with those of earlier studies, but need wider testing to establish the extent of their validity. The research indicates more definitely the usefulness of an automated system of content analysis in handling large bodies of text in an efficient and completely reliable way, and thus opens up a wide range of possibilities for further studies on this subject.

13

A Note on Fantasy Themes
in the Evolution of Group Culture

JOHN J. HARTMAN

GRAHAM S. GIBBARD

Fantasies, daydreams, and other imaginative productions shared on a group-wide basis provide an excellent medium for the study of the interface between personality and social structure. In small experiential groups, individuals often develop and express fantasies, hopes, and beliefs which become myth-like and which assume great importance for the group-as-a-whole in the maintenance of group equilibrium.

The purpose of this chapter is to explore distinct yet related sets of fantasies involving utopian, bisexual, and messianic themes. We shall propose two interlocking conceptual schemes. The first is a theory of group evolution, in which development is delineated as a progression from fusion with the group-as-a-whole to differentiation and autonomy. We have presented this model in more detail elsewhere (Gibbard and Hartman, 1973b; Hartman and Gibbard, this volume, Chapter 7). In this chapter the theory takes on a special focus—the vicissitudes of this movement toward and away from fusion with the group. The second scheme centers more specifically on the relationship between group development and the shared nature of the fantasies. This analysis attempts to account for the linkage between the individual's fantasies, the small social system, and larger collectivities. The individual employs daydreams; the small group creates myths (Kaplan and Roman, 1963; Dunphy, 1964, 1968); and the large collectivity supports a projective system (Whiting and Child, 1953) involving beliefs, folklore, mythology, art. Individuals can, for example, have wishful thoughts about an ideal existence. The members of a small group may develop the idea that their relationships can be free of strife and competition and that warmth and friendship will prevail as the value system of the group. A part of a nation, operating on an ideological assumption that perfection in human relations can be achieved, sets out to create a community which will match those ideals. How can we begin to forge conceptual bonds, motivational and structural, between these utopian ideas which exist in quite different units of the social system but seem interconnected in their content and aims?

Some clarification of terms is necessary at this point because, as we move to different levels in the social system, different terms begin to apply. By *fantasy* we mean conscious, nontask-directed thoughts, beliefs, or assumptions held by individuals. We do make a distinction between fantasy and unconscious fantasy and make specific note of that distinction. *Myth* or *mythology,* as used here, refers to Dunphy's (1968; this volume, Chapter 12) notion of an "overarching symbol system" which unifies small-group interaction by pooling individual fantasies. These myths, while conscious or nearly so, contain elements of unconscious fantasy and may further represent the pooling of unconscious fantasies of individuals. In larger collectivities, ideology and belief systems closely resemble the myths we note in small groups. That is, political and religious ideas, which are a matter of faith and belief, resemble individual fantasy and small-group myth.

In our view, fantasy, myth, and ideology all have a psychodynamic significance for individuals in that they represent the expression of certain wishes as well as defensive and adaptive ways of coping with those wishes. In addition, fantasies shared on a groupwide basis take on functions in the development of the collectivity, in the maintenance and fluctuation of social structure. Our initial focus will be a general scheme of group development, in which we trace a progression of shared fantasies. We shall utilize illustrative material from two self-analytic groups. We conclude with an analysis of the role of fantasy in small groups and suggest an analogy with the role of ideology in larger collectivities.

FROM FUSION TO INDIVIDUALITY

We have in Chapter 7 outlined a theory of group development which rests on the notion that change in small groups is a product of boundary evolution analogous to the development of self and object boundaries in individuals. We postulated that unstructured groups oscillate between a wish for differentiation and individuation and a regressive pull toward fusion and symbiotic relatedness with the group-as-a-whole. In the establishment of a sense of cohesiveness and identity, groups utilize splitting (into good and bad)', as well as exclusive and inclusive processes—just as splitting, introjection, and projection are employed by individuals, particularly in early childhood.

In the course of developing these notions, we were struck with the importance of the fantasies and myths that arose in the groups. We have discussed elsewhere the utopian and bisexual fantasies in these groups (Gibbard and Hartman, 1973b; Hartman and Gibbard, 1973). Our purpose here is to bring these observations about particular fantasy constellations into a more encompassing developmental context. We present in Table 1 an outline of our developmental scheme, with special focus on fantasies and myths that occur at particular phases of development.

Mystical Fusion

The fantasy of a mystical fusion with or a frightening envelopment by the group-as-a-whole has been described by several observers. Such fantasies do not, however, constitute an identifiable developmental stage, since they are largely unconscious in experiential groups.

Fantasies of fusion with the group operate at different stages of development but are most salient at the beginning and end, when

Table 1. FANTASY THEMES IN GROUP DEVELOPMENT

Myth	Mystical Fusion	Deification	Utopianism	Bisexuality	Messianism
STAGE	Beginning (unconscious) and termination (possibly conscious)	Early	After revolt	When group is threatened with dissolution and death	Late middle
			(revolt)		
BION'S ASSUMPTION	Fight/flight	Dependency	Dependency	Pairing	Pairing
POSITIVE AIMS	Peace, tranquility, no conflict or tension	Nurturance, support, guidance	Nurturance, warmth, pregenital sexuality, harmony, equality	Fusion of dependent and sexual needs without differentiation	Hope, new life, creativity, purpose
DEFENSIVE AIMS	Avoidance of emptiness, flight from conflict, avoidance of differentiation	Avoidance of depression, emptiness, helplessness	Avoidance of guilt, differences, competition, ambivalence, and heterosexuality	Avoidance of competition, oedipal guilt, sex differences, group death	Avoidance of oedipal guilt, group death, failure
OBJECT RELATIONS	Autistic	Anaclitic, ambivalent, symbiotic	Preambivalent symbiotic	Ambivalent symbiotic	Individuation

dissolution of group boundaries is an issue. The positive aim of fusion is the establishment of the peace, tranquility, and magical fullness of the early mother-child symbiosis. It is the return to Paradise, the achievement of Nirvana. Its defensive aims include coping with the inner hunger and emptiness and the chaotic distress which the original union with the mother warded off. It is also a flight from conflict and an avoidance of differentiation, which is inevitably accompanied by ambivalence and separateness. In developmental terms it corresponds to the state of primary narcissism and autism described in psychoanalytic writing (Mahler, 1968). In Bion's framework, it is closest to the fight/flight assumption, which can be seen as a means of dealing with and warding off fusion.

Deification

Many writers have noted the tendency for group members early in the group to ascribe fantastic, almost godlike, powers to the leader (Bion, 1959; Kaplan and Roman, 1963; Slater, 1966). Slater has expanded these observations and postulated the notion of deification of the group leader as an antidote to the felt deprivation of the early group. This is essentially Bion's dependency assumption in religious form.

This fantasy—that there is a godlike figure who knows all that is happening in the group and could potentially provide information, help, and nurturance—differs from the idea of mystical fusion in that the leader has been differentiated out of the mass and the group attempts to relate to him in a dependent fashion. In object-relations terms, the relationship of the dependent member to the leader-god is anaclitic, with self and object boundaries being much more differentiated. A process of splitting has taken place; in the process, the good has been projected onto the ideal leader, and the group hopes to be fed this goodness.

In Slater's scheme, the deification "decays," and the leader who fails to live up to this hope of salvation turns into a false god and becomes the object of hostility and revolt. In the revolt the splitting becomes reversed. All that is bad, frustrating, malevolent is put into the leader and he is symbolically destroyed. In the revolt the members introject his power, and the group becomes not only good but strong. The revolt leads to a "new order" in Slater's terms and to the resolution of authority problems in Bennis and Shepard's (1956) scheme. This revolt often catalyzes sexual fantasies in the group and ushers in the pairing assumption.

Utopianism

The fantasy that the group is, or could become, a utopia reflects the emergence, at both an individual and a collective level, of a variety of oedipal and preoedipal themes. More specifically, our experience suggests that the utopian hopes engendered by these and other groups center on an aspect of the largely unconscious fantasy that the group-as-a-whole is a maternal entity, or some facet of a maternal entity. Acting on this fantasy, the group members seek to establish and maintain contact with certain "good" (nurturant and protective) aspects of the group and to suppress or deny the existence of certain "bad" (abandoning and destructive) aspects of the group. The establishment of such a fantasied relationship appears to promise many positive gratifications. In addition, the fantasy offers some assurance that the more frightening, enveloping, or destructive aspects of the group-as-mother are held in check and that a host of oedipal feelings, libidinal and aggressive, will not become fully conscious and gain direct expression in the group. The essence of the utopian fantasy is that the good can be split off from the bad and that this separation can be maintained.

By our choice of the term *utopian* we mean to imply that the group members attempt to institute a state of affairs that is perfect or ideal, with conflict eliminated and replaced by unconditional and unlimited love, nurturance, and security. The utopian fantasy is most likely to appear when the positive and appealing aspects of the group-as-mother (warmth, security, protectiveness) seem to be attainable and the negative aspects (engulfment, malevolence, obliteration of self-object boundaries) appear to be well defended against. The emergence of the fantasy is made possible by the individual's use of the mechanism of splitting, which allows him to maintain a consistent separation of good and bad and thus to avoid a state in which good and bad cannot be differentiated and a state in which both are experienced at the same time (genuine ambivalence). From an interpersonal perspective, the utopian conception of the group-as-mother is contingent on the perception of the group entity as benevolent, with the abandoning and destructive potential of the group being split off from this benevolent object.

The utopian phase differs from deification in that all that is good is now seen to reside within the group. All that is bad has been projected onto the bad leader, who has been attacked in the revolt. Utopianism, then, seems to be a stage between the dependency of deification and the pairing of the sexually liberated group. In the utopian group, a diffuse pregenital love and an atmosphere of harmony, no competition, warmth, and nurturance prevail.

The positive aims of the utopian phase involve equality, fraternity, and a diffuse warmth and love. Its defensive aims include the avoidance of guilt about the revolt and an avoidance of anxiety about differences, competition, ambivalence, and heterosexuality. In object-relations terms, the utopian group resembles the more positive, preambivalent symbiotic relationship of the child and mother (Searles, 1965).

Other authors have specifically mentioned utopianism in their analyses of small groups. Bennis and Shepard (1956; this volume, Chapter 6), for example, in discussing the first subphase of "interdependence," refer to "the myth of mutual acceptance and universal harmony." This is a period characterized by a transfer of attention from problems of authority to problems of member-member intimacy. There is a serious attempt to minimize hostility or competition and to establish solidarity, harmony, and love. Dunphy (1968; this volume, Chapter 12), in his study of myth in self-analytic groups, identifies a phase dominated by the hope for a "utopian group and the messiah hero." In this phase, which comes after a long period of "group paralysis" and depression, the group begins thinking about "a new dawning" and is concerned again about member-member friendship and intimacy. There is an effort to create an atmosphere of warmth, mutual understanding, and harmonious living, which Dunphy describes as a wish for an idealized group in which spontaneity, sharing, and cooperation exist.

While our formulation parallels Bennis and Shepard's discussion of the relationship between the confrontation with the leader and the emergence of utopianism, our view does differ from that of

Dunphy. His utopian period comes later in the group and is more explicitly sexual; it corresponds to the phenomenon which we term *messianic* and comes at a later stage of group development. The utopianism we observe is a distinctively postrevolt phenomenon and is marked by a diffuse, pregenital sexuality.

In one group we observed, Kevin (pseudonyms are used for all group members) was the most salient and persistent advocate of the group as utopia. He endorsed the creation of mutually affectionate dyads, relationships characterized by consistent supportiveness, intense closeness, and a diffuse and essentially pregenital sexuality. His centrality in the second phase provided the group with an opportunity to respond in a variety of ways to his demands for closeness and nurturance. Some members encouraged him. Some attempted simply to placate him. Others were more openly hostile. There were moments at which almost everyone shared his vision of the utopian potential of the group. More concretely, however, his unconscious strategy was aimed at eliciting the nurturance of others with only a modicum of reciprocation, an unlikely foundation for a utopian group.

When we examine more closely the interpersonal positions of Kevin and the group, we find a close parallel to the relationship between a needy and demanding child and his mother. Kevin presented himself as confused, anxious, and empty. The group was asked to assume the role of a nurturant mother. Clearly, one problem with the utopian group, as exemplified by Kevin, is that the dependent and the nurturant roles cannot be assumed simultaneously. In this group, Kevin's centrality in this second phase can be understood as one attempted resolution of this problem. The group is experienced as a generous and protective mother, and one member acts out the complementary position. This informal designation of one member as a recipient of the group's nurturance serves several functions. It makes possible considerable expression of dependency in the group, even though some members would feel uncomfortable expressing such feelings themselves. In addition, it minimizes greatly the threat of competition for the attention and resources of the group. The group members can take on the supportive, nurturant role with respect to the dependent member and can at the same time identify with him and participate vicariously in the dependency he expresses and the feedback he receives. Finally, the designation of a single, highly dependent person can be understood as a self-protective localization of needs and feelings, a mechanism that gives the group additional control over them. In other words, if the members' dependency needs can be placed into a single person, then that person is available to express those feelings and the group is free to respond to them in a variety of ways, ranging from explicit endorsement or implicit identification to repudiation and ridicule. This latter possibility is suggestive of scapegoating, and that was Kevin's fate in the third phase of the group's development. The group's attitude toward Kevin during the period of heterosexual competition was one of impatient tolerance. He was scapegoated by the more sexually aggressive members, especially just prior to a group party. His fall from favor signaled the demise of the fantasy of the utopian group. Still, he was regarded with some reverence. He had, after all, made a real effort to create an unconditionally loving group, and in so doing he had acted out a utopian fantasy which was widely shared in the group. Ironically, it was this effort itself which demonstrated to the other members how unrealistic such a group would be.

The second phase of group 2 was also marked by the adoption of warmth, closeness, equality, noncompetition, and honesty as group goals. In this group the role of architect for the utopia was split between two members. Larry offered himself in one session as a "subject" for group investigation—in order, he felt, to bring honesty to the group. He endorsed closeness, warmth, and honesty as worthy goals and was supported in this by many group members. His "analysis" never came about, and the group was thrown into a depressed disappointment. Some sessions later, Larry and another active member, Harvey, were compared. The core of this comparison was the issue of dependency. Harvey, who was described as "dependent" and "weak," appeared to represent one extreme position, which most members attempted to disown and reject. Larry was perceived as stronger, more independent, and more attractive. Again it seemed possible that the recruitment of Larry as a peer leader would usher in the utopian goals which the members had agreed were desirable. This did not happen, of course; but it was Harvey who was scapegoated in the phase of sexual competition, and Larry remained in his role as attractive male peer leader.

Very similar conflicts characterized the second, postrevolt period in both groups. There was an obvious desire for closeness without competition and for a relatively undifferentiated and pregenital sexualization of the group. There was also a great deal of uneasiness about this idealized state of affairs, with obvious anxiety over the rearousal of dependency feelings. This phase was also marked by an avoidance of sexual competition and rivalry.

Bisexuality

We have previously identified a fantasy which we called bisexual and which appears to be a variant of the messianic fantasy of the pairing group (Hartman and Gibbard, 1973). The bisexual fantasy involves pairing with aspects of *oneself,* the self being experienced in fantasy as both masculine and feminine. This bisexual fantasy arises when the group is threatened with dissolution and death and when more usual realistic means or the more usual heterosexual and messianic fantasies are not available. The bisexual fantasy is a "regressed" (in object-relations terms) form of the messianic fantasy described by Bion as accompanying the pairing group. Bion's observations have been given some confirmation by Slater (1966) and Dunphy (1968; this volume, Chapter 12).

The bisexual fantasy involves the bringing together of dependent and sexual needs without clear differentiation. As such, this fantasy, too, has a not-quite-individuated quality. It harks back to the time when the individual has an undifferentiated sense of sexual identity or has regressed to that point because of fears about sexual differentiation and oedipal rivalry. In its defensive aspects the bisexual fantasy is an avoidance of competition, oedipal guilt, and sexual fears, and serves as a way of suppressing an awareness of group dissolution. It is the expression of the omnipotent wish not to need other people for love, support, or even procreation. It says, in effect, "I have everything I need to take care of myself, to love myself, and even to reproduce myself." It is thus a symbiotic pairing fantasy in which self and object are not fully differentiated.

We shall present some of the observations on which our previous work was based; a more extensive discussion can be found in our original report of those observations.

In group 2 the group members were confronted with a crisis which cast doubt on the viability of the group itself. Prior to this crisis the group had been struggling with issues related to self-revelation and the way the group had been progressing. Members expressed concern about whether the group was in control of itself and whether "defenses" could or should be "broken down." Session 25 began with a discussion of motherhood led by the three married women in the group. After one of them expressed concern about the "passivity" of the men in the group, the group began to discuss the question of whether men could form close relationships with other men and whether such relationships were "good" or "bad." This concern with control, the stability of the group, and male passivity culminated when Norm delivered a diatribe against the group and the leader. Norm said that he had discussed the group with several faculty members and his own psychiatrist, and all agreed that the group was stirring up some very dangerous feelings that group members were not aware of. He implied that his own mental health was endangered and that the leader could not be trusted. The rest of the hour was spent dealing with this "bombshell." The leader attempted to deal with Norm's distress realistically, while at the same time pointing out that the group itself was in no real danger of collapse. There were several suggestions to end the session early and perhaps an implicit wish to end the class permanently, since anxiety was running high. It was immediately apparent that the group members felt threatened by Norm's disclosure and perceived the group as being in grave danger of dissolution. Norm absented himself from the group for the next several weeks but did return for the last four sessions of the class.

The next two sessions were devoted to the question of whether or not the group was harmful and whether or not the leader would step in to prevent anything "really bad" from happening. Most members felt that the leader had "handled" Norm well and that the leader was now closer to the group and cared about it. It was also noteworthy that two vocal females, who had previously been quite challenging toward the leader, "admitted" their attraction for and "dependence" on the leader. The males seemed to resent these displays of interest in the leader on the part of these two active females. It was as if the distress caused by Norm's departure had generated fantasies with sexual, rivalrous, and hostile content.

In session 28 Jeffrey played a tape recording of comedian Bill Cosby's account of Noah and the Flood: "Noah was bringing two hippopotamuses onto the Ark and God stopped him. Apparently both were males, and God had requested Noah to find a male and a female of the various animal species. Noah said that he was too tired after all his work and asked God simply to change the sex of one of them. God replied: 'You know I don't work like that.' " Jeffrey felt that this was a perfect description of the leader's style: "You know Mr. Hartman might have the power to do lots of things in here, but he'd rather let us struggle with them rather than telling us what to do." The conversation went immediately to the grading procedure in the course. The grading of the final examination was characterized as being like God's punishment. One member felt that at the end of the course each student would be "face to face" with the leader and his judgment. Several voiced the hope that the leader would give more individual feedback. Others expressed the feeling that members were guarding their insights about the group so that they could write them in their logs and get better grades. This raised the issue of competition and rivalry, which one member termed the "competitive instinct for self-survival." Beatrice likened the group rivalry to sibling rivalry in the family and again brought up Noah: "I still think this is connected with the Noah thing because think about being Noah and being the one God loved and everyone else is destroyed and I really think there is a feeling in this group that you want to be the one that Hartman loves and the heck with the rest of them." She was immediately attacked for advancing this theory, and many members denied any competitive feelings for grades, attention, or anything else.

It is interesting to note that the initial reactions to the playing of the Noah story centered around competition and dependency. No mention was made of the sexual implications of the story. In the following sessions the issue of rivalry continued to be discussed, but members gradually became more aware of an explicitly sexual theme—group intimacy and its dangers. In one session Vickie and Al had a heated argument about the possibility of understanding the group. Larry interpreted Al's anger as masking an underlying sexual attraction for Vickie. Another member pointed out that if any of the females expressed any positive interest in the leader, this was tantamount to emasculating the other males. In the next session the group dealt with the dangers of group intimacy. Natalie said that, in her opinion, it was better to establish intimate relationships with friends outside of the group. Others talked about the costs of personal involvement with people in the group because it was ending soon and because such involvement would mean revealing secrets and being subjected to "analysis." It was as if group intimacy and closeness involved oedipal, rivalrous, and other dangerous feelings which needed to be avoided.

Session 32 saw a return to the story of Noah and the emergence of material relating to the meaning of bisexuality in groups. This session began with one member's assertion that "potency" rather than "dependency" had become the central issue in the group. Russ asserted that the group did little to promote group intimacy. He said that he felt "restricted" about asking a girl in the group for a date. Mara then related a dream in which she was "left out" of a frisbee game Joan was playing with "some guy." These sexually tinged themes were dropped in favor of discussing the many absent members, which included Norm. The leader asked whether the concern with absent members was related to concerns about the end of the group. There was general agreement with this interpretation. Vickie noted that Eileen had suggested continuing the group into the next semester. She wondered whether the group could change people. There followed a discussion about whether the leader was "omnipotent" or "impotent." The leader observed that perhaps there was an unconscious fantasy that he had given birth to the group and could also kill it. A heated discussion ensued, with Al and Joan becoming vociferous about the leader's lack of importance in their group experience:

AL: Some things today say that you can't kill the group because it might go on.

MR. H.: Which is really a denial of the end of the group.

JEFFREY: Yeah. Why couldn't we have given birth to ourselves?
. . . Maybe it was a computer in the administration
building.

AL: Yeah. Hartman could have been replaced.

JOAN: *You* could have been replaced. [Laughter].

AL: Yeah, yeah. I know, but I was sitting here thinking it's
more like Hartman has been raped and he was forced
to give birth whether he wants to or not.

JOHN: Who raped him?

AL: Probably the administration or maybe Dr. M [an older,
more prestigious and quite popular campus figure who
taught another section of the course]. It's his basic idea
and he said, "Go teach it."

JOAN: It would be nice to think he was that submissive,
wouldn't it?

The group then discussed the leader's motives for teaching
such a course. Then the following interaction took place:

JEFFREY: We were saying that when you start thinking about
the group breaking up, one of the thoughts that goes
along with it is, uh, the generation so the group
doesn't die. Like you give birth to something else of
just that idea . . . I was thinking about that Noah
tape. [Laughter.] Like this is gonna sound crazy but
just for a minute I thought of Mr. Hartman as Noah.
There's good old Noah standing underneath the
elephant and pow—this little potential elephant—and
like there's this big computer and it's producing
groups.

BEATRICE: What have we generated? I think that's what's bother-
ing us. What is all this new life that was supposed to
come from putting us all in the Ark and then putting
Mr. Hartman in the Ark to watch over us?

JOAN: Maybe there's too much new life. Like is this a group
or isn't it? And is this gonna continue or isn't it and
what's going on and all that stuff?

JEFFREY: Yeah, well maybe. Does a baby often keep on living or does it die? Does it keep on growing?

AL: Suppose Hartman has another baby. That's what I was thinking. How about the group giving birth to itself? I studied Indian thought for awhile and I was trying to think of something that would be something like this. And all I can get is like a picture of Krishna is one impression I got, sucking his foot. And there's also a snake that eats himself.

The rest of the session was devoted to a discussion of feelings toward parents and to the question of gaining equality with or independence from them. Joan was concerned that people in the group could not relate to each other as mature people but had to be preoccupied with matters like "dependency" and "power."

The image of Noah as caretaker of pairs of animals or the group leader as chaperone for the pairing group is an expression of and a retreat from awareness of oedipal rivalry and competition for the attention of the leader-parent. No mention was made of sexuality. On one level the difficulties of the actual male-female relationships in the group are expressed in the sequence in which God refuses to change the sex of one of the hippopotamuses. The leader does not work this way either, someone mentioned—suggesting that the leader's passive noncooperation or perceived active interference was responsible for the lack of member-member sexuality in the group. God is standing in the way of the pairing up of the hippopotamuses. Members wish that the group can become a place of unconflicted sexuality and that the problems of rivalry and competition can be settled automatically by the leader-God (choosing pairs of each species). The oedipal theme is stated: God-leader-father is preventing sexuality. Resolution of the oedipal rivalry is also stated: Noah-leader-father grants a controlled and unrivalrous sexuality from which he excludes himself.

The group moved from a heterosexual pairing fantasy to an essentially unconscious bisexual fantasy because the former was too threatening. It is clear that the group was concerned with homosexual pairing as well. In one session the dangers of group "intimacy" were discussed. At the beginning of the next session Russ described his feeling "restricted" in dating a group member. The dream of feeling left out of a male-female game was reported. These details give us a glimpse of the rivalrous and incestuous connotation of intimacy within the group. The group was very resistant to recognizing any sexuality in the leader, since any such recognition might lead to an examination of hidden sexual feelings in the group. Any female expression of interest in the leader was resented by several males. However, in the fantasy of his rape the leader was defeated and emasculated by a more powerful leader, as well as by the conclusion that the group could reproduce itself without pairing. The rape fantasy points to an attempt to defeat the leader and to deny the oedipal implications of this defeat. The bisexual fantasy ensures the group's immortality without rivalry or sexuality. The pairing fantasy took on a bisexual character in this group because of the threat of dissolution by member withdrawal and because of the dangers of more usual heterosexual wishes.

Messianism

The wish for rescue from disruptive affects and realistic problems, as Bion (1959) has noted, is crystallized around the hope that a messiah will appear to save the group from disintegration and individual members from a loss of identity. Bion has identified this messianic wish as a hallmark of the pairing assumption. Whereas Dunphy describes one phase as both utopian and messianic, our scheme introduces a distinction between utopian and messianic paradigms.

The positive aim of the messianic fantasy is to create hope, new life, and a sense of purpose. The defensive aim is to ward off oedipal guilt aroused by pairing fantasies, and to avoid group death and a sense of failure. Messianism is to be distinguished from utopianism in our scheme by virtue of the fact that it becomes salient later in the group and represents, in psychosexual and in object-relations terms, a much more differentiated state of development.

FANTASY AND GROUP DEVELOPMENT

In this chapter we have recast the developmental scheme outlined in Chapter 7 to account for certain shared fantasies or myths which have consistently emerged from the study of self-analytic groups. We have postulated a progression from unconscious fantasies of fusion with the maternally perceived group-as-a-whole to the relatively conscious, individuated fantasy of messianism. Deification of the leader, the quest for a utopian group, and a bisexual solution to group stress are seen as way stations along this continuum. Utopianism and bisexuality can, in developmental terms, be placed between the dependency and pairing assumptions of Bion.

If our portrait of group development is reasonably accurate, how can we best understand the function of the fantasies and myths we have discussed and why do they arise instead of some other coping mechanism? In our view, these fantasies serve several functions. First, they offer ways of handling intense anxiety, usually of a depressive nature. The pairing group's messianic fantasies are primarily a defense against a depression associated with termination or are defenses against the guilt of the postrevolt period. Dunphy interprets the myth of the utopian group as an attempt to establish relationships based on mutual trust. In both of the groups he studied, these fantasies emerged after a long period of "group paralysis" and "depression." In addition, as we have noted, these fantasies help the group members deal with the conflict between desire for individuation and wish/fear for symbiosis with the group-as-mother.

Another theme implicit in the notion of the pairing group is the idea of reproduction. In many ways the purpose of the pairing group is to produce something—an idea, a symbolic baby—that will perpetuate the group. Reproductive fantasies and wishes counter the idea of group death with the idea that someone or something will carry on the tradition of the group and that it will not die. That such a fantasy will occur at just those times when the group is most threatened with death and destruction is not at all surprising. Moreover, fantasies of reproduction rather than rescue bear some similarity to the conscious and unconscious fantasies of many suicidal patients (Warburg, 1938), who view suicide as a step toward rebirth, a killing of the old self and the liberation of a new one. The crux of this fantasy is the hatred, disgust, and despair that the patient feels about himself. The fantasy of rebirth through suicide is a reflection of the desperation these patients experience.

Slater's account of the revolt bears some resemblance to a fantasy of rebirth through murder. In this context, the ritual murder of the leader makes possible the birth or rebirth of the group. It serves to counter both the fearful and the depressive feelings of the members. Perhaps there is a link between revolt, termination, and pairing fantasies. Not only is the revolt "oedipal" in the sense of the "primal horde" freeing libido for intermember sexuality, but that very sexuality may serve the defensive purpose of warding off fears of death through fantasies of reproduction.

In this scheme fantasy serves primarily as a vehicle for the expression of wishes and for defenses against them. This wish-defense scheme is applicable to both the individual and the group. In addition, fantasy, while at its base irrational, serves adaptive and group-maintenance functions.

Shared fantasy is the conscious expression of the pooled unconscious fantasies of individual members. It represents not only a compromise between internal agencies within an individual but also a distillation of such compromises involving all the individuals of the group. The myth thus has "universal" appeal, meaning, and function for at least most of the members of a particular group. The shared fantasy becomes part of the belief system or "projective system" (Whiting and Child, 1953) and plays a crucial role in the creation of group culture. Myth is analogous to ideology in that it binds people to common purposes through a similarity of belief. Our conclusion is that shared fantasy is essential to group formation. Fantasies and myths will reflect different stages of group development, particularly stages of the relationship of the individual to the group and to the leader.

UTOPIANISM AND MESSIANISM IN LARGE GROUPS

If we turn our attention to larger collectivities, we discover phenomena similar to those we have described for small groups, some of which we shall briefly explore here.

There is an extensive and fascinating anthropological literature on "messianic," "nativistic," and "millenarian" movements (Aberle, 1965; Barber, 1965; Linton, 1965; Slotkin, 1965; Talmon, 1965). Barber (1965), for example, discusses two American Indian messianic movements, the ghost dance and peyote cults, in terms of deprivation and hope. These movements arose in 1870 and 1890, respectively, after the military defeat of most of the Indian tribes and the destruction of the buffalo—hard times for most of the Indians. In this case the intrusion of white settlers was threatening to destroy the integrity of the tribes, so that in a very real sense many tribes were threatened with extinction. The mythology of the ghost dance fostered the belief that the Great Spirit would bring about a Golden Age through his human emissary. This age would be enjoyed by the living, and the dead would come back to life. The traditional values and ways of life would return, and the ways of the white man would be cast aside. The messianic movement thus instilled hope for the rebirth of a group threatened with destruction and for the return to a happier, more traditional time, before the onslaught of a foreign culture. The peyote cult was a more passive response to deprivation. It emerged, in fact, just after the ghost dance movement was destroyed by whites, who found its message too revolutionary. Withdrawal to the use of drugs offered a passive way of dealing with the deprivation (material and spiritual) which the Indians experienced.

Aberle (1965) has modified the deprivation theory of messianic movements by introducing the notion of *relative* deprivation. In his view, it is not the amount of absolute deprivation that determines whether a specific type of cult will evolve, but conditions of relative deprivation of many kinds. He suggests that cults arise because certain other options are not open. The peyote cult developed because the more active, militaristic, and potentially revolutionary ghost dance was undermined by anxious whites. It is our contention that the religiously oriented and messianic cults evolve when the usual political and military options are closed. The ghost dance arose after the military defeat of the Indians and at a time when other political channels were not open.

A comparable analysis can be applied to other religiopolitical groups such as the Black Muslims. The Black Muslim cult, a messianic movement that began in the ghettos of large American cities, appeals largely to migrants who have little access to traditional seats of political power and who have lost touch with traditional Christianity (Essien-Udom, 1962).

SUMMARY

We have argued that messianic fantasies appear at times when anxiety and depression, the psychological equivalent of the anthropologist's "spiritual deprivation," cannot be dealt with in a familiar and viable manner. Messianism should be most in evidence when "political," active, problem-solving behavior is not effective in coping with the problems confronting the group. The revolt in the self-analytic group can be considered political work in the sense of active manipulation of real events in order to bring about real change. Deification and messianism are more passive, fantasy-oriented, and future-oriented ways of dealing with problems. It is entirely understandable that, as Slater notes, pairing and messianic fantasies occur at those times when the group is most in danger of ending and dissolving.

For various reasons, group 2 had a more difficult time solving its problems through the realistic medium of interpersonal interaction and analysis than did group 1. These difficulties led to fantasy solutions in group 2, solutions which were significantly less necessary in group 1. What we are proposing is that there is a close parallel between individual, small-group, and large-group fantasy phenomena. Fantasy activity serves defensive and adaptive purposes of controlling anxiety, disruption, and anomie. When the usual, more rational problem-solving devices are, for various reasons, not open to people, fantasy on an individual or on a more widely shared group basis may provide the opportunity for solutions-in-fantasy and may even constitute the basis of a social movement.

This proposal points clearly to the centrality of faith, fantasy, and ideology in the genesis of group cohesion and on a larger societal scale in nation-building. Slater (1966) informs us that the evolution of religion is mirrored in the development of self-analytic groups. Perhaps an equally strong case can be made that the political evolution of the state is recapitulated in the development of such groups. The origin of the state is a topic of much interest to historians, sociologists, and anthropologists: How do a group of people come together to form a political entity larger than the family? How do strangers meeting together come to form a group? These questions are similar, and the role of shared fantasy in this process may offer an important source of understanding.

Other political problems—such as the integration of the social system, the response to deviance and minority views, the distribution of power and wealth—have to be dealt with in self-analytic groups. Problems of social control—the regulation of violence and sexuality—are also challenges common to many societies and groups. Tendencies toward the integration of races, nations, and classes have been countered by forces advocating segregation of separate political entities throughout history. Visions of One World without distinctions in nationality, class, and race vie with fierce nationalisms and racial pride. Phenomena such as political separation and political integration are processes of splitting and fusion, discussed earlier in relationship to individuation and symbiosis. There is, on the societal level, the same wish/fear regarding symbiosis which is central to utopianism in small groups.

These observations are not advanced as a complete or coherent theory of political evolution, but reflect impressions and speculations growing out of our studies of small groups. They are meant to extend Slater's conceptualization of religious evolution and to forge theoretical ties between political and religious processes. There are real problems in all groups, and they can be faced in a "political way" by alloplastic, rational, problem-solving activity. They may also be solved or alleviated by appeal to a higher authority, to wish and fantasy, which is more akin to the "religious way." We have described in detail how utopian and messianic fantasies evolve and the functions they serve. All groups are held together by irrational mechanisms of faith and belief, as well as by real capacity of the group to provide for its members.

PART FIVE

THE DYNAMICS
OF LEADERSHIP

Leadership styles have changed, in some instances quite dramatically, over the last decade or so. But it is not at all obvious that these highly visible shifts have been accompanied by more subtle and fundamental changes in authority and peer relations or by enhanced member learning or personal growth. At least one alternative hypothesis deserves investigation: that the almost exponential expansion of small-group technology and the frequent preoccupation with elaborate techniques is symptomatic of considerable uncertainty about the tasks, functions, and outcomes of experiential groups. This uncertainty has several roots, though the major source of difficulty is that experimentation and attempts at innovation have proceeded much more quickly than have theoretical and empirical work in this area. Thus, we find a proliferation of techniques and consultative activities with no coherent conceptual foundation and only isolated efforts to provide conceptual leadership.

Given this state of affairs, our aims here must be modest, realistic, and clearly articulated. We have chosen not to offer a balanced sampling of current work on leadership and technique. It would be impossible to choose three or four papers that could be defended as representative, and in any case a representative sampling might simply mirror the intellectual confusion described above. Instead, we have selected three contributions which we believe meet two important criteria. First, they deal with issues that have been relatively neglected by most writers and by many practitioners. Second, they raise questions that are relevant to a broad range if not perhaps the entire spectrum of leadership styles. Our primary purpose is to identify and explore some of the basic dimensions of leadership in experiential groups and to examine the obstacles to understanding which have made thoughtful conceptual and empirical work in this area so difficult and so rare.

Turquet's paper presents a model of effective leadership which centers on the establishment and maintenance of a clear definition of the primary task of the group. Adopting the social-systems perspective of A. K. Rice and E. J. Miller (Rice, 1963, 1965, 1970; Miller and Rice, 1967), he argues that the nature and the specific requirements of the task should determine the structure and composition of the group. Ideally, the nature of the task serves also to define the basic parameters for the exercise of authority and leadership. The leader, if he is to remain effective, must create and preserve for himself a unique psychosocial position in the group, struggling continually to synthesize participation and observation. Emotional immersion must be avoided, as must extreme detachment. The leader, since he is required to regulate transactions between his group and other groups, must be both in and out of the group. If he moves outside the psychological boundary of the group, he loses touch with the membership; if he becomes too deeply enmeshed in the dynamics of the group, he sacrifices his ability to initiate and monitor interactions with the external environment.

Turquet expands Bion's (1959) distinction between work and basic-assumption activity, emphasizing the differences in both leader and member roles in work and basic-assumption groups. In the work group the skills and interests of individual members are assessed rationally; role assignments are sensible; and individual efforts are coordinated in a productive way. The leadership of a work group shifts in accordance with the actual demands of the task. The leader's executive functions and the aptitudes and preferences of individual members are recognized and protected. Basic assumptions are mobilized, sublimated, and channeled into work activity. In the basic-assumption group, on the other hand, there is no acknowledged need for or tolerance of a complex view of interpersonal reality. The basic assumptions offer simplifying constructions of reality and relatively uncomplicated leader and member roles. The difficulty is that such simplification is inevitably accompanied by a profound "deskilling" of individuals and a constriction of role options for both leader and member. Individuals are seduced and locked into irrational and unsatisfying roles, and the basic-assumption leader is subjected to conflicting and fundamentally impossible demands—to provide unlimited nurturance, to fight and subdue imaginary enemies, to rescue the group from death and dissolution. The work leader must therefore define and defend an appropriate initial structure for the execution of the primary task and determine the scope and permeability of the initial boundary around the group. Throughout the life of the group he must continue to clarify the task and the nature of the work which it requires.

It is difficult enough to provide reliable work leadership in a group with visible "products" and outcomes, though in such a group it is at least conceivable that there can be some agreement about what constitutes success and failure. In an experiential group the products and outcomes are almost exclusively intangible—"cure," "personal growth," "insight," "learning," "joy." What is the task of such a group? What kinds of leadership are required? What kinds of organizational structures and procedures are permissible? Is there an optimal structure? One crucial difference between a work group and an experiential group is that work groups generally attempt to coordinate individual efforts to accomplish a *collective* task, whereas in experiential groups individuals are committed to more personal and *idiosyncratic* tasks—thus the persistent question, how does one maximize individual growth, therapeutic progress, or whatever, in a group? Obviously the group leader must provide some answer to this question.

Whitaker and Lieberman have presented one approach to some of these issues in their discussion of the role of the group therapist. Their priorities are clear. The overriding goal is individuation and the personal development of the individual member. Moreover, they do not overlook the fact that each patient brings to the group idiosyncratic aims, needs, characteristic perceptions and distortions of reality. The therapist's task is to foster a culture in which the skills (experiential and analytic) of every individual patient are protected and utilized, so that he will be enabled to develop in his own way and at his own pace without restricting the development of other members. If he conceptualizes his work in this way, the therapist must have enough confidence in the evolving work culture of the group, and in the members of the group, to endorse one central assumption: if the culture of the group is a generally enabling one, more circumscribed interpersonal and intrapsychic conflicts will be resolved without the direct, focused attention of the therapist. This assessment of the position of the therapist has much in common with Turquet's portrait of the leader operating on the boundary of the group. Whitaker and Lieberman also argue that the therapist is, at least initially, the only person who can serve this function.

Several implications of this point of view merit further exploration. One crucial difference between individual and group therapy, which has received very little attention in the literature, is that the dynamics of groups, small or large, are much more complex than the dynamics of the single psyche or of the dyad. There is simply much more to think about in a group, and it is not possible for the group therapist to work as thoroughly, with as deep an understanding of each individual or each relationship, as he can (or feels that he can) in a dyadic setting. Two related kinds of therapeutic error stem from this fact. First, as Whitaker and Lieberman observe, there are errors of understanding, emphasis, and timing which are attributable to the complexity of the phenomena rather than to what we ordinarily think of as countertransference. Second, unless the therapist understands and is able to accept the harsh reality that in the group he is even further from omniscience than in the dyad, he will be tempted to abandon his role as the leader of a working treatment group and to retreat to a dyadic stance, relating directly to individual group members.

Two other conclusions are implicit in this view. From the assumption that the therapist's primary responsibility is to the development of a therapeutic *group culture,* it follows that as time passes the patients assume more responsibility for the analysis of specific interpersonal issues. In addition, this observation helps us understand some of the pressures on the group therapist. The group leader cannot, as we have seen, be as consistently influential, as much in control, as he is in the dyadic relationship; yet he is the focus of even more intense and varied transference forces. Because of his position on the boundary of the group and the ambiguities and dissatisfactions which are inevitably catalyzed by his authority, power, and personal characteristics, he is the individual in the group most likely to be idealized, castigated, and misunderstood. We believe that it is this combination of circumstances—the complexity of the interpersonal phenomena, the persistent pressure of multiple transference reactions, and the leader's relative lack of power—which makes group therapy so difficult to do well.

To carry this argument one step further, it is plausible to conclude that, since the nature of the work is somewhat different, there are potentially identifiable differences in interpersonal style, temperament, or even cognitive style between effective individual and group therapists. This is obviously not to suggest that the same person cannot do both well, but only that the correlation is less than perfect. Some people may be more able than others to come to grips with the interpersonal complexity of the group and to meet the emotional requirements of group leadership. This is, or should be, a focus for systematic research and for more searching consideration in programs devoted to the training of clinicians.

The strength of O'Day's paper rests in his commitment to thoughtful, systematic, empirical examination of trainer behavior. Though we were able to include only a brief review of his methodology and a condensed presentation of his principal findings, it is important to recognize that his detailed, act-by-act coding of trainer activity is one of a mere handful of such studies. Why has this kind of research been so studiously avoided? The most common explanation is that the methodology and technology required for this type of process analysis are relatively new, and are expensive and time-consuming to employ. All of this is true, but does not speak to the fact that there is considerable resistance to the analysis of leadership behavior. This resistance and the underlying anxiety about such research have prevented the development and application of the research strategy which has *always* been available—the naturalistic, nonquantitative assessment of leadership assumptions and styles.

The literature is overflowing with idealized and prescriptive statements of what group leaders should do, are doing, have done, or are planning to do. Yet while the behavior of group members is often the focus of case studies and research reports, leader activity is very seldom subjected to the same type or degree of scrutiny. It seems to be assumed that everyone knows what group leaders do or that no one can find out what they do without undertaking a research project of monumental proportions.

The most intriguing substantive finding of O'Day's research involves the apparent collusion between the trainer and the group to protect the members' dependency while at the same time maintaining the illusion of participatory democracy and of a gradually evolving sense of member independence from the trainer. One way of understanding this collusion—and here our interpretation of the data departs somewhat from O'Day's thinking—is to view it as a reflection of a latent conflict, or confusion, about the primary task of the group. The trainers in this study seemed unable to identify such a conflict and were consequently unable to deal with it. They instead vacillated between "training" (which points the member toward autonomy) and "teaching" (which binds the member in a dependent position vis-à-vis the trainer-instructor). We are impressed with the very real ambiguity about the primary task of the training group, a source of conflict and confusion which is embedded in the group situation and which creates difficulties for the trainer as he attempts to order his own task priorities. As O'Day points out, the trainer *does* know more about groups than do most of the members, and it may well be legitimate for him to engage in activity which one might describe as teaching. The fact that what is usually considered teaching is not an acceptable aspect of his role activity, of his conception of himself as a trainer and a supporter of member autonomy, sets in motion a process of self-deception and collusion with the membership. This accounts for at least some of the difficulty which these four trainers experienced. Since the primary tasks of these training groups were not entirely clear, there was no way for the trainers to enter the groups with an explicit and consistent ordering of their own task priorities. Thus, they were forced to try to develop and negotiate such an ordering in their groups.

O'Day stresses the uncertainty and anxiety which trainers experience as they attempt to deal interpretively with dependency and counterdependency. The solution which these trainers were tempted to adopt seems quite typical. The groups moved toward a compromise formation in which pressures for nurturance, dominance, and direction become more subtle, allowing the leader to collude with some of these demands. If this kind of defensive compromise is to be avoided, O'Day concludes, leaders must become more able to recognize and frustrate member dependency and to deal firmly with the predictably hostile response to this frustration. Our interpretation is somewhat broader. We are less convinced than O'Day that it is always essential or productive to frustrate dependency and to activate members' fundamental ambivalence toward authority. We believe, though, that O'Day is essentially correct in his argument that dependent and counterdependent feelings and attitudes exist in every group, and that this ambivalence generates a whole set of conflicting pressures on authority—be strong, capitulate; be omnipotent, resign; nurture and love, remain aloof and impartial. There are a variety of possible responses to these pressures—they can be denied, interpreted, selectively recognized, or mobilized and channeled into work activity. The leader's preferred response will be determined by his strategy and style of intervention, or by his lack of a coherent strategy and style (see Klein and Astrachan, 1971). O'Day's observation that these trainers were conflicted in their response to members' authority conflicts is entirely accurate. Our point is simply that one crucial component of this conflict was that they had not formulated a clear sense of what work they hoped to accomplish in the area of authority relations.

Pagès (1971) has offered a provocative commentary on several of the themes explored by O'Day. Describing the "Bethel culture" (as he observed it in the summer of 1969), he suggests that the training culture and ideology of Bethel (that is, of the National Training Laboratories) operate to reinforce individual defenses against the painful affects which accompany many basic, universal, and inescapable human experiences.

[The Bethel culture is aimed] at alleviating individual
and group anxieties, particularly anxieties of isolation, destruc-

tion, and conflict. It does so by offering participants satisfactions of a defensive nature, particularly protective love, closeness, physical contact, and the feeling of a mystical union with the other, the group, and the community. . . . Powerful social norms, conscious and unconscious, centered around love, closeness, expression of feelings, directedness, reinforce the system. The staff group act as guardians of the norms; they also use their technical expertise to maintain their power over the community through constantly designing and structuring the work. In so doing, they protect the unity of the community— but the unity thus achieved is of a defensive nature, acquired at the expense of repressing conflicts, particularly social conflicts between rulers and ruled. The ultimate goal of training thus appears to be the maintenance of an artificially united community devout in the cults of its norms under its benevolent rulers [pp. 278–279].

Whatever the extent of one's agreement with Pagès' appraisal of the Bethel culture, it is fascinating to look more closely at what occurs when the collusion described by O'Day as characteristic of individual trainers and particular groups becomes *institutionalized* in a school of thought, a training center, or a network of professional colleagues. It is at this point that particular patterns of collusion become anchored in an overarching and self-perpetuating social system. Such patterns serve as a reminder that we must become much more attentive to the collusion and distortion of reality which are more than the product of an interaction between a single group and a single leader. Cadres of professionals create, inherit, and internalize their own blends of science, magic, and common sense. It may take some time—or some geographical concentration, such as that provided at Bethel—for the institutionalized bases of the shared defenses to become visible. We can safely assume, however, that any group leader who identifies himself with a tradition or a school of thought, orthodox or heretical, or even one who asks to be seen as eclectic and unique, carries with him an internalized reference group. This reference group may exert a significant influence on his self-image, role definition, and leadership behavior even when he works in isolation. Thus, a group leader, struggling alone with the challenges and demands of the group, may find himself listening more to the inner voice of his fellow professionals than to the members of his group.

We have at several points commented on the widespread and entrenched resistance to intensive empirical examination of the exercise of authority and leadership in experiential groups. This resistance is, we should add, characteristic of the field as a whole, and is certainly not limited to any particular school of thought. Even the Tavistock group-relations tradition, despite its commitment to the study of authority relations, has produced very little empirical work. By way of summary we shall focus on this resistance, in an effort to illuminate its roots and to identify some ways of beginning to work through and beyond it.

Self-analysis is never easy or comfortable, and one obstacle to research on leadership is that the group leader and the researcher are quite often similar in background, theoretical persuasion, and professional style. They may well be the same person, as is the case in virtually all the research that the three of us have undertaken during the last decade. It is not surprising that the trainer, teacher, or therapist is both eager to learn more about how his colleagues are working, how they are perceived by group members, and what they are accomplishing, and somewhat uneasy about what he might discover if he permits himself to look closely and analytically at the actual behavior of group leaders. Moreover, it is exceedingly difficult to feel confident and masterful as a group leader. There are many technical "errors" to be made in a group, and everyone makes at least his share of them. Our hunch is that clinicians trained primarily as individual psychotherapists, which probably includes the majority of group therapists, seldom feel that they are working as effectively in a group as they are with individuals. Groups present their leaders with many opportunities to look foolish or stupid; indeed, one measure of competence is the ability to trust one's judgment even at the risk of being "exposed" and appearing incompetent or misguided. This feeling helps explain, we believe, why many small-group researchers prefer to maintain some distance from the group interaction and the leadership behavior which they are studying.

As should be clear from our introduction to Part One, we

are convinced that at least some of the most sophisticated, set-breaking, and intellectually exciting writing on experiential groups is that of clinicians and other practitioners who have worked largely outside the conventions of what is usually considered scientific research. For many reasons, such contributions are rare, and it is worth noting what this synthesis of clinical and scholarly activities requires. It is difficult to remain reasonably objective and self-critical as a naturalistic observer or as a coder employing an act-by-act scoring system when one begins to examine an interaction which may have considerable personal significance. Here the researcher must, like the group leader, locate and operate on the boundary between participation and observation. Unless he is emotionally close to the data, he will be forced to sacrifice the kind of information that comes largely through emotional involvement. If he is too close to the phenomena, his work will be informed by his clinical expertise and intuition but may be simply a reflection of his thinking as a clinician-in-action, without the broader, long-range perspective which is possible only when one steps back from clinical involvement and becomes an observer. It is unrealistic to imagine that one can maintain this kind of boundary position without feeling pulled in both directions. A capacity to endure this tension is a prerequisite for doing this kind of research. One must alternate between intense participation and determined observation, and be able to manage both simultaneously.

It is understandable that one common alternative to the tension and complexity of research based on this kind of participant observation is a splitting of clinical and research activity. Such splitting, however, creates a barrier between practice and research and tends to isolate clinical inference and intuition from more public, objective, and "scientific" modes of thought. What is lost is the possibility for an integration of the two.

The resistance to research on leadership has in our estimation undermined attempts to look more closely at what leaders actually do in experiential groups. One recent contribution, however, may do a great deal to counteract this resistance and generate support for similar research: the detailed study by Lieberman, Yalom, and Miles (1973) of sixteen encounter group leaders of varied backgrounds and persuasions. They began by developing an em-

pirical taxonomy of leader behavior and then tried to relate behavioral differences among group leaders and different kinds or
degrees of member learning and personal growth. This was an important first step, and it yielded a wealth of data and some very
promising leads for future research. One of the most salutary effects
of the research was the discrediting of a number of assumptions
about the group experiences and the leadership styles which facilitate learning and personal change. Lieberman, Yalom, and Miles
have demonstrated quite convincingly that a variety of positive outcomes in these groups should be attributed at least as much to cognitive work as to emotional engagement. They also point out that a
strict adherence to a "here-and-now" format may constrict the development of a group or the self-exploration of an individual member, and argue that an inclusion of "there-and-then" topics is not
necessarily defensive. More generally, one of the most significant
implications of their research is that the group leader does not play
as crucial a role in group and individual change as many people
have assumed. The evidence, unfortunately too complicated to be
presented here, is that the dynamics of the group-as-a-whole and
the psychosocial relations among the members of the group are extremely important in the process of change.

Most group leaders—assuming that the sixteen studied by
Lieberman, Yalom, and Miles are reasonably representative—are
remarkably unaware of some quite basic elements of group process
and structure. They discovered, for example, that the leaders in
their sample were not much attuned to the fundamental shifts in
group norms, shared attitudes and fantasies, and relationship patterns that are usually subsumed under the general notion of group
development. The leaders also were not particularly aware of or
responsive to role differentiation, and they seemed to struggle with
the problems created by deviancy and scapegoating without a clear
and consistent conceptualization of those problems. In encounter
groups the most visible and disturbing deviants are the "casualties."
The authors suggest that the casualty rate in encounter groups
might be much lower if leaders were more aware of the significance
for the individual and the group of this particular role specialization
and if they were thus more able to view the casualty as symptomatic
of more widespread difficulties in the group. All in all, the authors

noted that these competent, effective, and well-respected clinicians frequently expressed only a vague, impressionistic conception of what made things go well, or badly, in their groups. It is informative (and reassuring) to learn that such vagueness does not vitiate successful leadership, but we suspect that it is accompanied by some anxiety and by a search for a more explicit and concrete theoretical orientation. It is this anxiety, we believe, that pushes leaders toward a preoccupation with epiphenomenal behavioral characteristics and techniques. This reliance on shared mythology and technical amulets is in itself relatively innocuous, but it does distract group leaders from learning more about group process and group structure and from forcing themselves to examine their own work from a variety of perspectives.

Our prescription is simple, and somewhat austere. What is needed is much more theoretical and empirical work on the dynamics of leadership in experiential groups. There is, as we have noted, a serious lack of information about the actual behavior of group leaders. We have urged researchers to alter their priorities and observational strategies somewhat and to make more use of naturalistic observation and of clinically based studies of group process. Both process and outcome research are, of course, essential to a thorough and sophisticated examination of leadership. Our view is simply that naturalistic observation and process studies have been avoided by group leaders and by group researchers and that the time has come to understand and overcome this avoidance.

14

Leadership:
the Individual and the Group

PIERRE M. TURQUET

By way of introduction, I would like to make three preliminary points.

First, I shall be describing, from personal experiences, small-group behavior; that is, the behavior of groups with eight to twelve members, with sixteen as the extreme upper limit. There is nothing mysterious about such numbers. Many a committee is so composed —the board of directors of a company, a selection committee for a post, the senior faculty of a university department, or a committee to plan and organize some event. Slightly larger groups—say, with a membership of twenty to thirty, the typical honorary committee for some event, or the board of governors of an institution—seem to get little or no work done. In my experience they live up to their "honorary" title all too easily. My advice to anyone invited to join such a committee is to recognize that he is being invited for his name, rank, or whatever, but not for work. If he has a taste for work, then he had better refuse this signal invitation to futility. In

This chapter is based on a lecture given to the Paris Society of Psychosomatic Medicine in November 1967. The essay is much indebted to the work of Bion (1959), Rice (1963), and Miller and Rice (1967).

fact, such moderately large committees tend to split into small executive committees; but then we are back to our original smaller numbers of eight to twelve. When groups reach even larger numbers (say, fifty to eighty, and eighty is the largest group that I have studied in detail), and so because of their size can no longer remain face-to-face groups, the presence of other phenomena intrude on the characteristics of the small group.

These new phenomena are of a different order from those of small groups and in part center around the question of the institutionalization of the individual as a means of saving the single person from annihilation, which constantly threatens. In part, the observable phenomena seem also to stem from the need of individual members to search for and find an encompassable whole. Another reason, it would seem, for preferring to work in a small group is that it is encompassable by each individual member, as well as being face-to-face. Hence a membership of twelve seems to be getting near the upper limit of a single member's capacity to encompass and take in, with sixteen as the extreme limit. It is perhaps relevant to point out that chess has sixteen pieces. But role differentiation on an institutional basis—that is, a large-group phenomenon—has already begun to crystallize out. On the other hand, and at the other extreme, if membership numbers are five or six, again phenomena of a different order appear—phenomena more directly related to the field of family dynamics and family fantasies.

My second introductory point is that a small group, if it is to be alive and active, must have a *primary task* (Rice, 1963)—a task that the group must carry out if it is to survive. Thus, a factory must produce goods, a businessman must make profits, a bank must show a return on its investments, a hospital must cure a visible number of its patients, a school must teach the subjects on its curriculum, a university must produce graduates from undergraduates. A functioning small group must therefore seek to know its primary task, both by definition and by feasibility. Failure in these matters inevitably leads to the dismemberment of the group, and hence to its final dissolution, or to the emergence of some other primary task unrelated to the one for which it was originally called into being.

Even though some groups or institutions may have more than one primary task, nevertheless, at any one moment in time they must decide which primary task to pursue. A surgeon can teach while operating, but teaching has to go by the board when the patient shows signs of vascular collapse, at least if the surgeon wishes to be able to continue to operate on a live patient—a matter of taste if you like. If the sales department of a factory is unable to sell the factory's goods, further attempts on the part of the personnel department to solve the local unemployment problem can lead to the bankruptcy court, which is no way of solving unemployment. In my opinion, universities, especially in England and the United States—the former less so than the latter—appear to have got themselves into a difficult situation by attempting to carry out two of the main contradictory primary tasks, to teach and to do research; or at least they appear to have failed to distinguish between them. They are different in that, for instance, each requires its own method of work, its own group membership, and its own leadership. To the research worker, the undergraduate is a chore, and the able teacher a second-class citizen, a mere "vulgarisateur" who waters down, if he does not actually distort, the research worker's valuable and fine ideas. For the teacher, the research worker is an ivory tower specialist, demanding more and more facilities and time for his own work, requiring more specialized and highly expensive equipment, thereby starving the departmental library of basic textbooks for the students, and increasingly making claim to professorial teaching chairs. In such a conflict situation it is no wonder that the undergraduate feels more and more disaffected.

Consider our prisons. If in recent months there has been an increase in prison escapes, it is perhaps because prison administrators are uncertain about which of their diverse primary tasks to implement. In a reformist prison, the uniformed disciplinary staff feel undervalued or unneeded. In a no-escape prison, the socializing reformer experiences the impossibility of his task. Thus the staff members become easy victims for the escaping prisoner. Only by drawing clear boundaries between conflicting primary tasks can a group resolve tensions and confusions. The implication here is that structure and primary task are internally linked, and that primary-task fulfillment requires an appropriate structure.

The first signs of group institutional failure can be sought in an examination of primary task "products": the ratio of satisfied to dissatisfied undergraduates in a university or of cured to dead patients in a hospital, the escape rate from prisons, the balance sheet of a commercial enterprise. That is, the groups or institutions that I have mentioned are *open-system groups,* interacting with the environment in which the group has its being. Hence, their primary-task products are to be found in their external environment. If no such products are externally detectable, then the group in question is probably a closed-system group (one of the basic-assumption groups discussed later). Because a group's primary task involves interactions with the environment, there will be a surface of interaction between the group and the environment. Such an interaction surface leads to the formation of a boundary between group and environment. Furthermore, because there is a boundary, there will be transactions across the boundary; and such transactions will require mechanisms of control—in particular, and in individual terms, the presence of a leader. A fundamental aspect of leadership, therefore, is boundary control at this interface.

Furthermore, the clearer the boundary, the easier it is for these transactions to be studied and, indeed, for the fact of their existence to be acknowledged. In the debate that took place in the House of Commons after World War II on the rebuilding of the House following its destruction by German incendiary bombs, Winston Churchill eloquently argued for a rectangular House on the grounds that such a House would inevitably highlight the act of "crossing the floor" as an open, deliberately taken decision—and he himself was well experienced in such political tergiversations—as against a semicircular House modeled, for instance, on the Continental or American examples where all that is required is a shifting movement of the bottom, the boundaries being so structurally indeterminate.

Open-system groups are involved not only in an internal/external world of differentiation but also in an internal-world differentiation, in the setting up of the internal processes of intake, conversion, and output. Such internal processes help in turn to strengthen the boundary between the internal and external worlds and thereby to support the exercise of the leadership function of boundary control. The complication for leadership is that, like the psychoanalytic model of the ego, it has to be Janus-like, looking both internally and externally, becoming both participant and observer. If the leader allows himself to become an observer gliding above the fray as a nonparticipant, he will deprive himself of knowledge of certain vital aspects of the group's activities. Hence, he will lose much of his evidence about the state of the group and especially the group's expectations with regard to his leadership. Indeed, there will be times when the only evidence available to him as to the state of the group's health will be his own personal experience of the group, what he feels the group is doing to him, and how he feels the group inside himself. Equally, of course, total immersion or loss of self in the group is destructive to leadership as a boundary function. It follows, too, that leadership has to act as a projection receptacle and to bear being used. As a motto for leadership, I would offer a saying attributed to Socrates: "It is never right to return a wrong or to defend ourselves against a wrong by threats of retaliation," for groups are beset by fears of such retaliations.

Furthermore, if I have in one and the same breath talked of groups and institutions, it is because more and more institutions are controlled and directed by small groups, as Galbraith for one points out in his recent book, *The New Industrial State*. Leadership of an institution is therefore apt to have two faces. On the one hand there is the leadership exercised by a small group, and so it becomes possible to think of group leadership. But there is also the personal leadership of an individual—a chairman, or director, or president—and hence it is possible to think in terms of the personal leadership of a small group. These two aspects can become disconnected, however, especially if the personal leadership is charismatic in quality.

Because in open systems there are interactional surfaces with exchanges across boundaries, and because primary-task products are detectable outside the group or institution, there is no place in such groups for secrecy. Leadership of a group or an institution, either as a group or as an individual function, is therefore a public function. Leadership which is not public belongs to a different order of phenomena, a point I will come back to later. Secrecy, like charisma, may be appropriate for a particular moment in the life of a group or an institution, but such moments are for obedience rather than for learning, more for the creation of beliefs than the establishment of demonstrable facts, more for the greater glory of one person than for the healthy development of the whole.

To illustrate, with an example from business: A family firm was profitably manufacturing and marketing a product that was sold under the family name, mostly by small retailers. The chairman and founder of the business, upon learning that several large distributing stores were interested in marketing the product under trade names of their own choosing, suggested to his fellow directors that they accept this departure from tradition, to seek greater profits. His suggestion was rejected: "Our unique product under somebody else's trade name? Allow control over our processes? Never." The chairman had done his charismatic job too well. Eighteen months later the firm was the object of a successful takeover bid; the directors lost their seats on the board, and the product is now being sold under new trade names. The directors had made their primary task the protection of a name, rather than the pursuit of profits through manufacture and selling.

My third and last introductory point relates to the work of Bion (1959)—specifically, his notion that a small group can exist in two states: as a sophisticated work group and as a basic-assumption group. The primary task of these two groups is different, and hence also the quality of the leadership required for primary-task implementation.

The sophisticated work group is a group called into being for a predetermined, clearly defined primary task which has been openly accepted, at least at the conscious level, by its members and at which, again consciously, they have agreed to work. *Ab initio,* therefore, such a group will be concerned with trying to define its primary task or, as work progresses, whatever discrete aspects of its primary task are on hand at that particular moment. Such a group is therefore concerned not only with definition but with a high level of self-awareness—an awareness concerning impingements between itself and the external world in which its work is taking place. Later, as "work" develops, the group will seek to maintain its relationship between its primary task and the external milieu, especially as this relationship undergoes change following on work. In this sense a work group behaves like an open-system group.

In its attitude to primary-task implementation—that is, to work—the work group is activated by a desire to know: to acquire insights, to discover and understand explanations, and to form hypotheses that can be tested. It will also be concerned with the consequences of its own behavior and actions—not only between individual members of the work group but also with the group's external milieu.

The members cooperate freely in primary-task implementation through the skills each brings to this task; indeed, each member is valued for the skills brought to its implementation. Furthermore, as part of the initial definition of the primary task, the work group will examine the skills present among its members to ensure at least the possibility of its fulfillment. A surgical team will require a surgeon; it may or may not need a physician. A society may or may not need a treasurer, depending upon the number of subscriptions and financial transactions involved. This preliminary examination of skills in relation to primary-task definition is especially crucial with regard to leadership. It is not self-evident that a chemical plant requires the leadership of a chemist, particularly if sales or profitability is its immediate current primary task.

Furthermore, a very important distinguishing feature of a work group is the freedom to associate enjoyed by its members. They are also free to resign, and resignation is not necessarily a threat to their personal existence; also, the work group is free to dissolve. Furthermore, the members of a work group assume responsibility for the group's interactions—both internally as between members, and externally as between themselves and the environment—and their consequences. The assumption of responsibility is a collective one, somewhat like the doctrine of collective responsibility which guides the British Cabinet, and is not left to become the sole responsibility of an individual. The notion of the leader, of a single member being solely responsible, is not only derogatory of the individual skills of the other members of the group but is also inimical to the task of inquiry. Particular experts may be necessary for specific functions, but their expertise has to be assessed by the group if the group is to flourish as a sophisticated work group and not to behave as something else. A board of directors may need an accountant, but disaster will ensue if he is the only member of the board who can read a balance sheet.

If a work group has structure—chairman, secretary, minutes, and the like—this structure is related to the needs of the primary task. Minutes of a meeting are not ends in themselves but are there to refresh memories of decisions taken and the reasons for those decisions being taken at that time. If there is a chairman, the implication is that there is a particular aspect of boundary control which requires such a role. When structure becomes an end in itself, it is most probable that we are dealing with a basic-assumption group. Similarly, if a group seeks to include some particular function without relating that function to the group's primary task, without taking into account the consequences of the inclusion for group functioning, or without investigating the skill contribution offered to primary-task fulfillment, then again we may find ourselves in a world other than that of the work group.

Work groups are not mutual admiration societies. Though they may contain friends, they can and should be able to tolerate and contain disagreements. Implicit, too, in the notion of freedom of association is freedom for disassociation, for work-group dissolution. A classical illustration—to put the point the other way round —is the tendency of research teams to perpetuate themselves. Initially a research team will come into being for some clear-cut purpose, perhaps at the request of another research group. Though it may take time, the purpose for which the group was formed is accomplished. But because its members have been successful, perhaps also because they are now familiar with each other's quirks, are now "friends," there is a marked tendency for such groups to perpetuate themselves by finding another project to work on. It is seemingly easier for them to carry on "as before" than to consider self-dissolution or to examine the skill requirements of the further project. Under these circumstances it is more than likely that the second project will not be as successful as the first, particularly if the primary-task requirements for the second project favor a different member composition.

BASIC-ASSUMPTION GROUPS

Let us now turn to the basic-assumption group and its way of life, which is very different from that of the sophisticated work group. In the first place, its primary task arises entirely from within its own midst and is pursued solely for the satisfaction of the internal needs of the group. The *basic-assumption dependency group* (the

BD group) seeks to obtain security for its members, who are to be looked after, protected, and sustained by a leader and only by that leader. The *basic-assumption fight/flight group* (the BF group) pursues the aim of fighting or of flying from somebody or something —with the leader to ensure this necessary action, and the members to follow. The *basic-assumption pairing group* (the BP group) strives to create something, some hope, some new idea or Messiah, to reproduce itself through a pair in the group, with all other members vicariously participating in this paired relationship. To these three basic-assumption groups described by Bion, I would add a fourth—the *basic-assumption oneness group* (the BO group), whose members seek to join in a powerful union with an omnipotent force, unobtainably high, to surrender self for passive participation, and thereby to feel existence, well-being, and wholeness.

Basic-assumption groups (hereafter referred to as Ba groups) require leaders, but it is a personified leadership located in one person, who is expected to do "all that is necessary" for accomplishing the group's basic-assumption primary task. The group may have to adopt special methods to persuade the leader to act accordingly. Thus, a member of a BD group may offer himself or herself as a sick person to be looked after and thereby seek to move the leader to providing succourance. Similarly, a BF leader, if he cannot find enemies to fight or fly from for himself, will be offered suitable candidates to stimulate the necessary paranoid qualities through "atrocity stories" of the stupidity of a therapeutic colleague in another hospital, the iniquitous sales campaign techniques of a rival firm, the alleged absence of the necessary culture in another group or nation, and so on.

Here I must emphasize four points.

First, in such Ba groups it is entirely a question of leader and led, with a collusive interdependence between the two. It is never a question of equals, nor is the leader a "first among equals." He is there by kind permission of the group and will survive as long as he fulfills the primary task of the Ba group. However, since this task contains impossible elements—to be omnipotent; to know without being told; to find and lead into a promised land; to be constantly active with regard to potential enemies; to foster new hopes and ideas, which in themselves are doomed to die; to face impossible unfriendly odds—failure is his future and his replacement is inevitable. (It is true that he may be deified for worship, or changed into a book, or become the subject of much textual exegesis, as Freud was; but appreciation of such consolations is not easy from beyond the grave.) Such groups are therefore often unstable because of changes in leadership; a new leader must be found to replace the old failing one, but the new leader fails too and is replaced, and so it goes.

Second, such groups are not primarily interested in interactions with their environment. They are self-contained, closed systems and, as such, are not like the sophisticated work group, which is interested in predictions and consequences. Hence, they have little or no desire to know, since knowledge might be an embarrassment, might cause disturbance in the internal harmony or "groupiness" of the group. Their motto might be "Don't confuse me with facts; I have my own ideas." Their attitude toward knowledge is very similar to Goebbels' attitude toward art. Being fearful of and aggressive toward knowledge, lacking the necessary predictive techniques, scornful of hypotheses, hence uninterested and unaware of consequences, they have little or no sense of collective responsibility. In the main, responsibility is left to the leader. External reality is regarded as a potential source of sudden unpleasantness and therefore to be avoided. All coldness is outside; all warmth is inside, with members huddling together like so many babes in the wood, especially in BD. Outside is death; inside is life.

Third, such groups appear to come into existence spontaneously, with no preparatory formulation, no expectations to be fulfilled. Hence they act on an "as-if" basis—as if things will come to pass because they are so and so; as if their leader has but to act, which as a good leader he obviously will do. No effort seems to be required for their emergence, and they have a full dynamic energy of their own. Such groups are indeed lively affairs. Equally, the group seems to know what to do, and no previous training of its members seems to be required. In addition, the assumptions on which the members act are rarely formulated, certainly not by one particular member. Intellectually, their task is neither troublesome nor thought-provoking. Their primary task is simply to be carried out, not developed and not the object of adaptive processes.

Fourth, these leadership concepts, brought into being by the interpersonal relations between the members of the group, contain a mythical quality. As myths they have such universality that major sections and institutions of a community—hospitals, church, and clergy for BD, army for BF, aristocracy or ruling intellectual families for BP, the "mysteries" for BO—represent and embody those myths on behalf of society. These institutions often have the characteristics of closed systems—their leadership recruitment, for instance, comes from within, their sense of time is oriented toward the past or an out-of-time timelessness, and their failures at crisis moments, when called on to fulfill their primary tasks, are notable. But the further point, both theoretical and technical, is that our attention is drawn by the presence of such myths to the dynamic, myth-making quality of interpersonal, interface relations.

For instance: For the dyadic relationship, there are the myths of Penelope, of "marriages made in heaven," of marriage as an exposed, eternally available breast, and the myth of the birth of a savior. For the triadic relationship, there is the oedipal myth. For the family groups, there is the revengeful "Urvater" who watchfully encourages sibling self-destruction, or the all-embracing succouring mother. For the small group, there are the Ba leader myths already described. For the large group, there is the errant mob so aptly displayed in Goya's painting of Rumor. For the individual seeking his identity in group situations, there is the myth of Odysseus. And for each situation there are others. Technically these myths have to be elucidated because by their binding together quality, they contribute to the perpetuation of fruitless non-adaptive systems.

The members of such Ba groups are both happy and unhappy. They are happy in that their roles are simple, requiring little skill and no great soul-searching. In BD the role is to be looked after, to be the "casualty" for the exercise of the leader's thoughtful expertise in caring and the object of the group's concern. Though there may be competitiveness for such a role, the criterion for success—command of the leader's attention—is simple. In BF it is to be a member of a combat team for courage and obedience; though casualties—to be neglected and treated as malingerers—may abound, they are compensated for by the great sense of camaraderie, of action, of doing something, even though it may be over the cliff or into the mouth of the cannon. (Watching such a group in action, I have often sympathized with the French general in the Crimean War who, on observing the famous Charge of the Light Brigade at Balaklava, is reported to have said, "C'est beau, mais ce n'est pas la guerre"—It is nice, but it is not war. Clearly for him war was a matter for a sophisticated work group.) In BP the member is either one of the pair or part of the vicarious participating audience, in either case lost in the ongoing activity, buoyed up by hope, like the characters in a Chekov play expecting that "spring will come," the total atmosphere being of bated breath, as in a Flemish picture of the Adoration. In BO the group member is there to be lost in oceanic feelings of unity or, if the oneness is personified, to be part of a salvationist inclusion.

With these levels of simplicity there is little need for personal assessment of whether individual members possess the skills needed for task implementation. Throughout, the member gets his task from the group, and his social role is defined by the group. It may not always be pleasant to be the objector, the interpreter, or the buffoon. But better such roles than none at all, which may be a consequence of membership of a work group. In such a role a member may be missed. Thus, in committee, when the objector is absent, confusion ensues, so that a decision is postponed until he returns, when the matter is quickly settled and the objections promptly overcome.

On the other hand, there are difficulties and unhappinesses. Participation in Ba groups results in individual members' becoming deskilled in varying degrees. Memories become poor. Time sense is impaired: "Some time back somebody said so and so." Living in the here and now seems very difficult, and there is a marked tendency to go back over past events: "What did we do last time?" There is a disturbed location of speaker: "Somebody over there, I forget who, said. . . ." Sentences, especially if they seek to convey an explanation or insight, have to be simple and relatively short. The preference is for the leader to act without the group's having to indicate its action wishes: "How clever he is; see, he knew it all along." Indeed, in a BD group so strong is the wish for magic that all disasters are treated as signs of the most thoughtful planning. If

I go to America and leave a group with my assistant, the comment is "See how thoughtful he is? It is all for our own good."

The deskilling of the individual member can be great. Thus, a group of analysts, psychologists, and social workers, all well versed in psychoanalytic theory, meeting for the primary task of studying group processes, on one occasion decided that one of my wrists was swollen, and perhaps my ankles also, and expressed concern. When I suggested that there might be some oedipal significance to this discussion, I was greeted with looks of frank amazement. Very painfully and slowly they gradually reestablished the fact that they had been talking about swollen ankles. Then a member remembered that there was a link between Oedipus and swollen ankles. But they were quite insistent that it was the father who had killed the son. Such deskilling can be in favor of group cohesiveness. For instance, a member of a similar study group commented, "Why is the group wearing black ties?" Only with difficulty did they discover that of the ten people present only three seemed to be wearing black ties and that one of these ostensibly black ties was not black, since it had a dark-purple stripe. The black ties were clearly wanted—in the name of cohesiveness and uniformity.

An additional cause of pain is the concreteness of the situation in these groups. It is not that there is a picture of an angry Dr. Turquet, but that Dr. Turquet is in fact angry. An interpretation from a consultant is often treated as a rebuke: "We have got it wrong again." It may also be treated as a specific instruction to do something. Thus when a whole conference membership of fifty or so, assembled to study intergroup relations, heard the statement "It seems that in order to carry out this exercise some process of small group formation will have to be thought about," it was taken as an instruction to divide, and the room cleared itself in a matter of seconds. Army commanders of small units are well aware of the dangers arising from the concrete interpretation put on orders. Thus when a platoon pinned down on a machine-gun swept beach, unable to move, was given the order "forward march," the men all stood up and marched, and were killed to the last man. In addition, this concreteness makes the assumption of responsibility particularly difficult and painful.

Nor is the individual member there for his own sake. Like the leader, he is given his role for the fulfillment of the group's purpose, and only for that purpose. If the member oversteps the mark and behaves idiosyncratically, then he is out. Thus, in a psychotherapy group a patient was encouraged to tell her story in the hope that the consultant would demonstrate his skill and do something about her pain. At first she was very inhibited and apologetic, particularly at taking up the group's time, but the group encouraged her to talk. Finally she told the group that after many hesitations because of her sexual shyness, she had accepted an invitation from a man in her office to meet him for a drink. She had arrived a half hour late—which the group accepted as a woman's privilege. Then she said she had been seized by fear, and claiming that she had to make a telephone call, she had slipped out by another door, leaving the man stranded. This proved too idiosyncratic for the group, and she was left for the rest of the session neglected and crying in her corner. Equally, in BF anyone who gets sick is treated as a malingerer, as asserting individual values over and against the group's supremacy. One member, with the group's approval, tried to form a pair with me. He got much encouragement from the group in this new plot, despite my interpretations. The matter turned sour on him when he asked me for a private consultation. Gods can be public but not private. Such groups can be ruthless toward their members; and members can avoid receiving such treatment only by fitting in with the group's roles and requirements.

Consolation for each member would seem to come from the group's undoubted action nature. There is no time for pausing or thinking and no sympathy with such activities. Thinking is referred to as "introspective nonsense," particularly in the BF group, where "Rome is always burning and the work group fiddling." There are frequent statements such as "We are getting nowhere" and "Where does that get us?" Although a group may ostensibly be seeking to understand itself, the consultant's explanations in these circumstances are described as "Our consultant is always blocking us," leading to "We've got to do something." This kind of phenomenon may become acute, as in the general practitioner's surgery with the anxious wife questioning the husband after his visit: "Well, what did he do?" Indeed, often the general practitioner, while having diagnosed his patient's condition as psychological, and after having discussed with him the relevant emotional problem, finds himself forced to give him a bottle of medicine in the name of having done something. To talk is not to do anything.

Such basic-assumption groups, then, are very cohesive and coherent, full of energy and life. They are helped in this by having a structure, though the structure becomes an end in itself. The committee has a treasurer even though the budget is very small. Minutes become laws rather than aids to memory; often the minutes seem written to provide a "full record" rather than a summary of actions taken. The chairman directs and the members rubber-stamp. Members seem to be required to sit in the same chairs. The chairs of absent members are removed to close the ranks, on an "out of sight out of mind" basis, a further example of concreteness. Structure and cohesion are also reinforced by the tendency of these groups to use broad generalizations and clichés. There are to be no divergencies.

WORK GROUPS VERSUS BASIC-ASSUMPTION GROUPS

What then is the relationship between the work group and the basic-assumption group? Here I would suggest the dream as a paradigm. Just as the manifest content of the dream is suffused with latent content, so the work group is constantly suffused with basic-assumption elements. Just as it is impossible to have a dream of manifest content alone, so a pure work group is very rare. On the other hand, it is possible to have a dream of latent content only. So, too, a pure basic-assumption group can come into being and remain in being for some time.

The question of the relationship between the two groups, especially how a work-group atmosphere can be sustained with few lapses into basic-assumption modes of behavior, can be further explored through an examination of the phrase "sophisticated work groups." The sophistication of work groups is expressed in four principal ways.

First, a work group is sophisticated in the use it makes of leadership. The leader of a work group is a "first among equals," having, like the other members of the group, skills for primary-task implementation; he is not the only member of the group who has skills. In Ba groups the leader is believed to be the only one who matters, and is in fact the only one who is listened to; and though other members can be insightful, their contributions remain virtually ignored. The work-group leader's primacy is in defining and maintaining the primary task in relationship to the environment. As new and different facets of the primary task emerge, changes in leadership may be required. For instance, in an operating team, under normal conditions the surgeon is probably in charge. If, however, respiratory embarrassment occurs, the anaesthetist may take over while the surgeon packs the operating site and perhaps acts as assistant to the anaesthetist. When the respiratory crisis is overcome, the surgeon will again assume the leadership role and continue his operation. Thus, in a sophisticated work group, though there may be shifts in leadership, the nonoperant leader does not become a discarded and rejected member of the group. In contrast, in a Ba group his nonuse amounts to defeat or annihilation—as, for instance, is the case with politicians voted out of executive office. The work group will indeed be anxious to preserve the leader's skills since they are not pure leadership skills but have another component which initially was concerned with the group's primary task, as with the anaesthetist in the operating team. In the Ba group it is a question of sacking and dismissal; in the work group it is a question of shift of emphasis. Furthermore, the need for such shifts is not the responsibility of the leader alone. Members of a work group have also to assess the nature of the leadership required at any particular moment in relation to the discrete aspects of the primary task on hand at that moment. In addition, an outside observer will be able to detect some of the reasons for this shift in leadership in the work group. This is not so with the Ba group, whose leaders come and go for no externally discernible reason, the reasons being purely those of failing to satisfy internal needs.

Second, in contrast to the Ba group, the work group seeks in a sophisticated way to protect the skills of its individual members. Moreover, each member must constantly assess and reassess himself in skill terms for primary-task implementation. Such a reassessment may require the painful decision to withdraw from the work group on the grounds of lack of skill; this is bound to be painful because no one can easily accept the rupture of member-to-member continuity which group life contains. Because of role simplicity, no such self-evaluation is required in Ba groups, and hence that kind of life is less painful. It is a function of the work-group leader to help group members in this type of assessment.

Perhaps, however, the most important area of skill preservation in leadership is over the leader's inalienable right to executive action. The nature and grounds of his decision making may be questioned, but not his right to make decisions or to ensure their implementation. Ideally, the decision-making process should center around predictions and their testing. In practice no group can afford to wait for definitive certainty, and decisions have to be taken on incomplete knowledge. One aspect, therefore, of the work leader's skill is his capacity to tolerate anxiety and doubt. In this connection very noticeable efforts are often made to deskill the leader by various members of the group, who fill him up with their anxieties and their fantasies. As a result, his threshold for anxiety and doubt may become so lowered that his skill for taking executive action becomes impaired, resulting in his becoming a leader by permission of the group. That is, a Ba group leader may become so involved in the group's internal life that he is no longer able to preserve the necessary boundary between himself as an individual and the group as a whole. He then becomes the prey of the group's action requirements, pausing and thinking together, with work going by the board. Of course, what can happen to the leader by way of filling up can also happen to other members of the group. It is therefore in the mutual interest of all that the skills of all should be preserved. The sophisticated preservation of the leader's skill therefore involves self-containment by each member. Each work-group member has to learn to think in "appraisal" terms and not in "discharge" terms; to extract and appraise the relevant information rather than give an excited discharge through a detailing of all the minutiae of the event. This latter process is Ba-group behavior; in essence, it leaves appraisal to the group leader, and by using "discharge" rather than "appraisal," treats him as akin to a bottomless wastepaper basket. Appraisal requires skill and familiarity with the primary task as well as the exercise of personal responsibility, but without these safeguards, survival of member and leader can be in doubt.

Third, a work group is sophisticated in that it uses predictions. That is to say, the leader furthers the work of the group around testable hypotheses. All successful businesses have predictive aspects—what stocks of which raw materials will be needed when, sales expectations, preparation of budgets, rate of personnel replacement, and so on. Hospitals will develop notions about bed occupancy rates; general practitioners are interested in seasonal morbidity rates and the like. Similarly, in training seminars the leader of the seminar says in essence: "If you do or say so and so, such and such will follow." The most important predictive leader statement is the "because" clause, since the statement that so and so *is*—because of this or that—enables the leader's sense of reality, his "intouchness," to be seen and tested. In the absence of such predictions, a group lapses into hunches or is ruled by one experience. In extreme cases of absence of testable hypotheses, and many an example can be found, Ba ways of life come to dominate such groups. Here universities could be quoted. Predictions at admission are in the main rarely related to the results three or four years later. Worse, little is known about the rejectees—what proportion might have done better than those accepted. In these circumstances, Ba ways of life—with more and more insistence on higher intake standards— tend to take over, with schools accused of not giving these young people the right grounding, though little work is done to demonstrate that universities know how to use the material that is offered them, and little predictive testing is carried out to support their contention that higher standards are needed. Much of the trouble between the so-called schools of psychiatry stems from the absence of testable predictions, so that psychiatric clinics oscillate between BD development toward their patients—trying to give better and better care to more and more sick patients—and BF development toward other clinics, who are treated as foolish rivals who have not seen the light. Indeed, it is not too much to say that the degree of arbitrariness with which a point of view is held, particularly in medicine, is directly related to the extent to which it can be, or has been, tested.

A further essential point here is the time span of predictability; that is, how soon in time can predictions be verified? In a sense, the shorter the time between prediction making and verification, the better placed the group is to adapt and correct its behavior.

The longer the time span, the more likely Ba ways of thinking are to develop. Most sales departments have not only annual forecasts but also monthly checks. And similarly, with annual budgets, most firms have cash flow accounting or similar systems. Psychotherapy presents the contrary picture. A time span of three years or more between taking in a patient and thinking about discharge allows the psychotherapeutic institution to go its own way unchecked, so that it becomes more and more devoted to a BD way of life. In fact, it has nothing else.

Fourth and last, the work group seeks to make a sophisticated use of the relevant Ba group for the implementation of its primary task. It seeks to mobilize the relevant Ba group in support of its work, and to keep any Ba group which would be inimical to its primary task, at bay. For instance, a surgical team will seek to mobilize BD through its ward structure, the efficiency of its organization, the calm routine it provides, the detailed preliminary knowledge the doctors, nurses, and auxiliaries have of the patient and his circumstances, so that the patient can give himself over to the situation in a trusting, dependent way. Often the BD is reinforced by BP, the patient pairing with a nurse or ward orderly. So, doubly fended off, BF is kept at bay.

There also have to be sophisticated changes in Ba-group mobilization to meet shifts in primary-task implementation. Thus, in schools, too much fighting against the teacher hampers learning. BD is mobilized, as is BP, through individual attention from teacher to single pupils. Most schools in England try to get away from the large classroom teaching situation in favor of smaller groups, where the BD content of the situation can be more adequately controlled. Hence, too, the development of the seminar system in universities. But BD is of no use in the examination situation. It is not realistic to expect the examiner to look after the candidate—or such has been my experience. With medical examinations, for instance, there is a sophisticated mobilization of BF. Back papers are gone over, the pet subjects of the examiners are discovered, and in general the examinations are treated as an enemy offensive, which must be turned back by a strategy based on counterintelligence. BP may also be mobilized through two candidates examining each other.

In addition, the mobilization of Ba-group ways of life helps give to the work group its liveliness, warmth, and sense of cohesion. The inevitable suffusion by Ba elements is thus used constructively by the work group. But only a work group can do this, the sophisticated use of basic-assumption ways of life being an outstanding characteristic of work groups.

A classic example of the sophisticated use of basic-assumption ways in the service of work can be found in Thucydides' *History of the Peloponnesian War*, in connection with that shattering event, the defeat of the Spartans by the Athenians at Sphacteria. The Athenians held the mainland shore at Pylos and the Spartans the island of Sphacteria. The Spartans are about to force a landing and Demosthenes, the Athenian general, addresses his troops thus: "Soldiers, all of us together are in this: I do not want any of you in our present awkward position to try to show off his intelligence by making a precise calculation of the dangers which surround us. Instead we must simply make straight at the enemy and not pause to discuss the matter, confident in our hearts that these dangers too can be surmounted. For when we are forced into a position like this one, nice calculations are beside the point." Needless to say, he was addressing the intellectual elite of the ancient world; it is to be presumed that the Spartans neither needed nor would have understood such language.

THE INDIVIDUAL AND THE GROUP

Essentially, the single individual who joins a group is in a dilemma. He wishes to be part of the group and at the same time to remain a separate, unique individual. He wants to participate, yet observe; to relate, yet not become the other; to join, but to preserve his skills as an individual. He wants the Ba-group way of life for the satisfaction of his own basic-assumption needs, for the security such groups afford, for their simple ways of living, for their recuperative contribution to man's ultimate aim—to establish his uniqueness while maintaining his relatedness to others.

Initially, the individual achieves a sense of belonging through his identification with the leader. The leader helps the joining member to reality-test his perception of the primary task. Joining will be reinforced by the new member's personal affinity for one of the Ba-group ways of life. Therefore, the work group's implicit Ba culture must coincide with the individual's preferred interrelational method of work. Doctors must have an affinity for BD, physicians more so than surgeons. But woe betide the prison governor who expects his prisoners to look after him. He requires a strong "valency" (Bion's term) for BF. A salesman should have a strong liking for BP, since both he and his client have to pair to create the myth that the article is worth buying. The individual's later belongingness depends on work-group satisfactions, the development of his skills in primary-task implementation, and on the satisfaction of his group needs. Moreover—and this is the dangerous element—if his work-group skills are not satisfied, or if he lacks the necessary skills for the primary task, he may be tempted to remain because of this satisfaction of his Ba-group needs.

The individual's apartness from the group is brought about through splitting and projection, projection into an individual group member or into the group as a whole. Hence we see the development of a "nothing to do with me" attitude and a group's capacity to offer the individual opportunities for opting out. The use of these two mechanisms—splitting and projection—has important consequences. They tend to increase the absence of responsibility; responsibility is elsewhere linked to the disowned parts of the self, which are also projected elsewhere. They increase the power of, and hence the dependency on, the leader. For, by projection, the leader becomes the sole repository of power, skills, and reality testing. They also increase the cold, unfriendly, even persecutory nature of the world outside the group, leading to various fears (Will the boundary hold? What will happen when that which has been projected returns?), fears which again increase the strength of the centripetal forces within a Ba group.

And so the single individual struggles. As he leaves the Ba-group way of life, he experiences loss: loss of satisfaction of his needs to belong; loss of a sense of unity, cohesiveness, camaraderie, of being a part of something bigger than himself; loss of a determined, unargued role; and loss of opportunities for action, to "feel" that he is doing something, together with a sense of vitality and excitement. Confronting these losses, he is attracted back into Ba-group ways. And so he oscillates, first leaving Ba-group life and then returning to it, returning to fraternize with death by exclusion from the group, or by nonfulfillment, or idiosyncratic use of a group role, or by attempting to lead—and inevitably dealing with death in ways fit not for high tragedy but more for low comedy, expiring "Not with a bang but a whimper."

And so he pulls out again, to meet loneliness and isolation, to face alone Camus' "Absurdo"; to know things that cannot be shared, to search for what cannot be found; to be solely responsible for his actions, and even more for his knowledge and what he does with it; to have constantly to reassess himself vis-à-vis others, and perhaps to withdraw; to face relatedness with consequences for pain and pleasure; and to experience a future over which he has little control. And so back to the Ba-group life, where the one for whom the bell tolls never seems to be him, and where there is a myth of life and no mention of death. Basic-assumption groups are defenses against death, but like all psychological defenses, Ba-groups have a content, which in fact *is* death. All nonconforming members die of exclusion in the cold outside world. Failure in flight or in fight is death. The not-looked-after group member dies. The Ba-group leader dies, martyred or otherwise, crushed by the impossibility of his task.

What lives on for the support of future generations are the myths the group creates. Bruno Snell has aptly written of the Greek myths: "The reflection which the Greek myths are designed to assist usually produces a greater sense of humility. The majority of paradigms teach men to realize their status as men, the limitations upon their freedom, the conditional nature of their existence. They encourage self-knowledge in the spirit of the Delphic motto 'Know thyself,' they extol measure, order, moderation." Such knowledge and experience, offered through myths, are the ultimate contribution of the Ba group's way of life to man's endeavor.

Many words dominate Greek Tragedy—Sophia, Hubris, Sophrosuno, Time, and Aristeia—but not least in importance is Anake, or necessity: all these unalterable, inescapable facts that constitute the human conditions of living, the double yoke of man's own nature and a world he never made. As Arrowsmith writes: "Necessity is first of all death; but it is also old age, sleep, the reversal of fortune and the dance of life: it is thereby the fact of suffering as well as pleasure, for if we must dance and sleep, we must also suffer, age, and die."

It is Oedipus' necessity—he is Anake—to strive stubbornly, to know and to face the consequences of his knowledge and "by asserting his total, utter responsibility for his own fate, to win victory over a necessity that would have destroyed another man." Thus, Hamlet and the duel scene: "Ripeness is all." The victory is the broadening and deepening of compassion (so Oedipus at Colonnus), compassion experienced as shared suffering that makes men "endure with love in a world which shrieks at them to die," which gives dignity to the human struggle and thus saves it from futility. The Ba group way of life, however brief its occurrence, is a reprieve in this struggle. It gives man a breathing space and enables him to return refreshed by the strength of fraternity to face his aloneness. So refreshed, he endures and survives to demonstrate "the dignity of significant suffering" which alone gives a man his crucial victory over his Anake, his fate—a victory impossible without opportunities for the basic-assumption way of life. Hence man is a "political animal," a fact which, as Bion points out, we neglect at our peril.

15

Strategy, Position, and Power

DOROTHY STOCK WHITAKER

MORTON A. LIEBERMAN

*T*he therapist's goal is to facilitate the therapeutic process for each patient in the group. With this end in mind, he brings particular individuals together into a group and makes certain overall policy decisions about meeting time and place, frequency of sessions, and the general manner in which he plans to conduct the group. Once the sessions begin, he makes continual decisions about which aspects of the session are important to attend to and when and how to intervene.

The group therapist is likely to approach his task from either of two points of view. He may focus primarily on individual patients, proceeding much as he would in a two-person therapeutic situation, or he may focus primarily on the group processes. We shall explore the latter approach, in which the group processes are

Reprinted from Dorothy Stock Whitaker and Morton A. Lieberman, *Psychotherapy Through the Group Process* (New York: Atherton Press, 1964), pp. 189–203. Copyright © 1964 by Atherton Press. Reprinted by permission of the authors and Aldine Publishing Company.

seen as having a critical effect on each person's therapeutic experience.

In order to clarify similarities and differences in these approaches, consider Bob, a patient in a newly formed therapy group. Let us assume that, as the group therapist gains experience with Bob, he comes to understand that one of Bob's central problems is the severe suppression of sexual impulses. For Bob to think of himself as an adult, sexual person or to experience heterosexual feelings is to court rejection and punitive retaliation. Bob does not seem to recognize this as a problem. He moralizes about the sexual behavior of others and explains his own abstinence and lack of experience in highly intellectual, philosophical terms. He tells the other group members that he has entered therapy because he feels anxious and is vaguely dissatisfied with his life. To himself, the therapist might summarize Bob's situation as a sexual conflict which involves some fear of the consequences of recognizing or expressing sexual feelings appropriate to an adult male. The therapist might perceive that Bob has dealt with this conflict by repressing sexual feelings, adopting a moralistic stance, and maintaining intellectual rationalizations. Let us assume that this sexual issue is a dominant motif in Bob's life and that the therapist slowly comes to understand the ramifications and expressions of this problem, as well as its probable roots in Bob's past. Along with hypotheses about the nature of Bob's problem, the therapist also develops ideas about what needs to happen to Bob if therapeutic progress is to take place. Perhaps he forms the conviction that therapeutic growth would occur if Bob came to understand that his problems concern anxiety about sexual impulses or if he came to realize that the retaliation he fears is not likely to occur. Or the therapist might decide that it would be a good thing if Bob experienced sexual feelings in a setting which did not elicit punitive retaliation, or he might feel that it would be beneficial if Bob experienced affect related to the core conflicts which led him to adopt such drastic defensive measures. When the therapist begins to think in these terms, he has proceeded to the point of formulating a general prescription. Now the issue is how to put this prescription into operation. What can the therapist do that will enable the patient to gain the experience or insight which the therapist feels is required in order for positive therapeutic change to take place?

It is at this point that the two therapeutic approaches diverge. The therapist who thinks in terms of directly dealing with each patient might try to help Bob by introducing interventions aimed at coping with his resistance to sexual exploration. Bob's defensive maneuvers would surely be elicited in the group, thus giving the therapist the opportunity to observe and interpret them. The therapist might point out to Bob certain characteristic defensive operations and suggest the reasons that Bob may have found it necessary to maintain them. Or the therapist might use the relationship which has developed between him and Bob in order to point out that the fears of retaliation which the patient experiences about the therapist actually belong to someone in his primary family. Such an interpretation might lead the patient to the recognition that the fears which keep him from experiencing sexual feelings are unrealistic. Or the therapist might use the positive relationship which he has developed with the patient in order to provide the support required for Bob to take what he regards as the dangerous step of exploring his sexual feelings. These and other operations might be introduced or considered by a therapist whose basic strategy is geared toward dealing with a patient's problems by interventions specifically directed toward the individual.

In general, a therapist who focuses directly and specifically on individual patients is likely to offer direct personal interpretations to the patient, probe into the history of the patient in order to clarify links between current and past situations, use dream material, encourage other patients to provide feedback and interpretations, and try to develop a relationship which provides sufficient support to explore anxiety-laden areas. A therapist following such an approach is likely to perceive the principal advantage of the group as its capacity to evoke the patterns which are the heart of the patient's neurosis. The group is helpful to the therapist primarily because it provides him with extensive information on which he can base interpretations. Secondly, the group is useful because it includes auxiliary therapists—the other patients—who can also offer interpretations and reactions to the patient. A therapist operating from this orientation is not likely to pay much attention to group forces unless they interfere with his therapeutic work.

A therapist whose approach focuses on the group processes might see Bob as sharing the group's inability to talk and think about a variety of human issues, be it sex, anger, or affection. This inability would be characteristic of Bob, yet supported by a restrictive group atmosphere. In focal conflict terms, Bob's fears of rejection and retaliation are also experienced by the others and are dealt with by a group solution which may alleviate fears but also prevents free expression of the underlying issues. The therapist might direct his efforts to encouraging the modification of the group solution, substituting an enabling solution for the restrictive one. If he could accomplish this, a number of consequences would follow, making a therapeutic experience for Bob as well as for others more likely to occur. For example, under free group conditions, issues relating to sexuality are more likely to come to the forefront in an explicit manner. Bob would be exposed to affect in the forbidden area. He would have the opportunity to listen to the explorations and feelings of others and perhaps observe that others are able to admit to sexual feelings without eliciting punishment. Some of Bob's underlying fears might be brought out. If this occurs and if Bob has gained some sense of safety from the group culture, he might be able to experience the disconfirmation of his fears and examine them for their real or unreal character. He might reveal enough about himself so that it becomes possible for others in the group to make suggestions and interpretations and to offer feedback. In general, if the appropriate group cultural conditions evolve, Bob is certain to be confronted with experiences relevant to his underlying conflict, might be able to undergo a corrective emotional experience, and might be directly and indirectly exposed to information relevant to his own concerns.

In general, a therapist who emphasizes the group processes may encourage the development of a group culture which allows the patient to reexperience crucial conflicts in the group setting; he may attempt to influence the general anxiety level of the group, so that the individual need not flee from the group or psychologically insulate himself; he may encourage group conditions which provide a sense of mutual support and safety; he may direct his interventions toward freeing the group and widening the boundaries within which it operates; and he may at times point out to patients unique qualities of their own participation and feelings. A therapist with such an approach sees the group as an ever changing context for the patient's behavior and the group forces as having a direct impact on the patient's therapeutic experience. The group's eliciting effect is perceived as important, but is regarded as merely the first of many ways in which the group forces may have an impact on the individual's therapeutic experience. The therapist with this orientation is likely to attend to the overall characteristics of the group as they unfold, as well as to the manner in which each patient contributes to and is influenced by these processes. The individual is viewed in the context of the group.

These approaches have the same goal—promoting the growth of the patient. We emphasize this point because it has sometimes been assumed that to emphasize the group processes means that the therapist is interested in or is treating the group rather than the individual. To state matters as a choice between the individual and the group sets up a false issue. It implies that therapists disagree about goals and that the goal of some therapists is to treat the individual, whereas the goal of others is to treat the group. Actually, the distinction is between means. In one case, the therapist believes that the most appropriate strategy is one which deals directly and specifically with each patient in the group. In the other case, the therapist believes that attention to the group as a whole will create conditions which will facilitate therapeutic change in each patient. In both instances the therapist's goal has to do with the individual and not the group.[1]

Nor can the two approaches be differentiated on the basis of the target of the therapist's interventions. The therapist who emphasizes attention to the group will sometimes introduce inter-

---

[1] To suggest that "the individual versus the group" is a false issue does not imply that the therapist is never faced with choices in strategy which take on the character of a choice between an individual and some aspect of the group. For example, the therapist may avoid interpreting some specific point to a patient because of a potentially negative effect on the group process, or he may be careful about the manner in which he refers to a group issue because of its meaning for a particular patient. This choice is the same that is faced by a therapist whose individual patient is presenting him with complex material which could be exploited in several directions. The group therapist who does not think in terms of total-group aspects of the situation is continually faced with decisions about which patient to concentrate upon. These are all choices in strategy which face any therapist no matter what his theoretical orientation or whether he is dealing with an individual or a group.

pretations directed to individuals; the therapist who concentrates on individual patients will at times attend—often implicitly, sometimes explicitly—to group phenomena. Apart from this, a comment directed to the group may nevertheless have significance for some patient; a comment directed to a specific individual will inevitably have an impact on the group process. For example, a therapist who invites a patient to report a dream is not only interacting with that patient but also may be stirring up competitive feelings in others, thereby rendering ineffective some previously established group solution for dealing with competitive feelings. A therapist who calls attention to the sexual feelings of one patient toward another may be interpreting a shared disturbing motive and thereby interfering with a group solution which involved denial of sexual feelings in the group. A particular intervention may refer to the group, an individual patient, several patients, an individual in relation to the group, subgroups, or any other element or combination of elements in this complex situation. It may be directed toward an individual, the whole group, or a portion of the group. It may take the form of interpretation, comment, reaction, or question. It may even take the form of a *failure* to intervene. Whatever its character, form, or target, however, an intervention is likely to have an impact on the group process. Thus, although the therapist may not think in terms of group forces and may not direct his comments to the whole group, he nevertheless cannot escape the fact that what he says or does not say affects the group process.

In order to understand the kind of influence which the therapist can deliberately exert on the group, it is necessary to understand the position from which he operates. His position in regard to the patients and the emotional forces of the group is not directly comparable to his position in a two-person therapeutic situation. Nor is it the same as that of the patients. Similarly, the therapist's power to influence the situation must be examined anew, for it is not analogous to the therapist's power in individual therapy or to the patient's power in the group.

The therapist's position in the group permits him to view group events from a unique perspective. He is in emotional touch with the forces which operate in the group, but at the same time can stand aside and observe them in a way which is not ordinarily possible for the patients. This unique position makes it possible for the therapist to empathize with the patients' affective experience and yet be able to comment on rather than associate to the material which emerges. One of our basic theses is that powerful emotional forces emerge and significantly affect the behavior, feelings, and experience of the patients. A focal conflict which involves, for example, powerful competitive feelings versus nearly overwhelming guilt has an impact on each patient. None can escape its impact, though each has contributed to the shared group feeling in a different way and each reacts to it in his own unique way. A focal conflict which involves sexual feelings about one another versus fears of retaliation from the therapist is experienced and reacted to in some way by each person in the group. The therapist is also affected by these emotional forces but does not share in them in the same way that the patients do. In his own way, each patient shares in the wishes and fears that comprise the group focal conflict. Each patient wants the therapist for himself, feels angry, fears retaliation, worries about getting out of control, urgently wants the therapist to come to his rescue, reacts strongly to a deviant member, collaborates to maintain an apathetic mood, experiences relief when a successful solution is achieved, and so on. As such forces find expression in the group, the therapist can hardly expect to remain unaffected by them. Not only does he observe the apathy or panic or relief, but to some extent he experiences them. But, if he is able to maintain an appropriate therapeutic stance, he is not a part of them in the same way. He is touched by the emotional forces in the group but does not participate in them. Under ordinary circumstances, the therapist does not share in the wish for special recognition in the group; he does not share the fear of retaliation.[2] It is the therapist's capacity to be affected by the emotional forces in the group which makes it possible for him to intuitively grasp the nature of the emotional events. And it is his capacity to stand aside from these emotional forces which makes it possible for him to control his interventions:

[2] There are times when such sharing does occur and the therapist gets caught up in the wishes and fears of the group. When this happens, one is inclined to say that the therapist has lost his perspective or that he is experiencing countertransference feelings. This is discussed more fully later in the chapter.

to assess the prevailing group forces and guide his participation in terms of certain therapeutic goals.

> *The therapist views the group from a unique position. Though not usually participating in the generation or expression of the group focal conflict, he experiences the affect involved in it. Thus, he is in emotional touch yet stands outside the conflict and can observe its character and course.*

Assuming the therapist's awareness of the character of group events, an important issue is the extent to which the therapist, operating on this knowledge, can influence the course of group events. If the therapist has no power to influence the group, his awareness of the group processes is merely an intellectual exercise with no consequences for the patients' therapeutic experience. The therapist's power comes into play long before the first session of the group; in fact, it is then that his power is clearest, for it is the therapist alone who makes the important decisions about who is to be in the group (subject, of course, to the policies of his work setting and to the available patients). It is also up to the therapist to make decisions concerning the manner in which the group is to be structured and conducted.

The therapist's ability to influence the course of group events, by interventions and style of participation, is a more complex issue. The character and extent of the therapist's power in the group can be understood partly in terms of real power and partly in terms of imputed power. Because of his special training, experience, and perspective in the group, the therapist is in a position to see aspects of the group that the patients cannot see. He is likely to view the group in a broader perspective, noting relationships between current and past events. He is more likely to be aware of characteristics of the group as a whole, and he is in a better position to observe how individual patients participate in and contribute to the group processes. The special perspective of the therapist is as important as his special training and experience, for without this unique perspective, his special training and experience would be of little value. When the therapist participates in other kinds of group situations, such as a staff or committee meeting, his special training does not prevent him from participating in the group forces in ways similar to the patients' participation in the therapy group. But in the therapy group the therapist's unique perspective makes him the only person who can intervene from a position outside the group focal conflict.[3]

Another aspect of the therapist's influence in the group has its source in the fact that patients are likely to attribute special powers to the therapist and, therefore, are inclined to involve him in successive group focal conflicts and solutions in special ways. From the patients' point of view, the therapist is endowed with unique powers. In part, this endowment of special power is realistic. For example, the therapist has placed the patient in the group and presumably could also ask him to leave. He is unlikely to utilize his power punitively, but the patients may assume that he will. Another source of his imputed power is his status as an expert. Although the therapist does have special training and experience, patients are likely, especially during the early phases of the group, to endow him with omniscience and misunderstand the character of his expert knowledge. That is, the patients are likely to assume that, if only the therapist has sufficient data, he will be able to explain them to themselves or give them advice and that, once this is done, improvement will occur. They are likely to assume that the therapist can handle anything that comes up in the group as well as any problem of their own. Such expectations amount to a magical belief that the therapist can understand and fix everything. It is the patients' tendency to attribute such powers to the therapist that accounts for the way the therapist is often involved in the group focal conflicts. For example, the disturbing motive "wish to have a special relationship with the therapist" would be unlikely to develop were it not for the assumption that something special can be gained from the therapist, compared with the others. The reactive motive "fear of retaliation from the therapist" could not arise were it not for the assumption that the therapist possesses special powers that he may use destructively. The therapist is often perceived as a potential source for solutions. Frequently, the patients attempt to utilize the therapist to cope with

[3] With reference to individual patients, the therapist is not the only person in the group who stands in an observer's role. Thus he shares with patients the function of commenting on and offering interpretations about *individual* behavior and processes.

particular focal conflicts. The patients assume that the therapist has the power to control the uncontrollable impulse, deal with the deviant patient, or explain each person and thus bypass the otherwise extended and painful path to therapeutic change.

When the therapist is the object of the wish or fear in a focal conflict or when he is the potential source of a solution, he is in a position to have a special impact on the group. For example, in a focal conflict in which the patients share a wish to have a special relationship with the therapist, any intervention which pays special attention to a particular patient may have a more than ordinary degree of influence on the others. In a focal conflict in which the reactive motive involves fear of retaliation from the therapist, any interpretation on the part of the therapist may be perceived as a negative judgment and intensify the reactive fears. If the therapist introduces an interpretation to an individual patient at a time when the group is operating on a solution which involves perceiving the therapist as an expert, he may find the patient taking the therapist's comments very seriously, for to do so is to contribute to the maintenance of the group solution. If the group is pushing toward a solution the success of which requires the active collaboration of the therapist, withholding such collaboration will have a potent blocking effect in the group. When the latter occurs, the therapist is in the position of a deviant and is exerting the influence of a deviant. This source and character of influence corresponds exactly to that exerted by a patient when he is in a deviant position. That is, if a solution cannot be established without the cooperation of some patient and that patient withholds his cooperation, he is in a position of power. Whether the deviant is a patient or the therapist makes no difference, for the degree and source of influence are the same. In general, we have observed that the therapist's influence on the course of group events is, in many cases, no different from that of the patients. Both may influence the group by blocking an emerging group solution, both may make a comment which increases the reactive fears or the intensity of the wish, both may introduce a comment which leads to the modification of the group culture. Just as the patients sometimes succeed and sometimes fail in their attempts to influence, so does the therapist.

Sometimes the patients respond to the therapist's comments

exactly as he intended; at other times, the group feels like a stubborn mass, and no efforts on his part can move it from its current state. Success or failure in influencing the group depends, as is the case for patients, on the state of the group forces when the intervention is made. The principles which govern the degree and character of the therapist's influence on the group focal conflict are the same as the principles which govern the influence of other participants in the group.

Yet, even casual observation reveals that on the whole the therapist does exert greater influence on the course of the group than does any patient.[4] This apparent contradiction is resolved if one keeps in mind that the therapist is more likely than a patient to be an object of shared wishes and fears and more likely to be perceived as a source of solutions, because special powers are more often attributed to the therapist than to a patient. Under such conditions, the therapist's interventions have a special impact because of their relevance to the group forces. It is in this sense that the therapist "counts more" in the group and is more often in a position to influence the situation than are the patients. In this sense, attributed power is translated into actual power to influence the processes of the group.

The therapist's power to influence the group derives from (1) the unique position from which he views the group focal conflict and which permits him to intervene on the basis of information unavailable to the patients and (2) from the frequency with which the patients impute to the therapist the power of gratification, threat, and magical solutions. On this basis, the therapist becomes an object of impulses involved in the group focal conflict and a source of solutions. On such occasions, the therapist is in a position of special influence in the group.

The extent and character of the therapist's power in the group situation has to be understood in its own terms, distinct from

[4] Short-term exceptions occur, as when a deviant patient dominates a session or when the experience of one individual has a potent effect on the character of the entire group focal conflict. Over an extended period of time, however, the therapist is more influential.

the extent and character of his power in a two-person therapeutic relationship. In individual therapy, the extent, if not the character, of the therapist's influence is taken for granted. It is generally recognized that with only two people present, both play a significant though different role in affecting the character and course of the therapeutic situation. Questions about the influence of the therapist are not so likely to focus on the extent of his influence, but on its character and source. In the multiple-person situation of the group, the issue of how much influence the therapist can exert becomes more critical, for he is only one of a number of people whose participation has an impact on the course of group events. In the group, no individual has as much consistent influence on the character of the situation as either the patient or the therapist in the two-person relationship. As we have just suggested, certain real powers and consequences of imputed powers put the therapist in a position of special influence in the group. But in quantitative terms, the extent of his influence is never so great as that which can be exerted by a therapist in individual therapy. He is confronted with a control and influence problem which radically differs from that which faces the individual therapist.

A therapist who undertakes a therapy group is confronted with pressures and requirements which are unique to the group situation. These are such that he cannot realistically expect to avoid making errors from time to time. Therapeutic error can occur because the therapist has failed to understand the character of the group situation or the meaning of an individual's behavior in the context of the group. Such errors are errors of understanding. The therapist has failed to be sufficiently in touch with everything that is happening and thus misses significant aspects of the situation. In so complex a situation, such errors are inevitable. Other errors can more properly be regarded as countertransference errors. In focal conflict terms, countertransference can be described as occurring when the therapist loses or temporarily abandons the perspective appropriate to his role and participates from within the group focal conflict. Rather than operate on appropriate therapeutic goals, the therapist is driven by attempts to establish group conditions which are personally viable. The specific point at which a therapist is most vulnerable to the group forces and most likely to lose appropriate perspective will, of course, vary from person to person. That is, the particular ways in which the therapist may participate in a group focal conflict and the particular situations under which he is motivated to move the group in directions which are viable to him rather than useful to the group will depend on the therapist's personality and the way it interacts with the group forces.

It is often difficult to differentiate errors which have their source in countertransference reactions from errors which have their source in faulty understanding of the group situation. One might take the position that all errors can be regarded as countertransference errors, since a failure in understanding is inevitably attributable to some countertransference reaction. However, this view assumes that the therapist is equipped with superb and unfailing intellect and sensitivity. Any human being who decides to conduct a therapy group will certainly make errors of understanding from time to time, entirely apart from his possible affective involvement in the group forces. It is often a matter of definition and choice to decide whether a particular error is based on faulty understanding or on countertransference. For example, a common therapeutic error during the early group sessions is impatience with the group for operating on restrictive solutions and premature efforts to widen the group's boundaries. Such efforts may unduly increase the anxiety in the group and interfere with the necessary development of conditions of safety. Often it is appropriate for the therapist to accept the operation of restrictive solutions during the early period and wait until later to encourage shifts toward enabling solutions. It is very difficult to say whether this error is rooted in countertransference reactions or whether the therapist has simply misjudged the group situation. For different therapists it could be one or the other or both. It seems preferable to view errors on a scale ranging from misunderstanding to loss of appropriate therapist perspective.[5]

---

[5] Loeser and Bry have emphasized that it is difficult to differentiate countertransference and noncountertransference factors. They say, "As we explored the subject further, testing, observing, and collecting data, it became increasingly clear to us that the data being accumulated dealt with the total impact of the therapist upon the group and that any attempt to restrict our interest to one aspect of the problem would be difficult. Our study would indicate that there is no sharp demarcation between countertransference and noncountertransference factors, that they merge by gradation over a wide

It would not be useful to discuss the multitude of qualities of the therapist's personality which might lead to his losing appropriate therapeutic perspective and become involved in the group focal conflict. Countertransference involvements vary from therapist to therapist. However, it does seem useful to mention certain aspects of the group situation which may present particular challenges to the therapist.

There are times when the therapist operates under special pressures because of the manner in which he is built into the group focal conflict. The therapist may become the object of pressures from the patients, who perceive him as a potential savior, punisher, or source of gratification. He may be built into the disturbing motive by being the object of hostile, sexual, or succorant drives; he may be built into the reactive motive by being perceived as the source of punishment, envy, or retaliation. He may be built into the solution by being pressed to share his supposed omniscience with the group. Whenever anything of this sort happens, the therapist may feel great pressure because of the unanimity of the patients' feelings toward him. The group as a collective body is perceiving him in a particular way or is pressing him to behave in a particular way. If these pressures coincide with vulnerabilities in his own personality, he may find it especially difficult to maintain a proper perspective.

The therapist may feel vulnerable and threatened because of the character of his influence and control in the group situation. As we have pointed out, the amount and kind of influence and control which the therapist has in the group are radically different from the influence he can exert in the two-person therapeutic situation. Because the therapist may be accustomed to a two-person situation or is making inappropriate analogies from the one situation to the other, he may expect to have more impact or a different kind of impact on the group situation than is really possible. For example, he may feel that he ought to be able to exploit all the personal material which the patients reveal. This last point is very much related

---

scale" (Loeser and Bry, 1953, p. 389). They suggest that it is more appropriate to think in terms of the therapist's position in the group rather than in terms of countertransference. Ross and Brissenden (1961) have followed the same line of thought.

to another possible source of pressure. In the two-person therapeutic situation, the therapist is dealing with only one person and can pursue the material being introduced by his patient in any manner he wishes. He may assume that the therapeutic tactics appropriate to individual therapy are also appropriate to the group or should be modified as little as possible. If he makes this assumption, the therapist will be confronted with continual frustration, for, in the group setting, individual patients are continually presenting data about themselves which cannot be pursued on a one-to-one basis. If the therapist assumes that this is the only road to therapeutic improvement, he operates at a decided disadvantage. Logically, he is forced to the conclusion that he must fail and that he is offering second-rate treatment to the individual.

The therapist may perceive the group situation as one in which he is the primary source of interpretations and the security that the patients need in order to express themselves and explore their concerns freely. If so, he is again certain to experience failure and frustration. As we have suggested throughout, the individual therapeutic situation is an inappropriate model for the group. If crucial differences between the individual and the group therapeutic situation are not recognized, the therapist will not recognize that his role and task cannot be the same in both situations. In our view, the therapist has a significant role in the group, but it is not the same as his role in individual therapy. In the group, the therapist's primary task is that of influencing the interpersonal conditions under which the therapeutic experience occurs and of exploiting the group situation appropriately for the benefit of each patient. In this view, the therapist's role is conceptualized, in large part, as that of influencing the group situation. Some of the functions which belong primarily to the therapist in the individual therapeutic situation will, in the group therapeutic situation, be assumed by the patients. What remains the unique province of the group therapist is attention to the group forces, for this is essential to the movement of the group and cannot readily be undertaken by the patients. We perceive this not only as the unique role of the therapist, but also as one which makes a crucial difference in each patient's therapeutic experience.

The T-Group Trainer: A Study
of Conflict in the Exercise of Authority

RORY O'DAY

*T*he focus of this discussion is on sensitivity training groups (T-groups), particularly the behavior of those responsible for conducting these groups (trainers). During recent years the variety of group experiences has expanded greatly; and since theory and research about several types of groups will be introduced at various points in the discussion, it is important to begin with some terminological distinctions. The term *self-analytic group* is used here in a generic way to refer to all types of experiential group situations that are designed to achieve educational, remedial, or therapeutic aims by encouraging participants to discuss their performances and perceptions in the immediate context of the group.

One type of self-analytic group, the *learning group,* has evolved within educational settings. The leader-teachers of these groups are concerned primarily with teaching the members, through a direct experience, about the complexity of interpersonal relationships. These leaders are not much involved in trying to change the behaviors or attitudes of the members in any particular direction

387

except insofar as they want the members to examine group process. They do not provide a therapeutic experience that promises to alleviate the personal sufferings of the members. The participants tend to be college students, and the group experience is usually part of a course on group and interpersonal relationships (Bales, 1970; Mann, 1967; Mills, 1964; Slater, 1966). Another type of self-analytic group is the *encounter group*. Encounter group experiences have been developed largely within the personal-growth movement and represent an attempt to help participants more easily express their emotions and become more aware of their emotional life. The guides and facilitators in these encounter experiences are concerned with developing techniques and creating group climates that assist members to express and become conscious of intense but suppressed feelings about other group members or significant others in their lives. Typically, these encounter group experiences are conducted at "growth centers" (Back, 1972; Rogers, 1970; Schutz, 1967, 1971).

The term *T-group,* or sensitivity training group (the focus of our discussion), is used here to refer to group experiences designed to foster and develop interpersonal and social effectiveness among the participants. The trainers, as educators, are concerned that the members learn from the group experience how to be productive and effective member-leaders in their back-home work and community settings. The participants tend to come to the T-group experience as members of organizations in which they hold supervisory, managerial, or instructional positions. They hope that the experience will help them become more effective in their work roles, so that their contributions will enhance the overall effectiveness of their organizations and communities (Back, 1972; Bradford, Gibb, and Benne, 1964; Schein and Bennis, 1965).

During the past twenty years, the sensitivity training group has become a popular and widely used method of experiential learning. Participants are encouraged to become involved in the ongoing dynamics of group life in order to learn to become more effective and innovative members of work groups and larger organizations. Only quite recently, however, has much empirical attention been paid to the activities of the trainer and the contribution he does or does not make toward changing the members' behaviors and attitudes in particular directions (Bolman, 1971; Cooper, 1969; Culbert, 1968; Fiebert, 1968; Lundgren, 1971; O'Day, 1969; Pino and Cohen, 1971; Powers, 1965; Psathas and Hardert, 1966; Reisel, 1962; Sampson, 1972). For many years most T-group proponents never seriously raised questions about how effective different training styles were because they believed they knew how good trainers conducted groups.

This widely shared belief about the characteristics of the typical T-group trainer seems to have been based in large measure on the early case study of one trainer by Deutsch, Pepitone, and Zander (1948). This particular trainer was observed to be a model of friendliness—relaxed, easygoing, sincere, giving the impression of quiet self-assurance. The trainer refrained from expressing value judgments or his own opinion, and he tried to stay clear of intermember conflict, being careful not to take sides when he did arbitrate. He kept his comments on a relatively concrete level and tended to avoid higher-order conceptualizations in his summary of group process. In his capacity as resource person, he presented only factual information and highly qualified opinions and research findings. This trainer seldom gave directions; when he did present alternative means and goals to the group, or summarized discussion, or referred to agenda, or opened and terminated the sessions, he did so in an unassertive manner. He asked questions in order to orient the members to think more deeply about the issues facing the group.

Deutsch, Pepitone, and Zander observed and described the perfect trainer in terms of what the developing rationale for the T-group method required. Subsequent theoretical and instructional writings on what the effective trainer should and should not do tended to accept this image without seriously questioning its validity. Just as Thelen and Dickerman (1949) demonstrated that T-groups do, in fact, develop over time in ways that enhance democratic and collaborative functioning, Deutsch, Pepitone, and Zander provided an important justification for the use of T-groups by showing that the trainer they observed did behave according to prescribed theory and method.

It is true, of course, that there are serious methodological difficulties involved in categorizing the flow of interaction in a T-group and in conceptualizing the complexity of trainer interventions. These difficulties do make the researching of training styles

problematical (Stock, 1964). Wechsler, Massarik, and Tannenbaum (1962) argue, however, that investigations into training styles
and their possibly different influences on T-group processes and outcomes have not been particularly encouraged because T-group
practitioners are reluctant to admit that the trainer exerts any direct influence on group processes and member learnings.

My experience as a participant in various self-analytic
groups and my own work as a trainer led me to think about the
kinds of influences the trainer exerts and about how closely actual
trainer behavior corresponds to the generally accepted description
presented by Deutsch, Pepitone, and Zander. My growing doubts
about the veridicality of this ideal trainer model were supported
by the research findings of Reisel (1962) and Mann (1967).

Reisel, utilizing a postsession interview procedure with two
trainers, found that their dominant personality needs conditioned
how intensely they experienced problems common to all trainers.
One trainer's strong need to be liked proved to mask an underlying
anxiety about the expression of hostility. He reported feelings of
anxiety, depression, and self-deprecation whenever he was faced
with the issues of self-disclosure and personal vulnerability. He
became upset when he had to decide just how personally involved
he was going to become in the group, because this involvement
could expose him to the hostile feelings of the members. The other
trainer, who hid a fear of failure with a strong manifest need to
achieve and produce, reported similar feelings as well as anger. For
him these feelings were in response to such issues as whether the
group was conforming to his particular model of group behavior,
whether he had been successful in overcoming member resistance to
a process orientation, and whether he had set realistic learning goals.

Mann (1967) investigated the styles of leaders in four classroom groups by categorizing their interventions in order to determine how frequently they attended to various dimensions of the
member-leader relationship and which of these member performances they approved of, disapproved of, or were indifferent to.
Member expressions of dependency, withdrawal, direct anger, and
anxiety all received more attention than did expressions of member self-esteem and expressions of affection for the leader. The
leaders were more likely to intervene when a member was not in-

volved in the group process; when he was suppressing his feelings; or when he was either overdependent or counterdependent in his relationship with the leader. Mann observed that the leaders changed from an initially neutral stance in the group to a stance that discouraged member rebellion and supported loyalty performances in the latter phases of the group. The leaders approved of member expressions of independence and various forms of affection, self-esteem, depression, and anxiety; they disapproved of member expressions of hostility, counterdependency, and denial of anxiety and depression. The leaders supported members' adoption of the leaders' interpretive style and the members' definition of the leader role as being somewhere between an authority and a peer. They pressured members toward involvement in the group process, and they rewarded the expression of feelings. The leaders expressed dislike at being characterized by the members as manipulative and devious, and they discouraged denial of feelings and moralistic or judgmental attitudes on the part of group members.

Reisel found that trainers reported being upset and angry when they encountered T-group issues which threatened the satisfaction of their strong personal needs. Mann found that the leaders of learning groups encouraged, discouraged, or ignored various members' performances depending on their own definition of meaningful work. Both studies reported behavior of leaders and trainers that was discrepant with the idealized image of the group leader. Reisel's trainers tended to be of the personal-growth/emotional-expression orientation to sensitivity training, and Mann's leaders were of the social-relations/learning-group orientation. My primary research interest was to discover whether the leader and trainer behaviors they observed were peculiar to these particular variations of the self-analytic group situation or whether trainers of the National Training Laboratories/social-effectiveness orientation also exhibited styles that departed from the Deutsch, Pepitone, and Zander model. The opportunity to follow up the leads of these investigations with a more systematic and intensive examination of training styles presented itself in the form of sound recording tapes of four T-groups led by experienced and highly regarded trainers, professional psychologists associated with the National Training Laboratories (NTL). They had agreed to conduct a laboratory together because, although each represented, to some extent, different orientations to T-groups, they respected each other's talents and believed that they could learn from each other.

THE TRAINING STYLE SCORING SYSTEM

Although my intention here is not to present a detailed description of the categories that were developed to analyze the verbal interventions of the trainer, I will touch on the most salient features of the scoring system. More methodologically inclined readers are encouraged to read the original report of this research (O'Day, 1969) or more recent presentations (O'Day, 1972, 1973). My research interest was to examine as closely as possible what trainers actually said throughout the course of a group. It was my belief that since so little was known empirically about trainer behavior, a significant contribution to the assessment of training style could come only from a methodology based on an act-by-act analysis of trainer comments. At this stage of my research, what the trainers thought they were doing or what the members thought the trainers were doing, while not irrelevant, was of secondary importance. Moreover, the best evidence so far suggests that there is no necessary relationship between how people think they behave and how they actually do behave (Mann, 1959; Milgram, 1965).

Training style is a mix of three components: the *definitional* (how the trainer defines the group situation at any moment in time and the particular issue or event that the trainer calls to the members' attention), the *behavioral* (the various forms from which the trainer can choose to make his interventions—interpretations, questions, or reflections), and the *emotional* (the range and intensity of feelings which the trainer expresses as part of his interventions—is he pleased, anxious, angry, depressed, or indifferent?). In developing the category system, I had to devise a set of categories small enough in number to be useful as a research tool and yet numerous enough to capture the complex meanings of trainer comments. The categories selected were derived from T-group theory about what all trainers ought to do and from the available research about what some trainers actually seem to do.

The coding system developed to score the dimensions of the

definitional component assumes that the members' relationship to the trainer, the members' relationship to the training experience, and the members' relationships to each other involve most, if not all, of the group issues and member performances on which a trainer might comment. The issues of primary concern in the member-trainer relationship are those of dependency, counterdependency, and independence. The member-group relationship involves the quality of the members' performance in and attitudes toward the unstructured group situation. The three issues of importance here are the extent of the individual's personal confrontation with the group, the degree of emotional expression on his part, and the quality of his understanding regarding his experience and performance and those of others in the group. The member-member relationships involve most directly what is typically referred to as the "climate" of the group. The degree of trust and openness that members express in their transactions with each other, the amount and quality of helpfulness they show toward each other as colleagues in a common endeavor, and the way the members resolve the difficulties surrounding the distribution of power and control in the group are three important dimensions of the climate of the T-group to which a trainer might address himself.

The various categories which describe the manner in which the trainer might make his interventions were derived from a consideration of the metaconcepts (Bradford, 1964) that the laboratory experience is assumed to convey and the various roles or functions that the trainer can perform that either facilitate or hinder the members' learning of these concepts. The first concerns the process of discovery, in which the members learn how to identify those aspects of the multifaceted group events which are of particular importance for achieving greater insight into and understanding of the group's behavior. The second metaconcept deals with the development of a group climate that facilitates the expression of feelings—the basic data of the group experience; the third concerns the process of understanding the dynamics of the group situation. An important trainer function is assisting the members in arriving at personally meaningful conceptions of their feelings and behaviors without at the same time assuming complete responsibility for that task. The final metaconcept concerns the most effective locus of power, control, and decision making for a successful T-group experience. That is, who is responsible for what happens in the group (the trainer or the members) and to what extent does the trainer encourage the members to look to themselves for goals and direction and to explore and discover their own personal and group strengths in order to resolve the dilemmas they will face in the group?

The emotional component of training style was assessed by means of the coding system developed by Mann (1966, 1967, 1970) for his investigations of the member-trainer and student-teacher relationships. This system (expressing hostility and affection; showing dominance, counterdominance, and independence; expressing and denying anxiety and depression; and expressing self-esteem) was chosen because it includes all the usual facilitative feelings that trainers are supposed to express (according to the training literature) as well as those feelings considered nonfacilitative in the training literature but which, the studies by Mann and Reisel suggest, are expressed by trainers and leaders at different periods in the life of various self-analytic group experiences and in response to particular member performances.

The statistical reliability of the training style scoring system (interrater and intrarater agreement) was sufficient to indicate that the content-analytic descriptions of the four trainers' styles would be accurate (O'Day, 1969). The reliability and range of the categories, coupled with the recognized competence of these four experienced NTL trainers, provided some assurance that the findings of this research project would reflect what it is that competent trainers actually do when conducting groups.

TRAINING STYLES: FINDINGS

The results of an exhaustive analysis of the trainers' interventions revealed some striking similarities in styles, some very important differences, and, above all, patterns of training style that are much more complex than has been generally suggested by the training literature.

None of the trainers demonstrated a clear progression from early attention to nonfacilitative performances to later attention to facilitative performances, as is suggested by those models of group development that propose a set of phases through which a group passes on its way to an ideal level of functioning (Bennis and Shepard, 1956; Thelen and Dickerman, 1949; Tuckman, 1965). The trainers were continually concerned with those activities of the members which indicated that they had not yet achieved a maximal learning experience. On the whole, the trainers directed most of their attention throughout the groups to those member performances which involved dependency, counterdependency, lack of personal involvement, suppression of feelings, personal defensiveness, and mistrustful and hostile transactions between members.

The trainers were attentive to individual members' responses to the unstructured group situation and the dynamics of the member-trainer relationship. The fact that the trainers directed the least amount of their attention toward aspects of the members' relationships with each other also casts some doubt on the idealized developmental model, which suggests that the members move from an initial preoccupation with the trainer and with themselves as individuals to a final stage of mutually collaborative work.

The trainers did not, as the hypothetical ideal model proposes, respond uniformly to all individual and group issues. They did not always respond in the same manner to the same issue at different time periods in the group. It was possible to identify four distinct types of issues: those that the trainers completely ignored; those that they handled comfortably throughout the group; those that they handled comfortably in the early phases of the group, but less comfortably in the later phases of the group; and those that gave them difficulty throughout the group.

Ignored Issues

For the most part, each trainer ignored the members when they were being complimentary about his ability in general or his interpretive and analytic skills in particular, and when they engaged in various forms of imitation of his style. This can be understood as an attempt to discourage member dependency (Mann, 1967). The trainers also ignored those transactions among the members indicative of collaborative problem solving and shared decision-making processes. This is somewhat less understandable, since an important aim of the training group is learning how to develop effective working groups. It is possible that the trainers did not want to interfere with the process involved in the development of collaborative problem-solving relationships. Interference in this sense would entail an endorsement of analysis of collaboration instead of collaboration as such. Trainer attention at this point might make the members so self-conscious that the process of building cooperation in the group breaks down. It is also possible that the trainers did not perceive the members as behaving in a shared decision-making manner, or that the members rarely if ever behaved in this way. What does seem clear is that these various issues were ignored for reasons other than that they presented difficulty for the trainers.

Comfortable Issues

The trainers were accepting and tolerant of the difficulties that members faced in overcoming their reluctance to share their feelings openly. They directly encouraged and approved of the members when they were demonstrating personal involvement in the group, when they were expressing their feelings, when they were attempting to arrive at personally meaningful analyses of their own behavior, and when they were showing trust and openness. Like the leaders in Mann's study, these trainers overtly pressured members to become involved, to express feelings, and to take on and utilize an intellectual, analytical style.

While the trainers were not overjoyed at member suppression of feelings, they did express tolerance and tried to convey to the members that they were aware of the initial difficulty of expressing feelings in a group of strangers. In order to encourage member expression, the trainers questioned the members and offered tentative interpretations about the nature of their feelings and the probable reasons why it was difficult to express those feelings. The fact that the trainers were not flustered by this type of member performance (suppression of feelings) indicates that this behavior is expected and encountered frequently and that experienced trainers know how to deal with it. This being the case, they respond more as trainers would be expected to respond—accepting but resisting, allowing the member to talk but probing for the underlying feelings.

The trainers functioned primarily as detached observer-commentators, making nonevaluative descriptive comments on the trusting and generally helpful and considerate aspects of members' performances. The trainers were comfortable and competent in dealing with these aspects of member-member relationships. While Argyris (1966, 1967) and Schein and Bennis (1965) suggest that this mirroring activity is very common, apparently it is primarily when the members are interacting with each other in particular ways at particular times that trainers distance themselves sufficiently from the ongoing interaction to function in this capacity.

One important way in which trainers assist the members in developing an independent member-training relationship is by reinforcing those member perceptions which characterize the role of the trainer as being somewhere between a peer and an expert (Mann, 1967). In this regard, the four trainers were able to encourage the members to perceive them as resource helpers and as knowledgeable facilitators while ignoring those positive perceptions of them which could mask dependency.

Ambivalent Issues

The trainers seemed able to deal with some issues reasonably comfortably when they occurred early in the groups but reacted with some anxiety when the same issues were manifested in later sessions. In the early sessions, apparently, these issues were expected to be salient; but their presence near the end of the group cast both the success of the group and the skill of the trainers into question—and therefore caused the trainers some measure of difficulty. These issues involve performances in which the members attempt to structure the group in ways that would seal off the anxiety elicited by the uncertainty of the relatively unstructured nature of the T-group situation. By denying that behavior and feelings are affected by the ambiguous situation or other members, by attempting to force the trainer into a traditional leader-director role, or by attempting to maintain one's involvement with other members at the level of strangers or passing acquaintances—in these various ways the members tried to control their feelings of anxiety by not admitting the experiental demands of the T-group.

When the members were defensive or resistant to analytic work, the trainers responded with a variety of interpretations in order to clarify to the members the defensive nature of their activities. By focusing on the feelings of vulnerability underlying the members' defensive performances, the trainers transformed the issue into one of how people cope with their anxiety. To do this the trainers frequently played an assertive and directing role in their interchanges with the members. But by attending to the feelings underlying the defensiveness, the trainers did not get trapped in a struggle of trying to involve the members against their will. Changing the focus from a normative level (members should be involved because it will be good for them) to an examination of what was inhibiting the members had the consequence of freeing them enough so that they were able to admit their fear and anxiety in the situation. However, in response to these same defensive performances later in the group, the trainers became directly angry and moralistic and sought to discourage the members from avoiding work by asserting their role dominance vis-à-vis the members. The trainers acted very much like outraged traditional leaders/teachers who become angry and disappointed at the less than perfect performance of their subordinates/pupils.

In summary, when the relationships among the members were characterized by a lack of trust and emotional superficiality in the early sessions, the trainers were tolerant but resistant, and tried to show the members how and why they were dealing with each other in a mistrustful way. They did this both by reflecting back to the members in a nonevaluative and descriptive manner what they, as trainers, perceived the members to be doing and by asking questions in order to get the members to think more deeply about their superficial relationships with each other. However, if the nontrustful and emotionally shallow interactions among the members continued into the later sessions, the trainers became openly disapproving of and personally angry toward the members and tried to make them feel ashamed of their conduct.

The other area which received inconsistent responses on the part of the trainers was dependency, which split from a combined control/knowledge base in the early sessions to a primary concern with expertise at the end of the group. While the members no longer

looked to the trainer to direct the group's proceedings, in part because the group was ending and they no longer needed him in this
supervisory capacity, they did continue to relate to the trainer as the
expert. The members were dependent on the trainers both as a
source of control and as a source of knowledge, with the former
becoming less important as the groups neared termination. The upsurge of member dependency near the end of the group elicited expressions of depression on the part of the trainers, apparently because the members' continuing preoccupation with them as experts
demonstrated that they, as trainers, had not been as successful as
they would have liked to be. The resolution of the dependency problem in groups is not a simple process, and the centrality of the
trainer does not completely vanish by the end of the group, as has
been suggested by a number of writers who postulate a final stage
of member autonomy and independence in T-group development
(Bennis and Shepard, 1956; Frank, 1964; Miles, 1964; Thelen and
Dickerman, 1949; Tuckman, 1965).

In part, the resilience of member dependency in these T-
groups was due to certain activities of the trainers, activities that
condoned and even encouraged a highly dependent member-trainer
relationship. In the first place, these trainers frequently functioned
as experts, authority figures, and evaluators in response to a wide
range of member performances. Instead of limiting their interpretations of various member performances to those that members could
consider and evaluate before rejecting or accepting them, the trainers made frequent unequivocal interpretations as they gained more
information about the characteristic interpersonal styles of members. The trainers rarely revealed their own feelings so that the
members could utilize these feelings as phenomena to be analyzed.
All of these activities have been characterized as dependency-pro-
ducing (Argyris, 1966, 1967; Deutsch, Pepitone, and Zander, 1948;
Gibb, 1964; Schein and Bennis, 1965; Semrad and Arsenian, 1962;
Whitman, 1964).

More important is the fact that the trainers responded in-
consistently to direct manifestations of dependency. On the one
hand, the trainers ignored member requests to make sense of group
phenomena through their analytic skills; they refused to take control of the group, to set up proceedings, or to explain events to the

members when the members wanted them to do so. On the other hand, the trainers frequently exercised control over the group, directed proceedings, and instructed the members. This inconsistency can be better understood if we keep in mind the explicitness of member dependency that is exhibited in a T-group in its early sessions, where members are openly and often shamelessly dependent upon the trainer. The trainer openly refuses to reciprocate and satisfy those needs. However, as the members come to express their dependency in less explicit and more subtle ways, the trainer begins to act more and more as the authoritative expert directing the proceedings. Of course, it is difficult for a trainer to make what are often subtle distinctions between the dependent pleas and the independent requests occurring within the context of the ongoing activity of the group. Therefore, as the subtlety of the members' dependency increases, trainers are more likely to mistake dependency for independence and find themselves unwittingly being the traditional leader the members want. Also, since trainers are competent professionals and do know more than the members about the dynamics of group processes and how to run a group, they want to do what they know best. However, when the members are openly dependent on them, the values of member-centered learning are placed in direct conflict with the trainers' desire to help the member perform effectively in their particular group. Only when the dependency is less obvious can its presence be denied or ignored, so that the trainers are free to function as traditional leaders when they consider it appropriate to keep the group's process flowing.

Some form of collusion, then, seems to occur between members and trainer: the trainer agrees to function as a traditional group leader if the members will refrain from explicitly asking him to do so. What often passes for successful resolution of the "authority problem" in T-groups could very easily be this kind of collusion. The members learn that if they want the trainer to take control and to explain things to them, they had better stop being so obvious. This "arrangement" frees the trainer to function as a fairly traditional task-group leader while maintaining the image of participatory democracy. This analysis is not meant to characterize trainers as hypocritical in their adherence to the values of member-centered learning or to question their sincerity when they assert that they unilaterally resist all member attempts to set up a dependent leader-follower relationship. The point is rather that—in the context of the unstructured T-group situation, with all its demands and pressures—trainers frequently take over control of the group, and they even set up the conditions which will permit them to be more assertive and directing in the group whenever they feel it is necessary for them to do so. While the finding that trainers do not consistently resist member dependency clearly runs counter to the usual description of the trainer performance found in the training literature, the fact that trainers do frequently encourage and condone member dependency helps account for the upsurge of expressed member dependency near the end of the group, as found here and in other studies (Mann, 1966, 1967; Mills, 1964).

Difficult Issues

Those issues with which the trainers consistently experienced difficulty involved either overt or covert expressions of member-to-trainer hostility. For the most part, the members accused the trainers of being unhelpful, uncaring, and self-centered but rarely if ever of being confused. The trainers were characterized as being in control of themselves and as having good reasons for the ways they behaved, even if the members did not particularly like that behavior. Member counterdependency was expressed through attacks on the competence of the trainers and by accusations that the trainers were acting in response to their own personal needs and not out of concern for the welfare of the members. The members rarely questioned the adequacy of the trainers' personal strengths to withstand the tensions of the unstructured group situation. It was too anxiety-provoking for the members to accuse their trainer of lacking the necessary strengths to lead the group, because that analysis would place them in the uncomfortable position of being the blind led by the blind.

The trainers found it difficult to allow a full expression of counterdependent hostile feelings on the part of the members. Each trainer tried to undo some of the members' negative perceptions of him by expressing anxiety and projecting the image of a facilitator-helper who felt bad about not being more helpful to the members.

When these attempts at muffling hostility failed, the trainers eventually lost patience and reacted as outraged experts at having their actions questioned and criticized. Moreover, it was only in response to direct member counterdependency that the trainers engaged in any significant amount of personal disclosure. The value of trainer self-disclosure has been reported by Culbert (1968), and Argyris (1966, 1967) has recommended that trainers should function in this way to model effective group membership. In general, though, the trainers were more often trying to justify their actions to hostile members than attempting to illustrate a strategy of participation by which the members could begin to clarify and understand the dynamics of interpersonal relationships.

It was also difficult for the trainers to examine various aspects of the member-member relationships that suggested underlying (or displaced) member-to-trainer hostility and resentment. Semrad and Arsenian (1962) contend that the trainer should consider the hostility in member-member relationships as a manifestation of the displacement of member anger from the trainer onto other members. The members fight with each other in order to eliminate competition for the affection, attention, and special knowledge of the trainer. They also attack each other because they cannot directly express anger toward the trainer for not being nurturant and benevolent with every member. While they want a special relationship with the trainer, they dare not attack him openly because he may retaliate by denying them access to his favors. In order to prevent scapegoating, Semrad and Arsenian argue, the trainer must redirect the hostility onto himself. This the trainers did not do.

It was only with the mistrustful, emotionally superficial, and dominance-submissive aspects of the members' relationships with each other that the trainers did any significant amount of interpreting. Here the trainers focused on the ways in which the members protected themselves from the unstructured nature of the T-group and dealt with the feelings of anxiety and uncertainty that were elicited by the ambiguous situation. More specifically, all the trainers directly interpreted instances of an authoritarian relationship in the group (where some individual assumes control over the group's proceedings with or without the consent of the other members). There were two orders of interpretations. One was that the individual asserting this control was acting out of his anxiety about the unstructured nature of the group. Control in this case was an active strategy to cope with feelings of distress. The second type of interpretation was that the other members, by permitting someone else to become leader or chairman, were employing a passive strategy that would hold their anxiety in check. In both cases the trainers focused on reasons why the members resisted confronting the unstructured group situation.

The trainers did not try to interpret the dynamics underlying those transactions among the members that were characterized by indifference; unsupportiveness; evaluative, nonspecific descriptions; and depth interpretations of one another's personalities and performances. It was easier for the trainers to focus on member anxiety and the defenses used to control that anxiety than it was to highlight the instances and sources of member hostility, particularly when some or all of that hostility might well be displaced from the member-trainer relationship. The trainers apparently attributed members' nonspecific and evaluative comments about each other to the members' lack of knowledge about the value and the technique of specific and nonevaluative feedback. Such an assumption seems warranted because, in response to instances of ineffective feedback, the trainers played the role of expert-instructor rather than analyst and proceeded to teach the members the skills of giving effective feedback. By assuming that the members were giving each other inappropriate feedback because they did not know any better, or by trying to view all the hostile give-and-take between members from an effective/ineffective feedback perspective, the trainers excluded from consideration the possibility that the members were indeed feeling hostile toward each other—in large part because of the unacknowledged resentment they felt toward their trainer.

The trainers' reluctance to recognize the existence of member-to-trainer hostility was also evident in their failure to interpret or even ask leading questions whenever members were expressing a lack of interest in the group or investing little or no energy in its proceedings. Withdrawal is an obvious form of passive hostility through which the members can express their resentment toward their trainer without risking the possible wrathful consequences of a more direct confrontation. However, instead of analyzing or questioning the members in order to get them to think more deeply about the reasons for their noninvolvement and their passivity, the trainers first tried to shame the members into becoming involved; when that failed, they began to demand that the withdrawn members become active participants. The most characteristic response of the trainers to member passivity seemed to be to try to get them moving, involved, or active. What was noticeable in this regard was the absence of any interpretive or mirroring activity on the part of the trainers, indicating that the trainers had difficulty in utilizing these kinds of member performances and the feelings involved for analysis and insight. Part of the difficulty the trainers manifested in response to withdrawal was that they saw it as a threat to the entire learning experience. Trainers sense that what is learned in the group has to be the result of a cooperative venture; if the members do not take the group experience seriously, then there is little that they, as trainers, can do to make the members see it as important. Change agents can influence people who want to be influenced, but it is extremely difficult to influence someone against his will. Therefore, when members withhold their energies from the group situation, they are striking the trainer in his area of greatest concern—how to get the members involved without taking over complete control of the group's proceedings and thereby violating the norm of member-centered learning.

Another reason why member noninvolvement presents difficulties for trainers is that trainers apparently use the dimension of member involvement/noninvolvement as another measure of their own competence. When members are not involved, trainers experience a sense of incompetence or impotence; they feel that the members are not involved because they, as trainers, have not done their job well. It follows, then, that trainers are more likely to interpret member withdrawal as being a result of their own incompetence as trainers if the withdrawal continues into the later sessions of the group. Member withdrawal can also represent a strategy by which the members force the trainers to take control of the proceedings. It is, in essence, a waiting game on the part of the members, in which they reason that if they do nothing themselves, the trainers will be forced to initiate activities in the service of learning. The findings of this study indicate that this waiting-game strategy of the members is to some degree successful, because the trainers did become more directive when faced with member passivity.

Withdrawal is also a safe way for the members to express hostility toward the trainer and the whole group experience, because the covert hostility is masked by overt expressions of boredom, dissatisfaction, and noninvolvement. The expression of hostility is indirect; that is, instead of attacking the trainer outright, the members simply withhold something that would please him. If the trainer were to interpret the withdrawal as hostility, the members could easily deny it and in effect say, "No, we are just bored because nothing is happening; when something exciting happens, we'll be interested and involved." The members punish the trainer by making him feel impotent and ineffective while at the same time protecting themselves from his wrath. The fact that member withdrawal masks hostility toward the trainer helps account for the absence of any trainer analysis of this kind of member performance. The trainers colluded (apparently unconsciously) with the members to ignore the hostile elements in their withdrawal because of their own reluctance to discover just how angry the members really were. This collusion occurred whenever the trainers—instead of focusing on the causes of withdrawal—chose to guilt-induce, pressure, or cajole members into becoming involved. It must be pointed out, however, that passive aggression is a particularly difficult pattern of member resistance to unravel, because of the complex mixture of hostility and fear—hostility toward the trainer for not satisfying their dependency needs, and fear of the consequences of displeasing him. When the members were too fearful to confront the trainer and the trainer was reluctant to encourage the members to verbalize and explore their hostility toward him, the unexpressed hostility continued to erode the members' energies. This process of energy erosion was accelerated when the trainers responded to withdrawal in disparaging tones that made the members even more fearful and more reluctant to express their anger. In this vicious circle, the trainers and the members gnawed away at each other's sense of vitality and competence.

The trainers not only tried to ignore the existence of member-to-trainer hostility and to dispose of it quickly when it appeared more directly; they also tried to prevent its appearance in the first

place. Semrad and Arsenian (1962) recommend that trainers analyze the members' needs for nurturance in order to prevent a sibling-
like rivalry from becoming so intense as to inhibit any real learning.
The findings reported here indicate that the trainers either resisted
or satisfied member demands that they function as familiar traditional leaders, but they did not interpret the dependent nature of
the member-trainer relationship. It seems that the trainers were
more likely to set up conditions so that the members fought with
each other than they were to ensure that the members focused their
hostility onto the trainers themselves. It has also been argued that
the amount of hostility the members feel toward the trainer is a
direct function of the degree of frustration they experience in trying
to get the trainer to take control and direct the group's proceedings
(Bennis and Shepard, 1956; Mann, 1966, 1967; Mills, 1964;
Slater, 1966). It seems plausible, then, to conclude that the trainers'
inconsistent response pattern to member dependency (first resisting
it, then satisfying it) was the result of their reluctance to have the
members become intensely angry at them. The trainers frustrated
the members only up to some level which was safe for themselves,
and then they acquiesced to the dependent demands of the members.

DISCUSSION

The focus of this presentation has been on characteristics of
style found to be common to the four trainers under examination.
The research findings suggest that these shared patterns of training
style are more complex than has been generally acknowledged in the
training literature. Interestingly, the area of greatest difficulty for
the trainers, that of member-to-trainer hostility, seemed to be most
critical for the process of member independence and for generating
emotional involvement in the group experience. While it is not
possible to discuss in detail here the stylistic differences among the
four trainers, it can be noted that the most successful trainer was
the least active (number of interventions) in the early sessions; focused directly on the counterdependent hostile components of the
member-trainer relationship in an interpretive, self-confident manner; and tended to ignore direct instances of member dependency.

This combination of frustrating member attempts to establish a familiar authority relationship early in the group and then responding to the consequent member hostility in a personally confident and accepting manner accounted for the greater effectiveness of this trainer (O'Day, 1969, 1972).

The importance of the role the trainer plays in encouraging and accepting the direct expression of the hostility the members come to feel toward him as a function of the initial frustration of dependency has been stressed by Bennis and Shepard (1956), Mann (1966, 1967), Mills (1964), Semrad and Arsenian (1962), and Slater (1966). More recently Lundgren (1971) has compared the developmental patterns in two human relations training groups. In one of these groups the co-trainers were initially inactive and nondirective. The members became increasingly hostile toward these trainers over the early sessions; and, as their confrontation with the trainers increased, the members simultaneously showed increasing solidarity and openness of communication with each other. Following the session of greatest confrontation with their trainers, the members exhibited high cohesiveness and productivity. A second pair of trainers, considerably more active and directive, elicited a hostile encounter with the members in the first session and, as a result, generated initially positive attitudes between members and trainers. The following group sessions, however, involved little confrontation of the trainers by the members and less solidarity, openness of communication, and productivity. It does seem that a critical condition for the effectiveness of a T-group experience is the extent to which the members are able directly to express their resentment of and their opposition to their trainer and to rebel collectively against him. The effectiveness of the T-group situation as a method of experiential learning is curtailed to the extent that trainers and members are willing to share in the illusion of experiencing confrontations with and successful resolutions of the authority problem instead of actively engaging in the actual process of achieving independence from each other. If the pattern of trainer reluctance to frustrate member dependency, in conjunction with an avoidance of and/or punitive response to member-to-trainer hostility, is at all widespread among trainers, then the power inherent in the sensitivity training group situation as a medium through

which people can learn to analyze and modify their own interpersonal styles and those of others will be greatly reduced. It seems
reasonable to speculate that T-groups could fall into disfavor principally because of the increasing boredom and superficiality of the
experience, resulting from the trainers' reluctance to risk the hazards
of exposing themselves to the overdetermined dependent and counterdependent feelings of the members.

The real educational and therapeutic value of any self-
analytic group experience lies in the opportunity it provides for the
participants to be brought face to face in an undeniably involving
way with the discrepancies between self-image and actual performance. The importance of the trainer in a T-group is his ability
to help the members face these discrepancies and then continue the
hard work of resolving the contradictions between how they see
themselves as behaving, how they would like to behave, and how
they actually do behave. The task of the trainer is to guide the
members through a meaningful self-analysis while eschewing the
familiar and comfortable protections offered by a traditional leader/
director role.

If the proponents of T-groups as vehicles for social and personal change are serious about fostering change, then they should
be creating group conditions that will lead the members to challenge and rebel against the group leader. It is precisely in this way
that the T-group members experience the power of collective human energy and will and the exhilaration of taking control over a
disagreeable and frustrating situation, of being courageous enough
to confront authority directly, and of meeting each other as peers
instead of as competing subordinates.

The "social-effectiveness school" (Lomranz, Lakin, and
Schiffman, 1972), while emphasizing group and interpersonal conflicts, has really underestimated the critical need for member rebellion in the service of collective work. It has tended to gloss over
the "authority problem" by advocating models of T-group development which characterize the member-trainer confrontation as an
early phase involving easily resolved issues that do not recur (Bennis
and Shepard, 1956; Thelen and Dickerman, 1949; Tuckman,
1965). By undercutting the important role of member confrontation
of the trainer, these T-group practitioners will be left only with

the appearance of collaborative problem solving in their groups. What has often been overlooked by the proponents of this orientation is that revolts against the trainer are important instances of collaborative problem solving by the members and are not simply preliminary cathartic exercises.

The proponents of the "personal-growth school" or encounter group movement (Lomranz, Lakin, and Schiffman, 1972) have developed a wide range of imaginative methods to foster emotional expressiveness on the part of participants. The leader here functions as a facilitator; and, although the sessions involve a group situation, in reality the experience tends to be that of an individual performing in front of a live audience. The leader becomes the focus of direct member attention only if that is somebody's particular "hang-up." There is no real possibility for collective confrontation with the leader and hence no opportunity to function collaboratively with one's peers.

As vehicles of personal and social change, these two types of self-analytic group experiences do not seriously try to help participants work through the greatest taboo of all—collective rebellion against authority. As the proponents of T-groups and encounter groups continue to avoid the issues of power and authority, the trainers and facilitators of these experiences will increasingly become one of two types—either the "benevolent authority figure" or the "he hurts me for my own good" type. The first type will not prepare people to confront authority which is not benevolent or reasonable, and it will mislead people into believing that one can quite easily become attitudinally and behaviorally independent of authority. The second type will teach people to obey severe demands of authority because such obedience helps one "grow and become a better person." Both of these views are dangerously naïve when it comes to dealing with authority figures who have actual power over people. Neither approach will develop in people the ability or even the desire to evaluate critically the actions of authority as they affect one's life situation, to challenge and confront authority which is perceived as arbitrary and totalitarian, and to take control and direction over one's situation and experiences. The benevolent-authority type of trainer will permit group members to mistake dependency for independence. The "it may hurt but you're becoming

a more authentic growing person" type of trainer will lead participants to believe that through dependency they will achieve personal independence.

The process of achieving independence is a continuous struggle against the seductive simplicity of a dependent relationship with
authority as the solution to many personal and social problems. The
trainer must allow members to confront his authority, thereby encouraging them to become intensely aware of the complexities surrounding authority relations. Through the confrontation, the members come to realize that the important themes of the group, power
and authority, are also the important themes of their organizations
and their communities. The sensitivity training group can be a valuable medium for enhancing personal awareness and promoting
individual and collective changes if the trainer and the members
face up to the central reality of the authority relationship. The self-
analytic potential of the T-group experience is reduced whenever
the process of independence is confined to an early phase through
which one is expected to pass easily or is subordinated to a devo-
tional relationship with a charismatic leader.

Bibliography

ABERLE, D. "A Note on Relative Deprivation Theory as Applied to Millennarian and Other Cult Movements." In W. A. Lessa and E. Z. Vogt (Eds.), *Reader in Comparative Religion: An Anthropological Approach.* New York: Harper, 1965. Pp. 537–541.

APPELBAUM, S. A. "The Pleasure and Reality Principles in Group Process Teaching." *British Journal of Medical Psychology,* 1963, *39,* 49–56.

APPELBAUM, S. A. "The Kennedy Assassination." *Psychoanalytic Review,* 1966, *53,* 393–404.

ARGYRIS, C. "Explorations and Issues in Laboratory Education." In *Explorations in Human Relations Training and Research,* Vol. 3. Washington, D.C.: National Training Laboratories–National Education Association, 1966. Pp. 1–41.

ARGYRIS, C. "On the Future of Laboratory Education." *Journal of Applied Behavioral Science,* 1967, *3,* 151–183.

ARLOW, J. A. "Ego Psychology and the Study of Mythology." *Journal of the American Psychoanalytic Association,* 1961, *9,* 371–393.

ARSENIAN, J., SEMRAD, E. V., AND SHAPIRO, D. "An Analysis of Integral Functions in Small Groups." *International Journal of Group Psychotherapy,* 1962, *12,* 421–434.

ASTRACHAN, B. M. "Towards a Social Systems Model of Therapeutic Groups." *Social Psychiatry,* 1970, *5,* 110–119.

BACK, K. W. *Beyond Words.* New York: Russell Sage Foundation, 1972.

BACK, K. W. "The Experiential Group and Society." *Journal of Applied Behavioral Science,* 1973, *9,* 7–20.

411

BALES, R. F. *Interaction Process Analysis: A Method for the Study of Small Groups.* Reading, Mass.: Addison-Wesley, 1950(a).

BALES, R. F. "A Set of Categories for the Analysis of Small Group Interaction." *American Sociological Review,* 1950(b), *15,* 257–263.

BALES, R. F. "The Equilibrium Problem in Small Groups." In T. Parsons, R. F. Bales, and E. A. Shils (Eds.), *Working Papers in the Theory of Action.* New York: Free Press, 1953. Pp. 111–161.

BALES, R. F. "Adaptive and Integrative Changes as Sources of Strain in Social Systems." In A. P. Hare, E. F. Borgatta, and R. F. Bales (Eds.), *Small Groups.* New York: Knopf, 1955. Pp. 127–131.

BALES, R. F. *Personality and Interpersonal Behavior.* New York: Holt, 1970.

BALES, R. F., AND SLATER, P. E. "Role Differentiation in Small Decision-Making Groups." In T. Parsons, R. F. Bales, and others (Eds.), *Family, Socialization, and Interaction Process.* New York: Free Press, 1955. Pp. 259–306.

BALES, R. F., AND STRODTBECK, F. L. "Phases in Group Problem Solving." *Journal of Abnormal and Social Psychology,* 1951, *46,* 485–495.

BALES, R. F., STRODTBECK, F. L., MILLS, T. M., AND ROSEBOROUGH, M. E. "Channels of Communication in Small Groups." *American Sociological Review,* 1951, *16,* 461–468.

BARBER, B. "Acculturation and Messianic Movements." In W. A. Lessa and E. Z. Vogt (Eds.), *Reader in Comparative Religion: An Anthropological Approach.* New York: Harper, 1965. Pp. 506–509.

BARKER, R. G. *The Stream of Behavior.* New York: Appleton-Century, 1963.

BENNIS, W. G. "Patterns and Vicissitudes in T-Group Development." In L. P. Bradford, J. R. Gibb, and K. D. Benne (Eds.), *T-Group Theory and Laboratory Method: Innovation in Re-education.* New York: Wiley, 1964. Pp. 248–278.

BENNIS, W. G., AND SHEPARD, H. A. "A Theory of Group Development." *Human Relations,* 1956, *9,* 415–437.

BERLIN, I. *The Hedgehog and the Fox.* New York: Mentor, 1957.

BIBRING, E. "The Mechanism of Depression." In P. Greenacre (Ed.), *Affective Disorders.* New York: International Universities Press, 1953. Pp. 13–48.

BIBRING, E. "Psychoanalysis and the Dynamic Psychotherapies." *Journal of the American Psychoanalytic Association*, 1954, 2, 745–770.

BION, W. R. "Experiences in Groups: I." *Human Relations*, 1948(a), 1, 314–320.

BION, W. R. "Experiences in Groups: II." *Human Relations*, 1948(b), 1, 487–496.

BION, W. R. "Group Dynamics: A Re-View." *International Journal of Psycho-Analysis*, 1952, 33, 235–247.

BION, W. R. *Experiences in Groups*. New York: Basic Books; London: Tavistock, 1959.

BION, W. R. *Learning from Experience*. London: Heinemann, 1962.

BION, W. R. *Transformations: Change from Learning to Growth*. New York: Basic Books, 1965.

BION, W. R. *Attention and Interpretation: A Scientific Approach to Insight in Psycho-Analysis and Groups*. New York: Basic Books, 1970.

BIRDWHISTELL, R. L. *Introduction to Kinesics*. Louisville: University of Louisville Press, 1952.

BOLMAN, L. "Some Effects of Trainers on Their Groups." *Journal of Applied Behavioral Science*, 1971, 7, 309–325.

BORGATTA, E. F., COUCH, A. S., AND BALES, R. F. "Some Findings Relevant to the Great Man Theory of Leadership." *American Sociological Review*, 1954, 19, 755–759.

BRADFORD, L. P. "Membership and the Learning Process." In L. P. Bradford, J. R. Gibb, and K. D. Benne (Eds.), *T-Group Theory and Laboratory Method: Innovation in Re-education*. New York: Wiley, 1964. Pp. 190–215.

BRADFORD, L. P., GIBB, J. R., AND BENNE, K. D. *T-Group Theory and Laboratory Method: Innovation in Re-education*. New York: Wiley, 1964.

BRIERLY, M. *Trends in Psychoanalysis*. London: Hogarth, 1951.

CAMPBELL, J. *The Hero with a Thousand Faces*. New York: Meridian, 1956.

CARSON, R. C. *Interaction Concepts of Personality*. Chicago: Aldine, 1969.

CHIN, R. "The Utility of Systems Models and Developmental Models for Practitioners." In W. G. Bennis, K. D. Benne, and R. Chin (Eds.), *The Planning of Change*. New York: Holt, 1961. Pp. 201–204.

CLEAVER, E. *Soul on Ice*. New York: McGraw-Hill, 1967.

COOLEY, C. H. "The Roots of Social Knowledge." *American Journal of Sociology,* 1926, *32,* 59–65.

COOPER, C. L. "The Influence of the Trainer on Participant Change in T-Groups." *Human Relations,* 1969, *22,* 515–530.

COOPER, L. "Systematic Use of Groups in an Acute Psychiatric Unit." *Group Analysis,* 1971, *4,* 152–156.

CULBERT, S. A. "Trainer Self-Disclosure and Member Growth in Two T-Groups." *Journal of Applied Behavioral Science,* 1968, *4,* 47–73.

DEUTSCH, H. *Selected Problems of Adolescence.* New York: International Universities Press, 1967.

DEUTSCH, M. A., PEPITONE, A., AND ZANDER, A. "Leadership in a Small Group." *Journal of Social Issues,* 1948, *4,* 31–40.

DITTMAN, A. T., AND WYNNE, L. C. "Linguistic Techniques and the Analysis of Emotionality in Interviews." *Journal of Abnormal and Social Psychology,* 1961, *63,* 201–214.

DORSON, R. M. "Theories of Myths and the Folklorist." In H. A. Murray (Ed.), *Myths and Mythmaking.* New York: Braziller, 1960.

DUNPHY, D. C. "Social Change in Self-Analytic Groups." Unpublished doctoral dissertation, Harvard University, 1964.

DUNPHY, D. C. "Social Change in Self-Analytic Groups." In P. Stone, D. C. Dunphy, M. Smith, and D. Ogilvie (Eds.), *The General Inquirer: A Computer Approach to Content Analysis.* Cambridge, Mass.: M.I.T. Press, 1966. Pp. 287–340.

DUNPHY, D. C. "Phases, Roles, and Myths in Self-Analytic Groups." *Journal of Applied Behavioral Science,* 1968, *4,* 195–226.

DUNPHY, D. C., STONE, P. J., AND SMITH, M. S. "The General Inquirer: Further Developments in a Computer System for Content Analysis of Verbal Data in the Social Sciences." *Behavioral Science,* 1965, *10,* 468–480.

DURKIN, H. E. *The Group in Depth.* New York: International Universities Press, 1964.

DURKIN, H. E. "Analytic Group Therapy and General Systems Theory." In C. J. Sager and H. S. Kaplan (Eds.), *Progress in Group and Family Therapy.* New York: Brunner/Mazel, 1972. Pp. 9–17.

EDELSON, M. *Sociotherapy and Psychotherapy.* Chicago: University of Chicago Press, 1970.

ERIKSON, E. H. *Childhood and Society.* New York: Norton, 1950.

ERIKSON, E. H. "Identity and the Life Cycle." *Psychological Issues,* Monograph 1. New York: International Universities Press, 1959.

ESSIEN-UDOM, E. U. *Black Nationalism: A Search for an Identity in America.* Chicago: University of Chicago Press, 1962.

EZRIEL, H. "A Psychoanalytic Approach to Group Treatment." *British Journal of Medical Psychology,* 1950, *23,* 50–74.

EZRIEL, H. "Notes on Psychoanalytic Group Therapy: II. Interpretation and Research." *Psychiatry,* 1952, *15,* 119–126.

EZRIEL, H. "The Role of Transference in Psychoanalytical and Other Approaches to Group Treatment." *Acta Psychotherapeutica,* 1957, *7,* 101–116.

FAIRBAIRN, W. R. D. *An Object-Relations Theory of Personality.* New York: Basic Books, 1954.

FANON, F. *The Wretched of the Earth.* New York: Grove, 1963.

FERENCZI, S. *Thalassa: A Theory of Genitality.* New York: Norton, 1968. Originally published 1938.

FIEBERT, M. "Sensitivity Training: An Analysis of Trainer Intervention and Group Process." *Psychological Reports,* 1968, *22,* 829–838.

FOULKES, S. H., AND ANTHONY, E. J. *Group Psychotherapy.* London: Penguin Books, 1957.

FRANK, J. D. "Training and Therapy." In L. P. Bradford, J. R. Gibb, and K. D. Benne (Eds.), *T-Group Theory and Laboratory Method: Innovation in Re-education.* New York: Wiley, 1964. Pp. 442–451.

FRANKFORT, H., FRANKFORT, H. A., WILSON, J. A., AND JACOBSON, T. *Before Philosophy.* London: Penguin Books, 1949.

FRENCH, T. M. *The Integration of Behavior,* Chicago: University of Chicago Press, 1954. Vols. I and II.

FREUD, S. *The Interpretation of Dreams.* In *The Standard Edition of the Complete Psychological Works of Sigmund Freud* (James Strachey, editor), Vols. 4, 5. London: Hogarth, 1953. Originally published 1900.

FREUD, S. "Fragment of an Analysis of a Case of Hysteria." *Standard Edition,* Vol. 7. London: Hogarth, 1953. Pp. 7–122. Originally published 1905.

FREUD, S. "Hysterical Phantasies and Their Relation to Bisexuality." *Standard Edition,* Vol. 9. London: Hogarth, 1959. Pp. 155–166. Originally published 1908.

FREUD, S. "Analysis of a Phobia in a Five-Year-Old Boy." *Standard Edition,* Vol. 10. London: Hogarth, 1955. Pp. 5–149. Originally published 1909(a).

FREUD, S. "Notes upon a Case of Obsessional Neurosis." *Standard Edi-*

tion, Vol. 10. London: Hogarth, 1955. Pp. 155–249. Originally published 1909(b).

FREUD, S. "Psychoanalytic Notes upon an Autobiographical Account of a Case of Paranoia." *Standard Edition,* Vol. 12. London: Hogarth, 1958. Pp. 9–82. Originally published 1911.

FREUD, S. "Totem and Taboo." *Standard Edition,* Vol. 13. London: Hogarth, 1955. Pp. 1–161. Originally published 1913.

FREUD, S. "Mourning and Melancholia." *Standard Edition,* Vol. 14. London: Hogarth, 1957. Pp. 239–258. Originally published 1917.

FREUD, S. "From the History of an Infantile Neurosis." *Standard Edition,* Vol. 17. London: Hogarth, 1955. Pp. 7–122. Originally published 1918.

FREUD, S. "Group Psychology and the Analysis of the Ego." *Standard Edition,* Vol. 18. London: Hogarth, 1955. Pp. 69–143. Originally published 1921.

FREUD, S. "Inhibitions, Symptoms, and Anxiety." *Standard Edition,* Vol. 20. London: Hogarth, 1959. Pp. 77–174. Originally published 1926.

FREUD, S. "Moses and Monotheism." *Standard Edition,* Vol. 23. London: Hogarth, 1964. Pp. 3–137. Originally published 1939.

FRIEDMAN, L. J., AND ZINBERG, N. E. "Application of Group Methods in College Teaching." *International Journal of Group Psychotherapy,* 1964, *14,* 344–359.

GIBB, J. R. "Climate for Trust Formation." In L. P. Bradford, J. R. Gibb, and K. D. Benne (Eds.), *T-Group Theory and Laboratory Method: Innovation in Re-education.* New York: Wiley, 1964. Pp. 279–309.

GIBBARD, G. S. "The Study of Relationship Patterns in Self-Analytic Groups." Unpublished doctoral dissertation, University of Michigan, 1969.

GIBBARD, G. S. "Bion's Group Psychology: A Reconsideration." Unpublished paper, 1972.

GIBBARD, G. S. "Role Differentiation in Small Groups: A Psychodynamic Interpretation." *Human Relations,* in press.

GIBBARD, G. S., AND HARTMAN, J. J. "Relationship Patterns in Self-Analytic Groups." *Behavioral Science,* 1973(a), *18,* 335–353.

GIBBARD, G. S., AND HARTMAN, J. J. "The Significance of Utopian Fantasies in Small Groups." *International Journal of Group Psychotherapy,* 1973(b), *23,* 125–147.

GIBBARD, G. S., AND HARTMAN, J. J. "The Oedipal Paradigm in Group Development: A Clinical and Empirical Study." *Small Group Behavior,* 1973(c), *23,* 305–354.

GITLIN, T., AND HOLLANDER, N. *Uptown: Poor Whites in Chicago.* New York: Harper, 1970.

GOSLING, R., MILLER, D., TURQUET, P. M., AND WOODHOUSE, D. L. *The Use of Small Groups in Training.* London: Tavistock Institute, Codicote Press, 1967.

GOULDER, A. *Wildcat Strike.* Yellow Springs, Ohio: Antioch Press, 1954.

HARTMAN, J. J. "The Role of Ego State Distress in the Development of Self-Analytic Groups." Unpublished doctoral dissertation, University of Michigan, 1969.

HARTMAN, J. J. "The Case Conference as a Reflection of Unconscious Patient-Therapist Interaction." *Contemporary Psychoanalysis,* 1971, *8,* 1–17.

HARTMAN, J. J., AND GIBBARD, G. S. "The Bisexual Fantasy and Group Process." *Contemporary Psychoanalysis,* 1973, *9,* 303–322.

HAYS, W. L. *Statistics for Psychologists.* Holt, 1963.

HEATH, E. S., AND BACAL, H. A. "A Method of Group Psychotherapy at the Tavistock Clinic." *International Journal of Group Psychotherapy,* 1968, *18,* 21–30.

HEIMANN, P. "Certain Functions of Introjection and Projection in Early Infancy." In M. Klein (Ed.), *Developments in Psycho-Analysis.* London: Hogarth, 1952(a). Pp. 122–168.

HEIMANN, P. "Preliminary Notes on Some Defence Mechanisms in Paranoid States." *International Journal of Psycho-Analysis,* 1952(b), *33,* 208–213.

HEINICKE, C., AND BALES, R. F. "Developmental Trends in the Structure of Small Groups." *Sociometry,* 1953, *16,* 7–38.

HENDERSON, L. J. "Procedure in a Science." In H. Cabot and J. H. Kahl (Eds.), *Human Relations: Concepts and Cases in Concrete Social Science,* Vol I. Cambridge, Mass.: Harvard University Press, 1953. Pp. 24–39.

HERBERT, E. L., AND TRIST, E. L. "The Institution of an Absent Leader by a Students' Discussion Group." *Human Relations,* 1953, *6,* 215–248.

HEYNS, R. W., AND LIPPITT, R. "Systematic Observation Techniques." In G. Lindzey (Ed.), *Handbook of Social Psychology,* Vol. I. Reading, Mass.: Addison-Wesley, 1954. Pp. 370–404.

HINTON, W. *Fanshen.* New York: Vintage, 1966.

HINTON, W. *Iron Oxen*. New York: Vintage, 1970.

HOLMES, R. "The University Seminar and the Primal Horde." *British Journal of Sociology*, 1967, *18*, 135–150.

HORWITZ, L. "Transference in Training and Therapy Groups." *International Journal of Group Psychotherapy*, 1964, *14*, 202–213.

HOWENSTINE, R. A., AND MILLER, J. C. "Group Development in Inter-Group Relations." Unpublished paper, 1971.

ISAACS, S. "The Nature and Function of Phantasy." In M. Klein (Ed.), *Developments in Psycho-Analysis*. London: Hogarth Press, 1952. Pp. 67–121.

JACOBS, R. H. "Emotive and Control Groups as Mutated New American Communities." *Journal of Applied Behavioral Science*, 1971, *7*, 234–251.

JAQUES, E. "Interpretive Group Discussion as a Method of Facilitating Social Change." *Human Relations*, 1948, *1*, 533–549.

JAQUES, E. "Collaborative Group Methods in a Wage Negotiation Situation." *Human Relations*, 1950, *3*, 223–249.

JAQUES, E. *The Changing Culture of a Factory*. London: Tavistock, 1951.

JAQUES, E. "On the Dynamics of Social Structure." *Human Relations*, 1953, *6*, 3–24.

JAQUES, E. "Social Systems as a Defense Against Persecutory and Depressive Anxiety." In M. Klein, P. Heimann, and R. E. Money-Kyrle (Eds.), *New Directions in Psychoanalysis*. New York: Basic Books, 1955. Pp. 478–498.

JAQUES, E., RICE, A. K., AND HILL, J. M. M. "The Social and Psychological Impact of a Change in Method of Wage Payment." *Human Relations*, 1951, *4*, 315–340.

JONES, R. M. *The New Psychology of Dreaming*. New York: Grune and Stratton, 1970.

KAPLAN, S. R. "Therapy Groups and Training Groups: Similarities and Differences." *International Journal of Group Psychotherapy*, 1967, *17*, 473–504.

KAPLAN, S. R., AND ROMAN, M. "Characteristic Responses in Adult Therapy Groups to the Introduction of New Members: A Reflection on Group Processes." *International Journal of Group Psychotherapy*, 1961, *11*, 372–381.

KAPLAN, S. R., AND ROMAN, M. "Phases of Development in An Adult Therapy Group." *International Journal of Group Psychotherapy*, 1963, *13*, 10–26.

KATZ, D. Review of G. Lindzey and E. Aronson (Eds.), *Handbook of*

Social Psychology. Contemporary Psychology, 1971, *16,* 273–282.

KENISTON, K. *The Uncommitted: Alienated Youth in American Society.* New York: Harcourt, Brace, 1964.

KLEIN, E. B., AND ASTRACHAN, B. M. "Learning in Groups: A Comparison of Study Groups and T-Groups." *Journal of Applied Behavioral Science,* 1971, *7,* 659–683.

KLEIN, M. *The Psycho-Analysis of Children.* London: Hogarth Press, 1932.

KLEIN, M. "Notes on Some Schizoid Mechanisms." In M. Klein (Ed.), *Developments in Psycho-Analysis.* London: Hogarth, 1952. Pp. 292–320.

KLEIN, M. *Contributions to Psycho-Analysis: 1921–1945.* London: Hogarth, 1948.

KLEIN, M. "The Oedipus Complex in the Light of Early Anxieties." In *Contributions to Psycho-Analysis: 1921–1945.* London: Hogarth Press, 1948(a). Pp. 339–390.

KLEIN, M. "A Contribution to the Psychogenesis of Manic-Depressive States." In *Contributions to Psycho-Analysis: 1921–1945.* London: Hogarth Press, 1948(b). Pp. 282–310.

KLEIN, M. "Mourning and Its Relation to Manic-Depressive States." In *Contributions to Psycho-Analysis: 1921–1945.* London: Hogarth Press, 1948(c). Pp. 311–338.

KLEIN, M. *Envy and Gratitude.* New York: Basic Books, 1957.

KLEIN, M. "Our Adult World and Its Roots in Infancy." In *Our Adult World.* New York: Basic Books, 1963. Pp. 1–22.

KRIS, E. *Psychoanalytic Explorations in Art.* New York: International Universities Press, 1952.

KULIK, J. A., REVELLE, W. R., AND KULIK, C. C. "Scale Construction by Hierarchical Cluster Analysis." Unpublished paper, 1970.

LAKIN, M. *Interpersonal Encounter: Theory and Practice in Sensitivity Training.* New York: McGraw-Hill, 1972.

LEARY, T. *Interpersonal Diagnosis of Personality.* New York: Ronald Press, 1957.

LEIGHTON, A. H. *The Governing of Men.* Princeton, N.J.: Princeton University Press, 1946.

LENNARD, H., AND BERNSTEIN, A. *The Anatomy of Psychotherapy: Systems of Communication and Expectation.* New York: Columbia University Press, 1960.

LEVINSON, D. J. "Role, Personality, and Social Structure in the Organizational Setting." *Journal of Abnormal and Social Psychology,* 1959, *58,* 170–180.

LEVY, C. J. *Voluntary Servitude: Whites in the Negro Movement.* New York: Appleton-Century-Crofts, 1968.

LEWIN, K., LIPPITT, R., AND WHITE, R. K. "Patterns of Aggressive Behavior in Experimentally Created 'Social Climates.'" *Journal of Social Psychology,* 1939, *10,* 271–299.

LIEBERMAN, M. A., YALOM, I. D., AND MILES, M. B. *Encounter Groups: First Facts.* New York: Basic Books, 1973.

LINTON, R. "Nativistic Movements." In W. A. Lessa and E. Z. Vogt (Eds.), *Reader in Comparative Religion: An Anthropological Approach.* New York: Harper, 1965. Pp. 499–506.

LOESER, L. H., AND BRY, T. "The Position of the Group Therapist in Transference and Countertransference: An Experimental Study." *International Journal of Group Psychotherapy,* 1953, *3,* 389–406.

LOFGREN, L. B. "Organizational Design and Therapeutic Effect." In *Task and Organization.* Memorial Volume to A. K. Rice. London: Tavistock Institute, in press.

LOMRANZ, J., LAKIN, M., AND SCHIFFMAN, H. "Variants of Sensitivity Training and Encounter: Diversity or Fragmentation?" *Journal of Applied Behavioral Science,* 1972, *8,* 399–420.

LUNDGREN, D. C. "Trainer Style and Patterns of Group Development." *Journal of Applied Behavioral Science,* 1971, *7,* 689–709.

MAHL, G. F. "Exploring Emotional States by Content Analysis." In I. De Sola Pool (Ed.), *Trends in Content Analysis.* Urbana: University of Illinois Press, 1959. Pp. 89–130.

MAHLER, M. S. *On Human Symbiosis and the Vicissitudes of Individuation.* New York: International Universities Press, 1968.

MALINOWSKI, B. *Magic, Science and Religion and Other Essays.* Boston: Beacon Press, 1948.

MANN, J. *Encounter: A Weekend with Intimate Strangers.* New York: Pocket Books, 1970.

MANN, R. D. "A Review of the Relationship Between Personality and Performance in Small Groups." *Psychological Bulletin,* 1959, *56,* 241–270.

MANN, R. D. "The Development of the Member-Trainer Relationship in Self-Analytic Groups." *Human Relations,* 1966, *19,* 85–115.

MANN, R. D., WITH GIBBARD, G. S., AND HARTMAN, J. J. *Interpersonal Styles and Group Development.* New York: Wiley, 1967.

MANN, R. D., ARNOLD, S. M., BINDER, J. L., CYTRYNBAUM, S., NEWMAN, B. M., RINGWALD, B. E., RINGWALD, J. W., AND ROSENWEIN, R. *The College Classroom.* New York: Wiley, 1970.

MEEHL, P. E. *Clinical Versus Statistical Prediction.* Minneapolis: University of Minnesota Press, 1954.

MENNINGER, R. W. "The Impact of Group Relations Conferences on Organizational Growth." *International Journal of Group Psychotherapy,* 1972, *22,* 415–432.

MENZIES, I. E. P. *The Functioning of Social Systems as a Defense Against Anxiety: A Report on the Study of Nursing Service of a General Hospital.* Tavistock Pamphlet No. 3, London: Tavistock Institute, 1967.

MILES, M. B. "The T-Group and the Classroom." In L. P. Bradford, J. R. Gibb, and K. D. Benne (Eds.), *T-Group Theory and Laboratory Method: Innovation in Re-education.* New York: Wiley, 1964. Pp. 452–476.

MILGRAM, S. "Some Conditions of Obedience and Disobedience to Authority." *Human Relations,* 1965, *18,* 57–75.

MILLER, E. J., AND RICE, A. K. *Systems of Organization: The Control of Task and Sentient Boundaries.* London: Tavistock Publications, 1967.

MILLER, J. C. "Psychological Aspects of System Analysis." Unpublished paper, 1972.

MILLS, T. M. "Power Relations in Three-Person Groups." *American Sociological Review,* 1953, *18,* 351–357.

MILLS, T. M. "The Coalition Pattern in Three-Person Groups." *American Sociological Review,* 1954, *19,* 657–667.

MILLS, T. M. *Group Transformation: An Analysis of a Learning Group.* Englewood Cliffs, N.J.: Prentice-Hall, 1964.

MILLS, T. M. *The Sociology of Small Groups.* Englewood Cliffs, N.J.: Prentice-Hall, 1967.

NEUMANN, E. *The Origins and History of Consciousness.* New York: Pantheon, 1954.

NEUMANN, E. *The Great Mother.* New York: Pantheon, 1955.

O'CONNER, G. "The Tavistock Method of Group Study." In J. H. Masserman (Éd.), *Techniques of Therapy.* New York: Grune and Stratton, 1971. Pp. 110–115.

O'DAY, R. "Training Styles in Self-Analytic Groups." Unpublished doctoral dissertation, University of Michigan, 1969.

O'DAY, R. "Differences in Trainers' Styles and Interpersonal Orientations and Participant Evaluations of Self and Trainer." Unpublished manuscript, 1972.

O'DAY, R. "Training Style: A Content Analytic Assessment." *Human Relations,* 1973, *26* (in press).

PAGÈS, M. "Bethel Culture, 1969: Impressions of an Immigrant." *Journal of Applied Behavioral Science,* 1971, *7,* 267–284.

PALM, R. "A Note on the Bisexual Origin of Man." *Psychoanalysis,* 1957, *5,* 77–80.

PARK, R. E. *Society.* New York: Free Press, 1955.

PECK, H. B., ROMAN, M., KAPLAN, S. R., AND BAUMAN, G. "An Approach to the Study of the Small Group in a Psychiatric Day Hospital." *International Journal of Group Psychotherapy,* 1965, *15,* 207–219.

PHILP, H., AND DUNPHY, D. C. "Developmental Trends in Small Groups." *Sociometry,* 1959, *22,* 162–174.

PIAGET, J. *The Moral Judgement of the Child.* London: Kegan Paul, 1932.

PINO, C. J., AND COHEN, H. "Trainer Style and Trainer Self-Disclosure." *International Journal of Group Psychotherapy,* 1971, *21,* 202–213.

PITTENGER, R. E., HOCKETT, C. F., AND DANEHY, J. J. *The First Five Minutes.* Ithaca, N.Y.: Paul Martineau, 1960.

POWERS, J. R. "Trainer Orientation and Group Composition in Laboratory Training." Unpublished doctoral dissertation, Case Institute of Technology, 1965.

PSATHAS, G. "Interaction Process Analysis of Two Psychotherapy Groups." *International Journal of Group Psychotherapy,* 1960(a), *10,* 430–445.

PSATHAS, G. "Phase Movement and Equilibrium Tendencies in Interaction Process in Psychotherapy Groups." *Sociometry,* 1960(b), *23,* 177–194.

PSATHAS, G., AND HARDERT, R. "Trainer Interventions and Normative Patterns in the T-Group." *Journal of Applied Behavioral Science,* 1966, *2,* 149–169.

RANK, O. *The Myth of the Birth of the Hero and Other Writings* (P. Freund, Ed.). New York: Vintage Books, 1959. Originally published 1914.

RATTRAY, R. S. *Ashanti.* Oxford: Clarendon Press, 1923.

REDL, F. "Group Emotion and Leadership." *Psychiatry,* 1942, *5,* 573–596.

REDL, F. "The Psychology of Gang Formation and the Treatment of Juvenile Delinquents." *The Psychoanalytic Study of the Child,* Vol. I. New York: International Universities Press, 1945. Pp. 367–377.

REDL, F. "The Impact of Game Ingredients on Children's Play Behavior." In B. Schaffner (Ed.), *Group Processes: Transactions of the Fourth Conference.* New York: Macy Foundation, 1959(a). Pp. 33–81.

REDL, F. "Implications for Our Current Models of Personality." In B. Schaffner (Ed.), *Group Processes: Transactions of the Fourth Conference.* New York: Macy Foundation, 1959(b). Pp. 83–131.

REIK, T. *The Psychological Problems of Religious Ritual: Psychoanalytic Studies.* New York: Farrar, Strauss, 1946.

REISEL, J. "Observations on the Trainer Role: A Case Study." In I. R. Wechsler and E. H. Schein (Eds.), *Issues in Human Relations Training,* Vol. 5. Washington, D.C.: National Training Laboratories–National Education Association, Selected Reading Series, 1962. Pp. 93–107.

RICE, A. K. *The Enterprise and Its Environment.* London: Tavistock Publications, 1963.

RICE, A. K. *Learning for Leadership.* London: Tavistock Publications, 1965.

RICE, A. K. "Individual, Group, and Intergroup Processes." *Human Relations,* 1969, *22,* 565–584.

RICE, A. K. *The Modern University.* London: Tavistock Publications, 1970.

RINGWALD, B., MANN, R. D., ROSENWEIN, R., AND MC KEACHIE, W. J. "Conflict and Style in the College Classroom." *Psychology Today,* February 1971, p. 45.

RIOCH, M. J. "Group Relations: Rationale and Techniques." *International Journal of Group Psychotherapy,* 1970(a), *20,* 340–355.

RIOCH, M. J. "The Work of Wilfred R. Bion on Groups." *Psychiatry,* 1970(b), *33,* 56–66.

RIOCH, M. J. " 'All We Like Sheep' (Isaiah 53:6): Followers and Leaders." *Psychiatry,* 1971, *34,* 258–273.

ROGERS, C. R. *Carl Rogers on Encounter Groups.* New York: Harper, 1970.

ROSE, H. J. *A Handbook of Greek Mythology.* New York: Dutton, 1959.

ROSENFELD, F. "The American Social Scientist in Israel: A Case Study in Role Conflict." *American Journal of Orthopsychiatry,* 1958, *28,* 563–571.

ROSS, D. W., AND BRISSENDEN, A. "Some Observations on the Emotional Position of the Group Therapist." *Psychiatric Quarterly,* 1961, *35,* 516–522.

RUIZ, P. "On the Perception of the 'Mother-Group' in T-Groups." *International Journal of Group Psychotherapy,* 1972, *22,* 488–491.

RUNKEL, P. J., LAWRENCE, M., OLDFIELD, S., RIDER, M., AND CLARK, C. "Stages of Group Development: An Empirical Test of Tuckman's Hypothesis." *Journal of Applied Behavioral Science,* 1971, *7,* 180–193.

SAMPSON, E. E. "Leader Orientation and T-Group Effectiveness." *Journal of Applied Behavioral Science,* 1972, *8,* 564–575.

SCHAFER, R. *Aspects of Internalization.* New York: International Universities Press, 1968.

SCHEIDLINGER, S. "The Concept of Identification in Group Psychotherapy." *American Journal of Psychotherapy,* 1955, *9,* 661–672.

SCHEIDLINGER, S. "Group Process in Group Psychotherapy." *American Journal of Psychotherapy,* 1960, *14,* 104–120.

SCHEIDLINGER, S. "Identification: The Sense of Belonging and of Identity in Small Groups." *International Journal of Group Psychotherapy,* 1964, *14,* 291–306.

SCHEIDLINGER, S. "The Concept of Regression in Group Therapy." *International Journal of Group Psychotherapy,* 1968, *18,* 3–20.

SCHEIN, E. H., AND BENNIS, W. G. *Personal and Organizational Change Through Group Methods.* New York: Wiley, 1965.

SCHMIDEBERG, M. "The Role of Psychotic Mechanisms in Cultural Development." *International Journal of Psycho-Analysis,* 1930, *11,* 387–418.

SCHUTZ, W. C. "What Makes Groups Productive?" *Human Relations,* 1955, *8,* 429–465.

SCHUTZ, W. C. *FIRO: A Three-Dimensional Theory of Interpersonal Behavior.* New York: Holt, 1958.

SCHUTZ, W. C. *Joy: Expanding Human Awareness.* New York: Grove Press, 1967.

SCHUTZ, W. C. *Here Comes Everybody: Bodymind and Encounter Culture.* New York: Harper, 1971.

SEARLES, H. F. *Collected Papers on Schizophrenia and Related Subjects.* New York: International Universities Press, 1965.

SEMRAD, E. V., AND ARSENIAN, J. "The Use of Group Processes in

Teaching Group Dynamics." In W. G. Bennis, K. D. Benne, and R. Chin (Eds.), *The Planning of Change*. New York: Holt, 1962. Pp. 737–743.

SHILS, E. "The Calling of Sociology." In T. Parsons, E. Shils, K. Naegele, and J. Pitts (Eds.), *Theories of Society*, Vol. II. New York: Free Press, 1961. Pp. 1405–1448.

SINGER, J. L. *Daydreaming: An Introduction to the Experimental Study of Inner Experience*. New York: Random House, 1966.

SLATER, P. E. "Role Differentiation in Small Groups." *American Sociological Review*, 1955, *20*, 194–211.

SLATER, P. E. "Parental Role Differentiation." *American Journal of Sociology*, 1961, *67*, 296–311.

SLATER, P. E. *Microcosm: Structural, Psychological and Religious Evolution in Groups*. New York: Wiley, 1966.

SLOTKIN, J. S. "The Peyote Way." In W. A. Lessa and E. Z. Vogt (Eds.), *Reader in Comparative Religion: An Anthropological Approach*. New York: Harper, 1965. Pp. 513–517.

SMITH, E. W. *The Golden Stool*. Garden City, N.Y.: Doubleday, 1928.

SMITH, L. *Killers of the Dream*. Garden City, N.Y.: Doubleday, 1963.

STERN, M. M. "Ego Psychology, Myth and Rite: Remarks About the Relationship of th Individual and the Group." In W. Muensterberger and S. Axelrad (Eds.), *The Psychoanalytic Study of Society*, Vol. III. New York: International Universities Press, 1964. Pp. 71–93.

STOCK, D. "Interpersonal Concerns During the Early Sessions of Therapy Groups." *International Journal of Group Psychotherapy*, 1962, *12*, 14–20.

STOCK, D. "A Survey of Research on T-Groups." In L. P. Bradford, J. R. Gibb, and K. D. Benne (Eds.), *T-Group Theory and Laboratory Method: Innovation in Re-education*. New York: Wiley, 1964. Pp. 395–441.

STOCK, D., AND LIEBERMAN, M. A. "Methodological Issues in the Assessment of Total Group Phenomena in Group Therapy." *International Journal of Group Psychotherapy*, 1962, *12*, 312–325.

STOCK, D., AND THELEN, H. A. *Emotional Dynamics and Group Culture*. New York: New York University Press, 1958.

STOCK, D., WHITMAN, R. M., AND LIEBERMAN, M. A. "The Deviant Member in Therapy Groups." *Human Relations*, 1958, *11*, 341–372.

STONE, P. J., DUNPHY, D. C., SMITH, M. S., AND OGILVIE, D. M. *The General Inquirer: A Computer Approach to Content Analysis*. Cambridge, Mass.: M.I.T. Press, 1966.

STRUPP, H. H. "The Experiential Group and the Psychotherapeutic Enterprise." Unpublished paper read at the American Psychological Association Convention, September 2, 1972.

SULLIVAN, H. S. *Conceptions of Modern Psychiatry.* Washington, D.C.: William Alanson White Psychiatric Foundation, 1940.

SULLIVAN, H. S. "Tensions, Interpersonal and International." In H. Cantril (Ed.), *Tensions That Cause Wars.* Urbana: University of Illinois Press, 1950. Pp. 79–138.

SUTHERLAND, J. D. "Notes on Psychoanalytic Group Therapy: I. Therapy and Training." *Psychiatry,* 1952, *15,* 111–117.

TALLAND, G. A. "Task and Interaction Process: Some Characteristics of Therapeutic Group Discussion." *Journal of Abnormal and Social Psychology,* 1955, *50,* 105–109.

TALMON, Y. "Pursuit of the Millennium: The Relation Between Religious and Social Change." In W. A. Lessa and E. Z. Vogt (Eds.), *Reader in Comparative Religion: An Anthropological Approach.* New York: Harper, 1965. Pp. 522–537.

THELEN, H. A. "Methods for Studying Work and Emotionality in Group Operation." Unpublished manuscript, Human Dynamics Laboratory, University of Chicago, 1954.

THELEN, H. A., AND DICKERMAN, W. "Stereotypes and the Growth of Groups." *Educational Leadership,* 1949, *6,* 309–399.

TRIST, E. L., AND SOFER, C. *Exploration in Group Relations.* Leicester: Leicester University Press, 1959.

TURQUET, P. M. "Leadership: The Individual and the Group." Lecture delivered to the Paris Society of Psychosomatic Medicine, 1967.

TURQUET, P. M. "Threats to Identity in the Large Group: A Study in the Phenomenology of the Individual's Experience in Groups." Unpublished paper, 1969.

TUCKMAN, B. W. "Developmental Sequence in Small Groups." *Psychological Bulletin,* 1965, *63,* 384–399.

WARBURG, B. "Suicide, Pregnancy, and Rebirth." *Psychoanalytic Quarterly,* 1938, *7,* 490–506.

WECHSLER, I. R., MASSARIK, F., AND TANNENBAUM, R. "The Self in Process: A Sensitivity Training Emphasis." In I. R. Wechsler and E. H. Schein (Eds.), *Issues in Human Relations Training,* Vol. 5. Washington, D.C.: National Training Laboratories–National Education Association, Selected Reading Series, 1962. Pp. 33–46.

WECHSLER, I. R., AND REISEL, J. *Inside a Sensitivity Training Group.*

Industrial Relations Monograph, No. 4. Los Angeles: Institute of Industrial Relations, University of California, 1959.

WEICK, K. E. "Systematic Observational Methods." In G. Lindzey and E. Aronson (Eds.), *Handbook of Social Psychology,* Vol. II. (Rev. Ed.) Reading, Mass.: Addison-Wesley, 1968. Pp. 357–451.

WHITAKER, D. S., AND LIEBERMAN, M. *Psychotherapy Through the Group Process.* New York: Atherton, 1964.

WHITE, R., AND LIPPITT, R. "Leader Behavior and Member Reaction in Three 'Social Climates.' " In D. Cartwright and A. Zander (Eds.), *Group Dynamics.* Evanston, Ill.: Row, Peterson, 1960. Pp. 527–553.

WHITING, J. W. M., AND CHILD, I. L. *Child Training and Personality.* New Haven: Yale University Press, 1953.

WHITMAN, R. M. "Psychodynamic Principles Underlying T-Group Process." In L. P. Bradford, J. R. Gibb, and K. D. Benne (Eds.), *T-Group Theory and Laboratory Method: Innovation in Reeducation.* New York: Wiley, 1964. Pp. 310–335.

WHITMAN, R. M., LIEBERMAN, M. A., AND STOCK, D. "Individual and Group Focal Conflicts." *International Journal of Group Psychotherapy,* 1960, *10,* 259–286.

WHITMAN, R. M., AND STOCK, D. "The Group Focal Conflict." *Psychiatry,* 1958, *21,* 269–276.

WHYTE, W. F. *Patterns for Industrial Peace.* New York: Harper, 1951(a).

WHYTE, W. F. "Observational Fieldwork Methods." In M. Jahoda, M. Deutsch, and S. Cook (Eds.), *Research Methods in Social Relations,* Vol. II. New York: Dryden, 1951(b). Pp. 493–511.

WINNICOTT, D. W. "Transitional Objects and Transitional Phenomena." *International Journal of Psycho-Analysis,* 1953, *34,* 89–97.

WINNICOTT, D. W. *Collected Papers.* New York: Basic Books; London: Tavistock, 1958.

WINTER, S. K. "Black Man's Bluff." *Psychology Today,* September 1971, p. 39.

ZINBERG, N., AND FRIEDMAN, N. "Problems in Working with Dynamic Groups." *International Journal of Group Psychotherapy,* 1967, *17,* 447–456.

ZINNER, J., AND SHAPIRO, R. "Projective Identification as a Mode of Perception and Behavior in Families of Adolescents." *International Journal of Psycho-Analysis,* 1972, *53,* 523–530.

Indexes

NAME INDEX

A

ABERLE, D., 332, 333
ANTHONY, E. J., 106, 113
APPELBAUM, S. A., 106, 116, 119
ARGYRIS, C., 397, 399, 402
ARLOW, J. A., 113, 118-119, 121, 271
ARSENIAN, J., 106, 184, 399, 402, 406, 407
ASTRACHAN, B. M., 343

B

BACK, K. W., 388
BALES, R. F., 3-4, 7, 9, 11, 16n, 26, 162, 388; esteem of for group members, 28; as group leader, 301; on group struggle, 32; interaction process analysis of, 49-54, 61, 180, 198-199, 249; on polarity, 174; on role differentiation, 186, 194, 265; on role structure, 180-181; on social change and group equilibrium, 87, 156-157; on study of fantasy, 273; three-man problem-solving groups of, 30
BARBER, B., 332-333
BARKER, R. G., 56

BAUMAN, G., 106
BENNE, K. D., 37, 94, 388
BENNIS, W., 5, 27, 37, 76, 81, 185, 388, 395, 397, 399, 406, 407, 408; developmental model of, 84, 249, 320; editors' discussion of, 92-93, 185; epigenetic model of, 265; on oedipal paradigm, 89; on role differentiation, 93, 189, 190; on utopian subphase, 321
BERLIN, I., 2
BERNSTEIN, A., 49n
BERNSTEIN, M., 24
BETTLEHEIM, B., 80
BIBRING, E., 27, 160
BION, W. R., 6, 27, 37, 76, 277, 349n; "basic-assumption" theory of, 4, 5, 86, 111n, 155, 158, 179, 183, 214, 215, 272, 287, 318-319, 338, 354; on group as oedipal mother, 89, 175, 271; on group culture and mentality, 58, 178; group-process approach of, 106; on group task, 32, 183, 338, 354; on individual's ambivalence toward group, 178; on individuation, 262-263; on messian-

ism, 324, 330; pendular model of, 86; Slater's interpretation of, 157-158; testing theories of, 8, 9, 61, 156; theories of, 11n, 129, 157-158; on white male leader, 206
BIRDWHISTLE, R. L., 56
BOLMAN, L., 388
BORGATTA, E. F., 181
BRADFORD, L. P., 94, 113, 388, 393
BRIERLY, M., 108
BRISSENDEN, A., 385
BRY, T., 384n-385n

C

CABOT, R., 220
CARSON, R. C., 8
CHILD, I. L., 316, 332
CLEAVER, E., 211
COHEN, H., 389
CONN, L. K., 217
COOLEY, C. H., 43
COOPER, C. L., 388
COUCH, A. S., 181
CULBERT, S. A., 388-389, 402

D

DANELY, J. J., 24, 56
DANIELS, R. S., 62n
DAVIS, H., 197n
DEUTSCH, M. A., 389, 390, 391, 399
DICKERMAN, W., 389, 395, 399, 408
DITTMAN, A. T., 56
DORSON, R. M., 119
DUNPHY, D. C., 5, 7, 11, 55, 162, 220, 302n, 324; editors' discussion of, 273, 275; on General Inquirer, 301; on group myth, 156, 210, 228, 273, 316; on myth, definition of, 316; on oedipal paradigm, 89; phase-movements study by, 301-302n, 303; role-structure study by, 186-190, 191, 221, 241, 247, 253; on termination of group, 86; on utopian phase, 321-322
DURKIN, H. E., 89, 175

E

EZRIEL, H., 58-59, 106
ERICKSON, E., 84, 87, 92, 116, 265

F

FANON, F., 31, 32
FIEBERT, M., 389
FOULKES, S. H., 106, 113
FRAENKEL, M., 217
FRANK, J. D., 94, 399
FRANKFORT, H., 115
FRANKFORT, H. A., 115
FRENCH, T. M., 59, 62n
FREUD, S., 31, 76, 80, 84, 87, 109, 119; on artificial group, 297; on authority relations, 130; on expression of feelings, 18; on group and leader, 129, 139, 249, 279, 280; on identification relations, 120, 249, 280; on myths, 114; on neurosis in group, 123; oedipal paradigm of, 88; primal-horde concept of, 81, 88, 138-139; on symptoms, 21-22
FRIEDMAN, N., 94, 111, 123, 124-125

G

GIBB, J. R., 94, 388
GIBBARD, G., 9, 17n, 24, 162, 165, 168, 220-221; editors' discussion of, 194-195, 275; epigenetic model of, 180, 187; on group as mother, 89, 93; on hero role, 191, 195; on oedipal paradigm, 88; pendular developmental model of, 87, 93; process analysis scoring by, 160, 190; on regression, 195; role-differentiation theory of, 190, 194, 241; on Slater, 157n
GITLIN, T., 31, 32
GREENE, D., 197n

H

HARDERT, R., 389
HARTMAN, J., 9, 17n, 24, 162, 168, 177, 220n, 221; editors' discussion of, 275; on fantasy, 275, 317; on group as mother, 89; on oedipal paradigm, 88, 93, 168; pendular developmental model of, 87, 93; on phases of group development, 165; process analysis scoring by, 160, 190, 222; on Slater, 157n
HAYS, W. L., 222

HEIMANN, P., 277n, 280, 284
HEINICKE, C., 30
HENDERSON, L. J., 42
HEYNS, R. W., 49n
HERBERT, E. L., 186
HILL, J. M. M., 288n, 294
HINTON, W., 31, 32, 33, 34, 37
HOCKETT, C. F., 24, 56
HOLDEN, J., 62n
HOLLANDER, N., 31, 32
HORWITZ, L., 94, 116, 125
HOWENSTINE, R. A., 172

I

ISAACS, S., 281

J

JACOBSON, T., 115
JAQUES, E.: on anxiety as source of
group development, 87, 93, 154,
155, 179, 272, 277, 299; editors'
discussion of, 274-275; on group as
mother, 89; on social change, 159;
on study of Glacier Metal Co.,
288, 294
JONES, R. M., 268

K

KAPLAN, S. R., 94, 106, 107, 316, 319;
on dependency, power, and intimacy, 93, 123; linear progression
model of, 84, 92, 93; on new group
members, 114, 118
KATZ, D., 27
KLEIN, E. B., 343
KLEIN, M., 21, 27, 154, 155, 156, 161,
271; on controlling others, 220,
277n; on depressive anxiety, 286,
291n; on introjection, 280-281,
297; mother focus of, 274-275; on
mourning, 289; on persecutory
anxiety, 285
KULIK, J. A., 222

L

LAKIN, M., 408, 409
LE BON, 150
LEARY, T., 4, 6
LEIGHTON, A. H., 140

LENNARD, H., 49n
LEVINSON, D. J., 179, 192
LEVY, C. J., 209, 217n
LEWIN, K., 182
LIEBERMAN, M. A., 9, 11, 60, 72, 73,
106, 184; editors' discussion of, 11-
12, 339-342; on encounter leaders,
346-347; on focal conflict, 249
LINTON, R., 332
LIPPITT, R., 49n, 182
LOESER, L. H., 384n-385n
LOMRANZ, J., 408, 409
LUNDGREN, D. C., 89, 389, 407

M

MAHL, G. F., 56
MALINOWSKI, B., 80, 311
MANN, J., 33
MANN, R. D., 4, 9, 11, 12, 16n, 17n,
167, 198, 220, 222; commitment
theme of, 28-29, 32; on hero role,
253; leader study by, 388, 390-
391, 392, 395, 397, 401, 406, 407;
life-cycle model of, 85-86; member-leader scoring system of, 156,
160, 390-391, 394; on oedipal paradigm, 89; on productive work, 169;
role-differentiation study by, 188-
191, 221, 228, 240, 247, 253; on
scoring group interaction, 164
MASSARIK, F., 125, 390
MATHIS, A., 62n
MEEHL, P. E., 2
MILES, M. B., 346-347, 399
MILGRAM, S., 392
MILLER, E. J., 338, 349n
MILLER, J. C., 172, 183
MILLINGER, H., 197n
MILLS, T. M., 4, 7, 11, 12, 16n, 32, 37,
76, 88, 388, 406, 407; on boundaries and group development, 93,
157; on death of group, 35, 401;
life-cycle model of, 85, 174; on
role differentiation, 181; sign process analysis of, 4, 55, 157, 195;
social-change theory of, 87, 159,
167, 174
MONEY-KYRLE, R. E., 277
MURRAY, H., 17, 18

N

NEUMANN, E., 6, 76

O

O'DAY, R., 89, 389, 392, 394; editors' discussion of, 341-343
OGILVIE, D. M., 55, 187, 301, 302n

P

PAGES, M., 343-344
PALAMAS, C., 197n
PECK, H. B., 106
PEPITONE, A., 389, 390, 391, 399
PETTINGER, R. E., 24, 56
PIAGET, J., 6, 76, 80
PINO, C. J., 389
POWERS, J. R., 389
PSATHAS, G., 49n, 389

R

REDL, F., 106, 109; on central persons, 131, 182, 183, 249; on group formative processes, 108n; on role suction, 209
REIK, T., 268
REISEL, J., 5, 389, 390-391, 394
REVELLE, W. R., 222
RICE, A. K., 177, 288n, 294, 338, 349n
RINGWALD, B., 190, 192-194, 240
ROGERS, C., 388
ROMAN, M., 94, 106, 107, 316, 319; on intimacy in groups, 123; linear progression model of, 84, 92; on new members, 114, 118
ROSEBOROUGH, M. E., 53
ROSS, D. W., 385
RUIZ, P., 89, 175

S

SAMPSON, E. E., 389
SCHEIDLINGER, S., 89, 120, 121, 122, 171, 175, 195
SCHEIN, E. H., 388, 397, 399
SCHIFFMAN, H., 408, 409
SCHMIDEBERG, M., 277
SCHUTZ, W., 4, 33, 37, 88, 388; on body awareness, 38; on end of group, 86; FIRO test of, 131n; on group compatibility, 129; recurring-cycle model of, 86
SEARLES, H. F., 31-32, 33, 34
SEITZ, P., 62n
SEMRAD, E. V., 106, 184, 399, 402, 406, 407
SHAPIRO, D., 106, 184
SHAPIRO, R., 275
SHEPARD, H. A., 5, 27, 76, 81, 395, 399, 406, 407, 408; developmental model of, 84, 249, 320, 321; editors' discussion of, 92-93, 185; epigenetic model of, 265; on oedipal paradigm, 89; on role differentiation, 93, 189, 190
SHILS, E., 49n
SINGER, J. L., 268, 270
SKINNER, B. F., 24
SLATER, 5, 6, 12n, 16n, 17, 32, 34-35, 37, 88, 167, 168, 174, 198, 324; attitude of toward group members, 28; on boundaries, 93, 154, 157-158, 174, 214-215; change theory of, 159; on deification of leader, 272, 319; developmental model of, 87; editors' discussion of, 272; on end of group, 86; on experimenter myth, 30, 166; on group as mother, 89, 158, 175, 272; on individual's ambivalence toward group, 177; on individuation, 251, 262-263; on leaders, 388, 406, 407; on myths and religious beliefs, 272, 334; on revolt against leader, 87, 89-90, 93; on role differentiation, 53, 186, 194, 247, 251-252, 264, 265
SLOTKIN, J. S., 332
SMITH, L., 80
SMITH, M. S., 55, 187, 301, 302n
SNELL, B., 370
STOCK, D., 5, 9, 11, 37, 60, 61, 72, 73, 184, 390; on "bridging" members, 186; group-process approach of, 106; testing of Bion's theory by, 156
STONE, P. J., 55, 187, 301, 302n
STRODTBECK, F. L., 52-53
SULLIVAN, H. S., 128, 139, 142

T

TALLAND, G. A., 49n
TALMAN, Y., 332-333
TANNENBAUM, R., 125, 390
THELEN, H. A., 4, 5, 9, 61, 106, 389,
    395, 399, 408; on role specialists,
    186; testing of Bion's theory by, 156
TOLSTOY, L., 1-2, 7
TRIST, E. L., 186
TUCKMAN, B. W., 83-84, 89, 395, 399,
    408
TURQUET, P. M., 177, 338-339

V

VEBLEN, T., 80

W

WARBURG, B., 331
WECHSLER, I. R., 5, 125, 390

WEICK, K. E., 4, 49n
WHITAKER, D. S., 9, 106, 184, 249,
    339-342
WHITE, R., 182
WHITING, J. W. M., 316, 332
WHITMAN, R. M., 60, 62n, 72, 73, 89,
    106, 184, 399
WILSON, J. A., 115
WINNICOTT, D. W., 31, 90, 270-271, 272
WINTER, S. K., 190-191, 247
WYNNE, L. C., 56

Y

YALOM, I. D., 346-347

Z

ZANDER, A., 389, 390, 391, 399
ZINBERG, N., 94, 111, 123, 124-125
ZINNER, J., 275

SUBJECT INDEX

A

Absenteeism, 100-103, 213, 306
Act-by-act scoring. *See* Scoring
Additive approach, 61
Anxiety: as barrier to communica-
    tion, 152; as basis for group be-
    havior, 155, 159, 277-278; black
    leader's, 200; coping with, 200,
    208; depressive, 155, 277, 285-287,
    291-293, 295, 299; about feeling
    expression, 224; about fusion, 263-
    264; as growth preventer, 127;
    about intimacy, 146; about lack of
    structure, 224, 244, 313; paranoid,
    155, 277, 282-285, 291-293, 299;
    role of in early stages, 132, 171;
    scoring of, 156, 160-161
Authority problem, 129, 408-410. *See
    also* Dependency

B

Barometric events, 131, 139, 141,
    152-153
Basic-assumption groups, 4, 5, 86,
    111n, 155, 158, 179, 183, 214, 215,
    272, 287, 318-319, 338, 352, 354;
    action orientation of, 362; as de-
    fense against death, 370; depen-
    dency in, 184, 356, 357, 358, 359,
    360, 366, 367, 369; deskilling of
    members in, 360-361; fight/flight
    in, 184, 357, 359, 362, 367, 369;
    happiness in, 359-360, 362; in-
    dividual's relation with, 368-371;
    leader of, 184, 357-358, 364; myths
    in, 359; oneness in, 357, 359, 360;
    pairing in, 357, 359, 360, 366, 367,
    369; roles in, 359, 360, 362; struc-
    ture of, 356, 363; types of, 356-

357; used by work group, 367-368; vs. work group, 338-339, 363-368

Belief systems, 316, 332

Bethel culture, 334-344

Bisexuality fantasy, 275, 318, 324-330

Black Muslims, 333

Boundaries, 47-48, 86, 87, 157; defined, 154-155, 172-173; and ego-state distress, 159, 171, 174-175; evolution of, 89; exclusive and inclusive transformations in, 174; in group development, 87, 93, 156, 174-175, 195, 317; individual, 90, 214-216, 303, 304, 313; in interracial groups, 192; leader control over, 339, 352; nonlinear course of, 173-174; in open-system groups, 352, 353; strains on, 88, 91, 159; study of, 195

C

Catalyst role, 131, 136-138, 141, 148, 152-153

Cathartic period, 139-140

Central figures, study of: anxiety in, 224-225; applicability of, 245; categories in, 193; conclusions of, 244-246; detachment in, 230-231, 235; leaders in, 231-233; methodology of, 221-222; norms in, 238; role-differentiation theory in, 220-221, 241-242; role image disagreements in, 235-237, 241; solidarity in, 244

Central person: defining, 307; limitations on emphasizing, 251, 261; types of, 193, 307

Clinical/naturalistic approach: assumptions of, 63-67; description of, 2-3, 5-7; fantasy in, 269; to group focal conflict, 62; to leadership analysis, 341, 346; reliability and validity of, 11, 70; with statistical approach, 7-12

Closed-system group, 352, 358, 359

Communication goal, 128, 142, 148-149, 152

Compatibility theory, 129

Conflicts, group, 102, 134-136; as catalyst for role differentiation, 250; over individuation/fusion, 260-261, 262, 263; splitting response to, 250; over structure, 135; over task vs. integrative activities, 262

Conformity, study of, 60

Consensual validation, 128, 129, 147-149

Contamination of data, 78-80

Countertransference, 383-385

D

Defense mechanisms, 91; fantasy as, 281, 287, 290-291, 295; need for, 227; against psychotic anxieties, 282-287, 291-296, 299

Deification of leader, 157, 232, 272, 318-320

Dependency, 83, 84, 88, 92-93; as "basic assumption," 111n; and deification fantasy, 319; and group compatibility, 129; in group formative process, 106-107; group/leader collusion to preserve, 342, 400, 409; hostility and, 407; leader's attitude toward focus on, 141; personal attitude toward focus on, 141; personal conflict about, 130-132; as phase in group development, 128-130, 132-142; in self-analytic classroom group, 326; sexual, 205-206; Slater's view of, 158, 215; summary of, 143, 152; on therapist, 96-99, 110; on trainer, 96-99, 106-108, 132-142, 395, 397, 398-410; in utopian-phase group, 322-323

Depression, study of, 156, 160, 164, 171

Deviancy: of encounter group "casualty," 347; in group focal conflict, 60, 72; of peer hero, 261; of therapist, 381

Displacement concept, 96, 109, 110

Division of labor. See Role differentiation

E

Ego development, early, 175-176, 280n
Ego ideal, 279n-280n; instructor as, 249, 313; replaced by an object, 280, 297; role of 242, 244, 280
Ego psychology applied to groups, 118, 121, 122, 154
Ego-state distress: and boundary evolution, 159, 171, 174-176; defined, 154; expression of, 164; in group change, 159; peaks of, 166; sources of, 166, 174; study of, 156, 160, 163-178
Emotions, group, 118-119, 122-125
Encounter group(s): defined, 388; member-leader relations in, 409; as social movement, 38; study of leaders of, 345-347
Epigenetic model, 186, 190, 265
Equilibrium, group, 87, 90; disruption of, 91; lack of structure as threat to, 244; maintained through role differentiation, 181, 185, 194, 250; race issues as threat to, 213
Experimental groups: clinical writing on, 346; compared with work groups, 339; products and outcomes of, 339; uncertainty about tasks of, 337

F

Factor analysis, 7, 8, 10, 304-306
Fantasy, 59; as avoidance of conflict, 243; bisexual, 259; case study of, 291-295, 297-299; and childhood ego processes, 276; conscious, 268, 272, 281; controversy about, 269; as defense vs. adaptation, 270, 275, 281, 286-287, 290, 297-299; defined, 267-268, 273-274, 316, 332; dreams and daydreams as, 268, 270, 275; and experimenter myth, 166; function/aims of, 170, 243, 287, 291, 295, 316, 318, 331-332, 334; of fusion with group, 158, 263, 264, 272, 315, 317-319, 335; in group development, 155, 178, 317-

318, 334-335; by individual, group, and larger society, 272-273, 316, 334-335; about intimacy goals, 214; about leader, 166, 252, 310; nonrational role specialists as representatives of, 156; oedipal, 268; in psychoanalytic terms, 267, 271-272, 275, 281; psychological and sociological views of, 269, 273, 275; quantifying, 7; vs. rational problem-solving, 334, 335; of reproduction and rebirth, 258-259, 331-332; sexual, 320; shared, 273-276; in social change, 299; social form and content of, 281, 298-299; sources of, 269; themes in, 318; in training group, 111; of utopian group, 310; as wish defense, 3
Fight-flight behavior: and fusion, 318-319; in group development phase, 132-136; in interracial group, 215; Slater's view of, 158, 215. See also Basic-assumption groups
Focal conflict, individual, 59. See also Group focal conflict
"Foxes," 2-7
Free association, 63
Fusion: aim of, 319; fantasy of, 158, 263, 264, 272, 315, 317-319, 335; fear of, 263-264

G

General Inquirer technique, 55, 187, 301-307
Ghost dance, 333
Glacier Metal Co., 288-296
Grading and evaluation, 148, 153, 232
Group-as-a-whole: change in, 125; characteristics of, 57-58; clinical approach to, 106; communication, evaluation, and control in, 50-53; culture of, 57, 58, 178, 272, 340, 386; emotions of, 118-119, 122, 123-125; fusion with, 90, 263-264; mature and primitive, 91; as mother, 89-91, 158, 260, 276, 320; myths about, 113-115, 117, 121,

271; as nuclear family, 91; object relations with, 92, 271; as omnipotent self, 276; progress as goal of, 85; projections into, 272, 275; as social system, 50, 112-116; structure, process and content in, 113; study of, 38, 72-73; work goal of, 122, 125

Group culture, 58, 178, 272, 340, 375, 386

Group development: absenteeism issue in, 100; affection/love phase in, 142, 144, 152; anxiety as basis of, 155-156, 272, 278, 297; approval-seeking theme in, 133-134; barometric events in, 131, 139, 141, 152; boundaries in, 6, 154, 156, 159, 172-175; catalysts in, 131, 136-138, 152; collaboration model of, 295; counterdependence-flight phase in, 134-136, 141; covert processes of, 94; dependence-interdependence theory of, 6, 128-153; dependency, power, intimacy theory of, 96-115; evaluation stage in, 147-149; ego-state distress aspects of, 155-157, 159, 166, 171, 174-176; formative processes of, 105-126; global theories of, 7; goal-searching in, 132, 231; "group focal conflict" aspects of, 71-72; independence phase of, 142, 144-151; and individual ego development, 84-85, 115-116, 175; individuation/fusion theory of, 175, 263-266, 272, 315, 317, 331; Kleinian theories of, 155-156; leader-testing in, 133; life-cycle models of, 85-86; linear-progression models of, 83-84, 115; moderation and compromise in, 190; myths and fantasies in, 156, 164, 273-275, 311-314, 317, 331, 334; norming behavior in, 144; oedipal aspects of, 88-91; pendular or recurring cycle models of, 86-88, 174, 264; personality effects on, 130-132; phase theory of, 162-166, 222, 300, 303-304, 309-310; psychosexual

sexual stages in, 116, 119; regression in, 171-172, 175, 195; resolution and catharsis in, 136-141, 147; revolt against leader in, 137-139; role recruitment in, 196; self-esteem concerns in, 146-147, 148; solidarity stage in, 142, 144-145; splitting phenomenon in, 172, 175, 176; stages in, 83-85, 115-116, 130, 165; structure conflicts in, 135; subgroup role in, 109, 134, 136, 141, 145-146, 172; termination phase in, 147, 149, 165, 166, 168-169, 171, 173, 174; in training and therapy groups, 94; traumatic events in, 141-142; turning points in 139, 227; utopian stage in, 165, 167, 169-170

Group focal conflict, 11; analytical procedure for locating, 67-70; applications of theory of, 60, 71-73; cues for discovering, 65-66; defined, 57-60, 61; examples of, 60, 184-185, 375, 378; and individual benefit, 73; methodology for studying, 62-70; prediction based on analysis of, 71; reliability and validity of study of, 70-73; subgroup role in resolving, 93; therapist as focus of, 380-382, 385; therapist as participant in, 383-385

Group formative process: ambivalence and hostility to leader in, 108, 110; dependency stage of, 106-107; determinants of, 107; ego-adaptive aspects of, 110, 118, 119, 122; hypothesis of, 105; identification relations in, 110, 120-122, 125; as influence on individual emotions, 118; intimacy and pairing in, 111; leader-group relations in, 108, 110, 118, 119-120; motivation for, 120-122; myths in, 113-115; new members in, 114-115, 118; norms in, 110; power stage in, 108-111; scapegoating in, 109; shared needs in, 101, 107, 109; structural aspects of, 111n, 113, 123; study of, 124,

125; subgroup formation in, 109, 110-111

Group members. *See* Individual member/patient

Group mentality, 178, 243-244, 246

Group therapist: countertransference by, 383-385; as deviant, 381; dyad approach of, 374, 376, 386; errors of, 383-384; and focal conflict, 380-385; fostering of group culture by, 375, 386; group-process approach of, 374-376; vs. individual therapist, 340-341, 345, 377, 383, 385-386; interventions of, 377-379, 382; patients' magical expectations of, 380-382; perspective of, 379-380, 385; power of, 379-383, 385; role of, 339-340, 386; task of, 372, 376, 386; therapeutic stance of, 377-378, 383

Group therapy: absenteeism in, 100, 104; communication barriers in, 153; compared with other groups, 94, 112, 123-125, 248; context of, 65; dependency stage in, 96-99, 110; deviance in, 381, 382n; displacement in, 69, 110; emotional forces in, 378; focal conflict in, 59-72, 375, 378, 380-385; free association in, 63; goals of, 124; mythopoeic thinking in, 122; observation of by training group, 95; pairing in, 112; power theme in, 99-104, 110, 381; regression in, 103, 110; restricting and enabling solutions in, 384; subgroup formation in, 110; trust in, 105, 112

Guilt, study of, 162-163, 168, 169, 173

H

"Hedgefoxes," 3, 7, 7-11

"Hedgehogs," 2-3, 5-7

Hero, peer, 189, 191, 193, 194, 241-242; case study of, 254-260; characteristics of, 253; compared with black leader, 253; compared with seducer, 253; declining importance of, 264; as deviant, 261; as drama-

tizer of individuation struggle, 260-261, 263; relations of with instructor, 254-260, 263; symbiotic relation of with group, 260, 263

Historical causation, 1-2

I

Identification, 120-121, 122, 125; introjective and projective, 251, 252, 279-281

Ideology, 316, 332, 334

Impulse-expression struggle, 188-189

Independent, role of, 131, 136-138, 141, 148, 152

Individual member/patient: ambiguous feelings of toward group, 177-178, 368-370; autonomy of, 342, 370, 379, 409-410; entering group, 195; and group, 368-371; growth of, 152, 339-340, 376; identification of with leader, 368; individuation of, 339; responsibility of, 340; skills of, 340, 364-365; therapeutic benefits to, 73

Individuation: as central concern of small groups, 260, 265; compared with role differentiation, 251-252; decline of anxiety over, 264; defined, 262; facilitated by identification with leader, 252; and fusion, 241, 242, 253, 259, 262; hero role in, 253, 260-261; how to study, 195, 265; linear development of, 194, 252; and personal boundary maintenance, 214; Slater on, 251-252

Interaction (process), group: analysis of, 3-5, 7-8; Bales' analysis of, 54-55; categorizing overt, 49-54; defeatist fantasies about, 37; disorder in, 45-46; fears about, 21; free association in, 63; as iceberg, 55; love and hate in, 27-28; problem-solving in, 50-54; among researchers, 62; role of revolt in, 79-81, 87, 89; selecting examples of, 75-78; self-revelation in, 45; shared anxieties in, 72; as struggle to work, 32; universals in, 8; variables affecting, 53; verbal, 4-5, 7;

work and emotionality aspects of, 61; working through in, 77

Interaction process analysis, 3-4, 7; description of, 49-54; ego-state categories in, 160; as example of "additive" approach, 61; scoring of, 52, 54, 160-166, 221, 272; value of, 54

Interracial groups, 190-191; aggression in, 208, 209, 214; black male leader of, 198-208; black men in, 202; black women in, 202-203; compared with all-white group, 208; denial of white female sexuality in, 205; fantasy goals of, 214; findings on, 217-218; impotence in, 205, 207; pairing and intimacy in, 214; racial myths in, 210-219; role persistence in, 202, 209; role structure in, 208-212; sexual dependency in, 205, 206; sexuality in, 200, 204-207, 209; solidarity in, 213-214, 218; white male leaders in, 206; white men in, 205-206; white women in, 203-204

Interdependence: consensual validation phase of, 147-149; disenchantment phase of, 145-147; enchantment phase of, 142, 144-145, 147; personal conflict about, 130-131, 149; personality influences on resolution of, 149; as stage in group development, 128-130; summary of, 150-153

Intimacy, 84, 85, 88, 92-93; group discussion of, 124; subgroup conflict over, 146; in training group, 104-105, 111, 142, 144-149

Introjection, 91; in case study, 290-293; to establish group identity, 317; identification through, 171, 173-176, 274, 278, 280, 282-285; summary of, 297

L

Leader(ship): absence of, 98-99, 137-138; ambivalence toward, 98, 102-103, 108-109, 134-135, 138; of basic-assumption group, 184, 338-339, 357, 364; black, 198-202, 219; on boundary of group, 340-341, 352-353; in central-figure study, 223; closeness to, 104; as conqueror of maternal mass, 263; decision-making by, 365; deification of, 157, 232, 272, 319; double (co-), 101, 103; in encounter group, 409; expressive (social-emotional), 180-181, 187, 193, 197, 208, 262; as father, 89, 91, 117-118, 158; fear of, 30, 101, 102, 108; female as, 190, 218; as focus of group formative processes and feelings, 96, 106, 108, 120, 158, 182, 183, 231-233; Freud on, 249; function of, 184; as great-man, 181, 182; group control of, 98-99, 110, 232; guilt of treatment of, 168; hostility toward, 108-109, 157, 166-167, 232; internal questions of, 19; as instructor (formal), 248n, 252, 263, 301, 312, 327-328; instrumental (task-oriented), 180-181, 187, 197, 208, 262; laissez-faire vs. democratic, 182; Lieberman, Yalom, Miles study of, 341, 345-347; magical powers of, 106, 108, 121, 136, 140, 214, 380; models of, 183, 186; as mother of group, 327-328; myths about, 312-313; nondirective, 157, 166, 231, 244, 248, 312; as obstacle to group purpose, 231-232, 234; as organizer, 182; overestimation of, 97, 99, 102-103, 108, 111; peer as, 180, 193, 323; power of, 133, 327-328; as projection object, 353; punishment of, 135-136; reference group of, 344; as representative of deified institution, 121; research on, 341, 345-347; as researcher, 33, 35, 204, 345; as rule-giver, 133; sexual dependence on, 205-206; as shared ego ideal, 249, 313; studying interventions of, 73; styles of, 337; symbolic significance of, 117-121; task of, 30, 342; task-oriented, 338; traditional conceptions of, 249; unawareness of group process among, 347-348; of unstructured groups, 182; upward-positive-forward dimensions of, 198n, 199, 208; of work group, 338-339, 354-355, 363-365. *See also* Group therapist, Revolt against leader, Trainer

Learning group. *See* Self-analytic classroom group

Life-cycle models, 85-86, 157

Linear-progression models, 83-85

Logs, member, 223, 232, 254

M

Magical powers of leader, 106, 108, 121, 136, 140, 214, 380

Maturity, group, 127, 128, 157

Member-leader scoring, 156, 188, 221

Messianism, 275, 318; bisexuality as variance of, 324; as fantasy theme, 330-334; in large groups, 332-334

Methodological strategy: for central-figures study, 221; of General Inquirer, 301, 314; for group focal conflict study, 62-70; for interpersonal styles and group structure, 192; for leadership study, 341; needed for study of individuation and role differentiation, 265; participant observer in, 198, 301; for phase-movement study, 301-302. *See also* Clinical/naturalistic approach, Statistical/quantitative analysis

Myths: adaptive function of, 271; in basic-assumption group, 370; as collective projections, 212; cultural, 113-114, 191; defined, 273, 311, 316; function of, 273, 359; ghost dance as, 333; group development role of, 273, 313-314; group emotions expressed in, 120; group-evolved, 113-115, 117, 121, 156, 273, 275; heroic, 139, 313; insight into, 218-219; about leader, 113, 311-315; persistence of, 211-214; in phase movements, 312-313; primal horde as, 138-139; racial, 191, 210-219; role specialists as actor of,

186-187, 311, 314; sexual idols as focus of, 228, 230; shifts in, 313-314. *See also* Fantasy

N

National Training Laboratories, 343-344, 391

Norms, group, 60, 72, 83, 144; external, 305-306; group acceptance of, 190; white middle-class, 208; in self-analytic group, 238

Nuclear conflict, 59

O

Object relations, 89, 92, 107, 121, 175, 318; in deification fantasy, 318-319; identification types of, 120, 280n; regression in, 120; in utopian fantasy, 318, 321

Observation: act-by-act, 160; barriers to, 44-49; of clinical material, 156; postmeeting logs of, 6; quantitative vs. clinical approach to, 3-4, 156; reliability and validity of, 11 by scientist/professional, 39; o self-analytic groups, 6, 156

Observer: barriers to group relationship of, 44-48; boundary problems of, 47-48; members' observation of, 47-48; as participant, 198, 346. *See also* Researcher

Oedipal conflicts, 88-91, 93, 117, 155, 173, 188

Open-system groups, 352, 353

Outcomes, 348, 388

P

Pairing: Bion's theory of, 111n; bisexual, 324, 329; in interracial group, 214; and reproduction, 331; after revolt, 320, 321; Slater's view of, 158, 215; symbiotic, 324. *See also* Basic-assumption groups

Pendular or recurring cycle models, 86-87, 93, 174

"Personal growth" school, 391, 409

Personality, member: "conflicted," 131; dependent and counterdependent, 130, 133, 149, 228; as focus of second stage of development, 153; independent, 131, 136-138, 141, 148, 152, 228; overpersonal and counterpersonal, 130, 146; related to group development, 130-132, 149, 153; in training vs. therapy group, 123

Phase movements, 300-314; analysis of variance in, 302-304; defined, 302; description of, 303-304, 306, 309; factor analysis of, 305-306; hypotheses about, 302; related to myth, 312-314; related to role differentiation, 306-307, 309-311

Political phenomena, 176, 278, 334-335

Postmeeting ratings, 5, 6, 223, 232, 254

Power: fantasies of, 141; in group development, 7, 92-93, 134, 142; and responsibility, 138; in therapy group, 110; in training group, 98-104, 108-111

Prediction, 366-367

Preoedipal paradigm, 89-91, 93

Primal horde myth, 81, 88, 138

Projection, 91, 171, 173, 176, 178, 209-210, 250-251; in case study, 290-293, 295; defined, 280; examples of, 282-284; general discussion of, 297, 369; identification by, 274-275, 278

Psychoanalytic theory, 112, 116, 119-120, 122, 279-281; of normal behavior, 122; of role differentiation, 262-266

R

Racial concerns. *See* Interracial groups

Recruitment, 193-194, 196

Regression, 90, 92, 103; extent of 121; individual, 119; mechanisms associated with, 175; to prescientific social order, 115; and progression, 122, 141; resulting from group formative process, 119, 171, 195; types of, 171

Religious evolution, 334-335

Research: additive approach to, 61; aims of, 21-22; alienating aspects of, 31; category systems in, 27; clinical/naturalistic, 2-3, 21; contamination problems in, 78-79, 82; on covert behavior, 55-56; data collection in, 49-54, 61; defeatist fantasies in, 37; definition and conduct of, 13; familiarity with phenomena in, 42, 44-49; "good," 38-39; on leaders, 341, 345-346; literature on, 30, 33-35, 40-41; as love, 28-29; major issues in, 1; outcome of, 348; participation in, 40; people-oriented, 23, 32; purpose of, 16; reliability and validity issues in, 11; scientific, 14-15, 17-18. *See also* Methodological strategy

Research group, 356

Researcher: as apprentice, 45-46; as artist, 27, 39; category development by, 27; as clinician, 346; colleague relations of, 35-36; commitment of, 22, 32; egocentric view of, 20; as exploiter, 31, 46; flooded by meaning, 23-24; functioning range of, 27; goals of, 16, 21, 22, 39; group relations of, 15-16, 33, 39, 43-44; identity of, 15-16, 22, 24, 29, 39; myths about, 46; naturalistic, 21, 346; as part of social movements, 36, 38; as participant observer, 346; people orientation of, 28-29; as professional, 39-40; reports of, 34-36; roles of, 39; root experiences of, 16; as scientist, 14-15, 23, 40, 48; in search of order and laws, 26-27, 36; self-loss by, 24-25; skills needed by, 20, 23-24; subjectivity of, 15; use of form by, 25-27; values of, 33; as voyeur, 46. *See also* Observer

Responsibility: ambiguous locus of, 178, 394; collective, 355; leader's, 138, 358; peer leader's, 239; and power, 138; shared, 140, 142; and splitting and projection decrease, 369

Revolt against leader, 79-81, 87, 332;

cohesiveness as result of, 407; as collaborative problem-solving, 409; compared with deification, 334; guilt over, 168, 169; need for, 408-409; oedipal complications of, 89-90, 168; readiness for change after, 140; in self-analytic classroom group, 165, 166, 168, 169; theory of, 157-158, 172-173, 319-320

Role(s): commonality of across groups, 185, 192, 193, 241; components of, 179, 192-193; concept of, 179-180; evolution of, 190; influences on assignment of, 197; intermittent playing of, 201; persistence of, 202, 209; recruitment for, 193-194, 196; repertory of, 187; suction into, 209

Role differentiation, 179-182; as acting out focal conflicts, 194, 266; adaptive function of, 250-251; and boundary maintenance, 193; costs of, 250; and developmental process, 185, 194, 249-250, 264-265; Dunphy and Mann on, 188-190; ego-psychology approach to, 241-242; epigenetic model of, 186, 190, 265; evolutionary tree model of, 186, 190, 265; expression/suppression in, 189; Freud on, 249; function of, 182, 185, 194, 250, 266; generalized, 263; and individuation/fusion conflicts, 194, 214, 252, 260-264; in interracial groups, 191, 197; intrapsychic and group process in, 249; pendular movement of, 194, 252, 264, 266; in phase movements, 306-307, 309-311; by projection into central persons, 220-221, 241-242, 251, 260-261; psychoanalytic theory of, 262-266; race-linked, 208; Redl on, 249; replaced by behavioral flexibility, 252; research on, 182-185, 186, 249; as response to group conflict and disequilibrium, 182, 185, 194, 250; as response to lack of norms, 193; sex basis of, 197; in self-analytic

groups, 247-248; for task needs, 262, 355; wave of, 264

Role image: group reactions to, 246; hypotheses about, 306, 310-311; individual's vs. group's, 187, 193, 223, 235, 241, 245-246

Role specialist(s): aggressor, 188, 189, 307-313; anxious dependent, 240; anxious participator, 193, 222, 223-226, 240; black male leader, 198-208; catalyst, 185-186, 189, 228; central person, 182, 220, 307; changes in relative importance of, 311; conflicted person, 131, 185, 307n; counterdependent, 130, 185, 241; deviant, 185; distressed female, 193, 240; ego ideal, 242, 244, 280, 313; fall guy, 223, 233-234, 242; hero, 189, 191, 193, 194, 241-242; idol, 307-310; independent, 131, 185-186, 189, 228; instructor, 307-312; leader, 180-187, 249; nonrational, 186-187, 189, 221, 309; as object of group projections, 283, 297-298; outsider, 194, 223, 234-237, 242, 244; personal/overpersonal, 130; prophet, 193, 223, 237-240, 241, 243-244; resister, 189; respected enactor, 193, 223, 226-228, 240; scapegoat, 172, 173, 181, 188, 189, 193, 234, 236-237, 242, 307, 310, 312, 323, 324; seducer, 188, 189, 191, 253, 307-312; sex idol, 193, 223, 228, 231, 243; as symbol of group emotion, 309; as symbol of response to focal conflict, 306, 307; white male leader, 206, 208

S

Scapegoat(ing), 172, 173, 181, 188, 189, 193, 234, 236-237, 242, 243, 307, 310, 312, 323, 324, 402; as example of group exploitation, 250; by individual, 178; of minority groups, 285-286; leaders' lack understanding of, 347

Science: vs. art, 27; building a, 42-43; denial of knowledge by, 23;

experimental rigor in, 78; form in, 26, 34; grandiosity of, 34; as hiding place, 33; limitations of, 26, 34, 36; official code of, 24-36; separativeness of, 24; and values, 33

Scoring: act-by-act, 3-4, 9, 11, 26, 155, 188, 190, 221, 392; based on psychodynamic theories, 10; categories for, 27, 160-161; of clinical variables, 9-10; in interaction process analysis, 52, 54, 160-166, 195, 221; member-leader and member-member, 4, 7, 160; in sign process analysis, 195; stresses involved in, 24-25; of trainer-style study, 341, 392-394; training for, 162

Self-analytic classroom group, 4, 9, 16n, 17, 171-173; central-figures study in, 220-246, 261; compared with other groups, 248, 263; defined, 247n, 300n, 301; evaluation and grading in, 147-148; format of, 162, 198, 254, 301; General Inquirer method in, 301-304; goal of, 152; hero's importance in, 260; histories of, 166-170; interracial, 190-192; members' reports on, 198, 301, 302; Mills and Mann on, 4; myth in, 311-314; nondirective formal leadership of, 157, 248, 301; participant observation in, 198; phase movements in, 165-166, 303-304, 314; role differentiation in, 186-187, 197, 247-248; role specialists in, 306-314; scoring interactions in, 9, 17, 160-164; self-observation by, 169, 170; as setting for studying role differentiation, 247, 248, 263; status and power in, 218; study of, 127n, 162, 186, 188, 247, 301. See also Interracial groups

Self-analytic group: defined, 247n, 300, 387; and evolution of religion, 334; value of, 408

Sensitivity training group. See Training group

Separation anxiety, 100

Sexuality: and aggression, 208-209;

in bisexual fantasy period, 327-330; as center of discussion, 327; expressed in roles, 193, 223, 228-231, 241; and fear of intimacy, 327, 329; in interracial group, 192, 200, 204-209; myths about, 211, 212; shared fantasies on, 241; in utopian fantasy, 322

Sign process analysis, 4, 55, 157, 195

Size, group, 248, 349-350

Social (group) change: cultural diffusion explanation of, 80; as product of equilibrium maintenance, 87; resistance to, 278, 297, 299; role adjustments in, 296-297; role of emotional tension in, 140; theories of, 159. See also Group development

"Social effectiveness" school, 391, 408

Social institutions, 279

Social problems, 278

Social structures, 279

Social system, 50, 112-116, 183, 195, 263

Social-systems approach, 338

Splitting mechanism, 171-172, 175-176, 281, 285n, 369; and deification of leader, 319; examples of, 233, 291; in individual, 178; in minority groups, 285; political separation as, 335; as response to group conflict, 317; in utopian fantasy, 320

State, origin of, 334-335

Statistical/quantitative analysis, 2-5, 7-11; "additive," 61; analysis of variance as, 302-304; Bales' work as example, 3-4, 7, 61; basis of, 4, 7; cluster analysis as, 222; combined with clinical approach, 7-12; factor analysis as, 7, 8, 10, 304-306; postmeeting variables in, 5; reliability of, 394; of role and group structure, 192; of subjective behavior, 8-9, 55-56, 156, 269; of verbal interaction, 4-5, 156. See also Methodological strategy, Scoring

Structure, group: anxiety over, 224, 244, 313; based on task, 338, 355-

356; boundaries as, 155, 159, 174, 195; conflicts over, 135; theories of, 269, 271. *See also* Group development

Study group, 248

Subgroups, 109: as avoidance of intimacy, 145-146; as boundaries, 172; conflicts over structure expressed in, 135; evolution of, 190; leaders of, 141; mutual support in, 136; phase dominance by, 185, 190; preventive action of, 148; as response to leader failure, 134-135

T

Task, group: accomplishment of, 84; of basic-assumption group, 356; collective vs. idiosyncratic, 339; commitment to, 7; complexity of, 248; concept of sophisticated, 287, 295-296; linked to structure, 351; necessity of primary, 350-352; products of, 351-353; sublimation of group drives in, 310, 314; of work group, 354-356

Task-oriented groups, 180-182

Tavistock tradition, 248, 345

Time factor, 124

Trainer, T-group: ambivalent issues for, 397, 401; comfortable issues for, 396-397; dependency on, 395, 397, 398-400, 406-407; difficult issues for, 401-406; feeling-expression by, 392, 394; hostility toward 401-403, 405-408; ignored issues by, 395-396; importance of, 408; influence of, 390; and members' feeling-expression, 396, 398; mirroring by, 397, 404; as observer-commentator, 397; personality of, 390-391; problems of research on, 389-390; self-disclosure by, 402; styles of, 390, 392-394; success of, 406-407; task of, 397, 408; as traditional leader, 400, 406, 408; as "typical" ideal, 389; and withdrawal, 403-405

Training group: absenteeism in, 100-103; accomplishment in, 97, 100; ambivalence toward leader in, 98, 102-103, 108, 134-135, 138; anxiety in, 402-403; authority problem ignored in, 408-409; climate of, 393; collaborative functioning in, 389, 396, 409; compared with other groups, 94, 112, 123-125; conflict in, 102, 134-136; counterdependency in, 401; defined, 388; dependency there in, 98-99, 106-108, 393, 398-410; discovery process in, 393; end of, 105, 111, 132-143, 147-149, 399, 401; feeling expression in, 393, 396; format of, 95; goal of, 80, 124-125, 393, 396; group emotions in, 111; high regard for leader in, 97, 99, 102, 103, 108; honeymoon period in, 100; hostility in, 401-408; intimacy theme in, 104-105, 111, 142, 144-149; leadership in, 124; metaconcepts of, 393; mythopoeic thinking in, 122; pairing in, 111-112; power theme in, 98-104, 108-111, 138, 141, 142, 393, 394; scapegoating in, 102, 103, 109, 402; as self-analytic group, 301; setting of, 95, 112; shared needs in, 101, 109; success of, 407-408; task of, 342; as therapy group, 104, 124-125; unstructured nature of, 397, 402-403; waiting game in, 404-405; withdrawal in, 403-405

Transference neurosis: dealing with, 341; in group formative process, 107, 116-118, 120n; misapplied to groups, 124; sibling, 118

U

Unity, group, 309-310, 313-314

Utopianism: aims of, 321-323; failure of, 239; as fantasy theme, 275, 318, 320-325, 335; following revolt, 321-322; individual, group, and national, 316, 335; in interracial groups, 192, 214; oedipal aspects of, 320; phase of, 165, 167-170, 173, 304, 313

V

Validity, 11-12, 71-72

Values, 33
Verbal interaction, study of, 4-5

W

Work, productive, 148, 168-169, 183, 190
Work group, 183-184; barriers to, 155; description of, 354-356; leader of, 363-365; predictions in, 366; primary task of, 354; skill preservation in, 364-365; sophistication of, 363; use of basic assumptions by, 367-368; vs. basic-assumption groups, 338-339, 354, 363, 368